Texts in Theoretical Computer Science.
An EATCS Series

More information about this series at http://www.springer.com/series/3214

Dennis Komm

An Introduction to Online Computation

Determinism, Randomization, Advice

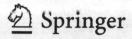 Springer

Dennis Komm
Department of Computer Science
ETH Zürich
Zürich
Switzerland

ISSN 1862-4499
Texts in Theoretical Computer Science. An EATCS Series
ISBN 978-3-319-82653-0   ISBN 978-3-319-42749-2   (eBook)
DOI 10.1007/978-3-319-42749-2

Printed on acid-free paper

This Springer imprint is published by Springer Nature
The registered company is Springer International Publishing AG
The registered company address is: Gewerbestrasse 11, 6330 Cham, Switzerland

My parents,
my brothers,
my love.

Preface

The design and analysis of algorithms deals with extracting certain information from instances of computational problems. In a way, this information is "hidden" in the instances, and usually the aim is to come up with a clever way to obtain the desired information with as little effort (for instance, using as little space and time) as possible. In *online computation*, we are facing a situation that somewhat diverges from this setting. Here, the instance is not known in advance, but we gradually get to know it piece by piece over time. However, parts of the final output must already be created before the whole input is known. As an example, consider the *paging problem*, which we will study in the first three chapters of this book. In a nutshell, the task is to manage the *cache* of a computer that can contain a small fraction of the data that is needed during computation. All the data is stored in the larger and much slower main memory, and our goal is to minimize the number of accesses to this slow memory. In other words, the cache should be managed with the goal in mind that the required data is available in the cache as often as possible. The smallest unit of data that can be moved from the main memory to the cache is called a *page*. If a requested page is currently not in the cache, it must be loaded into the cache by replacing another page, since we assume that the CPU can only directly access the cache but not the main memory. This must of course be done *during runtime*, that is, the pages are requested while the operating system is running and executing programs that require different pages in some order. Thus, the basic question that we ask when dealing with this problem is "Which page should be replaced if we do not know anything about the pages that are requested afterwards?"

In this book, we study online computation in different settings. The book it organized as follows. Every chapter begins with an overview of its content and concludes with some bibliographical remarks, historical notes, and literature for further reading. The first three chapters each introduce a different model of computation in an online environment—deterministic, randomized, and with advice. We use the paging problem to serve as an example for each of them.

We start with a very brief description of computing problems and then focus on the concept of computing online. Chapter 1 investigates what can be done in this setting when assuming that the requested data arrives in a worst possible manner. Such a *worst-case analysis* will be used throughout this book. The output of an online algorithm is compared to that of an optimal (offline) algorithm for the given problem; this approach is known as *competitive analysis*. In this context, "optimal" means that the algorithm knows the whole input, and thus has an enormous advantage compared to the *online algorithm* which is analyzed. To model worst-case instances, we introduce an *adversary* that knows the given online algorithm, and constructs the input such that it makes the online algorithm perform as badly as possible compared to an optimal algorithm. Of course, the existence of such an optimal algorithm is merely hypothetical, and it usually obtains a solution quality that cannot be reached when computing online. We illustrate what can be done when dealing with such a situation for the aforementioned paging problem. In particular, we survey different strategies to manage the cache, such as *first in first out*, *last in first out*, *least frequently used*, and *least recently used*. More over, we analyze a broad class of online algorithms for paging called *marking algorithms*.

We study the power of *randomized computation*, that is, algorithms that produce output that is based on randomness, in Chapter 2. In this case, we assume that the adversary still knows the algorithm, but it does not know the outcomes of the random decisions. Here, we compare the expected value of the online algorithm's solution quality to an optimal output on instances which are again constructed by the adversary in a worst-case manner. We will see in Section 2.2 that this allows the design of online algorithms which are exponentially better (in expectation) than any online algorithm that does not use randomness. To show that this result cannot be asymptotically improved, we learn about a lower-bound technique for randomized (online) algorithms, called *Yao's principle*. Moreover, the *ski rental problem* is used as another example in order to compare deterministic and randomized online computation.

A major focus of this book which distinguishes it from other works (and there are very good ones, see Section 1.7) is that we will always try to be very specific about the information which is hidden in a given instance. In online computation, we usually do not care about the running time of the algorithms we construct or study; we are more interested in what we are losing due to computing without knowing the whole input (one might say "the future"). The *advice complexity* of an online algorithm, which is introduced in Chapter 3, measures the amount of information that is needed to obtain a given solution quality. For every online problem we study, we will pose the question of how much we must know about the input to perform well; in a way, this is the *information content* of the problem. Knowing some simple characteristic helps a lot in some cases; in others, full knowledge of the input is required. This additional knowledge is called *advice*, and as a measurement, the advice complexity (in simple words, the size of the advice) tries to gain some insight into what makes an online problem hard. We first investigate how much advice is both necessary and sufficient to design online algorithms for the paging problem that achieve a certain (for instance, optimal) solution quality. Then we make a general observation that connects online algorithms with advice and randomized online algorithms.

The following five chapters are each devoted to a single online problem, each of which is investigated with respect to the above three models of computation.

Chapter 4 studies the *k-server problem*, which is one of the most prominent online problems. It is of particular interest since, unlike the paging problem, it is not fully understood. This is remarkable as the question "How well can a deterministic or randomized online algorithm perform for the *k*-server problem?" is unanswered for more than 25 years. We first study some simple subclasses of the problem, and then focus on what can be done when given advice. These results have some interesting implications for randomized online algorithms for the *k*-server problem.

Chapter 5 deals with a special variant of *online scheduling* where two partially unknown sequences of tasks should be processed in such a way that as much work as possible is parallelized. For this problem, we are mostly interested in comparing randomized online algorithms to those with advice. It turns out that, for this problem, the difference between whether information about the yet unknown parts of the input is supplied or just guessed is rather small.

In Chapter 6, we study an online version of the *knapsack problem*, and our aim is to give a complete picture of what is possible in each of the above three cases. This is done for both the simple and the general version of the problem. In particular, the former has an intriguing behavior when it comes to how much advice is both sufficient and necessary to obtain a certain solution quality. On the one hand, the case of no additional information leads to a situation where any deterministic online algorithm can be forced by the adversary to perform arbitrarily badly. On the other hand, as little as one single bit of advice allows for a solution that is never worse than twice as bad as an optimal one. Any additional bit of advice does not change this until advice is given which has a length that is logarithmic in the input length; this much advice can be used to get a solution that is worse than an optimal one only by a constant factor arbitrarily close to 1. However, to be optimal instead of almost optimal, linear advice is necessary instead of only logarithmic advice.

Chapter 7 studies the *bit guessing problem*, which is a very generic problem that basically captures the essence of what it means to "compute online." Results about deterministic and randomized online algorithms for the problem can be obtained in a rather straightforward manner. However, our main focus is to use results on the hardness of bit guessing to allow statements about the hardness of other online problems by a special kind of reduction. We construct such reductions for three online problems, namely the *k*-server problem, the online set cover problem, and the disjoint path allocation problem.

Finally, we study different *online graph problems* in Chapter 8. In the online setting considered, the vertices arrive in an online fashion; a vertex is revealed together with all edges that connect it to previously revealed vertices. We start with the coloring problem and present results for both deterministic online algorithms and online algorithms with advice. Last, we investigate an online version of the *minimum spanning tree problem.* Here, we are particularly interested in connections between the online and offline versions of the problem when dealing with special graph classes.

This book by no means claims or even tries to be complete in any sense. It should be understood as an introduction to a selected set of topics that are met in online computation. There are, however, many other topics that are not addressed. For a start, there are many different models that are all worth studying but which are not investigated here. There are, for instance, different types of adversaries when dealing with randomization in online computation that do have knowledge about some of the random decisions made by the online algorithms. Furthermore, there are approaches different to that of competitive analysis such as assuming some probability distribution over inputs instead of having an adversary pick one. As a matter of fact, competitive analysis was often criticized for being too pessimistic, which is why a large number of refined models were introduced; this is also one of the reasons why we study the advice complexity as a complementary measurement asking questions that go beyond "How good can an online algorithm be for a given problem?" and that are more along the lines of "What is it that makes a given problem hard?" However, there are also different models of computing with advice that we will not study in detail in this book; they are described in Section 3.6. Last, there are of course many other online problems out there, many of which both pose and answer interesting questions about the power of determinism, randomization, and advice in online settings.

The Audience

This book is intended for computer science students that have some basic knowledge in algorithmics and discrete mathematics; for instance, it is assumed that the reader knows what a binomial coefficient is, how the expected value of a discrete random variable is computed, how to read and apply the Landau symbols (big-$\mathcal{O}$ notation), and how a worst-case analysis of a given approximation algorithm is done. Basically, the reader should be familiar with how theoretical computer scientists see the world. However, most of the ideas and techniques presented in this book are built on basic fundamentals. All in all, a sufficient preparation should been given by an undergraduate course on theoretical computer science, algorithms and data structures, and discrete mathematics.

At any point, the notation is kept as simple and basic as possible, and the intuition behind the proofs is given, and not just the mathematical details. There are, however, some theorems that are stated without a proof. In this case, pointers to these proofs can be found in the section "Historical and Bibliographical Notes" at the end of the corresponding chapter. Sections marked with "$\star$" are technically advanced, but should still be suitable for students on a graduate level.

Another goal of this book is to be useful to researchers who are interested in the concept of advice complexity, and how to apply it. To this end, the basic principles are discussed in detail, and put into context. Different techniques to obtain lower and upper bounds are described and used, and the reader is challenged to apply her or his knowledge in the exercises. Altogether, there are 101 of them; the solutions are given at the end of this book. The idea behind these exercises is to gain a deeper insight into some details, to try alternative proofs, and, most importantly, to get a good intuition and technical understanding of the results. Most exercises can be answered by readers at an undergraduate level. Exercises that are technically more challenging are again marked with "$\star$."

Acknowledgment

There are many people who increased the quality of this book a lot. First, I would like to thank Juraj Hromkovič for encouraging me to write a book on this topic and for supporting me all the way. Second, I am very grateful to Meike Akveld, Paola Bianchi, Elisabet Burjons, Jérôme Dohrau, Heidi Gebauer, Philipp Hupp, Nils Jansen, Tobias Kohn, Rastislav Královič, Richard Královič, Sacha Krug, Tobias Lieber, Jesper Mikkelsen, Tobias Mömke, Marcel Schöngens, Jasmin Smula, and especially Hans-Joachim Böckenhauer for proofreading parts of the manuscript.

Some chapters of this book are based on parts of my dissertation [97], which I defended in December 2011 at ETH. I had the great pleasure to have Georg Schnitger and Peter Widmayer as co-referees, and I am very thankful for their comments.

Moreover, I had the opportunity to test the material contained in this book in a course "Approximation and Online Algorithms" at ETH, which was so far held in 2013, 2014, 2015, and 2016. The German lecture notes of this class [98] contain a subset of the material that is presented in this book. Some of the students who attended this class contributed a lot to improve this book, especially Tatjana Brülisauer, Mathias Jostock, Sven Hammann, Dominik Müller, and Philipp Schmid.

I am very thankful to Ronan Nugent of Springer for his support.

Last but not least, I want to thank all the people with whom I worked on online algorithms with advice in the last eight years. Without all the discussions we had, this book would not have been possible.

The typesetting of this book was done with LaTeX.

Finally, I hope you enjoy reading this book as much as I enjoyed writing it.

Zürich, September 2016   *Dennis Komm*

Contents

Introduction

1

This chapter introduces the concept of computing online, after briefly looking at algorithms from a more general perspective. As a starting point, we consider optimization problems and $\mathcal{NP}$-hardness on a very high level. Next, we describe one of the strategies used to attack such problems, namely approximation algorithms. As an example, we have a quick look at the simple knapsack problem, which is one of the most famous $\mathcal{NP}$-hard maximization problems. We study this problem as we will meet it again later in this book; in Chapter 6, we formulate an online version of the problem where we make use of our insights into the greedy strategy for the offline version. The goal is to quickly recall what we understand as computing problems and algorithms, not to give an introduction to the topic; we assume that the reader is already familiar with these concepts. The objective of these first few pages is to put into context what we learn next.

After that, we formally introduce the main topic of this book: *online computation*, that is, algorithms that work on problem instances which they do not know from the start, but that get revealed piece by piece. These algorithms are called *online algorithms*, and they are commonly analyzed using so-called *competitive analysis*, which compares their solution to an optimal one; this is a concept that is strongly related to studying the approximation ratios of algorithms described in the afore-mentioned setting. We start by giving a formal definition, which we link to the paging problem. Paging, as it is defined in this book, is a very simplified version of what is met in practical settings; a simple two-level memory hierarchy is assumed that consists of a small fast memory, called the *cache*, and a larger slow memory. The objective is to manage the memory such that the slow memory is accessed as rarely as possible. The problem is motivated by the difference in speed between the main memory and the CPU. Note that, from a practical point of view, we should be speaking of caching in this context, but we use the terminology that is established in the area of online algorithms. We are not concerned with the technical details of this problem, but we want to break it down to its essence. Paging will accompany

© Springer International Publishing Switzerland 2016
D. Komm, *An Introduction to Online Computation*,
Texts in Theoretical Computer Science. An EATCS Series,
DOI 10.1007/978-3-319-42749-2_1

us in Chapters 2 and 3, where we introduce two different models of computation, namely randomized computation and computation with advice. In this chapter, we state some basic results and present fundamental techniques to analyze deterministic online algorithms, and make clear to which points we need to pay special attention. For paging, we introduce some important strategies and give upper and lower bounds on their competitive ratios (analogously to the approximation ratio, the competitive ratio roughly corresponds to the factor by which a solution computed by an online algorithm is worse than an optimal solution). To analyze the latter, we consider worst-case instances and introduce a hypothetical *adversary* that tries to make the online algorithm at hand perform as badly as possible. We show an upper bound on the competitive ratio that solely depends on the given cache size k; this is done by proving that an online algorithm that implements a simple *first in first out* (FIFO) strategy (basically treating the cache like a queue) achieves this competitive ratio. This bound is tight as there is an adversary that can make sure that no online algorithm can be more successful in general. Interestingly, we also show that FIFO's counterpart, that is, a *last in first out* (LIFO) strategy, is a lot worse, as is a *least frequently used* (LFU) strategy. After that, we introduce the general concept of *marking algorithms* for the paging problem. This class of algorithms, which contains algorithms that implement a *least recently used* (LRU) strategy, is also shown to achieve a competitive ratio of k. Finally, we quickly touch upon two ideas to possibly grant an online algorithm an advantage over the adversary, namely seeing into the future for a little bit, or having a larger cache than the optimal algorithm that the online algorithm is compared against.

1.1 Offline Algorithms

The term *algorithm* may without hesitation be called the central notion of computer science; it is the formal description of a strategy to solve a given instance of a problem. It is important to point out that this description is finite, but it should be applicable to *every* instance of the problem although there may be infinitely many. The origin of the word dates back to Muḥammad ibn Mūsā al-Khwārizmī, a Persian mathematician, who lived in the eighth and ninth century. In computer science, we are concerned with the study of these algorithms to both explore what is doable by means of computers, that is, which kind of work can be automated, and how well it can be done when satisfying certain conditions such as, for instance, bounding the time spent to solve the problem.

The investigation of the first point is based on one of the major breakthrough results of twentieth-century science. There are well-defined problems that cannot be solved algorithmically, that is, no matter how powerful a computer's resources will be at some point, it will not be able to answer these questions. In 1936, Alan Turing wrote his pioneering paper "On computable numbers with an application to the Entscheidungsproblem," introducing a formal definition of the notion of *algorithm* and then (using arguments similar to those in the proof of Gödel's fundamental

Incompleteness Theorem) showing that, for some particular problems, algorithms cannot give a correct answer. Today, we call his formalization the *Turing machine* in his honor. The informal term *algorithm* is formalized by Turing machines that always finish their work in finite time (they "halt"). Most computer scientists agree that these hypothetical machines do indeed formalize what we understand as algorithms. Since then, a lot of effort has been made to further refine Turing's result, and nowadays the field of *computability* is one of the cornerstones of theoretical computer science.

One such question that we cannot answer algorithmically in general is the *halting problem*, which asks

> *Does a given Turing machine halt on a given input or does it run forever?*

Even though there are only two possible answers, namely "yes" and "no," no algorithm can figure out the correct answer for all possible Turing machines. We call such a problem a *decision problem*. In this book, we only deal with computable problems, that is, problems for which, in principle, algorithms can compute a solution. As an example, such a computable decision problem can be given by the question

> *Is a given natural number a prime number?*

Obviously, there are infinitely many instances of this problem, namely all natural numbers. Moreover, we can find a finite description to answer this question for any given such number $x \in \mathbb{N}$. If x is either 0 or 1, we answer "no," and otherwise we check for every number $y \in \{2, 3, \ldots, \lfloor \sqrt{x} \rfloor\}$ whether it divides x. If we find such a y, we answer "no," otherwise we answer "yes."

In what follows, we usually ask questions that do not have a simple answer like "yes" or "no," but are more involved. A typical such question is

> *Given a traffic network, what is the fastest tour that visits all cities on the map exactly once and returns to the starting point?*

The above problem is the famous *traveling salesman problem* (TSP) and we know that, given enough time, we can answer it with the fastest tour there is, for any given instance. The next definition formalizes such an *optimization problem*; there are two different objectives, either to minimize some cost or to maximize some gain; we thus speak of *minimization* or *maximization problems*. For the TSP, we want to minimize some cost, namely the total traveling time that is associated with every tour.

Definition 1.1 (Optimization Problem). An *optimization problem* Π consists of a set of *instances* $\mathcal{I}$, a set of *solutions* $\mathcal{O}$, and three functions sol: $\mathcal{I} \rightarrow \mathcal{P}(\mathcal{O})$, quality: $\mathcal{I} \times \mathcal{O} \rightarrow \mathbb{R}$, and goal $\in \{\min, \max\}$. For every instance $I \in \mathcal{I}$, $\mathrm{sol}(I) \subseteq \mathcal{O}$ denotes the set of *feasible solutions* for I. For every instance $I \in \mathcal{I}$ and every feasible solution $O \in \mathrm{sol}(I)$, quality(I, O) denotes the *measure* of I and O. An *optimal solution* for an instance $I \in \mathcal{I}$ of Π is a solution $\mathrm{OPT}(I) \in \mathrm{sol}(I)$ such that

$$\text{quality}(I, \mathrm{OPT}(I)) = \text{goal}\{\text{quality}(I, O) \mid O \in \mathrm{sol}(I)\} \ .$$

If goal $=$ min, we call Π a *minimization problem* and write "cost" instead of "quality." Conversely, if goal $=$ max, we say that Π is a *maximization problem* and write "gain" instead of "quality."

We call an algorithm *consistent* for a given problem Π if it computes a feasible solution for every given instance (input). We denote the solution computed by an algorithm ALG on an instance I by ALG(I). When, for instance, considering a minimization problem, we denote the cost incurred by ALG on the instance I by cost$(I, \mathrm{ALG}(I))$; likewise, for maximization problems, we write gain$(I, \mathrm{ALG}(I))$ for the gain of ALG's solution when given I. To have an easier notation, we usually simply write cost$(\mathrm{ALG}(I))$ or gain$(\mathrm{ALG}(I))$, respectively.

We now have a framework of (computable) optimization problems and algorithms to solve them. However, not only from a practical point of view, we are typically not satisfied to merely know that we are able to design an algorithm to solve some given problem; we would also like to get the solution while obeying some given restrictions. One such restriction might be an upper bound on the running time of the algorithm at hand. Here, computer scientists consider an algorithm *efficient* if its running time is in $\mathcal{O}(n^k)$ for all inputs of length n and some natural number k which is independent of n; we call such algorithms *polynomial-time algorithms*. Consider our algorithm for testing whether a given natural number is a prime number, and let us call this algorithm PRIME. Furthermore, assume that the input x is encoded as a binary string of length n. We can roughly estimate the running time of PRIME as follows. Due to its length, x has a size of around 2^n; if x is prime, PRIME tests the divisibility of x for roughly $\sqrt{2^n} = 2^{n/2}$ natural numbers and thus its running time grows exponentially in n; hence, PRIME is not efficient. Of course, if x is not a prime, but, say, divisible by 2, PRIME finishes with the answer "no" very quickly; but we are interested in the worst-case behavior of the algorithms we study, and we keep this point of view throughout this book.

All decision problems that can be solved in polynomial time are members of the class $\mathcal{P}$. The class $\mathcal{NP}$ contains all decision problems Π for which we can *verify* in polynomial time that, for all instances of Π that have the answer "yes," the answer is indeed "yes." The exact relation between the two classes $\mathcal{P}$ and $\mathcal{NP}$ is surely one of the most important and famous questions in computer science and mathematics.

It is easy to see that $\mathcal{P} \subseteq \mathcal{NP}$; of course, if we can decide whether a given instance of a decision problem is a "yes" instance, we can also verify that this is the case. However, we do not know yet whether the above inclusion is strict, that is, whether

$$\mathcal{P} \subsetneq \mathcal{NP} \quad \text{or} \quad \mathcal{P} = \mathcal{NP}$$

is true. In the following, we will assume the former, that is, $\mathcal{P} \neq \mathcal{NP}$. To at least identify a class of problems in $\mathcal{NP}$ that are promising candidates to be outside $\mathcal{P}$, one defines a class of problems that are "hard" in the sense that the ability to solve any of them in polynomial time immediately allows us to solve all problems in $\mathcal{NP}$ in polynomial time. These problems, which are not necessarily decision problems, are called $\mathcal{NP}$-*hard*. The TSP is such a problem; primality testing is not. If a problem is $\mathcal{NP}$-hard and a member of $\mathcal{NP}$, it is called $\mathcal{NP}$-*complete*.

Unless $\mathcal{P} = \mathcal{NP}$, we cannot hope for an algorithm that works in polynomial time for an $\mathcal{NP}$-hard optimization problem. We can, however, sometimes at least hope to get a "good" solution in a time that is acceptable. This means that we pay with accuracy (such a solution will not be optimal in general), but we can get a satisfactory upper bound on the time we need to spend; such solutions are computed by *approximation algorithms*, which we formally define in what follows.

Definition 1.2 (Approximation Algorithm). Let Π be an optimization problem, and let ALG be a consistent algorithm for Π. For $r \geq 1$, ALG is an *r-approximation algorithm* for Π if, for every $I \in \mathcal{I}$,

$$\text{gain}(\text{OPT}(I)) \leq r \cdot \text{gain}(\text{ALG}(I))$$

if Π is a maximization problem, or

$$\text{cost}(\text{ALG}(I)) \leq r \cdot \text{cost}(\text{OPT}(I))$$

if Π is a minimization problem.

The *approximation ratio of* ALG is defined as

$$r_{\text{ALG}} := \inf\{r \geq 1 \mid \text{ALG is an } r\text{-approximation algorithm for } \Pi\}\,.$$

In general, r (and thus r_{ALG}) is not necessarily constant, but may be a function that depends on the input length n. Intuitively, a 2-approximation algorithm for a minimization problem Π is thus an algorithm that computes, for any instance I of Π, an output such that the cost of this solution is never more than twice as large as the cost of an optimal solution. What we want are of course approximation algorithms that are efficient, that is, work in polynomial time. For the TSP, which we described above, there is, for instance, a polynomial-time 3/2-approximation algorithm, known as the *Christofides algorithm*, if the input satisfies certain natural conditions. However, if these conditions are not met, it can be proven that there are instances of the TSP of length n such that there is no polynomial-time approximation algorithm with an approximation ratio bounded by any polynomial in n.

Now let us consider the following maximization problem. Suppose you want to pack a number of objects into a knapsack with a given weight capacity. Each such object has an assigned weight that also corresponds to its value and is given by a positive integer. The input is described by the weights of the objects and the weight capacity of the knapsack. The goal is to maximize the total value of the objects packed.

Definition 1.3 (Simple Knapsack Problem). The simple knapsack problem is a maximization problem. An instance I is given by a sequence of $n + 1$ positive integers $B, w_1, w_2, \ldots, w_n$, where we consider w_i with $1 \leq i \leq n$ to be the weight of the ith object; B is the capacity of the knapsack. A feasible solution for I is any set $O \subseteq \{1, 2, \ldots, n\}$ such that

$$\sum_{i \in O} w_i \leq B .$$

The gain of a solution O and a corresponding instance I is given by

$$\mathrm{gain}(I, O) = \sum_{i \in O} w_i .$$

The goal is to maximize this number.

In the following, we assume that the weight of every object is smaller than B. This makes sense as all objects that are heavier than the knapsack's capacity cannot be part of any solution and may thus be neglected. It is well known that there is no polynomial-time algorithm for the simple knapsack problem that solves every given instance optimally, unless $\mathcal{P} = \mathcal{NP}$. This problem will be very interesting for us later in a different setting; for now, we just want to give an easy idea of how to approximate optimal solutions in reasonable time. More precisely, we give a simple 2-approximation algorithm that works in polynomial time. The idea is to first sort the objects $w_1, w_2, \ldots, w_n$ in descending order (with respect to their weights) and then follow what is called a *greedy strategy*.

This simply means to pack objects into the knapsack starting with the heaviest one, then the second heaviest, and so on, as long as there is space left in the knapsack; the corresponding algorithm KNGREEDY is shown in Algorithm 1.1.

It is easy to see that the running time of KNGREEDY is in $\mathcal{O}(n \log n)$. Sorting n integers can be done in $\mathcal{O}(n \log n)$ and after that, every object is inspected at most one more time. It is not much more difficult to show that the gain of any solution computed by KNGREEDY is at least half as large as the optimal gain.

Theorem 1.1. KNGREEDY *is a polynomial-time 2-approximation algorithm for the simple knapsack problem.*

```
O := ∅;                              // Initialization
s := 0;
i := 0;
sort w₁, w₂, ..., wₙ;                // Preprocessing; we assume that
                                     // now w₁ ≥ w₂ ≥ ... ≥ wₙ
while i < n and s + w_{i+1} ≤ B do    // Pack objects greedily
    O := O ∪ {i + 1};
    s := s + w_{i+1};
    i := i + 1;
output O;
end
```

Algorithm 1.1. KNGREEDY for the simple knapsack problem.

Proof. Consider any instance $I = (B, w_1, w_2, \ldots, w_n)$ of the simple knapsack problem, and assume without loss of generality that $w_1 \geq w_2 \geq \ldots \geq w_n$. We distinguish two cases with respect to the total weight of the objects in I.

Case 1. If all objects fit into the knapsack, then KNGREEDY is even optimal, as it packs all of them.

Case 2. Thus, we assume that the total weight is larger than B, and distinguish two more cases depending on the weight of the largest object in I.

Case 2.1. Suppose there is an object w_i of weight at least $B/2$. We then have $w_1 \geq B/2$ and w_1 is always packed into the knapsack. Since B is an upper bound for any solution, it follows that the approximation ratio of KNGREEDY is at most 2 in this case.

Case 2.2. Suppose that the weights of all objects are smaller than $B/2$, and let j be the index of the first object that is too heavy to be packed into the knapsack by KNGREEDY. It follows from our assumption that $w_j < B/2$, and this implies that the space that is already occupied by the objects $w_1, w_2, \ldots, w_{j-1}$ must be larger than $B/2$. Thus, we immediately get an approximation ratio of at most 2 also in this case.

We conclude that KNGREEDY is a polynomial-time 2-approximation algorithm for the simple knapsack problem. □

An example instance and the corresponding solution computed by KNGREEDY are shown in Figure 1.1. Note that the greedy strategy works due to the preceding sorting of the weights of the objects. We now quickly discuss the tightness of our analysis of this algorithm. For any $n \geq 3$ and any arbitrarily large even B, consider an instance I that consists of a capacity B and the sequence

$$\frac{B}{2} + 1, \underbrace{\frac{B}{2}, \frac{B}{2}, \ldots, \frac{B}{2}}_{n-1 \text{ times}} \tag{1.1}$$

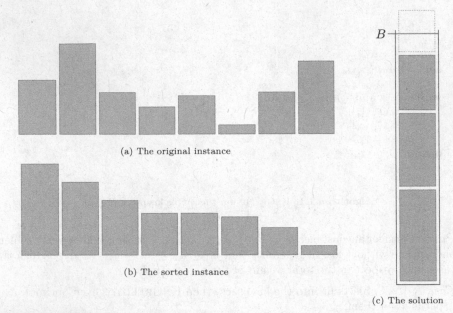

(a) The original instance

(b) The sorted instance

(c) The solution

Figure 1.1. The greedy strategy; first sort, then pack greedily what fits.

of weights. If given I as input, KNGREEDY packs the first object into the knapsack, which results in a situation where no more objects may be packed; thus, we have gain(KNGREEDY(I)) = $B/2 + 1$. On the other hand, any optimal solution OPT(I) for I may safely pack any two objects into the knapsack except the first one, and therefore gain(OPT(I)) = B. It follows that

$$r_{\text{KNGREEDY}} \geq \frac{\text{gain(OPT}(I))}{\text{gain(KNGREEDY}(I))} = \frac{B}{\frac{B}{2} + 1} = \frac{2}{1 + \frac{2}{B}} \, ,$$

which tends to 2 with increasing B.

This sums up our first ideas of how to deal with optimization problems that are in general regarded as *infeasible*. We pay with accuracy, and we gain speed in return. Of course, there are smarter methods to deal with the (simple) knapsack problem than just following a simple greedy approach. In particular, there is an algorithm that achieves an approximation ratio of $1+\varepsilon$ running in time $\mathcal{O}(n^3 \cdot 1/\varepsilon)$, for every constant $\varepsilon > 0$; such an algorithm that achieves an arbitrarily good approximation ratio $1 + \varepsilon$ in a time that is polynomial both in n and $1/\varepsilon$ is called a *fully polynomial-time approximation scheme* (FPTAS).

Exercise 1.1. Algorithm 1.1 shows a very naive implementation of KNGREEDY as it already stops packing objects into the knapsack after one object is encountered that is too heavy. However, there might still be smaller objects in the input. Would it help to consider them? How would the analysis change?

Exercise 1.2. As an input, an algorithm for the TSP expects a complete graph with edge weights that are positive real numbers; a feasible solution is a Hamiltonian cycle in the given graph, and the goal is to output such a cycle with minimum cost (the cost being the sum of all weights of edges that it consists of). The greedy algorithm TSPGREEDY starts with an arbitrary vertex and follows an edge of minimum weight to a yet unvisited neighboring vertex; this is iterated until all n vertices are visited. Then, the last and first vertex are connected to obtain a Hamiltonian cycle. Argue on an intuitive level why this approach is bad for the TSP.

We will revisit TSPGREEDY in Chapter 8. Although greedy strategies are bad for many other optimization problems, they will play an important role throughout this book. Let us therefore end this section with the remark that there are optimization problems for which they work quite well. One such problem is the *minimum spanning tree problem* (MSTP) to which we will also return in Chapter 8.

Exercise 1.3. An algorithm for the MSTP also expects a complete graph G with edge weights that are positive real numbers as input. The goal is to compute a minimum spanning tree of G, that is, a subgraph of G that is connected, does not contain any cycles, contains all vertices, and that has minimum cost. Consider the following greedy algorithm KRUSKAL. If n denotes the number of vertices of G, KRUSKAL works in $n - 1$ rounds. In every round, an edge e of G is chosen to be part of the solution; e is an edge of minimum weight that is not yet chosen and that does not close a cycle with respect to the already chosen edges. Prove that KRUSKAL always computes an optimal solution.

1.2 Online Algorithms and Paging

As described above, an algorithm computes a well-defined output for any given instance of a computational problem. In this context, we have, so far, briefly spoken about efficient approximation algorithms for $\mathcal{NP}$-hard problems. In other words, we have imposed certain requirements on the algorithms we want to study; we demanded that they have a polynomial running time while producing an output for any instance of the given problem. If $\mathcal{P} \neq \mathcal{NP}$, we may thus only hope to get an approximate solution. In the following, we want to focus on another restriction that we encounter in practice. Here, we are not concerned with not taking too much time, but with the fact that we do not know the whole instance of the problem at hand in advance. Until now, we assumed that from the start we have all information available that we need to compute a solution.

This assumption may be unrealistic in scenarios such as the following. From a practical point of view, the basic design principle of modern computers follows the *von Neumann architecture*. Computers suffer from the fact that the CPU is usually a lot faster than its main memory, which leads to a bad overall performance as

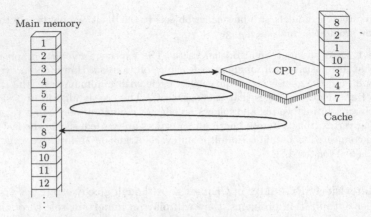

Figure 1.2. A schematic view of an environment in which we study paging. In the main memory, pages with indices $1, 2, \ldots, m$ are stored, while a small subset of them is currently stored in the cache of size $k \ll m$.

the CPU cannot be utilized to its full extent. To overcome this drawback, another memory, the so-called *cache*, is introduced. This memory is a lot faster than the main memory; however, it is therefore also a lot more expensive and thus smaller.

Now we consider the important task of an operating system to manage the cache in such a way that we need to access the main memory as rarely as possible. We want to study the essence of what makes this problem hard, and thus we look at a simplified version of the problem; see Figure 1.2. In a practical setting, we are confronted with a much more complicated situation, and there are usually many different levels of caches; here, we only deal with a two-level memory hierarchy. More precisely, for our theoretical investigations, we make the following assumptions.

- There are two different types of memory, namely the aforementioned main memory and the cache.

- Both of them may store chunks of data of a fixed size, which we call *pages*; we assume that each page has a size of 1.

- The main memory can store m pages, denoted by $p_1, p_2, \ldots, p_m$, the cache can store k pages; we assume that there are m pages in total.

- As the cache is a lot more expensive than the main memory, we have $m \gg k$.

- The input is subdivided into discrete *time steps* $T_1, T_2, \ldots, T_n$. During such a time step T_i with $1 \leq i \leq n$, exactly one page is *requested*, that is, needed in the ongoing computation.

- The CPU can only access pages that are stored in the cache.

- As a consequence, if a requested page is not in the cache in the corresponding time step, it needs to be loaded into it from the main memory, which causes a *cost* of 1; we call this situation a *page fault*. In this case, if there is no space left in the cache, a *victim page* has to be selected and removed from the cache to make room.

- Conversely, accessing a page from the cache does not induce any cost.

This problem is called the *paging problem*. For convenience, we will simply refer to it as "paging." An algorithm for paging is basically defined by the strategy it uses to choose the victim pages, that is, which page it replaces in the cache if a page fault occurs.

Paging is a prominent member of a broad class of problems for which the concrete input is revealed piecewise at runtime. Such problems are called *online problems*, and it is obvious that we encounter them in many practical situations, when, for instance, humans frequently interact with computers. We will see many other examples throughout this book. However, at first, we need a formalism that enables us to study strategies to handle such problems. Similarly to "offline" problems, which we described in the previous section, the objective in online problems can either be to minimize some cost or to maximize some gain; for instance, for paging we want to minimize the number of page faults that occur.

We start by defining online problems formally. The following definition is similar to that of offline problems from Definition 1.1, but here we need to introduce the two notions *request* and *answer*, which will be crucial for our further formalizations.

Definition 1.4 (Online Problem). An *online problem* Π consists of a set of instances $\mathcal{I}$, a set of *solutions* $\mathcal{O}$, and three functions sol, quality, and goal with the same meaning as for general optimization problems according to Definition 1.1. Every instance $I \in \mathcal{I}$ is a sequence of *requests* $I = (x_1, x_2, \ldots, x_n)$ and every output $O \in \mathcal{O}$ is a sequence of *answers* $O = (y_1, y_2, \ldots, y_n)$, where $n \in \mathbb{N}^+$ (thus, all instances and solutions are finite). An *optimal solution* for an instance $I \in \mathcal{I}$ of Π is a solution $\mathrm{OPT}(I) \in \mathrm{sol}(I)$ such that

$$\mathrm{quality}(I, \mathrm{OPT}(I)) = \mathrm{goal}\{\mathrm{quality}(I, O) \mid O \in \mathrm{sol}(I)\}\,.$$

If goal $=$ min, we call Π an *online minimization problem* and write "cost" instead of "quality." Conversely, if goal $=$ max, we say that Π is an *online maximization problem* and write "gain" instead of "quality."

As in the case of offline problems, we usually simply write $\mathrm{cost}(O)$ instead of $\mathrm{cost}(I, O)$ if I is clear from the context. Definition 1.4 does not yet formalize what we mean by online computation; namely, that the output must be computed with incomplete information. In particular, we want to model that an algorithm that works on such a problem

1. only knows a prefix of the input in every given time step,
2. makes decisions that are based only on this knowledge, and

3. may not revoke any decision it already made.

We formalize these rules in the following definition of online algorithms, which are the main objects of study throughout this book.

Definition 1.5 (Online Algorithm). Let Π be an online problem and let $I = (x_1, x_2, \ldots, x_n)$ be an instance of Π. An *online algorithm* ALG for Π computes the output $\text{ALG}(I) = (y_1, y_2, \ldots, y_n)$, where y_i only depends on $x_1, x_2, \ldots, x_i$ and $y_1, y_2, \ldots, y_{i-1}$; $\text{ALG}(I)$ is a feasible solution for I, that is, $\text{ALG}(I) \in \text{sol}(I)$.

Although the notion *time step* is not explicitly used in Definitions 1.4 and 1.5, we implicitly assign the ith request x_i and the corresponding answer y_i to time step T_i.

How do we assess the output quality of an online algorithm? A natural approach is to have a definition analogous to the approximation ratio defined in Definition 1.2 for offline algorithms. As a matter of fact, we are facing a similar situation. The approximation ratio formalizes what we can achieve for an $\mathcal{NP}$-hard problem when computing in polynomial running time (if we assume $\mathcal{P} \neq \mathcal{NP}$). In the context of online computation, we ask what we can achieve when we do not know the whole input in advance. So there are two different restrictions, and in both cases we want to know what we pay for obeying them. In Definition 1.2, we compared the cost or gain of a solution computed by an algorithm to the cost or gain of an optimal solution. This is exactly the same thing that we do with online algorithms. More specifically, we now define the term *competitive ratio* analogously to the approximation ratio; however, there are some small differences.

Definition 1.6 (Competitive Ratio). Let Π be an online problem, and let ALG be a consistent online algorithm for Π. For $c \geq 1$, ALG is *c-competitive* for Π if there is a non-negative constant α such that, for every instance $I \in \mathcal{I}$,

$$\text{gain}(\text{OPT}(I)) \leq c \cdot \text{gain}(\text{ALG}(I)) + \alpha$$

if Π is an online maximization problem, or

$$\text{cost}(\text{ALG}(I)) \leq c \cdot \text{cost}(\text{OPT}(I)) + \alpha$$

if Π is an online minimization problem. If these inequalities hold with $\alpha = 0$, we call ALG *strictly c-competitive*; ALG is called *optimal* if it is strictly 1-competitive.

The *competitive ratio* of ALG is defined as

$$c_{\text{ALG}} := \inf\{c \geq 1 \mid \text{ALG is } c\text{-competitive for } \Pi\}.$$

If the competitive ratio of ALG is constant and the best that is achievable by any online algorithm for Π, we call ALG *strongly c_{ALG}-competitive*.

Note that, in online computation, the term *optimal solution* even has a somewhat stronger meaning than in the context of offline algorithms. In the latter case, optimal solutions to instances of "hard" problems were those that can hypothetically be computed when we are given more time (as opposed to polynomial time). In an online setting, an optimal solution even refers to solutions that usually can only be computed based on some knowledge (for instance, the complete instance) that we generally do not possess; therefore, we call $\text{OPT}(I)$ an *optimal offline solution* for I. Additionally, in online computation, we do not take the running time of the algorithms we study into account. For most of the problems we will investigate, the designed online algorithms will be efficient, but there will also be algorithms that take far longer to compute a solution. The same holds for the memory that our algorithms use. In particular, we will always assume that there are no space restrictions, and that an online algorithm is able to remember all choices that it made before in any time step. It is important to keep in mind that "optimal" refers to a solution quality we can generally not guarantee, although Definition 1.6 does speak about "optimal online algorithms." On the other hand, by "strongly competitive," we mean "best possible." Moreover, let us emphasize that the term "optimal" only corresponds to the output quality of an algorithm and is independent of any of its other parameters such as the aforementioned time and space complexities. We can think of $\text{OPT}(I)$ as being computed by a hypothetical *offline algorithm* OPT which is optimal in this sense. Throughout this book, we will either speak about OPT or $\text{OPT}(I)$ depending on what is more intuitive in the current situation.

Usually, ALG is clear from the context and we simply write "c" instead of "c_{ALG}." At times, we have to speak about the cost or gain of an online algorithm ALG on a subsequence of an instance I or even a single request; we will denote this by, for instance, $\text{cost}(\text{ALG}((x_j, x_{j+1}, \ldots, x_k)))$, for some j, k with $1 \le j \le k \le n$. Moreover, if we refer to a concrete instance I, we sometimes speak of the *performance of* ALG *on* I; this performance is a lower bound on ALG's competitive ratio.

Note that, similarly to the approximation ratio, an online algorithm has a better solution quality the smaller its competitive ratio c is, and that c is never smaller than 1. Furthermore, both measurements are *worst-case* measures, that is, we are interested in studying how well an algorithm works on its hardest instances for the given problem.

When analyzing and classifying online algorithms with respect to their competitive ratios, we speak of *competitive analysis*. As with the approximation ratio, the competitive ratio is not necessarily constant, but may be a function of the input length n. We use the following terminology.

- If the competitive ratio of some online algorithm ALG is at most c, where c is a constant, we call ALG *competitive* or (depending on whether this holds for $\alpha = 0$) *strictly competitive*. If an online algorithm does not possess a competitive ratio with an upper bound that is independent of the input length, we call it *not competitive*.

- It is fine to call an online algorithm competitive if its competitive ratio depends on some parameter of the studied problem such as, for instance, the cache size k when we are dealing with the paging problem. Such parameters are known to the online algorithm in advance.

- There are, however, problems where we have to be very careful with this classification. For instance, in Chapter 5 we will deal with a problem for which the input length is bounded from above by a parameter of the problem.

Another difference between the competitive ratio and the approximation ratio is that the former uses an additive constant α in its definition, which is not present in the definition of the approximation ratio. This constant plays an important role in an online setting. If we consider an (offline) approximation algorithm that works well on all but finitely many instances, we can always include finitely many exceptions in our algorithm. In an online setting, this is not possible since an online algorithm cannot distinguish these exceptional cases at the beginning of its computation. However, using an appropriate value of α, we can also cope with a finite number of exceptions here. To prove lower bounds, the constant α forces us to construct infinitely many instances with increasing costs or gains. It is not sufficient to construct a finite number of instances, not even an infinite number where the costs or gains are bounded by some constant. Let us give an example of a hypothetical online minimization problem to illustrate this point.

Example 1.1. Consider some online minimization problem Π and suppose we can show that, for every online algorithm ALG for Π, there is an instance I on which it has a cost of at least 10, while the optimal solution OPT(I) has cost 1. We are now tempted to conclude that every online algorithm for Π is at best 10-competitive. If we have a closer look at Definition 1.6, however, we see that this is actually not allowed. In fact, there may still be 1-competitive online algorithms for Π, because, if we choose $c = 1$ and $\alpha = 9$, the inequality

$$\text{cost}(\text{ALG}(I)) \leq 1 \cdot \text{cost}(\text{OPT}(I)) + 9$$

from Definition 1.6 still holds if we just plug in the values $\text{cost}(\text{ALG}(I)) = 10$ and $\text{cost}(\text{OPT}(I)) = 1$.

On the other hand, suppose we can give a set of infinitely many instances of Π such that, for every such instance of length n, every online algorithm has a cost of at least $10n$, while OPT has cost n. In this case, we may indeed state that every online algorithm for Π is at best 10-competitive. There is no constant α such that, for some arbitrarily small constant $\varepsilon > 0$ and any instance I from above, we have

$$\text{cost}(\text{ALG}(I)) \leq (10 - \varepsilon) \cdot \text{cost}(\text{OPT}(I)) + \alpha \,,$$

as

$$10n \leq (10 - \varepsilon)n + \alpha \iff \alpha \geq \varepsilon n$$

leads to a contradiction to the fact that α is constant. $\diamond$

Next, we formalize this observation; we start with online minimization problems. Suppose there is a set of instances $\mathcal{I} = \{I_1, I_2, \ldots\}$ such that $|I_i| \leq |I_{i+1}|$, and such that the number of different input lengths in $\mathcal{I}$ is infinite. Furthermore, suppose we can show that, for every online algorithm ALG,

$$\frac{\text{cost}(\text{ALG}(I_i))}{\text{cost}(\text{OPT}(I_i))} \geq c(n) \,, \tag{1.2}$$

where $n = |I_i|$ and $c \colon \mathbb{N}^+ \to \mathbb{R}^+$ is a function that increases unboundedly with n. If ALG were competitive, there would be two constants c' and α such that

$$\text{cost}(\text{ALG}(I_i)) \leq c' \cdot \text{cost}(\text{OPT}(I_i)) + \alpha \,,$$

and together with (1.2) we obtain

$$(c(n) - c') \cdot \text{cost}(\text{OPT}(I_i)) \leq \alpha,$$

which is a contradiction (under the reasonable assumption that the optimal cost is bounded from below by a positive constant). Therefore, whenever we show a lower bound on the competitive ratio that increases unboundedly with the input length, we do not need to consider α at all; in this case, we can conclude that the given online algorithm is not competitive. Note that the same argumentation holds for any function c' with $c'(n) \in o(c(n))$. Now let us consider competitive online algorithms.

Theorem 1.2. *Let Π be an online minimization problem, and let $\mathcal{I} = \{I_1, I_2, \ldots\}$ be an infinite set of instances of Π such that $|I_i| \leq |I_{i+1}|$, and such that the number of different input lengths in $\mathcal{I}$ is infinite. If there is some constant $c \geq 1$ such that*

(i) $\dfrac{\text{cost}(\text{ALG}(I_i))}{\text{cost}(\text{OPT}(I_i))} \geq c$ *, for every $i \in \mathbb{N}^+$, and*

(ii) $\lim\limits_{i \to \infty} \text{cost}(\text{OPT}(I_i)) = \infty$ *,*

for any online algorithm ALG, then there is no $(c - \varepsilon)$-competitive online algorithm for Π, for any $\varepsilon > 0$.

Proof. For a contradiction, suppose that both conditions (i) and (ii) are satisfied, but there still is a $(c - \varepsilon)$-competitive online algorithm ALG' for Π, for some $\varepsilon > 0$. Thus, by the definition of the competitive ratio, there is a constant α such that

$$\text{cost}\big(\text{ALG}'(I_i)\big) \leq (c - \varepsilon) \cdot \text{cost}(\text{OPT}(I_i)) + \alpha \,,$$

and thus (assuming that the optimal cost is never zero)

$$\frac{\text{cost}(\text{ALG}'(I_i))}{\text{cost}(\text{OPT}(I_i))} - \frac{\alpha}{\text{cost}(\text{OPT}(I_i))} \leq c - \varepsilon \,, \tag{1.3}$$

for every $i \in \mathbb{N}^+$. Due to condition (i), the first term of (1.3) is at least c. Furthermore, (ii) implies that there are infinitely many instances for which the second term of (1.3) is smaller than ε, which is a direct contradiction. $\square$

Instead of speaking of $c - \varepsilon$, we will sometimes (unless some ε is explicitly used in a proof) simply state that there is no online algorithm that is "better than c-competitive." However, formally it could still be the case that there is, for instance, some $(c - 1/n)$-competitive online algorithm. Then, (1.3) does not necessarily lead to a contradiction with (ii). Throughout this book, in this context "better than" will always mean "better by some arbitrarily small constant ε." Moreover, sometimes we will not define the set $\mathcal{I}$ explicitly, but only speak of one "representative" instance.

For maximization problems, we can prove a statement analogous to Theorem 1.2.

Theorem 1.3. *Let Π be an online maximization problem, and let $\mathcal{I} = \{I_1, I_2, \ldots\}$ be an infinite set of instances of Π such that $|I_i| \leq |I_{i+1}|$, and such that the number of different input lengths in $\mathcal{I}$ is infinite. If there is some constant $c \geq 1$ such that*

(i) $\dfrac{\mathrm{gain}(\mathrm{OPT}(I_i))}{\mathrm{gain}(\mathrm{ALG}(I_i))} \geq c$, *for every $i \in \mathbb{N}^+$, and*

(ii) $\displaystyle\lim_{i \to \infty} \mathrm{gain}(\mathrm{OPT}(I_i)) = \infty$,

for any online algorithm ALG, then there is no $(c - \varepsilon)$-competitive online algorithm for Π, for any $\varepsilon > 0$.

Proof. Again, we do not need to consider α when the given online algorithm is not competitive. For a contradiction, suppose that both conditions (i) and (ii) hold, but there is a $(c - \varepsilon)$-competitive online algorithm ALG' for Π, for some $\varepsilon > 0$. It follows that there is some constant α such that

$$\frac{\mathrm{gain}(\mathrm{OPT}(I_i))}{\mathrm{gain}(\mathrm{ALG}'(I_i))} - \frac{\alpha}{\mathrm{gain}(\mathrm{ALG}'(I_i))} \leq c - \varepsilon , \tag{1.4}$$

for every $i \in \mathbb{N}^+$. Since, due to (i) and (ii), ALG' would not be competitive if its gain were bounded by a constant, we can assume that

$$\lim_{i \to \infty} \mathrm{gain}\big(\mathrm{ALG}'(I_i)\big) = \infty . \tag{1.5}$$

Due to (i), the first term of (1.4) is at least c; due to (1.5), there are infinitely many instances for which the second term is smaller than ε, which is a contradiction. $\square$

To sum up, if we are not speaking about the strict competitive ratio, but allow $\alpha > 0$ when proving lower bounds, we will always try to construct an infinite set of instances such that the conditions (i) and (ii) of Theorem 1.2 (Theorem 1.3, respectively) are satisfied when dealing with online minimization (maximization, respectively) problems.

To this end, for paging, we will use the concept of *phases*, which consist of a number of consecutive time steps. We then show that every online algorithm is worse than an optimal solution by some factor c within one phase, and that it is possible to repeat phases for an arbitrary number of times. Thus, c is a lower bound on the competitive ratio of any online algorithm for paging. Before we start investigating the problem in terms of upper and lower bounds on the achievable competitive ratio, we define it formally.

Definition 1.7 (Paging). The *paging problem* is an online minimization problem. Let there be m memory pages $p_1, p_2, \ldots, p_m$, which are all stored in the main memory, where m is some positive integer. An instance is a sequence $I = (x_1, x_2, \ldots, x_n)$, such that $x_i \in \{p_1, p_2, \ldots, p_m\}$, for all i with $1 \leq i \leq n$, that is, the page x_i is requested in time step T_i. An online algorithm ALG for paging maintains a *cache* memory of size k with $k < m$, which is formalized by a tuple $B_i = (p_{j_1}, p_{j_2}, \ldots, p_{j_k})$ for time step T_i. At the beginning, the cache is initialized as $B_0 = (p_1, p_2, \ldots, p_k)$, that is, with the first k pages. If, in some time step T_i, a page x_i is requested and $x_i \in B_{i-1}$, ALG outputs $y_i = 0$. Conversely, if $x_i \notin B_{i-1}$, ALG has to choose a page $p_j \in B_{i-1}$, which is then removed from the cache to make room for x_i. In this case, ALG outputs $y_i = p_j$ and the new cache content is $B_i = (B_{i-1} \setminus \{p_j\}) \cup \{x_i\}$. The cost is given by $\text{cost}(\text{ALG}(I)) = |\{i \mid y_i \neq 0\}|$ and the goal is to minimize this number.

Note that our definition imposes some restrictions on algorithms designed for the problem, such as that it is impossible to remove pages if there is no page fault. We will see shortly that this is not as restrictive as it may seem; at some points, however, we will allow this constraint to be violated.

To consolidate our feeling for the problem, let us consider a simple instance of paging before we start the formal analysis.

Example 1.2. Suppose $k = 6$, there are m pages $p_1, p_2, \ldots, p_m$ in total, and according to Definition 1.7 the cache is initialized as

| p_1 | p_2 | p_3 | p_4 | p_5 | p_6 |

.

Now suppose that we are given an instance $I = (p_4, p_7, p_5, p_1, \ldots)$. In time step T_1, page p_4 is requested, which is already in the cache; thus, any online algorithm outputs "0" and there is no cost caused in this time step. The next request is page p_7, and therefore some page needs to be removed from the cache to make room. Assume page p_1 gets chosen to be replaced by p_7, which leads to the situation

| p_7 | p_2 | p_3 | p_4 | p_5 | p_6 |

.

After that, page p_5 can be loaded directly from the cache and again causes no cost. In time step T_4, however, the cache content needs to be changed once more, as p_1 is not present anymore. Hence, after four time steps, the cost is 2. It is easy to see that a strategy which replaced, for instance, p_4 instead of p_1 in time step T_2, only has a cost of 1 at this point. $\diamondsuit$

Having every algorithm start with the same pages in the cache seems to be a reasonable assumption. What we are interested in is to measure how well an online algorithm works compared to what it could hypothetically achieve in the given situation. Thus, we compare its solution to an optimal one that has the same starting situation. As a matter of fact, also this assumption is less restrictive than it seems, because the head start that may come with a different cache content at the beginning can be hidden in the constant α from Definition 1.6.

Moreover, as already discussed, Definition 1.7 implies that an online algorithm for paging only removes a page from the cache if the currently requested page is not already in the cache; we call such algorithms *demand paging algorithms*. Of course, we could also think of an alternative definition where a page, or even an arbitrary number of pages, may be removed from and loaded into the cache in every time step. However, it can easily be shown that this does not give an online algorithm any advantage.

Exercise 1.4. Suppose that we change Definition 1.7 such that algorithms may start with different cache contents. Prove that this does not change the competitive ratio of any online algorithm ALG. More precisely, show that if ALG is c-competitive for paging as formalized in Definition 1.7, then ALG is also c-competitive if OPT has a different set of pages in its cache at the beginning.

Exercise 1.5. Show that an online algorithm that is allowed to replace an arbitrary number of pages in every time step can be converted to a demand paging algorithm, that is, an online algorithm that is in accord with Definition 1.7, without increasing its cost. Of course, for such an online algorithm the cost measurement changes. Such an algorithm pays 1 for each replacement of a page in the cache.

Exercise 1.6. So far, it cannot happen that the cache contains empty cells at any point in time, as it is full initially (with the pages $p_1, p_2, \ldots, p_k$), and the only operation to change the cache is to replace a page with another one. In what follows, we will study an online algorithm that is allowed to remove some pages from the cache without loading other pages into it. Show that also such an algorithm can be converted into a demand paging algorithm without increasing its cost. Again, the cost measurement has to be changed. Here, the removal of a page from the cache is free, while loading a page into the cache causes cost 1.

As already mentioned, an (online) algorithm for paging is basically defined by the strategy that it follows when a *page fault* occurs and a page in its cache (the victim page) needs to be replaced. There are many different strategies an algorithm may follow; let us describe a few.

- *First In First Out (FIFO).* With this strategy, the cache is organized as a queue. If a page must be evicted from the cache, the one residing in the cache for the longest time is chosen. The first k pages may be removed arbitrarily.

- *Last In First Out (LIFO).* This strategy is the counterpart to FIFO since it organizes the cache as a stack. In case of a page fault, the page that was most recently loaded into the cache is removed from the cache. On the first page fault, an arbitrary page may be replaced.

- *Least Frequently Used (LFU).* On a page fault, the page is removed that was so far used least frequently. Ties are broken arbitrarily.

- *Least Recently Used (LRU).* Here, on a page fault, the page is removed that was last requested least recently. Also here, the first k pages may be removed arbitrarily.

- *Flush When Full (FWF).* The cache gets completely emptied ("flushed") if a page is requested that is not already in the cache and there is no empty cell. This strategy does not comply with Definition 1.7 since it is not a demand paging strategy; it may remove multiple pages on a page fault, but only loads pages into the cache if the requested page is not already present. As stated in Exercise 1.6, we assume that only loading a page into the cache causes cost 1. An online algorithm that uses the FWF strategy can be converted to be in accord with Definition 1.7 without increasing the cost (as stated in Exercise 1.6).

- *Longest Forward Distance (LFD).* Here, on a page fault, the page is removed whose next request will be the latest.

In what follows, we denote, for instance, by FIFO an (online) algorithm that implements the FIFO strategy. Clearly, LFD is an offline algorithm as it requires knowledge about the future input to replace a page. The other strategies are online strategies, but they have different solution qualities in terms of competitive analysis. The next sections are devoted to studying them in more detail.

1.3 An Upper Bound for Paging

In the preceding section, we defined that an online algorithm is competitive if its competitive ratio c is bounded by a constant with respect to the input length. For paging, this means that c may depend on both the cache size k and the size of the main memory m. Three of the above online algorithms are k-competitive, so their solution qualities do not at all depend on the number of pages that are available in total. As an example, we will consider FIFO; but before that, we introduce an important tool that will prove to be helpful in the subsequent analysis.

Definition 1.8 (k-Phase Partition). Let $I = (x_1, x_2, \ldots, x_n)$ be an arbitrary instance of paging. A *k-phase partition of I* assigns the requests from I to consecutive disjoint phases $P_1, P_2, \ldots, P_N$ such that

- phase P_1 starts with the first request for a page that is not initially in the cache. Then, P_1 contains a maximum-length subsequence of I that contains at most k distinct pages;

- for any i with $2 \le i \le N$, phase P_i is a maximum-length subsequence of I that starts right after P_{i-1} and again contains at most k distinct pages.

It is crucial to note that a phase does not necessarily end right after k distinct pages were requested, but right before a $(k+1)$th one is requested. The last phase of a k-phase partition is not necessarily complete. It is also important to note that a k-phase partition is defined on inputs, and not for algorithms; let us look at an example.

Example 1.3. Suppose we are dealing with paging with cache size 5, and we are given an input

$$(p_3, p_1, p_7, p_5, p_7, p_8, p_3, p_4, p_4, p_2, p_2, p_3, p_5, p_1, p_7, p_3, p_1, p_8, p_7, p_6) \ .$$

Recall that the cache is initialized as $(p_1, p_2, p_3, p_4, p_5)$. Then we obtain a k-phase partition

$$(p_3, p_1, \underbrace{p_7, p_5, p_7, p_8, p_3, p_4, p_4}_{P_1}, \underbrace{p_2, p_2, p_3, p_5, p_1, p_7, p_3, p_1}_{P_2}, \underbrace{p_8, p_7, p_6}_{P_3}) \ ,$$

where the last phase P_3 is incomplete. Observe that if we shift the phases by one, that is, if we consider the partition

$$(p_3, p_1, p_7, \underbrace{p_5, p_7, p_8, p_3, p_4, p_4, p_2}_{P'_1}, \underbrace{p_2, p_3, p_5, p_1, p_7, p_3, p_1, p_8}_{P'_2}, \underbrace{p_7, p_6}_{P'_3})$$

instead, there are still at least k distinct pages requested during any one phase (except during the last one P'_3). However, there are two differences between the previous phases and these ones. First, they do not have maximum length (with respect to containing k different pages) anymore; and second, since the first page requested in P_{i+1} was different from all pages in P_i, we observe that in P'_i there are k distinct pages requested that are different from the last page requested before P'_i starts. ◇

We now use a k-phase partition of the given input to analyze FIFO.

Theorem 1.4. FIFO *is strictly k-competitive for paging.*

Proof. Let $I = (x_1, x_2, \ldots, x_n)$ be any instance of paging and consider I's k-phase partition $P_1, P_2, \ldots, P_N$ according to Definition 1.8. Without loss of generality, we assume that $x_1 \notin \{p_1, p_2, \ldots, p_k\}$, that is, the sequence starts with a page fault for any algorithm.

Let us consider a fixed phase P_i with $1 \leq i \leq N$. First, we show that FIFO does not cause more than k page faults during P_i. By definition, there are at most k distinct pages requested during this phase. Let p be the first page that causes a page fault for FIFO during P_i. Then, out of all pages requested during P_i, p will be the first one that is removed again, and can thus cause a second page fault (for the same page). When p gets loaded into the cache, there are $k - 1$ pages in the cache that get removed from the cache before p. Thus, p stays in the cache for the next $k - 1$

page faults, and consequently no page causes more than one page fault during one phase. Therefore, there are at most k page faults in total during one phase.

Second, we argue that a fixed optimal solution $OPT(I)$ has to make at least one page fault for every phase. To this end, we shift all phases by one as in Example 1.3, leading to a new partition $P_1', P_2', \ldots, P_N'$, where P_N' might be the empty sequence; however, the first $N - 1$ shifted phases must be complete. As already observed, since the phases P_i with $1 \leq i \leq N - 1$ had maximum length, the phase P_i' now contains requests to k pages that differ from the page p' that was last requested before the start of P_i'. We know that p' is in the cache of OPT at the beginning of P_i'. Since there are k more requests different from p', OPT has to cause one page fault during P_i'. This adds up to $N - 1$ page faults for $OPT(I)$ plus an additional one on x_1 at the beginning of I.

Since $FIFO$ causes at most $N \cdot k$ page faults in total while OPT causes at least N, it follows that $FIFO$ is strictly k-competitive. $\square$

By similar reasoning to the preceding proof, it can be shown that LRU and (which might be surprising) FWF are also strictly k-competitive.

Exercise 1.7. Prove that LRU is strictly k-competitive for paging.

Exercise 1.8. Prove that FWF is also strictly k-competitive for paging. Recall that you need to change the definition of a paging algorithm for this case; FWF has cost 1 whenever it loads a page into the cache (see Exercise 1.6).

Exercise 1.9. We define a different phase partition to the one in Definition 1.8, which now depends on the online algorithm $FIFO$. The first phase $P_{FIFO,1}$ ends after the first page fault that is caused by $FIFO$. Every subsequent phase has a length that is such that $FIFO$ causes exactly k page faults in it; the phase ends right after the kth page fault occurred. Formally, phase $P_{FIFO,i}$ ends immediately after $FIFO$ made $(i-1)k + 1$ page faults. The last phase may be shorter. Use this phase partition to show that $FIFO$ is k-competitive.

Does your proof show that $FIFO$ is strictly k-competitive?

Exercise 1.10. $FIFO$ experiences a phenomenon that is known as *Bélády's anomaly*, which states that there are instances on which $FIFO$ causes more page faults if it has a larger cache. Find such an instance.

Hint. It suffices to consider two cache sizes 3 and 4 and a total number of nine pages.

1.4 A Lower Bound for Paging

We now know that there are k-competitive online algorithms for paging. But are these algorithms strongly competitive? In other words, is this the best we can hope for or are there online algorithms which outperform $FIFO$, FWF, and LRU?

The answer is that there is nothing better from a worst-case point of view. This means that, for every online algorithm ALG, there are infinitely many instances of paging for which ALG's cost is at least k times larger than the optimal cost. To model such hard instances, we think of an *adversary* that constructs a hard instance I while knowing the online algorithm ALG we want to analyze. In a way, ALG and the adversary are two players in a game and they have directly opposing goals (in Section 2.4, we will have a closer look at this point of view). As paging is an online minimization problem, this means that the adversary tries to make ALG have a cost that is as large as possible compared to the cost of an optimal solution OPT(I) for I and thereby to maximize the competitive ratio of ALG. If not stated otherwise, we will assume that we are dealing with demand paging algorithms as in Definition 1.7; with the considerations above (in particular, Exercises 1.5 and 1.6), we know that this does not cause any restriction.

Theorem 1.5. *No online algorithm for paging is better than k-competitive.*

Proof. Let $m = k+1$, that is, we only require that there are pages $p_1, p_2, \ldots, p_{k+1}$ in total; let n be some multiple of k. Recall that the cache is initialized as $(p_1, p_2, \ldots, p_k)$, and we consider an arbitrary online algorithm ALG for paging. Obviously, there is exactly one page, at any given time step, that is not in the cache of ALG. The whole idea is that the adversary always requests exactly this page to obtain an instance I of length n. Since it knows ALG, it can always foresee which page will be replaced by ALG if a page fault occurs.

```
output "p_{k+1}";                                    // Inevitable page fault
i := 1;
while i ≤ n − 1 do
        p := the page that is currently not in the cache of ALG;
        output "p";
        i := i + 1;
end
```

Algorithm 1.2. Adversary for any paging algorithm.

More formally, consider Algorithm 1.2, which creates the instance I of length n for ALG by following this strategy. It is easy to see that this instance causes a page fault for ALG in every time step, and thus a total cost of n. However, this is not sufficient to prove the claim. The competitive ratio compares this value to what could have been achieved on I if it had been known; in other words, we need to study the optimal cost on this instance as well.

To do so, we again divide the input into distinct consecutive phases. This time, one phase consists of exactly k time steps, that is, ALG makes exactly k page faults within a phase (recall that n is a multiple of k). If we can show that OPT causes at most one page fault in every phase, we are done. Consider the first phase P_1. In time step T_1, every algorithm causes a page fault as the requested page p_{k+1} is not in the cache by definition. OPT can now choose one of the pages $p_1, p_2, \ldots, p_k$ to be removed to load p_{k+1}. P_1 consists of exactly $k - 1$ more time steps, so at most

$k - 1$ more distinct pages are requested. Therefore, there is at least one page p' among $p_1, p_2, \ldots, p_k$ that is not requested during this phase, and OPT chooses p' to be removed in time step T_1. There may be more than one such page, in which case OPT chooses the page whose first request is the latest among all such pages (OPT therefore implements the offline strategy LFD).

We can use the same argument for any other phase P_i with $2 \leq i \leq N$. The only difference is that OPT does not surely cause a page fault in the first time step $T_{(i-1)k+1}$ of this phase, but it may cause a page fault later or even not at all. However, whenever a page fault occurs, by the same reasoning as for phase P_1, there must be some page that is not requested anymore during phase P_i and that may therefore be safely removed from the cache.

Finally, we need to deal with the additive constant α from Definition 1.6. If the number of page faults caused by OPT is constant, ALG is not competitive. On the other hand, if the number of page faults increases with n, Theorem 1.2 implies that ALG cannot be better than k-competitive. $\qquad\square$

We see that the adversary can guarantee that any online algorithm causes a page fault in every time step. Thus, with respect to the pure cost, all online algorithms are equally bad. Then again, for instance, FIFO outperforms LIFO when these strategies are analyzed according to their competitive ratios. This is due to the fact that FIFO keeps pages it just loaded in the cache for a longer time than LIFO.

Theorem 1.6. LIFO *is not competitive for paging.*

Proof. To prove the claim, we show that, for every n, there is an instance I of paging of length n such that $\text{cost}(\text{LIFO}(I))/\text{cost}(\text{OPT}(I))$ grows proportionally with n. To this end, we give an instance of length n that always requests the same two pages; again, it suffices to choose $m = k + 1$. The adversary again first requests p_{k+1}, and since all pages $p_1, p_2, \ldots, p_k$ are in the cache at the beginning, LIFO removes some fixed page from the cache, say p_i. Since the adversary knows that LIFO chooses p_i, it requests it in time step T_2 and LIFO removes p_{k+1}, which is now the page that was last loaded into the cache. Then, LIFO must remove p_i in time step T_3 when the adversary again requests p_{k+1}. The adversary continues in this fashion, that is, I is given by

$$(p_{k+1}, p_i, p_{k+1}, p_i, \ldots) \, .$$

In every time step, LIFO causes a page fault while there is an optimal solution OPT(I) that removes a page p_j with $j \neq i$ in time step T_1 and has cost 1 overall, because it has p_i and p_{k+1} in its cache from that point on. $\qquad\square$

So we see that there is a significant difference between FIFO and LIFO. This is not very surprising; intuitively it seems like a bad idea to immediately remove a page from the cache that was just loaded into it. What about LFU? Here, an intuitive point of view might suggest more success; we learn from what happened so far, namely, we replace a page that was in some sense the least valuable up to now. Unfortunately, this strategy is not much better in the worst case.

Theorem 1.7. LFU *is not competitive for paging.*

Proof. The proof is only slightly more complex than the one for LIFO from Theorem 1.6. For every n', consider the instance I given by

$$(\underbrace{p_1, p_1, \ldots, p_1}_{n' \text{ requests}}, \underbrace{p_2, p_2, \ldots, p_2}_{n' \text{ requests}}, \ldots, \underbrace{p_{k-1}, p_{k-1}, \ldots, p_{k-1}}_{n' \text{ requests}}, \underbrace{p_{k+1}, p_k, \ldots, p_{k+1}, p_k}_{2(n'-1) \text{ requests}})$$

of length $n := (k-1)n' + 2(n'-1)$. In the first $(k-1)n'$ time steps, no online algorithm causes a page fault, and after that, all pages in the cache have been requested n' times except for p_k. Thus, when p_{k+1} is requested in time step $T_{(k-1)n'+1}$, LFU removes p_k, which is the page in the cache that was used least frequently. Next, the adversary requests p_k, and this is iterated until both pages p_k and p_{k+1} have been requested exactly $n' - 1$ times each. Clearly, LFU makes a page fault in each of the last $2(n'-1)$ time steps. On the other hand, an optimal solution OPT(I) simply removes a page p_j with $j \neq k$ in time step $T_{(k-1)n'+1}$ and causes no more page faults. Since

$$n' = \frac{n+2}{k+1},$$

the competitive ratio of LFU can be bounded from below by

$$2(n'-1) = \frac{2(n-k+1)}{k+1},$$

which is a linear function in n. □

According to Definition 1.6, neither LIFO nor LFU are competitive; however, if we take a closer look, the lower bound on the competitive ratio of LIFO is stronger than that of LFU by a factor which tends to $(k+1)/2$ with growing n.

Exercise 1.11. We have defined LFU such that it keeps track of all m pages and removes one of the pages that was least frequently used in the sum. Suppose the algorithm forgets the number of accesses of pages that are not in the cache and initializes it with 1 for every page that is loaded. Does this give a stronger lower bound?

Exercise 1.12. Now consider the online algorithm MAX that always replaces the page in its cache that has the largest index, that is, for any cache content $p_{i_1}, p_{i_2}, \ldots, p_{i_k}$, the page p_j with $j = \max\{i_1, i_2, \ldots, i_k\}$ is removed in case of a page fault. Is MAX competitive? If so, prove an upper bound on the competitive ratio that is as good as possible. If not, show that MAX has no constant competitive ratio. How about an online algorithm MIN that is defined accordingly?

Exercise 1.13. Consider the following online algorithm WALK that replaces the page at position $1 + ((i-1) \bmod k)$ in the cache on the ith page fault. Less formally, it replaces the pages in the order they are stored in the cache, continuing with the first cell if it used the kth one for the preceding page fault. Argue why WALK is k-competitive.

Exercise 1.14. A phenomenon that is observed in practical settings is *locality of reference*, that is, that pages are likely to be requested consecutively if they are located next to each other. We want to make use of this fact and define an algorithm LOCAL that always removes the page whose page index is farthest away from the requested one on a page fault (ties are broken arbitrarily). Is LOCAL competitive?

1.5 Marking Algorithms

Now that we have established a lower bound on any paging algorithm and a matching upper bound for some specific strategies, we want to focus on a more general concept, the so-called *marking algorithms*. This class of algorithms plays an important role in the context of randomized computation for paging, which we will study in the following chapter.

A marking algorithm works in phases and *marks* pages that were already requested; it only removes pages that are not marked. If all pages in the cache are marked and a page fault occurs, the current phase ends, and a new one starts by first unmarking all pages in the cache. Before processing the first request, all pages get marked such that the first request that causes a page fault starts a new phase. The pseudo-code of a marking algorithm is shown in Algorithm 1.3.

```
mark all pages in the cache;                           // First page fault starts new phase
for every request x do
    if x is in the cache
        if x is unmarked
            mark x;
        output "0";
    else
        if there is no unmarked page
            unmark all pages in the cache;             // Start new phase
        p := somehow chosen page among all unmarked cached pages;
        remove p and insert x at the old position of p;
        mark x;
        output "p";
end
```

Algorithm 1.3. General scheme of a marking algorithm for paging.

We now show that this general concept allows for strongly competitive online algorithms by using the concept of phases as in the proof of Theorem 1.4. More precisely, we will prove that the phases of marking algorithms correspond to the phases of a k-phase partition from Definition 1.8. Except possibly the last one, a phase of a marking algorithm consists of a maximum-length sequence of requests for k different pages. This makes it very easy for us to argue why such an algorithm makes at most k page faults in one phase.

Theorem 1.8. *Every marking algorithm is strictly k-competitive for paging.*

Proof. Let MARK be a fixed marking algorithm; let I denote the given input and consider its k-phase partition into N phases $P_1, P_2, \ldots, P_N$ according to Definition 1.8. By the same argument as in the proof of Theorem 1.4, we conclude that any optimal algorithm OPT makes at least N page faults in total on I.

What remains to be done is to show that MARK makes at most k page faults in one fixed phase P_i with $1 \leq i \leq N$. We denote the $\overline{N}$ phases explicitly defined by MARK by $P_{\text{MARK},1}, P_{\text{MARK},2}, \ldots, P_{\text{MARK},\overline{N}}$ and claim that both $N = \overline{N}$ and $P_j = P_{\text{MARK},j}$, for all j with $1 \leq j \leq N$. Since MARK makes at most k page faults in one phase $P_{\text{MARK},i}$ (clearly, there cannot be more page faults than pages marked at the end of $P_{\text{MARK},i}$), the claim follows. We first observe that both P_1 and $P_{\text{MARK},1}$ start with the first request that causes a page fault. Every phase P_i except the last one is by definition a maximum-length sequence of k distinct requests. Every requested page gets marked by MARK after being requested. If k distinct pages were requested, all pages in MARK's cache are marked. With the $(k+1)$th distinct page p' being requested since the beginning of P_i, a new phase P_{i+1} starts. In this time step, MARK also starts a new phase $P_{\text{MARK},i+1}$, as there is no unmarked page left in its cache to replace with p'. Thus, the phases P_i and $P_{\text{MARK},i}$ coincide. As a consequence, MARK makes at most k page faults per phase and the claim follows. $\qquad\square$

It can be shown that some of the online algorithms we discussed are in fact marking algorithms, although they do not explicitly mark pages.

Theorem 1.9. LRU *is a marking algorithm.*

Proof. To prove the claim means to show that LRU never removes a page that is currently marked by some marking algorithm. For a contradiction, suppose that LRU is not a marking algorithm. Then there is some instance I such that LRU removes a page that is marked. Let p be the page for which this happens for the first time, and denote the corresponding time step by T_j with $1 \leq j \leq n$ during some phase P_i with $1 \leq i \leq N$. Since p is marked, it must have been requested before during P_i, say in time step $T_{j'}$ with $j' < j$. After that, p was most recently used; thus, if LRU removes p in time step T_j, there must have been k distinct requests following time step $T_{j'}$ that are all different from p; the first $k-1$ cause p to become least recently used afterwards, and on the kth such request p is removed according to LRU. As a consequence, P_i consists of at least $k+1$ different requests, which is a direct contradiction to the definition of a k-phase partition. $\qquad\square$

Exercise 1.15. Prove that FWF is also a marking algorithm.

Exercise 1.16. How about LIFO and FIFO? Justify your answer.

1.6 Refined Competitive Analysis

Competitive analysis, as we studied it so far, is a pure worst-case measurement; it formalizes a framework in which, for any given online algorithm, the worst possible situation is met. Actually, it might be quite a realistic setting to assume some additional knowledge about the input. There are numerous attempts to get a more realistic model for such situations. In Chapter 3, we will introduce a very general method to deal with additional information and its quantification. At this point, we only want to pick two more specific approaches to give more power to online algorithms for paging.

1.6.1 Lookahead

The straightforward approach to give an online algorithm an advantage compared to the classical model is to enable it to have some *lookahead*, that is, to allow it to look into the future for ℓ time steps. It might be surprising, but this knowledge does not help to improve the competitive ratio. Consider paging with lookahead ℓ; this means that, in any time step, an online algorithm ALG_ℓ sees the current request together with the subsequent ℓ requests. Since the adversary we use to model hard instances knows ALG_ℓ, it surely knows ℓ and may therefore proceed as follows.

Each request is repeated ℓ times such that ALG is still somewhat "in the dark" in the time step where it has to replace a page. We again only need to consider the case where $m = k + 1$. The first $\ell + 1$ requests all ask for the only page that is not in the cache initially, that is, p_{k+1}. In the first time step, ALG_ℓ must replace a page, but it cannot see which page is requested in time step $T_{\ell+2}$. Therefore, the additional knowledge is completely useless, and the adversary can simply request p_i which ALG_ℓ replaces in time step T_1. When ALG_ℓ then must find a page to replace with p_i, it only knows the prefix

$$(p_{k+1}, \underbrace{p_{k+1}, \ldots, p_{k+1}}_{\ell \text{ requests}}, p_i, \underbrace{p_i, \ldots, p_i}_{\ell \text{ requests}}, \ldots)$$

of the input I, which again does not help.

Continuing in this fashion, the adversary can ensure that ALG_ℓ causes a page fault every $\ell + 1$ time steps. With the same reasoning as in the proof of Theorem 1.5, $\text{OPT}(I)$ causes at most one page fault every $k(\ell + 1)$ time steps. For such inputs of length n, ALG_ℓ causes $n/(\ell+1)$ page faults, while $\text{OPT}(I)$ causes at most $n/(k(\ell+1))$. As a result, the competitive ratio of ALG_ℓ has a lower bound of k.

Theorem 1.10. *No online algorithm with lookahead ℓ for paging is better than k-competitive.* □

1.6.2 Resource Augmentation

Another principle to improve the chances of an online algorithm against the adversary is called *resource augmentation*. Here, we allow the online algorithm to use more resources than the optimal offline algorithm. What this means in detail depends on the problem at hand. For paging, OPT is only allowed to use a cache size of $h \leq k$ for the same input; this problem is called the (h, k)-*paging problem*. We assume that OPT's cache is initialized with the first h pages $p_1, p_2, \ldots, p_h$. This problem is a generalization of paging as we studied it until now, which can just be viewed as (k, k)-paging.

Theorem 1.11. *Every marking algorithm is $k/(k - h + 1)$-competitive for (h, k)-paging.*

Proof. The proof follows from an easy modification of the proof of Theorem 1.4. Let MARK be any marking algorithm. Once more, consider the k-phase partition of a given input I. For any given phase P_i with $1 \leq i \leq N$, we know that MARK causes at most k page faults as shown in the proof of Theorem 1.8.

To bound the number of page faults that OPT(I) causes, let us again shift the phases by one to obtain a new partition $P_1', P_2', \ldots, P_N'$; again, P_N' may be empty. Let p be the first request during the phase P_i. Then, OPT's cache contains $h - 1$ pages at the beginning of P_i' that are different from p, and since, for any i with $1 \leq i \leq N - 1$, k distinct pages (that are all different from p) are requested within P_i', OPT(I) has to make $k - (h - 1)$ page faults.

In the first $N - 1$ phases, MARK causes $(N - 1)k$ page faults whereas OPT(I) causes $(N - 1)(k - (h - 1))$ page faults. In P_N, MARK causes at most k page faults; on the other hand, OPT(I) causes one additional page fault with the first request of P_1. A competitive ratio of at most $k/(k - (h - 1))$ follows, where we set the additive constant α from Definition 1.6 to $k - 1$. $\square$

Observe that Theorem 1.11 does not claim *strict* competitiveness, whereas we know from Theorem 1.8 that the competitive ratio is indeed strict for $h = k$. This is due to the fact that we know that OPT(I) has to make one page fault right before P_1', which we can then assign to the at most k page faults a marking algorithm causes in the last phase P_N. Obviously, an analogous argument for $h < k$ does not work (we would have to assign $k - (h - 1)$ page faults of the optimal solution to the at most k page faults of the marking algorithm).

We will briefly revisit resource augmentation for the k-server problem in Chapter 4, and when studying the online knapsack problem in Chapter 6.

Exercise 1.17. What happens if we assume $k < h$ instead of $h \leq k$?

Exercise 1.18. Show that the bound of Theorem 1.11 is tight, that is, that no online algorithm is better than $k/(k - h + 1)$-competitive for (h, k)-paging.

1.7 Historical and Bibliographical Notes

As already mentioned, Turing machines were introduced by Turing [138] in 1936. Two major subjects in the kernel of theoretical computer science are *computability theory* and *complexity theory*, which are both basically built around this model. Of course, our introduction was extremely short and incomplete. There is a very rich literature on computability and computational complexity, for instance, the textbooks written by Arora and Barak [11], Hopcroft et al. [78], Hromkovič [79, 80], Papadimitriou [122], and Sipser [130]. As for approximation algorithms, both Hromkovič [79] and Vazirani [139] give very good introductions.

Today we know that testing whether a given number is prime can be done in polynomial time [1].

The algorithm KRUSKAL from Exercise 1.3 is known as *Kruskal's algorithm* and named after Kruskal, who first published it in 1956 [110]. In Chapter 8, we will introduce an online version of the MSTP and exploit KRUSKAL's optimality.

The decision version of the knapsack problem (more precisely, a variant that is called the *subset sum problem*) is among "Karp's 21 $\mathcal{NP}$-complete problems" [93]. In other words, it was one of the first problems ever to be proven to be $\mathcal{NP}$-complete. For the optimization version, there is a pseudo-polynomial-time algorithm that is based on dynamic programming [79, 139]. Ibarra and Kim [84] used this approach to design an FPTAS. Therefore, the offline version of the problem is one of the easier $\mathcal{NP}$-hard problems. More details about the knapsack problem and its variants are, for instance, given in the textbook by Kellerer et al. [94]. The Christofides algorithm for the TSP was introduced in 1976 by Christofides [44].

Competitive analysis was introduced in 1985 by Sleator and Tarjan [131]. The lower bound of k for paging was also proven in this paper (even the more general result from Exercise 1.18 that makes use of resource augmentation); the authors also showed that LRU is k-competitive. Bélády proved that LFD (which he called MIN, not to be confused with the online algorithm from Exercise 1.12) is an optimal offline algorithm for paging [18]. The terms *competitive* and *strongly competitive* were first used in this context by Karlin et al. [92].

"Online Computation and Competitive Analysis" from Borodin and El-Yaniv [34] is certainly the standard textbook on online algorithms and gives both a broad and deep introduction to the topic. Additionally, there are many excellent surveys on online algorithms by, for instance, Albers [4, 6], Fiat and Woeginger [63], and Irani and Karlin [86].

Although FIFO, FWF, and LRU achieve the same competitive ratio from our theoretical point of view, it has been pointed out that this does not reflect what is observed in practice [34, 47]. The criticism has been made that the idea of competitive analysis is not sufficiently fine-grained as it is, in general, too pessimistic [6, 20, 38, 54, 62, 86, 107]; in other words, many algorithms that perform very well in practice are considered to be very weak with respect to competitive analysis. A more detailed survey of the different refinements of competitive analysis that were proposed since its introduction is given by Fiat and Woeginger [62] and in Chapter 3 of the dissertation of Dorrigiv [56].

Bélády's anomaly (see Exercise 1.10) was first observed by Bélády, Nelson, and Shedler [19].

Due to the fact that a usual lookahead does not help, Albers followed a different approach by introducing and using a so-called *strong* lookahead that enables the algorithm to see ℓ pairwise distinct future requests [5]. This more powerful knowledge about the future does indeed help for paging. Let $\ell \leq k - 2$; then there is an online algorithm (basically a variant of the abovementioned strategy LRU) with strong lookahead ℓ that is $(k - \ell)$-competitive, and this bound is tight. The concept of resource augmentation was introduced by Kalyanasundaram and Pruhs [89, 90] (though implicitly used earlier [50, 131]), and since then used for a number of problems [50, 123]. Iwama and Zhang [88] and Han and Makino [75] used this relaxation of pure competitive analysis to study online versions of the knapsack problem; for this problem, we combine resource augmentation and computing with advice in Chapter 6.

Randomization

2

Now that we have established some basic ideas about online algorithms and competitive analysis, we introduce the concept of randomized online computation. Here, we basically allow an online algorithm to "flip a coin" from time to time and to continue its computation based on the outcome. The algorithms we studied so far were *deterministic*; this means that their actions were completely determined by the instance they were given. To distinguish these two different kinds of algorithms, we will now speak of deterministic online algorithms and *randomized online algorithms*. The output computed by a randomized online algorithm is not fully determined by the instance anymore, but there are different possible outputs, and therefore also different output qualities, when dealing with the same input. For a fixed input, we thus study the expected quality of a given randomized online algorithm. We again study worst-case inputs that are constructed by an adversary; the adversary model we use is called an *oblivious adversary*. Such an adversary is weak in the sense that it does not have any information about the random decisions made by the online algorithm.

We start by formally defining this model, and then continue by making some important observations on how to think about these algorithms. After that, we study randomized online algorithms for paging. An important result is that we can obtain an output that is exponentially better (in expectation) when computing using randomness instead of computing deterministically. Next, we learn a very central technique, known as *Yao's principle*, that allows us to prove lower bounds on the solution quality of randomized online algorithms by arguing about deterministic ones. First, we prove the statement for the special case where we have both a finite number of "coin tosses" and a finite class of instances; then, we generalize the results for an infinite setting. After that, we elaborate some interesting connections between online algorithms and two-person zero-sum games. Using what we have learned so far, we show a lower bound on the solution quality of randomized online algorithms for paging that asymptotically matches the preceding upper bound. Furthermore, as we are

© Springer International Publishing Switzerland 2016
D. Komm, *An Introduction to Online Computation*,
Texts in Theoretical Computer Science. An EATCS Series,
DOI 10.1007/978-3-319-42749-2_2

particularly interested in the number of random bits a randomized online algorithm has to use, we study so-called *barely random algorithms*, that is, algorithms that only use a constant number of random bits to create their output, independent of the input length. Last, we investigate deterministic and randomized online algorithms for a very generic online minimization problem that is encountered in many practical situations, namely the famous *ski rental problem*.

2.1 Introduction

The results of the previous chapter foreshadow the dilemma we are facing when computing online and considering worst-case instances; deterministic online algorithms may perform very poorly. Also, we have seen a possible way out by giving algorithms more power, for instance, by allowing resource augmentation or lookahead. However, for the latter idea, it turned out that it does not really help for paging with respect to competitive analysis. Of course, one might ask how realistic it is to perform such a worst-case analysis the way we do, or whether it is not sufficient to design algorithms that perform well for most instances. However, we want guarantees in the following sense. Our worst-case instances may seem artificial from a practical point of view, but maybe they are actually very natural for certain environments. In such a situation, there may exist a few hard inputs that always cause a given online algorithm to fail, although it performs a lot better on all other instances. The way we measure the solution quality of algorithms, such an algorithm is considered bad. In other words, we do not want that there are some instances of the given problem that *always* cause an online algorithm to perform poorly; even if our feeling is that these inputs do not occur very often.

However, in a randomized setting, it is acceptable if we design online algorithms for which we can guarantee that, for every given input, they perform well "on average." With this in mind, we use the following approach to enable online algorithms to obtain a higher output quality, that is, to overcome the drawback of not knowing the future, at least to some extent. We allow the online algorithm at hand to base its computations on randomness. So far, the output of a fixed algorithm was fully determined by its strategy and the input, which is why we call such algorithms *deterministic online algorithms*. We may think of *randomized online algorithms* as online algorithms that toss a coin from time to time and use the outcome of this coin flip to produce the output.

Formally, we need to introduce a *random source* which the algorithm may use; we neglect the potential difficulties of obtaining truly random numbers and simply suppose we have access to "real" randomness. In accordance with the model of Turing machines, we suppose that the random bits are read from a *tape* in a sequential manner. More precisely, the algorithm has access to a tape that is of unbounded length and that has an infinite binary string ψ written on it. Each bit of ψ is either 1 or 0 with a probability of $1/2$ each. Let us give a formal definition.

Definition 2.1 (Randomized Online Algorithm). Let Π be an online problem and let $I = (x_1, x_2, \ldots, x_n)$ be an input of Π. A *randomized online algorithm* RAND for Π computes the output $\mathrm{RAND}^\psi(I) = (y_1, y_2, \ldots, y_n)$, where y_i depends on $\psi, x_1, x_2, \ldots, x_i$ and $y_1, y_2, \ldots, y_{i-1}$; ψ denotes a *binary string*, where every bit is chosen with probability $1/2$ to be either 0 or 1, and each choice is independent of all other bits.

So the output created by randomized online algorithms does not simply depend on the input, but also on ψ. In other words, for a fixed randomized online algorithm and a fixed input, there may be different outputs. Of course, this needs to be reflected in the way we measure the solution quality of such an algorithm and we cannot simply apply Definition 1.6. To this end, cost(RAND(I)) (gain(RAND(I)), respectively) is now a random variable that corresponds to the cost (gain, respectively) of RAND on I. We measure the solution quality of a randomized online algorithm by comparing its expected cost (expected gain, respectively), that is, $\mathbb{E}[\mathrm{cost}(\mathrm{RAND}(I))]$ ($\mathbb{E}[\mathrm{gain}(\mathrm{RAND}(I))]$, respectively), to that of an optimal offline solution for I. It is important to note that the optimal cost (gain, respectively) is a fixed value and not a random variable in this setting. Also, we are still interested in worst-case analysis when it comes to the input. This means that we do not consider a probability distribution over the inputs, but over contents of the random tape ψ. A randomized online algorithm is consistent for an online problem if it computes a feasible solution for every ψ and every input. In the remainder of this book, we omit ψ for the sake of an easier notation. These ideas are formalized in the following definition.

Definition 2.2 (Expected Competitive Ratio). Let Π be an online problem, let RAND be a consistent randomized online algorithm for Π, and let OPT be an optimal offline algorithm for Π. For $c \geq 1$, RAND is *c-competitive in expectation* for Π if there is a non-negative constant α such that, for every instance $I \in \mathcal{I}$,

$$\mathrm{gain}(\mathrm{OPT}(I)) \leq c \cdot \mathbb{E}[\mathrm{gain}(\mathrm{RAND}(I))] + \alpha$$

if Π is a maximization problem, or

$$\mathbb{E}[\mathrm{cost}(\mathrm{RAND}(I))] \leq c \cdot \mathrm{cost}(\mathrm{OPT}(I)) + \alpha$$

if Π is a minimization problem. If these inequalities hold with $\alpha = 0$, we call RAND *strictly c-competitive in expectation*. The *expected competitive ratio* of RAND is defined as

$$c_{\mathrm{RAND}} := \inf\{c \geq 1 \mid \mathrm{RAND} \text{ is } c\text{-competitive in expectation for } \Pi\}.$$

If the expected competitive ratio of RAND is constant and the best that is achievable, we call RAND *strongly c_{RAND}-competitive in expectation*.

When proving lower bounds on the non-strict expected competitive ratio of some competitive randomized online algorithm, we can proceed analogously to deterministic online algorithms, that is, as we did in Theorems 1.2 and 1.3. More precisely, we again construct a set $\mathcal{I} = \{I_1, I_2, \ldots\}$ of instances and make sure that

$$\lim_{i \to \infty} \text{cost}(\text{OPT}(I_i)) = \infty$$

when dealing with a minimization problem, and

$$\lim_{i \to \infty} \text{gain}(\text{OPT}(I_i)) = \infty$$

when speaking about a maximization problem. All the other remarks we made in Section 1.2 about α can also be immediately transferred to the randomized setting.

For sure, one can easily think of alternative approaches to measure the solution quality of a randomized online algorithm; for instance, we could look at the competitive ratio that is achieved with some certain probability (which we will do in Section 2.7). Asking for an online algorithm to perform well in expectation is justified by the following reasoning.

- As mentioned above, if we consider a deterministic online algorithm ALG to be bad, there are infinitely many inputs for which ALG always produces some output of low quality, for instance, with large cost, compared to an optimal solution.

- For a good randomized online algorithm RAND, we require that it performs well on average. It may very well be the case that RAND produces a bad output for some instances, but only for some random decisions it makes. If the expected competitive ratio is small, however, we may hope that this does not happen too often for a fixed instance, or, if it does happen often, that RAND performs very well for the remaining random decisions. Thus, there are no hard instances that always cause RAND to fail, but, on each instance, RAND only fails sometimes. Of course, this "sometimes" comes in different flavors.

Similarly to deterministic online algorithms, we introduce an adversary that constructs the input in a malicious way. In accordance with the two points above, this adversary does not foresee the random decisions that are made by the algorithm; such an adversary is called an *oblivious adversary*. It knows all deterministic steps a given randomized online algorithm RAND makes. Thus, the adversary is aware of when RAND reads random bits, how many of them are used, and what is done depending on their values; but it has no clue about what these values will be. In the deterministic setting, we could think of the adversary as preparing the input in advance or as "reacting" to the algorithm's concrete answers. Here, we have to be more careful, because the adversary is not allowed to base the requests on the answers of the randomized online algorithm as they may depend on the values of the random bits; thus, the input has to be constructed in advance.

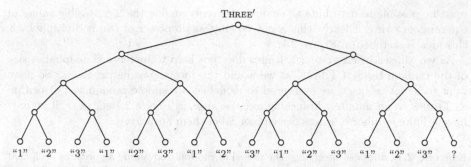

Figure 2.1. The randomized online algorithm THREE′.

A very important point which we need to consider when studying randomized online algorithms is the number of random decisions they make. An immediate problem is that we cannot always give an upper bound on the number of random bits used with absolute certainty. As an example, consider the simple randomized online algorithm THREE that does not get any input and only picks a number 1, 2, or 3 uniformly at random, that is, each with probability 1/3. How do we achieve this? Well, as THREE is a randomized online algorithm, it may read two bits from its random tape and simply map the outcome to "1," "2," or "3." Thus, as a straightforward implementation, THREE outputs

$$\boxed{0}\ \boxed{0}\ \diagdown \ldots \to \text{``1,''} \quad \boxed{0}\ \boxed{1}\ \diagup \ldots \to \text{``2,''} \ \text{and} \ \boxed{1}\ \boxed{0}\ \diagdown \ldots \to \text{``3''}$$

and all these decisions are made with probability 1/4 as the bits on THREE's random tape are 0 or 1 with probability 1/2 each. Obviously, this is not sufficient, because every outcome is supposed to have a probability of 1/3. In other words, what do we do if the two random bits are both 1? Clearly, we cannot map this event to any of the three outputs; actually, there only seems to be one meaningful option. If this case occurs, we read the next two bits from the random tape and follow the same strategy as above.

Then, however, the outcome might again be that both bits are 1. In this case, THREE has to read another two bits, which happens with probability 1/16, and so on. In general, the probability that we still do not have a result after n tries is $1/4^n$, which means that it tends to 0 exponentially fast; still, this does not suffice to say that THREE terminates with absolute certainty after n tries.

As a matter of fact, it is easy to see that we can never give any guarantee in such a case. For a contradiction, suppose there is a natural number n' such that there is a randomized algorithm THREE′ that uses n' random bits and outputs "1," "2," or "3" uniformly at random and with absolute certainty. THREE′ also does not get any input and therefore its behavior is fully determined by the values of the first n' bits on its random tape. This means that THREE′ may act in at most $2^{n'}$ ways. If there are three outcomes and each is supposed to be chosen with the same probability, it must be possible to distribute these outputs evenly among the $2^{n'}$ possible values of the random string. Clearly, this is not possible as no power of two is divisible by 3; this idea is sketched in Figure 2.1.

As we will see in Exercise 2.1, it also does not help to increase the alphabet size of the random tape of THREE$'$ as we would run into the same problems. So if we want to be really exact, we even need to model such a simple randomized algorithm as THREE$'$ as an infinitely branching tree, because, as Figure 2.1 suggests, if we only have a finite number of leaves, we cannot label them accurately.

Exercise 2.1. Suppose we change the model of randomized online algorithms such that the random tape does not contain bits, but symbols from an alphabet Σ with $|\Sigma| = \sigma$. Prove a result similar to the one for THREE$'$.

This behavior contradicts our notion as computer scientists of *algorithms*. As mentioned before, algorithms are those Turing machines that always halt, but here we are dealing with algorithms for which we cannot guarantee that they do. A possible way to cope with this problem is to analyze how many random bits we need in expectation; then we can apply Markov's inequality to derive a bound on the probability of taking t times as long, which is $1/t$. We can thus bound the number of random bits from above such that the probability that the considered randomized online algorithm uses more bits is very small. Then we will ignore this last uncertainty in a similar way that we ignore the probability of some hardware error during computation. Alternatively, we might be satisfied if the probabilities deviate very slightly from the ideal ones we assume theoretically. In what follows, we therefore assume that every randomized online algorithm that reads a finite input only uses a finite number of random bits.

To prove both lower and upper bounds on the expected competitive ratio of randomized online algorithms, we will often take the following point of view. Let $b\colon \mathbb{N} \to \mathbb{N}$ be a function that gives the maximum number of random binary decisions (figuratively speaking, the "coin tosses") of some given randomized online algorithm RAND for a given input length. As we have just discussed, for any natural number n, $b(n)$ is well defined, that is, $b(n)$ is some natural number as well. Therefore, we may say that RAND behaves in at most $2^{b(n)}$ different ways when reading some fixed input of length n. If we know RAND, we can compute $b(n)$ for every n. Furthermore, for every given instance of length n, we can simply simulate RAND for every possible random string of length $b(n)$, and thus study the behavior of the deterministic online algorithms we get as a consequence. The following observation is based on this idea and allows us to treat a randomized online algorithm as a set of deterministic algorithms.

Observation 2.1. *Every randomized online algorithm* RAND *that uses at most* $b(n)$ *random bits for inputs of length* n *can be viewed as a set* $\mathrm{strat}(\text{RAND}, n) = \{A_1, A_2, \ldots, A_{\ell(n)}\}$ *of* $\ell(n) \le 2^{b(n)}$ *(not necessarily distinct) deterministic online algorithms on inputs of length* n, *from which* RAND *randomly chooses one.*

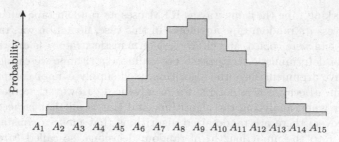

Figure 2.2. Schematic view of a randomized algorithm.

This point of view is shown schematically in Figure 2.2. To emphasize the context, we always write the names of deterministic strategies from the set strat(RAND, n) in italic letters. The probability distribution, on which RAND is based, is arbitrary; however, it must be possible to implement it with $b(n)$ random bits. We make another observation to again allow for an easier analysis. To this end, we note that every deterministic strategy is chosen with a probability that is a multiple of $1/2^{b(n)}$. Now let $a \in \{1, 2, \ldots, 2^{b(n)}\}$; instead of choosing a deterministic algorithm with a probability of $a/2^{b(n)}$, we can just choose a identical deterministic algorithms with a probability of $1/2^{b(n)}$ each. This leads to the following observation.

Observation 2.2. *Every randomized online algorithm* RAND *that uses at most* $b(n)$ *random bits for inputs of length n can be viewed as a set* strat(RAND, n) $=$ $\{A_1, A_2, \ldots, A_{2^{b(n)}}\}$ *of $2^{b(n)}$ (not necessarily distinct) deterministic online algorithms on inputs of length n, from which* RAND *chooses one uniformly at random with probability* $1/2^{b(n)}$.

Exercise 2.2. In Observation 2.2, we speak about "at most $b(n)$ random bits." But this means that the randomized online algorithm RAND may also use fewer bits. Don't we have to incorporate this fact? If so, the behavior of RAND can be different for all binary strings up to a length of $b(n)$. As a consequence, there would be

$$\sum_{i=0}^{b(n)} 2^i = 2^{b(n)+1} - 1$$

possibilities and not just $2^{b(n)}$. Argue why our reasoning is nevertheless correct, and why it is wrong to treat RAND as a set of $2^{b(n)+1} - 1$ deterministic algorithms.

Note that the point of view taken in Observations 2.1 and 2.2 is somewhat easier to see when speaking about offline algorithms instead of online algorithms. If we use the model of Turing machines, we can just modify a given randomized Turing machine RTM to another randomized Turing machine RTM$'$ in the following way. At the very beginning, RTM$'$ computes $b(n)$ and copies $b(n)$ bits from its random tape to an additional working tape. After that, RTM$'$ works exactly like RTM while using its working tape the same way as RTM uses its random tape whereas RTM′ does not access its random tape anymore. In this case, no action was taken before the random bits were copied, and clearly a deterministic strategy is drawn randomly from a set of deterministic strategies.[1] For online algorithms, we cannot use such a constructive argument since the algorithm itself simply cannot compute $b(n)$ at the beginning (because n is not known in advance). However, we can compute this number when analyzing the algorithm, and this is all that is needed in this case. Moreover, there are randomized algorithms that make a constant number (with respect to the input length) of random decisions (so-called *barely random algorithms*, which we will consider shortly). These algorithms can indeed read all random bits before starting the computation. For such a randomized algorithm RAND that reads at most b random bits, we simply define the set of deterministic strategies by $\text{strat}(\text{RAND}) = \{A_1, A_2, \ldots, A_{2^b}\}$.

Before we proceed to design randomized online algorithms for the paging problem, let us make some general statements. In Definition 2.2, we did not speak about *optimal* randomized online algorithms. In principle, there does not seem to be any immediate reason why we did not. So this would be a randomized online algorithm that, for *every* choice of random bits, produces an optimal solution for *every* input. However, if such an algorithm exists, we can immediately make an even stronger statement.

Theorem 2.1. *If, for some online problem* Π, *there is an optimal randomized online algorithm, then there also is an optimal deterministic online algorithm for* Π.

Proof. Suppose that RAND is an optimal randomized online for Π. Now suppose we simply design a deterministic online algorithm ALG that, whenever RAND reads a bit from its random tape, assumes that this bit is, without loss of generality, 1. Since RAND is optimal, it also has to be optimal in this (admittedly rather unlikely) case of "random" choices. Therefore, ALG is also optimal; moreover, we note that, for any fixed input length n, ALG is one of the strategies in $\text{strat}(\text{RAND}, n)$. □

As a consequence, if we show that there is no optimal deterministic online algorithm for some online problem, we can conclude that there also is no optimal randomized one. It is very important to note that the above argument only holds for optimality, and that there is no analogous argument for 1-competitive randomized online algorithms.

Example 2.1. Consider the following online minimization problem, for which we have an *almost* optimal randomized online algorithm, but for which any deterministic online algorithm is very bad. Let $\varepsilon > 0$ be arbitrary but fixed such that $1/\varepsilon \in \mathbb{N}^+$. The input $I = (x_1, x_2, \ldots, x_n)$ starts with a request $x_1 = n$, where n is a multiple of $1/\varepsilon$, and we have $n \gg 1/\varepsilon$. Every online algorithm has to give an answer y_1 when reading x_1 such that $1 \le y_1 \le n$. The second request is x_2 with $1 \le x_2 \le n$. If

---

[1]Note that computing $b(n)$ may increase the running time. Another issue is that such a construction does not necessarily work if the memory RTM uses is bounded.

$y_1 = x_2$, the algorithm has to pay a penalty of 1 in time step T_2 and every subsequent time step that is a multiple of $1/\varepsilon$, independent of its further answers. If, however, $y_1 \neq x_2$, the algorithm only pays 1 in total. Therefore, OPT always has cost 1; both the cost and the competitive ratio of any deterministic online algorithm are exactly εn.

Conversely, we can easily design a randomized online algorithm RAND that gives an answer y_1 with $1 \leq y_1 \leq n$ after the first request uniformly at random, that is, every value is given as an answer with probability $1/n$. The expected cost of RAND is therefore

$$\frac{1}{n} \cdot \varepsilon n + \left(1 - \frac{1}{n}\right) \cdot 1 \leq 1 + \varepsilon .$$

It directly follows that RAND is 1-competitive in expectation, according to Definition 2.2 for $\alpha = \varepsilon$.   ◇

Of course, our argument only works because the input length n is revealed to the algorithm in the first time step.

Note that there is a natural restriction on how much randomization can help in an online setting that we do not encounter in offline problems. When we deal with randomized offline algorithms, we can make use of the principle of *amplification*. The idea is to run a randomized algorithm multiple times on the same input to increase the probability of obtaining a correct answer for some decision problem. Let us stick to offline problems for a second and consider an easy example.

Example 2.2. In Section 1.1, we briefly discussed the decision problem of determining whether a given number is prime. The *Solovay-Strassen algorithm* SOST answers this question with "yes" or "no" as follows. If the input I is prime, the correct output "yes" is given with probability 1; if the input is composite, however, the correct output is given with probability at least $1/2$. This is, of course, unsatisfying. If the output is "no," I must be composite; if the output is "yes," however, it may very well be the case that I is also composite.

Then again, we have an additional promise, namely SOST only gives the wrong answer "yes" with a probability of at most $1/2$ if I is composite. Now suppose we run SOST t times on the same input. The probability that I is composite and "yes" is still given as an answer all t times is at most $1/2^t$. On the other hand, if during these t runs, an answer "no" is observed once, we know that I is composite.

Hence, a correct answer is given with probability at least $1 - 1/2^t$ if I is composite, and with probability 1 if I is prime. For any $\varepsilon > 0$, we can choose the number t of runs of SOST such that

$$1 - \frac{1}{2^t} > 1 - \varepsilon .$$

To this end, it suffices to set

$$t := \left\lfloor \log_2\left(\frac{1}{\varepsilon}\right) \right\rfloor + 1$$

to only allow an arbitrarily small (constant) error in the worst case.   ◇

When dealing with approximation algorithms for optimization problems, there is no simple "yes" or "no" and thus no right or wrong answer. Similarly to the expected competitive ratio of online algorithms, here, the expected approximation ratio is taken as a measurement. The nice thing is that through amplification a statement about some solution quality that is obtained in expectation also allows for a statement about which solution quality is obtained with an arbitrarily large (constant) probability. Suppose we are given a randomized offline r-approximation algorithm RAND for, say, a minimization problem Π. For any instance I of Π, let $d_I := r \cdot \text{cost}(\text{OPT}(I))$ where $\text{OPT}(I)$ is an optimal solution for I. Then, we have

$$\mathbb{E}[\text{cost}(\text{RAND}(I))] \le d_I ,$$

for every I. For any given $\delta > 0$, we can bound the probability that RAND has a cost that is a factor of $1 + \delta$ larger than d_I by

$$\Pr[\text{cost}(\text{RAND}(I)) \ge (1 + \delta) \cdot d_I] \le \frac{1}{1+\delta}$$

due to Markov's inequality. If we again run RAND t times and choose the solution with minimum cost at the end, we can bound the probability that the result has a cost that is at least $(1 + \delta) \cdot d_I$ in all t iterations by

$$\Pr[\text{cost}(\text{RAND}(I)) \ge (1 + \delta) \cdot d_I \text{ in all } t \text{ tries}] \le \left(\frac{1}{1+\delta}\right)^t ,$$

and we note that this upper bound does not depend on d_I. As in Example 2.2, we can choose the number of runs t of RAND such that

$$1 - \left(\frac{1}{1+\delta}\right)^t > 1 - \varepsilon .$$

A possible value is

$$t := \left\lfloor \log_{\frac{1}{1+\delta}} \left(\frac{1}{\varepsilon}\right) \right\rfloor + 1 .$$

In online computation, the technique of amplification unfortunately cannot be applied as online algorithms only have one shot to compute the output. Thus, a plain statement about the expected competitive ratio cannot be used in general to argue about the probabilities to compute a good or bad solution; for such statements we have to take a closer look.

2.2 A Randomized Online Algorithm for Paging

So far, we have learned that deterministic online algorithms are k-competitive at best for the paging problem. A general strategy to really obtain such a competitive ratio is that followed by marking algorithms. These algorithms only differ in the way unmarked pages are replaced. In this section, we design a randomized marking algorithm RMARK, which follows this concept and replaces the unmarked pages uniformly at random; the idea is shown in Algorithm 2.1.

mark all pages in the cache;   // *First page fault starts new phase*
for every request x **do**
    if x is in the cache
        if x is unmarked
            mark x;
        output "0";
    else
        if there is no unmarked page
            unmark all pages in the cache;   // *Start new phase*
        $p :=$ randomly chosen page among all unmarked cached pages;
        remove p and **insert** x at the old position of p;
        mark x;
        output "p";
end

Algorithm 2.1. Randomized online algorithm RMARK for paging.

Our hope is that no oblivious adversary can force RMARK to create an output that is too bad, because which pages reside in the cache at some given point in time partly depends on random decisions. For any $m \in \mathbb{N}^+$, let H_m denote the mth *harmonic number*, defined as

$$H_m := 1 + \frac{1}{2} + \frac{1}{3} + \ldots + \frac{1}{m} = \sum_{i=1}^{m} \frac{1}{i},$$

which we need to prove the following theorem.

Theorem 2.2. RMARK *is strictly* $2H_k$-*competitive in expectation for paging.*

Proof. Let I denote the given input, and let there be N phases (defined by the k-phase partition by both RMARK and Definition 1.8) in total. Note that the phases only depend on I and not on the random decisions of RMARK. Recall that, before the first request is processed, RMARK marks all pages in its cache; thus, the first page fault starts a new phase. For now, assume that all phases are complete.

Let us analyze a single phase P_j with $1 \le j \le N$. In this phase, exactly k distinct pages are requested; without loss of generality, we assume that no page is requested more than once during P_j. We call all pages that are already in the cache of RMARK at the beginning of P_j "old." Conversely, pages that are not old and that are requested during P_j are called "new." For every new page, an unmarked old page is removed from the cache. Since new pages cause page faults anyway, it is certainly a best strategy for the adversary to first request new pages and then old ones to increase the probability that some of the latter were removed before. Thus, we assume such an adversary for our analysis. Let l_j denote the number of new pages that are requested during P_j, leading to l_j page faults made by RMARK. Since P_j is complete, after the first l_j requests, there are $k - l_j$ unmarked old pages requested during P_j, and each one is in the cache of RMARK with a certain probability.

Consider the request for the first old page. In total, there are k unmarked old pages, some of which are still in the cache and some of which are removed at this point. More precisely, at the $(l_j + 1)$th time step of P_j, in which the first old page is requested, $k - l_j$ old pages have not yet been removed. Therefore, the probability that the page that is requested is still in the cache is

$$\frac{k - l_j}{k} .$$

After that, there are $k - 1$ unmarked old pages and $k - l_j - 1$ unmarked old pages that have not yet been removed from the cache. The probability that the page that is requested in the $(l_j + 2)$th time step is still in the cache is therefore

$$\frac{k - l_j - 1}{k - 1} ,$$

and in general we get that the ith requested old page is still in the cache of RMARK with a probability of

$$\frac{k - l_j - (i - 1)}{k - (i - 1)} .$$

Conversely, this page is not in the cache with a probability of

$$1 - \frac{k - l_j - (i - 1)}{k - (i - 1)} = \frac{l_j}{k - (i - 1)} ,$$

which then also denotes the probability that RMARK has cost 1 in the corresponding time step. Together with the cost l_j for the new pages which are requested at the beginning of P_j, we obtain a total expected cost for this phase of

$$l_j + \sum_{i=1}^{k-l_j} \frac{l_j}{k - (i - 1)} = l_j + l_j \left(\frac{1}{k} + \frac{1}{k - 1} + \ldots + \frac{1}{l_j + 1} \right)$$

$$= l_j + l_j \left(\underbrace{\frac{1}{k} + \frac{1}{k - 1} + \ldots + 1}_{H_k} - \left(\underbrace{\frac{1}{l_j} + \frac{1}{l_j - 1} + \ldots + 1}_{H_{l_j}} \right) \right)$$

$$= l_j (H_k - H_{l_j} + 1)$$

$$\leq l_j H_k .$$

(since $l_j \geq 1$ and thus $H_{l_j} \geq 1$ (every phase starts with a new page))

Now let $\text{cost}(\text{RMARK}(P_j))$ denote a random variable that is equal to the cost of RMARK in phase P_j. Due to linearity of expectation, the total cost of RMARK is

$$\mathbb{E}[\text{cost}(\text{RMARK}(I))] = \mathbb{E}\left[\sum_{j=1}^{N} \text{cost}(\text{RMARK}(P_j))\right]$$

$$= \sum_{j=1}^{N} \mathbb{E}[\text{cost}(\text{RMARK}(P_j))]$$

$$\leq \sum_{j=1}^{N} H_k l_j .$$

Next, we need to compute a lower bound on the cost of an optimal algorithm OPT. If we consider two consecutive phases P_{j-1} and P_j, at least $k + l_j$ distinct pages were requested. Hence, OPT has to make at least l_j page faults in these two phases. We can partition the phases in two different ways, either starting with phase P_1 or P_2, that is, we obtain

$$\underbrace{P_1, \; P_2,}_{l_2 \text{ faults}} \; \underbrace{P_3, \; P_4,}_{l_4 \text{ faults}} \; P_5, \; \dots \quad \text{or} \quad P_1, \; \underbrace{P_2, \; P_3,}_{l_3 \text{ faults}} \; \underbrace{P_4, \; P_5,}_{l_5 \text{ faults}} \; \dots \; .$$

Moreover, note that OPT causes l_1 page faults in P_1 since both RMARK and OPT start with the same cache content. We get

$$\text{cost}(\text{OPT}(I)) \geq \sum_{j=1}^{\lfloor N/2 \rfloor} l_{2j} \quad \text{and} \quad \text{cost}(\text{OPT}(I)) \geq \sum_{j=1}^{\lceil N/2 \rceil} l_{2j-1}$$

and therefore

$$\text{cost}(\text{OPT}(I)) \geq \max\left\{ \sum_{j=1}^{\lfloor N/2 \rfloor} l_{2j}, \; \sum_{j=1}^{\lceil N/2 \rceil} l_{2j-1} \right\}$$

$$\geq \frac{1}{2}\left(\sum_{j=1}^{\lfloor N/2 \rfloor} l_{2j} + \sum_{j=1}^{\lceil N/2 \rceil} l_{2j-1} \right)$$

$$= \sum_{j=1}^{N} \frac{1}{2} l_j .$$

Consequently, we obtain an upper bound on the strict expected competitive ratio of RMARK of

$$\sum_{j=1}^{N} H_k l_j \bigg/ \sum_{j=1}^{N} \frac{1}{2} l_j = H_k \sum_{j=1}^{N} l_j \bigg/ \frac{1}{2} \sum_{j=1}^{N} l_j = 2H_k .$$

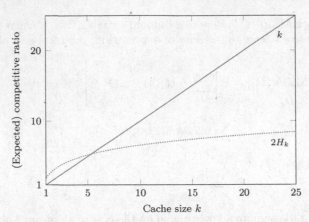

Figure 2.3. Comparison of the reachable competitive ratios of deterministic (solid) and randomized (dotted) online algorithms for paging.

To finish the proof, let us discuss the case where the last phase P_N is not complete. This means that, during P_N, there are $l_N \geq 1$ new pages requested and fewer than $k - l_N$ old pages. For the lower bound on $\mathrm{cost}(\mathrm{OPT}(I))$, nothing changes since it only incorporates the new pages of P_N. On the other hand, our upper bound on $\mathrm{cost}(\mathrm{RMARK}(P_N))$ decreases. $\qquad\square$

To better understand how much randomization helps us for paging, we note that

$$ H_m = \sum_{i=1}^{m} \frac{1}{i} \leq 1 + \int_1^m \frac{1}{i}\, \mathrm{d}i = \ln m + 1 \in \mathcal{O}(\log m) \ . $$

To sum up, we showed that no deterministic online algorithm is better than k-competitive, but there is a randomized online algorithm, which is $\mathcal{O}(\log k)$-competitive in expectation; see Figure 2.3. Hence, randomization allows for an exponential improvement of the asymptotic output quality in expectation.

In Section 2.5, we will show that, asymptotically, this is the best we can hope for when considering randomized online algorithms. However, before we show a lower bound on the expected competitive ratio of any randomized online algorithm for paging, we introduce a very general technique which often allows us to easily prove such bounds.

2.3 Yao's Principle

In this section, we study a connection between randomized and deterministic online algorithms. More precisely, the theorems below allow us to derive lower bounds on the expected competitive ratio of randomized online algorithms from bounds on the solution quality of deterministic online algorithms. It is of course not sufficient to show that all deterministic strategies are bad for a given problem. In general, we can prove such a claim using different worst-case instances. However, since these deterministic algorithms may perform well for many other instances, there still might be a "good" randomized online algorithm that chooses between them (basically, that is the point of randomized computation). We have to show something stronger; namely, we have to take into account all possible randomized online algorithms, that is, all distributions over all deterministic online algorithms, and for any of these distributions, we have to find a hard instance. Obviously, this can be very challenging since we generally do not know anything about these distributions. Yao's principle offers a way to significantly simplify this task. It essentially says that it is sufficient to show that, for a fixed probability distribution over some instances, all deterministic strategies give bad results. Intuitively speaking, we will show that we can use a distribution over instances to derive statements for distributions over deterministic online strategies. Surprisingly, we are allowed to pick *one* distribution over instances and obtain a bound on *all* distributions over deterministic algorithms.

2.3.1 Finite Problems

In this subsection, we take a first step by proving a restricted version of the claim; more specifically, we assume that both the number of different instances of the given problem Π and the number of different deterministic algorithms that are consistent for Π are finite; we call such problems *finite online problems*. In this context, by "deterministic algorithms" we mean *generic algorithms*; that is, two algorithms that produce the same output for every instance are considered to be the same algorithm. The adversary chooses the instances according to a probability distribution $\mathrm{Pr_{ADV}}$ over a finite set $\mathcal{I}$ of size μ of instances while the given randomized online algorithm implements a probability distribution $\mathrm{Pr_{RAND}}$ over strat(RAND). We denote the expected values with respect to $\mathrm{Pr_{ADV}}$ or $\mathrm{Pr_{RAND}}$ by $\mathbb{E}_{\mathrm{ADV}}$ or $\mathbb{E}_{\mathrm{RAND}}$, respectively. To have a notation that is consistent with that for deterministic algorithms, we write $\mathbb{E}_{\mathrm{ADV}}[\mathrm{cost}(\mathrm{ALG}(\mathcal{I}))]$ when we analyze the expected cost of ALG with respect to $\mathrm{Pr_{ADV}}$ for online minimization problems; likewise, we write $\mathbb{E}_{\mathrm{ADV}}[\mathrm{gain}(\mathrm{ALG}(\mathcal{I}))]$ for online maximization problems. Let $A_1, A_2, \ldots, A_\ell$ denote *all* deterministic strategies that are consistent for Π; without loss of generality, we consider an online algorithm RAND with strat(RAND) $= \{A_1, A_2, \ldots, A_\ell\}$.

Note that, since there is only a finite number of instances, any deterministic online algorithm for Π is 1-competitive since we can choose the additive constant α from Definition 1.6 such that it is equal to the worst possible cost (best possible gain, respectively) over all algorithms and instances from $\mathcal{I}$; this has to be a fixed constant (assuming that there are no infinite costs or gains, which is true for all problems considered in this book). As a consequence, we will assume that α is 0 in the following statements, that is, we consider strict competitiveness.

We start by proving two claims in terms of minimizing some cost; combining them yields Yao's theorem for finite minimization problems.

Lemma 2.1. *Let* Π *be a finite online minimization problem, and let* $\mathcal{I} = \{I_1, I_2, \ldots, I_\mu\}$ *be a set of instances of* Π*; let* $\mathrm{Pr}_{\mathrm{ADV}}$ *be a probability distribution over* $\mathcal{I}$*. If there is some constant* $c \geq 1$ *such that, for every deterministic online algorithm* ALG*, we have*

$$\mathbb{E}_{\mathrm{ADV}}[\mathrm{cost}(\mathrm{ALG}(\mathcal{I}))] \geq c \cdot \mathbb{E}_{\mathrm{ADV}}[\mathrm{cost}(\mathrm{OPT}(\mathcal{I}))] \,,$$

then, for every randomized online algorithm RAND*, there is an instance* $I \in \mathcal{I}$ *such that*

$$\mathbb{E}_{\mathrm{RAND}}[\mathrm{cost}(\mathrm{RAND}(I))] \geq c \cdot \mathrm{cost}(\mathrm{OPT}(I)) \,.$$

Proof. Following Observations 2.1 and 2.2, RAND can be seen as a probability distribution $\mathrm{Pr}_{\mathrm{RAND}}$, according to which one deterministic algorithm is chosen from a finite set $\mathrm{strat}(\mathrm{RAND})$. Now let us fix some arbitrary probability distribution $\mathrm{Pr}_{\mathrm{ADV}}$ over $\mathcal{I}$, such that every instance $I \in \mathcal{I}$ gets chosen with probability $\mathrm{Pr}_{\mathrm{ADV}}[I]$. We can then compute the expected cost of every deterministic online algorithm A_j with respect to $\mathrm{Pr}_{\mathrm{ADV}}$ as

$$\mathbb{E}_{\mathrm{ADV}}[\mathrm{cost}(A_j(\mathcal{I}))] = \sum_{i=1}^{\mu} \mathrm{Pr}_{\mathrm{ADV}}[I_i] \cdot \mathrm{cost}(A_j(I_i)) \,. \tag{2.1}$$

The expected cost of RAND with respect to $\mathrm{Pr}_{\mathrm{ADV}}$ is

$$\mathbb{E}_{\mathrm{ADV}}[\mathbb{E}_{\mathrm{RAND}}[\mathrm{cost}(\mathrm{RAND}(\mathcal{I}))]]$$

$$= \sum_{i=1}^{\mu} \mathrm{Pr}_{\mathrm{ADV}}[I_i] \cdot \mathbb{E}_{\mathrm{RAND}}[\mathrm{cost}(\mathrm{RAND}(I_i))]$$

$$= \sum_{i=1}^{\mu} \left(\mathrm{Pr}_{\mathrm{ADV}}[I_i] \sum_{j=1}^{\ell} \mathrm{Pr}_{\mathrm{RAND}}[A_j] \cdot \mathrm{cost}(A_j(I_i)) \right)$$

$$= \sum_{i=1}^{\mu} \left(\sum_{j=1}^{\ell} \mathrm{Pr}_{\mathrm{ADV}}[I_i] \cdot \mathrm{Pr}_{\mathrm{RAND}}[A_j] \cdot \mathrm{cost}(A_j(I_i)) \right)$$

$$= \sum_{j=1}^{\ell} \left(\sum_{i=1}^{\mu} \mathrm{Pr}_{\mathrm{ADV}}[I_i] \cdot \mathrm{Pr}_{\mathrm{RAND}}[A_j] \cdot \mathrm{cost}(A_j(I_i)) \right)$$

(by changing the order of summation)

$$= \sum_{j=1}^{\ell} \left(\mathrm{Pr}_{\mathrm{RAND}}[A_j] \sum_{i=1}^{\mu} \mathrm{Pr}_{\mathrm{ADV}}[I_i] \cdot \mathrm{cost}(A_j(I_i)) \right)$$

$$= \sum_{j=1}^{\ell} \mathrm{Pr}_{\mathrm{RAND}}[A_j] \cdot \mathbb{E}_{\mathrm{ADV}}[\mathrm{cost}(A_j(\mathcal{I}))] \,. \tag{2.2}$$

(due to (2.1))

Now suppose that every deterministic online algorithm has an expected cost that is at least c times larger than the expected optimal cost. Then we obtain

$$\mathbb{E}_{\mathrm{ADV}}[\mathbb{E}_{\mathrm{RAND}}[\mathrm{cost}(\mathrm{RAND}(\mathcal{I}))]] = \sum_{j=1}^{\ell} \mathrm{Pr}_{\mathrm{RAND}}[A_j] \cdot \mathbb{E}_{\mathrm{ADV}}[\mathrm{cost}(A_j(\mathcal{I}))]$$

$$\geq \sum_{j=1}^{\ell} \mathrm{Pr}_{\mathrm{RAND}}[A_j] \cdot c \cdot \mathbb{E}_{\mathrm{ADV}}[\mathrm{cost}(\mathrm{OPT}(\mathcal{I}))]$$

$$= c \cdot \mathbb{E}_{\mathrm{ADV}}[\mathrm{cost}(\mathrm{OPT}(\mathcal{I}))] . \tag{2.3}$$

(since the sum of all probabilities is 1)

At this point, we are not done yet as we considered a probability distribution over the set of inputs; this corresponds to a randomized adversary and this conflicts with our model where the adversary chooses one particular instance. However, we can easily "derandomize" the adversary by observing that (2.3) implies that there is a particular instance $I \in \mathcal{I}$ such that

$$\mathbb{E}_{\mathrm{RAND}}[\mathrm{cost}(\mathrm{RAND}(I))] \geq c \cdot \mathrm{cost}(\mathrm{OPT}(I)) .$$

To see this, assume the contrary; that is, for every instance $I_i \in \mathcal{I}$ with $1 \leq i \leq \mu$, we have $\mathbb{E}_{\mathrm{RAND}}[\mathrm{cost}(\mathrm{RAND}(I_i))] < c \cdot \mathrm{cost}(\mathrm{OPT}(I_i))$. Then it follows that $\mathrm{Pr}_{\mathrm{ADV}}[I_i] \cdot \mathbb{E}_{\mathrm{RAND}}[\mathrm{cost}(\mathrm{RAND}(I_i))] < c \cdot \mathrm{Pr}_{\mathrm{ADV}}[I_i] \cdot \mathrm{cost}(\mathrm{OPT}(I_i))$, for every i, and hence

$$\sum_{i=1}^{\mu} \mathrm{Pr}_{\mathrm{ADV}}[I_i] \cdot \mathbb{E}_{\mathrm{RAND}}[\mathrm{cost}(\mathrm{RAND}(I_i))] < c \sum_{i=1}^{\mu} \mathrm{Pr}_{\mathrm{ADV}}[I_i] \cdot \mathrm{cost}(\mathrm{OPT}(I_i)) ,$$

which is equivalent to

$$\mathbb{E}_{\mathrm{ADV}}[\mathbb{E}_{\mathrm{RAND}}[\mathrm{cost}(\mathrm{RAND}(\mathcal{I}))]] < c \cdot \mathbb{E}_{\mathrm{ADV}}[\mathrm{cost}(\mathrm{OPT}(\mathcal{I}))] ,$$

and therefore directly contradicts (2.3). As a consequence, it follows that there must be at least one instance $I \in \mathcal{I}$ such that

$$\frac{\mathbb{E}_{\mathrm{RAND}}[\mathrm{cost}(\mathrm{RAND}(I))]}{\mathrm{cost}(\mathrm{OPT}(I))} \geq c ,$$

which gives the claimed lower bound on RAND's strict expected competitive ratio.□

Lemma 2.1 makes a statement on the ratio of the expected cost of online algorithms to the expected optimal cost. This does not immediately allow us to speak about the expectation of the ratio of the costs. Let ALG be some arbitrary deterministic online algorithm for some online problem, and suppose we are given some probability distribution $\mathrm{Pr}_{\mathrm{ADV}}$ over a set $\mathcal{I}$ of inputs of this problem. Note that, in general, we have

$$\frac{\mathbb{E}_{\mathrm{ADV}}[\mathrm{cost}(\mathrm{ALG}(\mathcal{I}))]}{\mathbb{E}_{\mathrm{ADV}}[\mathrm{cost}(\mathrm{OPT}(\mathcal{I}))]} \neq \mathbb{E}_{\mathrm{ADV}}\left[\frac{\mathrm{cost}(\mathrm{ALG}(\mathcal{I}))}{\mathrm{cost}(\mathrm{OPT}(\mathcal{I}))}\right] .$$

With little effort, however, we now prove the following lemma similarly to Lemma 2.1.

Lemma 2.2. *Let* Π *be a finite online minimization problem, and let* $\mathcal{I}$ *and* $\mathrm{Pr}_{\mathrm{ADV}}$ *be as described above. If there is some constant* $c \geq 1$ *such that, for every deterministic online algorithm* ALG, *we have*

$$\mathbb{E}_{\mathrm{ADV}}\left[\frac{\mathrm{cost}(\mathrm{ALG}(\mathcal{I}))}{\mathrm{cost}(\mathrm{OPT}(\mathcal{I}))}\right] \geq c \,,$$

then, for every randomized online algorithm RAND, *there is an instance* $I \in \mathcal{I}$ *such that*

$$\mathbb{E}_{\mathrm{RAND}}[\mathrm{cost}(\mathrm{RAND}(I))] \geq c \cdot \mathrm{cost}(\mathrm{OPT}(I)) \,.$$

Proof. Let us consider a randomized online algorithm RAND that implements a probability distribution $\mathrm{Pr}_{\mathrm{RAND}}$ over a finite set $\mathrm{strat}(\mathrm{RAND})$ of deterministic online algorithms. Suppose that, for every deterministic online algorithm A_j, we have

$$\mathbb{E}_{\mathrm{ADV}}\left[\frac{\mathrm{cost}(A_j(\mathcal{I}))}{\mathrm{cost}(\mathrm{OPT}(\mathcal{I}))}\right] \geq c \,. \tag{2.4}$$

According to the definition of the expected value $\mathbb{E}_{\mathrm{ADV}}$, we further have

$$\mathbb{E}_{\mathrm{ADV}}\left[\frac{\mathrm{cost}(A_j(\mathcal{I}))}{\mathrm{cost}(\mathrm{OPT}(\mathcal{I}))}\right] = \sum_{i=1}^{\mu} \mathrm{Pr}_{\mathrm{ADV}}[I_i] \cdot \frac{\mathrm{cost}(A_j(I_i))}{\mathrm{cost}(\mathrm{OPT}(I_i))} \,. \tag{2.5}$$

Likewise, for RAND we get

$$\mathbb{E}_{\mathrm{ADV}}\left[\frac{\mathbb{E}_{\mathrm{RAND}}[\mathrm{cost}(\mathrm{RAND}(\mathcal{I}))]}{\mathrm{cost}(\mathrm{OPT}(\mathcal{I}))}\right]$$

$$= \mathbb{E}_{\mathrm{ADV}}\left[\frac{\sum_{j=1}^{\ell} \mathrm{Pr}_{\mathrm{RAND}}[A_j] \cdot \mathrm{cost}(A_j(\mathcal{I}))}{\mathrm{cost}(\mathrm{OPT}(\mathcal{I}))}\right]$$

$$= \sum_{i=1}^{\mu}\left(\mathrm{Pr}_{\mathrm{ADV}}[I_i] \cdot \frac{\sum_{j=1}^{\ell} \mathrm{Pr}_{\mathrm{RAND}}[A_j] \cdot \mathrm{cost}(A_j(I_i))}{\mathrm{cost}(\mathrm{OPT}(I_i))}\right)$$

$$= \sum_{i=1}^{\mu}\left(\mathrm{Pr}_{\mathrm{ADV}}[I_i] \sum_{j=1}^{\ell} \mathrm{Pr}_{\mathrm{RAND}}[A_j] \cdot \frac{\mathrm{cost}(A_j(I_i))}{\mathrm{cost}(\mathrm{OPT}(I_i))}\right)$$

$$= \sum_{i=1}^{\mu}\left(\sum_{j=1}^{\ell} \mathrm{Pr}_{\mathrm{ADV}}[I_i] \cdot \mathrm{Pr}_{\mathrm{RAND}}[A_j] \cdot \frac{\mathrm{cost}(A_j(I_i))}{\mathrm{cost}(\mathrm{OPT}(I_i))}\right)$$

$$= \sum_{j=1}^{\ell}\left(\mathrm{Pr}_{\mathrm{RAND}}[A_j] \sum_{i=1}^{\mu} \mathrm{Pr}_{\mathrm{ADV}}[I_i] \cdot \frac{\mathrm{cost}(A_j(I_i))}{\mathrm{cost}(\mathrm{OPT}(I_i))}\right) \,.$$

(by again changing the order of summation)

In the last line, we can plug in (2.5), which yields

$$\mathbb{E}_{\text{ADV}}\left[\frac{\mathbb{E}_{\text{RAND}}[\text{cost}(\text{RAND}(\mathcal{I}))]}{\text{cost}(\text{OPT}(\mathcal{I}))}\right] = \sum_{j=1}^{\ell} \Pr_{\text{RAND}}[A_j] \cdot \mathbb{E}_{\text{ADV}}\left[\frac{\text{cost}(A_j(\mathcal{I}))}{\text{cost}(\text{OPT}(\mathcal{I}))}\right]$$

and, due to (2.4), it follows that

$$\mathbb{E}_{\text{ADV}}\left[\frac{\mathbb{E}_{\text{RAND}}[\text{cost}(\text{RAND}(\mathcal{I}))]}{\text{cost}(\text{OPT}(\mathcal{I}))}\right] \geq \sum_{j=1}^{\ell} \Pr_{\text{RAND}}[A_j] \cdot c = c .$$

As before (in the proof of Lemma 2.1), from the definition of the expected value $\mathbb{E}_{\text{ADV}}$, we can immediately conclude that there is an instance $I \in \mathcal{I}$ such that

$$\frac{\mathbb{E}_{\text{RAND}}[\text{cost}(\text{RAND}(I))]}{\text{cost}(\text{OPT}(I))} \geq c$$

as we claimed. □

Combining Lemmata 2.1 and 2.2 results in Yao's principle for finite online minimization problems. Recall that $A_1, A_2, \ldots, A_\ell$ are all the deterministic online algorithms for Π, and that every randomized online algorithm for Π can be thought of as choosing between these algorithms.

Theorem 2.3 (Yao's Principle for Finite Min. Problems). *Let Π be a finite online minimization problem, and let $\mathcal{I}$, $\Pr_{\text{ADV}}$, and $\Pr_{\text{RAND}}$ be as described above. If there is some constant $c \geq 1$ such that*

$$\max\left\{\frac{\min_j(\mathbb{E}_{\text{ADV}}[\text{cost}(A_j(\mathcal{I}))])}{\mathbb{E}_{\text{ADV}}[\text{cost}(\text{OPT}(\mathcal{I}))]}, \min_j\left(\mathbb{E}_{\text{ADV}}\left[\frac{\text{cost}(A_j(\mathcal{I}))}{\text{cost}(\text{OPT}(\mathcal{I}))}\right]\right)\right\} \geq c ,$$

then, for every randomized online algorithm RAND for Π, there is an instance $I \in \mathcal{I}$, such that

$$\mathbb{E}_{\text{RAND}}[\text{cost}(\text{RAND}(I))] \geq c \cdot \text{cost}(\text{OPT}(I)) .$$ □

Obviously, we would like to have a similar statement for online maximization problems. This is indeed possible; we leave the proof of the following statement as an exercise for the reader.

Theorem 2.4 (Yao's Principle for Finite Max. Problems). *Let Π be a finite online maximization problem, and let $\mathcal{I}$, $\Pr_{\text{ADV}}$, and $\Pr_{\text{RAND}}$ be as described above. If there is some constant $c \geq 1$ such that*

$$\max\left\{\frac{\mathbb{E}_{\text{ADV}}[\text{gain}(\text{OPT}(\mathcal{I}))]}{\max_j(\mathbb{E}_{\text{ADV}}[\text{gain}(A_j(\mathcal{I}))])}, \min_j\left(\left(\mathbb{E}_{\text{ADV}}\left[\frac{\text{gain}(A_j(\mathcal{I}))}{\text{gain}(\text{OPT}(\mathcal{I}))}\right]\right)^{-1}\right)\right\} \geq c ,$$

then, for every randomized online algorithm RAND for Π, there is an instance $I \in \mathcal{I}$ such that

$$\text{gain}(\text{OPT}(I)) \geq c \cdot \mathbb{E}_{\text{RAND}}[\text{gain}(\text{RAND}(I))] .$$

Exercise 2.3. Prove Theorem 2.4.

Hint. For the second argument of the maximum function, consider the reciprocal of the strict competitive ratio as a measurement.

2.3.2 Infinite Problems

So far, our proofs only work if both strat(RAND) and $\mathcal{I}$ are finite. Indeed, if we assume they are infinitely large, we run into some problems. In this case, it is not justified anymore to ignore the additive constant α when computing a bound on the competitive ratio of the given online algorithms. This means that we now do not speak about the strict competitive ratio, and therefore we cannot simply show that there is one hard instance, but we have to prove the existence of infinitely many. Second, the expected values cannot necessarily be expressed as finite sums anymore. However, for many online problems, the number of instances of a given length is finite (or at least we can use finite subsets of instances of a given length for our lower-bound argument); for instance, for paging, for a fixed n, there is just a finite number of different sequences that request one of m pages in every time step, namely m^n. The number of possible answers to a given request is usually also finite, and thus, for a fixed n, there is also a finite number of *generic algorithms*. We again assume that strat(RAND, n) consists of all such algorithms. This way, we are able to apply Yao's principle for finite problems from the last subsection, yet implicitly define an infinite set of instances $\mathcal{I}$ and speak about an infinite set of algorithms. Moreover, if we can prove that the expected gain (when considering maximization problems) or the expected cost (when considering minimization problems) of an optimal offline algorithm tends to infinity, we can cover the case that α is positive; this is basically the same idea as used for Theorems 1.2 and 1.3. Subsequently, $\mathcal{I}_1, \mathcal{I}_2, \ldots$ denote infinitely many finite sets of instances of the given problem such that all instances in $\mathcal{I}_i$ have the same length, and, for every $I \in \mathcal{I}_i$ and $I' \in \mathcal{I}_{i+1}$, we have $|I| < |I'|$. Furthermore, for every input length n considered, there is only a finite number of deterministic online algorithms $A_1, A_2, \ldots, A_{\ell(n)}$. The adversary chooses the instances from $\mathcal{I}_i$ according to a probability distribution $\text{Pr}_{\text{ADV},i}$; the expected value is denoted by $\mathbb{E}_{\text{ADV},i}$. Now suppose we can construct $\mathcal{I}_1, \mathcal{I}_2, \ldots$ as above for an online minimization problem Π and show that

$$\max\left\{ \frac{\min_j(\mathbb{E}_{\text{ADV},i}[\text{cost}(A_j(\mathcal{I}_i))])}{\mathbb{E}_{\text{ADV},i}[\text{cost}(\text{OPT}(\mathcal{I}_i))]}, \min_j\left(\mathbb{E}_{\text{ADV},i}\left[\frac{\text{cost}(A_j(\mathcal{I}_i))}{\text{cost}(\text{OPT}(\mathcal{I}_i))}\right]\right) \right\} \geq c \, , \quad (2.6)$$

for every $i \in \mathbb{N}^+$. Applying either Lemma 2.1 or Lemma 2.2, there is an infinite set $\mathcal{I} = \{I_1, I_2, \ldots\}$ with $I_i \in \mathcal{I}_i$ and $|I_i| < |I_{i+1}|$ such that

$$\frac{\mathbb{E}_{\text{RAND}}[\text{cost}(\text{RAND}(I_i))]}{\text{cost}(\text{OPT}(I_i))} \geq c \, .$$

If $c = c(n)$ is an unbounded increasing function, then, by the same reasoning as for the deterministic case (see Section 1.2), RAND cannot be c'-competitive for any c' with $c'(n) \in o(c(n))$.

But what happens if c is constant? Suppose we can also show

$$\lim_{i \to \infty} \text{cost}(\text{OPT}(I_i)) = \infty \,,$$

for any choice of $I_i \in \mathcal{I}_i$. This implies that no randomized online algorithm for Π is $(c - \varepsilon)$-competitive in expectation, for any $\varepsilon > 0$; the arguments are exactly the same as in the proof of Theorem 1.2.

Analogous statements can easily be made for infinite maximization problems, which is left as an exercise for the reader. Next, we formulate an infinite version of Yao's principle where we bound from below the expected cost of an optimal offline algorithm. However, the proof (which uses a contradiction) only works for the first argument of the max-expression of (2.6).

Theorem 2.5 (Yao's Principle for Infinite Min. Problems). *Let Π be an online minimization problem, and let $\mathcal{I}_1, \mathcal{I}_2, \ldots$ and $\text{Pr}_{\text{ADV},i}$ be as described above. If there is some constant $c \geq 1$ such that*

(i) $\dfrac{\min_j (\mathbb{E}_{\text{ADV},i}[\text{cost}(A_j(\mathcal{I}_i))])}{\mathbb{E}_{\text{ADV},i}[\text{cost}(\text{OPT}(\mathcal{I}_i))]} \geq c$, *for every $i \in \mathbb{N}^+$, and*

(ii) $\lim\limits_{i \to \infty} \mathbb{E}_{\text{ADV},i}[\text{cost}(\text{OPT}(\mathcal{I}_i))] = \infty$,

then there is no randomized online algorithm for Π that is $(c - \varepsilon)$-competitive in expectation, for any $\varepsilon > 0$.

Proof. For a contradiction, suppose that both conditions (i) and (ii) are true, but there still is a randomized online algorithm RAND that is $(c - \varepsilon)$-competitive in expectation for Π, where $\varepsilon > 0$. In particular, there is a constant α such that, for every $i \in \mathbb{N}^+$ and every instance $I \in \mathcal{I}_i$, we have that

$$\mathbb{E}_{\text{RAND}}[\text{cost}(\text{RAND}(I))] \leq (c - \varepsilon) \cdot \text{cost}(\text{OPT}(I)) + \alpha \,.$$

Since this inequality holds for any $I \in \mathcal{I}_i$, we can immediately speak about the expected value with respect to $\text{Pr}_{\text{ADV},i}$, yielding

$$\mathbb{E}_{\text{ADV},i}[\mathbb{E}_{\text{RAND}}[\text{cost}(\text{RAND}(\mathcal{I}_i))]] \leq (c - \varepsilon) \cdot \mathbb{E}_{\text{ADV},i}[\text{cost}(\text{OPT}(\mathcal{I}_i))] + \alpha \,. \quad (2.7)$$

The same calculations as in the proof of Lemma 2.1 (more precisely, (2.2)) yield

$$\mathbb{E}_{\text{ADV},i}[\mathbb{E}_{\text{RAND}}[\text{cost}(\text{RAND}(\mathcal{I}_i))]] = \sum_{j=1}^{\ell} \text{Pr}_{\text{RAND}}[A_j] \cdot \mathbb{E}_{\text{ADV},i}[\text{cost}(A_j(\mathcal{I}_i))]$$

$$= \mathbb{E}_{\text{RAND}}[\mathbb{E}_{\text{ADV},i}[\text{cost}(\text{RAND}(\mathcal{I}_i))]] \,,$$

and thus it follows that

$$\mathbb{E}_{\text{RAND}}[\mathbb{E}_{\text{ADV},i}[\text{cost}(\text{RAND}(\mathcal{I}_i))]] \leq (c - \varepsilon) \cdot \mathbb{E}_{\text{ADV},i}[\text{cost}(\text{OPT}(\mathcal{I}_i))] + \alpha \quad (2.8)$$

51

has to be satisfied.

Since $\text{Pr}_{\text{ADV},i}$ is fixed, there is a "best" random choice for RAND, that is,

$$\min_j(\mathbb{E}_{\text{ADV},i}[\text{cost}(A_j(\mathcal{I}_i))]) \leq \mathbb{E}_{\text{RAND}}[\mathbb{E}_{\text{ADV},i}[\text{cost}(\text{RAND}(\mathcal{I}_i))]] . \tag{2.9}$$

The following steps are essentially the same as in the proof of Theorem 1.2. With (2.8) and (2.9), we get

$$\min_j(\mathbb{E}_{\text{ADV},i}[\text{cost}(A_j(\mathcal{I}_i))]) \leq (c - \varepsilon) \cdot \mathbb{E}_{\text{ADV},i}[\text{cost}(\text{OPT}(\mathcal{I}_i))] + \alpha ,$$

which is equivalent to (assuming that the expected optimal cost is not zero)

$$\frac{\min_j(\mathbb{E}_{\text{ADV},i}[\text{cost}(A_j(\mathcal{I}_i))])}{\mathbb{E}_{\text{ADV},i}[\text{cost}(\text{OPT}(\mathcal{I}_i))]} - \frac{\alpha}{\mathbb{E}_{\text{ADV},i}[\text{cost}(\text{OPT}(\mathcal{I}_i))]} \leq c - \varepsilon . \tag{2.10}$$

Due to (i), the first term of (2.10) is at least c. Additionally, (ii) implies that there are infinitely many sets of instances such that the second term of (2.10) is smaller than ε. Thus, for infinitely many $\mathcal{I}_i$, we get a contradiction. $\qquad \square$

The proof of the complementing statement for infinite maximization problems is also left as an exercise.

Theorem 2.6 (Yao's Principle for Infinite Max. Problems). *Let Π be an online maximization problem, and let $\mathcal{I}_1, \mathcal{I}_2, \ldots$ and $\text{Pr}_{\text{ADV},i}$ be as described above. If there is some constant $c \geq 1$ such that*

(i) $\dfrac{\mathbb{E}_{\text{ADV},i}[\text{gain}(\text{OPT}(\mathcal{I}_i))]}{\max_j(\mathbb{E}_{\text{ADV},i}[\text{gain}(A_j(\mathcal{I}_i))])} \geq c$, *for every $i \in \mathbb{N}^+$, and*

(ii) $\lim_{i \to \infty} \mathbb{E}_{\text{ADV},i}[\text{gain}(\text{OPT}(\mathcal{I}_i))] = \infty$,

then there is no randomized online algorithm for Π that is $(c - \varepsilon)$-competitive in expectation, for any $\varepsilon > 0$.

Exercise 2.4. For online maximization problems, we can make observations similar to those preceding Theorem 2.5. Discuss them.

Exercise 2.5. Prove Theorem 2.6.

⋆2.3.3 Unbounded Problems

In this subsection, we even go a step further and allow infinitely many sets of infinitely many instances and consistent algorithms. We even allow uncountably many instances and algorithms in each set, although this is somewhat "too general" as there is only a countable number of algorithms (to have an easier notation, we still speak of the jth algorithm A_j also in this case). As already mentioned in the previous subsection, in contrast to the finite case, the expected values may have to be expressed as infinite sums; even worse, we may be dealing with continuous random variables, whose expected values are given by integrals rather than sums. To study such a setting, we use the following variation of Tonelli's theorem, which we state without a proof; it will allow us to prove the "unbounded version" of Yao's principle by changing the order of taking the expectation (which so far simply meant to change the order of summation).

Theorem 2.7 (Tonelli's Theorem). *Let $\mathcal{X}$ and $\mathcal{Y}$ be probability spaces, and let $f \colon \mathcal{X} \times \mathcal{Y} \to \mathbb{R}^+$ be a non-negative measurable function. Then, we have*

$$\int_{\mathcal{Y}} \left(\int_{\mathcal{X}} f(x, y) \, \mathrm{d}x \right) \mathrm{d}y = \int_{\mathcal{X}} \left(\int_{\mathcal{Y}} f(x, y) \, \mathrm{d}y \right) \mathrm{d}x \, . \qquad \square$$

Since we are speaking about infinite sets, in the following we need to replace the maximum and minimum functions by supremum and infimum functions, respectively. Unlike in the previous two subsections, we use the limit inferior or limit superior of the fractions.

Moreover, we prove a more general claim by not grouping instances by their lengths, but by any suitable parameter. Consider (countably) infinitely many sets $\mathcal{I}_1, \mathcal{I}_2, \ldots$ of instances of an online minimization problem Π; each $\mathcal{I}_i$ may be of (even uncountably) infinite size. As always, let $\mathrm{Pr}_{\mathrm{ADV},i}$ be a probability distribution over $\mathcal{I}_i$. The following proof is obtained by slightly modifying that of Theorem 2.5.

Theorem 2.8 (Yao's Principle for Unbounded Min. Problems). *Let Π be an online minimization problem, and let $\mathcal{I}_1, \mathcal{I}_2, \ldots$ and $\mathrm{Pr}_{\mathrm{ADV},i}$ be as described above. If there is some constant $c \geq 1$ such that*

(i) $\displaystyle \liminf_{i \to \infty} \left(\frac{\inf_j (\mathbb{E}_{\mathrm{ADV},i}[\mathrm{cost}(A_j(\mathcal{I}_i))])}{\mathbb{E}_{\mathrm{ADV},i}[\mathrm{cost}(\mathrm{OPT}(\mathcal{I}_i))]} \right) \geq c$ *and*

(ii) $\displaystyle \limsup_{i \to \infty} (\mathbb{E}_{\mathrm{ADV},i}[\mathrm{cost}(\mathrm{OPT}(\mathcal{I}_i))]) = \infty \, ,$

then there is no randomized online algorithm for Π that is $(c - \varepsilon)$-competitive in expectation, for any $\varepsilon > 0$.

Proof. For a contradiction, suppose that both conditions (i) and (ii) are true, but there still is a randomized online algorithm RAND that is $(c - \varepsilon)$-competitive in expectation for Π, where $\varepsilon > 0$. By the same arguments as in the proof of Theorem 2.5, we get

$$\mathbb{E}_{\mathrm{ADV},i}[\mathbb{E}_{\mathrm{RAND}}[\mathrm{cost}(\mathrm{RAND}(\mathcal{I}_i))]] \leq (c - \varepsilon) \cdot \mathbb{E}_{\mathrm{ADV},i}[\mathrm{cost}(\mathrm{OPT}(\mathcal{I}_i))] + \alpha \, ,$$

and, together with Theorem 2.7 (the cost and the probabilities are always non-negative and measurable), it follows that

$$\mathbb{E}_{\mathrm{RAND}}[\mathbb{E}_{\mathrm{ADV},i}[\mathrm{cost}(\mathrm{RAND}(\mathcal{I}_i))]] \leq (c - \varepsilon) \cdot \mathbb{E}_{\mathrm{ADV},i}[\mathrm{cost}(\mathrm{OPT}(\mathcal{I}_i))] + \alpha \, . \quad (2.11)$$

Again using the same arguments as in the proof of Theorem 2.5 gives (assuming that the expected optimal cost is not zero)

$$\frac{\inf_j (\mathbb{E}_{\text{ADV},i}[\text{cost}(A_j(\mathcal{I}_i))])}{\mathbb{E}_{\text{ADV},i}[\text{cost}(\text{OPT}(\mathcal{I}_i))]} - \frac{\alpha}{\mathbb{E}_{\text{ADV},i}[\text{cost}(\text{OPT}(\mathcal{I}_i))]} \leq c - \varepsilon . \tag{2.12}$$

As a consequence of (i), there is an i_0 such that the first term of (2.12) is larger than c, for any $i \geq i_0$. Additionally, (ii) implies that there is an infinite increasing sequence $i_1, i_2, \ldots$, where $i_1 \geq i_0$, such that

$$\lim_{l \to \infty} \left(\frac{\alpha}{\mathbb{E}_{\text{ADV},i_l}[\text{cost}(\text{OPT}(\mathcal{I}_{i_l}))]} \right) = 0 .$$

Thus, for infinitely many $\mathcal{I}_i$, we get a contradiction. $\qquad \square$

One possible way to apply Theorem 2.8 is to define the sets to contain instances of the same length; however, we will use another partitioning of instances in Section 2.5, where we use Yao's principle to obtain a lower bound on the expected competitive ratio of every randomized online algorithm for paging.

Note that, for the last step of our argumentation in the proof above, we needed the fact that (i) speaks about the limit inferior. If, instead, we had used the limit superior (which is a weaker assumption), we could not argue the same way. In this case, we only know that the first term of (2.12) is larger than c for infinitely many i and the second one tends to 0 for a sequence of infinitely many i; however, the intersection of these two sets of input lengths is not necessarily infinite.

For maximization problems, we can prove an analogous statement. We again leave the proof to the reader.

Theorem 2.9 (Yao's Principle for Unbounded Max. Problems). *Let Π be an online maximization problem, and let $\mathcal{I}_1, \mathcal{I}_2, \ldots$ and $\text{Pr}_{\text{ADV},i}$ be as described above. If there is some constant $c \geq 1$ such that*

(i) $\displaystyle \liminf_{i \to \infty} \left(\frac{\mathbb{E}_{\text{ADV},i}[\text{gain}(\text{OPT}(\mathcal{I}_i))]}{\sup_j (\mathbb{E}_{\text{ADV},i}[\text{gain}(A_j(\mathcal{I}_i))])} \right) \geq c$ *and*

(ii) $\displaystyle \limsup_{i \to \infty} (\mathbb{E}_{\text{ADV},i}[\text{gain}(\text{OPT}(\mathcal{I}_i))]) = \infty ,$

then there is no randomized online algorithm for Π that is $(c - \varepsilon)$-competitive in expectation, for any $\varepsilon > 0$.

Exercise 2.6. Prove Theorem 2.9.

Before we apply Yao's principle, we will have a look at the game between a randomized online algorithm and the adversary from a different perspective. Our main reason to do this is to present an alternative proof of Yao's principle for finite minimization problems.

2.4 Another Point of View: Game Theory

Again, we consider a randomized online algorithm RAND and an adversary that tries to force RAND into creating an output that is as bad as possible compared to an optimal solution. Throughout this section, we will only consider finite online minimization problems; let Π be such a problem. RAND makes $b \in \mathbb{N}^+$ binary random decisions and, according to Observation 2.1, therefore picks one out of ℓ deterministic algorithms $A_1, A_1, \ldots, A_\ell$ from a set strat(RAND), where $\ell \leq 2^b$. Conversely, the adversary can choose an arbitrary input $I_1, I_2, \ldots, I_\mu$ from a set $\mathcal{I}$, which RAND then has to work on. We assume that ℓ and μ are arbitrarily large, but finite. For the same reasons as in Subsection 2.3.1, we thus assume that the additive constant α is 0.

In what follows, we call $A_1, A_2, \ldots, A_\ell$ the *strategies* of RAND and $I_1, I_2, \ldots, I_\mu$ the *strategies* of the adversary. Moreover, for all i and j with $1 \leq i \leq \mu$ and $1 \leq j \leq \ell$, we define the *strict performance* $c_{i,j}$ of A_j on I_i as

$$c_{i,j} := \frac{\text{cost}(A_j(I_i))}{\text{cost}(\text{OPT}(I_i))},$$

where $\text{OPT}(I_i)$ is an optimal solution for I_i. With these values, we can construct the following matrix $\mathcal{M}$.

	A_1	A_2	A_3	$\ldots$
I_1	$c_{1,1}$	$c_{1,2}$	$c_{1,3}$	$\ldots$
I_2	$c_{2,1}$	$c_{2,2}$	$c_{2,3}$	
I_3	$c_{3,1}$	$c_{3,2}$	$c_{3,3}$	
$\vdots$	$\vdots$			$\ddots$

For the moment, let us stick to the deterministic case, that is, RAND chooses one strategy with probability 1. We may think of RAND and the adversary as two players in a game. RAND chooses a column j from $\mathcal{M}$, which corresponds to a strategy A_j, and the adversary chooses a row i corresponding to an input I_i. In particular, RAND wants to choose j such that, whatever row i is chosen by the adversary, the value $c_{i,j}$ is as small as possible. Equivalently, we may say that RAND wants to maximize the value $-c_{i,j}$. Conversely, the adversary obviously wants to maximize the value $c_{i,j}$. We call $c_{i,j}$ and $-c_{i,j}$ the *payoff* of the adversary or RAND, respectively. Since, for a fixed column and row, RAND has a payoff which is exactly the negated payoff of the adversary, we call this game a *zero-sum game*; more specifically, as there are two players involved, such a game is called a *two-person zero-sum game*. In what follows, we say that RAND wants to minimize the adversary's payoff, which is, as just noted, the same as if RAND wants to maximize its own payoff, but yields a more intuitive point of view for our investigations.

We call the adversary the *row player* and RAND the *column player*, and we may assume that both players know the set of strategies of the opponent and therefore $\mathcal{M}$.

Example 2.3. Suppose the players have two strategies each, and consider the following matrix $\mathcal{M}_1$.

	A_1	A_2
I_1	1	2
I_2	2	1

The players now study all possible courses and payoffs according to $\mathcal{M}_1$, and then pick a best strategy based on their investigations, and we assume that they both have to reveal the chosen strategy at the same time. However, it turns out that one of them would always want to change its strategy. Suppose, for instance, that both have chosen their first strategy, that is, A_1 and I_1. In this case, the adversary has a payoff of $c_{1,1} = 1$ and RAND has a payoff of -1. Since the adversary knows the matrix $\mathcal{M}_1$, it wants to change its strategy to I_2 instead. In this case, RAND has a payoff of $-c_{1,2} = -2$, which is why it wants to change its strategy to A_2. If it does this, the adversary has an *incentive* to again change its strategy, and we see that we go round in circles; no matter which strategies are chosen, one player always has an advantage if it changes its strategy. We can illustrate this situation as follows, where the arrows point to the maximum values of the columns and the minimum values of the rows.

$\Diamond$

Let us give a different example that leads to a completely different situation.

Example 2.4. Consider the following matrix $\mathcal{M}_2$.

	A_1	A_2	A_3	A_4
I_1	7	2	3	1
I_2	1	4	5	4
I_3	10	9	6	9
I_4	6	3	2	11
I_5	12	1	2	5

In this example, there is a pair of strategies which, if chosen, lead to a situation in which neither of the players has an incentive to change its strategy, given that the other player sticks to its strategy. Specifically, this is the case if RAND chooses A_3 and the adversary chooses I_3; for all other choices, at least one player would want to change its strategy, as the following illustration shows.

In such a case, we say that the game is at an *equilibrium*, and we call $c_{3,3}$ the *value of the game*. We observe the following two facts.

1. If RAND chooses the strategy A_3, it can be sure that the adversary's payoff is not larger than 6; for instance, if RAND chose A_1 instead, the payoff of the adversary could be significantly larger, namely 12.

2. Conversely, if the adversary chooses the strategy I_3, it can be sure that its payoff is at least 6. If it chose I_5, its payoff could be a lot smaller, namely 1.

It follows that, in the above case, we can describe the strategies of both players that lead to an equilibrium as follows.

- RAND chooses its strategy A_{j^*} such that the maximum value over all entries in this column is as small as possible, that is,

$$j^* = \arg\min_j \{\max_i \{c_{i,j}\}\} \,,$$

and we set

$$v_{\mathrm{RAND}} := \max_i \{c_{i,j^*}\} \,.$$

- On the other hand, the adversary chooses its strategy I_{i^*} such that the minimum entry over the columns in this row is as large as possible, that is,

$$i^* = \arg\max_i \{\min_j \{c_{i,j}\}\} \,,$$

and we set

$$v_{\mathrm{ADV}} := \min_j \{c_{i^*,j}\} \,.$$

As we have just seen, we have

$$v_{\mathrm{ADV}} = v_{\mathrm{RAND}} = c_{3,3}$$

in this example. If i^* and j^* are played, neither player can obtain a larger payoff by changing its strategy (given that the other one does not change its strategy).   ◇

As Example 2.4 suggests, the value of the game can always be computed as above if the given game has an equilibrium. However, as Example 2.3 shows, this does not hold in general, although the values v_{RAND} and v_{ADV} always exist; we merely know that

$$v_{\mathrm{ADV}} \leq v_{\mathrm{RAND}}$$

is always true. Let us give one last example.

Example 2.5. Consider the following matrix $\mathcal{M}_3$.

	A_1	A_2	A_3	A_4
I_1	6	5	8	4
I_2	7	6	2	7
I_3	1	3	3	2

We can illustrate $\mathcal{M}_3$ as follows.

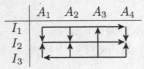

Suppose both players act according to the principle from Example 2.4. RAND can guarantee that the payoff of the adversary is at most 6 by playing A_2. Obviously, for the adversary it would then be best to choose the strategy I_2. However, in this case, RAND would want to change its strategy and play A_3 instead. On the other hand, by choosing the strategy I_1, the adversary can always guarantee that its payoff is at least 4. In this case, RAND would want to choose A_4 and the adversary has an incentive to change its strategy. As a consequence, the game is not at an equilibrium if the strategies I_1 and A_2 are chosen. $\Diamond$

Such a procedure does not seem very promising for analyzing deterministic algorithms, but this is not what we want anyway.[2] We want to speak about randomized online algorithms and, in what follows, let us also assume that the adversary chooses a strategy at random. If we transfer this model to our game, we are dealing with the following situation. RAND uses a probability distribution $\mathrm{Pr}_{\mathrm{RAND}} \colon \mathrm{strat}(\mathrm{RAND}) \to [0, 1]$ over the columns of a given matrix $\mathcal{M}$. We denote the probability $\mathrm{Pr}_{\mathrm{RAND}}[A_j]$ that RAND chooses the strategy A_j by $q_{\mathrm{RAND},j}$; the sequence $q_{\mathrm{RAND}} = (q_{\mathrm{RAND},1}, q_{\mathrm{RAND},2}, \ldots, q_{\mathrm{RAND},\ell})$ is called the *mixed strategy* of RAND. Conversely, the adversary uses a probability distribution $\mathrm{Pr}_{\mathrm{ADV}} \colon \mathcal{I} \to [0, 1]$ over the rows of $\mathcal{M}$. The probability $\mathrm{Pr}_{\mathrm{ADV}}[I_i]$ that the adversary chooses the strategy I_i is denoted by $q_{\mathrm{ADV},i}$; the sequence $q_{\mathrm{ADV}} = (q_{\mathrm{ADV},1}, q_{\mathrm{ADV},2}, \ldots, q_{\mathrm{ADV},\mu})$ is called the mixed strategy of the adversary. To distinguish these strategies from the deterministic setting above, we call the former strategies *pure strategies*. Since we are now dealing with a randomized setting, the payoff is modeled by a random variable $C \colon \mathcal{I} \times \mathrm{strat}(\mathrm{RAND}) \to \mathbb{R}^+$, which has an expected value of

$$\mathbb{E}[C] := \sum_{i=1}^{\mu} \sum_{j=1}^{\ell} q_{\mathrm{ADV},i} \cdot c_{i,j} \cdot q_{\mathrm{RAND},j} = q_{\mathrm{ADV}}^{\mathsf{T}} \cdot \mathcal{M} \cdot q_{\mathrm{RAND}} \,.$$

Obviously, RAND wants to minimize this expected value by choosing its probability distribution accordingly, and conversely, the adversary wants to maximize it. But what do concrete choices for the two players look like? We can argue as we did previously for deterministic strategies.

- RAND knows $\mathcal{M}$ and further knows that the adversary wants to choose its mixed strategy q_{ADV} such that $\mathbb{E}[C]$ is maximized for the given choice of q_{RAND}. Thus, RAND can choose a strategy q_{RAND}^* such that

$$q_{\mathrm{RAND}}^* = \arg \min_{q_{\mathrm{RAND}}} \{ \max_{q_{\mathrm{ADV}}} \{ q_{\mathrm{ADV}}^{\mathsf{T}} \cdot \mathcal{M} \cdot q_{\mathrm{RAND}} \} \} \,.$$

---

[2]If we consider a purely deterministic setting, the problem of Examples 2.3 and 2.5 does not appear anyway since the algorithm is fixed first, and the adversary chooses its strategy afterwards.

Therefore, the adversary has a payoff of at most

$$v_{\text{RAND}} := \max_{q_{\text{ADV}}}\{q_{\text{ADV}}^{\mathsf{T}} \cdot \mathcal{M} \cdot q_{\text{RAND}}^*\} \ .$$

- Conversely, the adversary can choose a mixed strategy q_{ADV}^* such that

$$q_{\text{ADV}}^* = \arg\max_{q_{\text{ADV}}}\{\min_{q_{\text{RAND}}}\{q_{\text{ADV}}^{\mathsf{T}} \cdot \mathcal{M} \cdot q_{\text{RAND}}\}\} \ .$$

This means that it can guarantee a payoff of at least

$$v_{\text{ADV}} := \min_{q_{\text{RAND}}}\{q_{\text{ADV}}^{*\mathsf{T}} \cdot \mathcal{M} \cdot q_{\text{RAND}}\} \ .$$

As with deterministic strategies, it is easy to see that we have $v_{\text{ADV}} \leq v_{\text{RAND}}$, but here, this holds with equality even if there is no equilibrium in pure strategies. The following theorem is one of the most important results from game theory and states that $v_{\text{ADV}} = v_{\text{RAND}}$. We will not prove it here.

Theorem 2.10 (Minimax Theorem). *For every two-person zero-sum game with finite strategies, we have*

$$\min_{q_{\text{RAND}}}\{\max_{q_{\text{ADV}}}\{q_{\text{ADV}}^{\mathsf{T}} \cdot \mathcal{M} \cdot q_{\text{RAND}}\}\} = \max_{q_{\text{ADV}}}\{\min_{q_{\text{RAND}}}\{q_{\text{ADV}}^{\mathsf{T}} \cdot \mathcal{M} \cdot q_{\text{RAND}}\}\} \ . \qquad \square$$

The minimax theorem states that, for any two-person zero-sum game, there is an equilibrium in mixed strategies q_{ADV}^* and q_{RAND}^* that are defined as above. Let us now go back to online algorithms and see what this implies.

We note that if one of the two mixed strategies q_{ADV} or q_{RAND} is fixed, the respective other player can maximize its payoff by choosing a deterministic strategy. Suppose that the strategy q_{RAND} is fixed; this corresponds to the situation we are dealing with in the context of randomized online algorithms, because the adversary chooses a deterministic strategy while knowing the probability distribution with which RAND chooses its deterministic strategies. Then

$$\mathcal{M} \cdot q_{\text{RAND}} = \begin{pmatrix} c_{1,1} & \cdots & c_{1,\ell} \\ \vdots & \ddots & \vdots \\ c_{\mu,1} & \cdots & c_{\mu,\ell} \end{pmatrix} \cdot \begin{pmatrix} q_{\text{RAND},1} \\ \vdots \\ q_{\text{RAND},\ell} \end{pmatrix} = \begin{pmatrix} c_1 \\ \vdots \\ c_\mu \end{pmatrix},$$

which means that the adversary can choose its strategy as a unit vector in which exactly that distinct entry is non-zero, for which the corresponding entry of the vector $(c_1, c_2, \ldots, c_\mu)^{\mathsf{T}}$ is as large as possible, to maximize its payoff

$$\left(q_{\text{ADV},1}, \ldots, q_{\text{ADV},\mu}\right) \cdot \begin{pmatrix} c_1' \\ \vdots \\ c_\mu' \end{pmatrix} \ .$$

Analogously, we can argue the other way around. If we combine this fact with Theorem 2.10, we obtain the following lemma, where e_i with $1 \leq i \leq \mu$ (e_j with $1 \leq j \leq \ell$, respectively) denotes the corresponding unit vector for which the ith (jth, respectively) entry is 1 and all other entries are 0.

Lemma 2.3 (Loomis' Lemma). *For every two-person zero-sum game with finite strategies, we have*

$$\min_{q_{\text{RAND}}}\{\max_i\{e_i^{\mathsf{T}} \cdot \mathcal{M} \cdot q_{\text{RAND}}\}\} = \max_{q_{\text{ADV}}}\{\min_j\{q_{\text{ADV}}^{\mathsf{T}} \cdot \mathcal{M} \cdot e_j\}\} \,. \qquad \square$$

Since, for every fixed mixed strategy q'_{ADV} for the adversary,

$$\max_{q_{\text{ADV}}}\{\min_j\{q_{\text{ADV}}^{\mathsf{T}} \cdot \mathcal{M} \cdot e_j\}\} \geq q_{\text{ADV}}^{\prime\mathsf{T}} \cdot \min_j\{\mathcal{M} \cdot e_j\} \,,$$

we can, using the minimax theorem (or rather Loomis' lemma), conclude that, for every q'_{ADV},

$$\min_{q_{\text{RAND}}}\{\max_i\{e_i^{\mathsf{T}} \cdot \mathcal{M} \cdot q_{\text{RAND}}\}\} \geq q_{\text{ADV}}^{\prime\mathsf{T}} \cdot \min_j\{\mathcal{M} \cdot e_j\} \,.$$

Now let q^*_{RAND} be a best mixed strategy for RAND; then we have

$$\max_i\{e_i^{\mathsf{T}} \cdot \mathcal{M} \cdot q^*_{\text{RAND}}\} \geq q_{\text{ADV}}^{\prime\mathsf{T}} \cdot \min_j\{\mathcal{M} \cdot e_j\} \,.$$

If we take a closer look, we observe that this inequality is exactly Yao's principle, which we introduced in Section 2.3. The statement is that, for a best randomized online algorithm (namely q^*_{RAND}), there is an input (namely e_i^{T}) such that the expected performance is at least as large as that of a best deterministic online algorithm (namely e_j, which induces minimum cost) on an arbitrary but fixed distribution over inputs (namely $q_{\text{ADV}}^{\prime\mathsf{T}}$).

2.5 A Lower Bound for Randomized Online Algorithms for Paging

Theorem 2.2 states that the randomized online algorithm RMARK for paging obtains an expected competitive ratio of at most $2H_k$. The next question is whether this is all we can do when allowing randomized computations. The following result gives the answer; as a matter of fact, the bound on the competitive ratio of RMARK is only a multiplicative constant of 2 away from a bound on what a randomized online algorithm can achieve at best. To prove the claim, we make use of Yao's principle, which we introduced in Section 2.3.

Theorem 2.11. *No randomized online algorithm for paging is better than H_k-competitive in expectation.*

Proof. As in the proof of Theorem 1.5, it is sufficient to assume that there are only $m = k + 1$ pages in total. We construct instances of the following form.

- In the first time step, page p_{k+1} is requested; by definition, it is not in the cache of any algorithm.

- In every subsequent time step, an arbitrary page is requested other than the one that was requested right before; each of these k pages is requested with probability $1/k$.

We now show that every deterministic online algorithm has a large expected cost compared to an optimal solution on these instances. Applying Yao's principle, we can then derive a lower bound on the expected competitive ratio of a best randomized online algorithm for paging.

Let ALG be some deterministic online algorithm for paging; without loss of generality (see Exercises 1.5 and 1.6), we restrict ourselves to demand paging algorithms. Thus, ALG has exactly k pages in its cache in every time step. In other words, every page that is requested in some time step is not in the cache with a probability of $1/k$ (an exception is, of course, the first time step).

We subdivide the input into phases; the number of phases is denoted by N. This is done similarly to Definition 1.8; however, the phases are now *stochastic*. By $\mathcal{I}_N$ we denote the set of all instances that contain N complete phases. Phase P_1 starts with time step T_1 and ends after time step T_r, where r is chosen such that in time step T_{r+1} all of the $k+1$ different pages were requested. After that, phase P_2, which is defined analogously, begins, etc. P_N ends right after time step T_{n-1}, which means that there is one more request after the last phase ends. We observe that $\mathcal{I}_N$ is well defined and contains infinitely many instances (of infinitely many lengths). However, there are instances that are not contained in any set.

Recall that, in every time step (except for T_1), ALG causes a page fault with probability $1/k$. This is true for every instance in $\mathcal{I}_N$, because the probability of reaching the Nth phase starting with any sufficiently short prefix and continuing by requesting pages as described is 1. Now let $\mathbb{E}_{\text{ADV},N}[\text{cost}(\text{ALG}(P_j))]$ denote the expected cost of ALG in phase P_j, and let $|P_j|$ denote the expected length of P_j with $1 \leq j \leq N$. Then we obtain

$$\mathbb{E}_{\text{ADV},N}[\text{cost}(\text{ALG}(P_j))] \geq |P_j| \cdot \frac{1}{k} . \tag{2.13}$$

Conversely, there is an optimal algorithm OPT that does not make more than one page fault in every single phase plus one additional page fault in T_n; in phase P_1, OPT causes a page fault in time step T_1 and it replaces the page that is requested at the beginning of phase P_2, and so on (in P_N, it replaces the page that is requested in T_n). As a result, we have

$$\mathbb{E}_{\text{ADV},N}[\text{cost}(\text{OPT}(P_j))] = 1 , \tag{2.14}$$

for every phase P_j with $1 \leq j \leq N$.

The key point is to compute the expected length of a single phase; recall that all phases are complete. Phase P_j ends when the next page that will be requested is the first occurrence of the $(k+1)$th different page since the beginning of phase P_j. Thus, we have to compute how long it takes in expectation until all pages $p_1, p_2, \ldots, p_{k+1}$

have been requested (a combinatorial problem, which is closely related to the well-known *coupon collector's problem*); the expected number of time steps of phase P_j is this number minus 1. To this end, let X_i, for any i with $1 \leq i \leq k+1$, denote a random variable that counts the number of steps that pass until the ith page gets requested after $i-1$ different pages were already requested (within P_j).

Let us first consider the corresponding probability q_i that the ith new page is requested when in the preceding time steps of P_j already $i-1$ different pages were requested. Clearly, $q_1 = 1$ and, since in the second time step of P_j the first page is not requested again, also $q_2 = 1$; furthermore, $q_3 = (k-1)/k$, $q_4 = (k-2)/k$, etc. In general, we have

$$q_i = \frac{k-(i-2)}{k} \, , \tag{2.15}$$

for $2 \leq i \leq k+1$. This is true for every phase including P_1. Now we can compute the expected value of X_i as follows. Suppose the $(i-1)$th page was just requested, and now we count the time steps that are needed until the ith new page is requested. The probability that this takes t time steps is $q_i \cdot (1-q_i)^{t-1}$; in other words, for $t-1$ steps, a page is requested that was already requested before, and then, in the tth step, a page is requested that was not requested yet. We get

$$
\begin{aligned}
\mathbb{E}_{\text{ADV},N}[X_i] &= \sum_{t=1}^{\infty} t \cdot q_i \cdot (1-q_i)^{t-1} \\
&= \sum_{t=0}^{\infty} (t+1) \cdot q_i \cdot (1-q_i)^t \\
&= \sum_{t=0}^{\infty} t \cdot q_i \cdot (1-q_i)^t + \sum_{t=0}^{\infty} q_i \cdot (1-q_i)^t
\end{aligned}
$$

(since none of the summands are negative)

$$
= (1-q_i) \cdot \sum_{t=1}^{\infty} t \cdot q_i \cdot (1-q_i)^{t-1} + q_i \cdot \sum_{t=0}^{\infty} (1-q_i)^t
$$

(since the first part is 0 for $t=0$)

$$
= (1-q_i) \cdot \mathbb{E}_{\text{ADV},N}[X_i] + \frac{q_i}{1-(1-q_i)} \, ,
$$

(using the closed form of the geometric series)

and therefore

$$\mathbb{E}_{\text{ADV},N}[X_i] = \frac{1}{q_i} \, . \tag{2.16}$$

Now let $X = X_1 + X_2 + \ldots + X_{k+1}$ denote a random variable that counts all time steps until $k+1$ different pages were requested since the beginning of P_j. Then, we have

$$\mathbb{E}_{\text{ADV},N}[X] = \mathbb{E}_{\text{ADV},N}[X_1 + X_2 + \ldots + X_{k+1}]$$
$$= \mathbb{E}_{\text{ADV},N}[X_1] + \mathbb{E}_{\text{ADV},N}[X_2] + \ldots + \mathbb{E}_{\text{ADV},N}[X_{k+1}]$$
(by linearity of expectation)
$$= 1 + \frac{1}{q_2} + \ldots + \frac{1}{q_{k+1}}$$
(as a consequence of (2.16))
$$= 1 + \sum_{i=2}^{k+1} \frac{1}{q_i}$$
$$= 1 + \sum_{i=2}^{k+1} \frac{k}{k - (i-2)}$$
(due to (2.15))
$$= 1 + k \cdot \sum_{i=2}^{k+1} \frac{1}{k - (i-2)}$$
$$= 1 + k \cdot \sum_{i=1}^{k} \frac{1}{k - (i-1)}$$
$$= 1 + k \cdot \sum_{i=1}^{k} \frac{1}{i}$$
$$= 1 + k \cdot H_k ,$$

and thus P_j ends after an expected number of kH_k steps. It is important to note that the above arguments are also true for the first and the last phase.

From (2.13), it follows that the expected cost of ALG in P_j is at least

$$\mathbb{E}_{\text{ADV},N}[\text{cost}(\text{ALG}(P_j))] \geq H_k . \tag{2.17}$$

As ALG is any deterministic online algorithm for paging, from (2.14) and (2.17) together with the fact that OPT causes a page fault in T_n, we obtain

$$\frac{\inf_j(\mathbb{E}_{\text{ADV},N}[\text{cost}(A_j(\mathcal{I}_N))])}{\mathbb{E}_{\text{ADV},N}[\text{cost}(\text{OPT}(\mathcal{I}_N))]} \geq \frac{\sum_{j=1}^{N} H_k}{1 + \sum_{j=1}^{N} 1} = \frac{NH_k}{N+1} ,$$

and since

$$\liminf_{N \to \infty} \left(\frac{NH_k}{N+1} \right) = H_k ,$$

it follows that (i) of Theorem 2.8 is satisfied. Moreover, note that the expected cost of OPT increases with N, that is,

$$\limsup_{N \to \infty} (\mathbb{E}_{\text{ADV},N}[\text{cost}(\text{OPT}(\mathcal{I}_N))]) = \infty \, ,$$

which means that also (ii) of Theorem 2.8 is true. Therefore, we can apply Yao's principle and conclude that no randomized online algorithm has an expected competitive ratio better than H_k. $\qquad\square$

⋆2.6 A Barely Random Algorithm for Paging

We now have gained some insight into the paging problem. In particular, we know that there is a randomized online algorithm that is exponentially better than all deterministic ones. If we take a closer look, we also realize that the algorithms we have dealt with so far are clearly efficient (in terms of their time complexity). Now we ask how much randomization we need to be this good. The randomized marking algorithm RMARK that we discussed in Section 2.2 obviously uses a number of random bits that increases with the input length n. In this section, we show that this is not necessary; we only need a constant number (with respect to n) of random bits to obtain (asymptotically) the same competitive ratio. To this end, we design a so-called *barely random algorithm* RMARKBARELY that chooses randomly between some deterministic marking algorithms. Formally, we have

$$\text{strat}(\text{RMARKBARELY}) = \{Mark_1, Mark_2, \ldots, Mark_{2^b}\} \, ,$$

where the online algorithms $Mark_i$ with $1 \leq i \leq 2^b$ are marking algorithms that replace unmarked pages in the cache in such a way that if a page is requested, this page is in the cache for a large number of them. Let us first try to explain the idea with an example.

Example 2.6. Suppose we read two random bits and thus pick one out of four algorithms $Mark_1$, $Mark_2$, $Mark_3$, and $Mark_4$. Moreover, suppose the cache has a size of 7 and is initialized with the pages $p_1, p_2, \ldots, p_7$ such that we are facing the situation

p_1	p_2	p_3	p_4	p_5	p_6	p_7

at the beginning. All algorithms memorize these pages in this order. Now, the page p_8 is requested, which is not in the cache. Then $Mark_i$ replaces p_i with p_8, which leads to the following situation; we color marked pages gray.

$Mark_1$:
p_8	p_2	p_3	p_4	p_5	p_6	p_7

$Mark_2$:
p_1	p_8	p_3	p_4	p_5	p_6	p_7

$Mark_3$:
p_1	p_2	p_8	p_4	p_5	p_6	p_7

$Mark_4$: | p_1 | p_2 | p_3 | p_8 | p_5 | p_6 | p_7 |

If the page p_9 is requested next, all algorithms remove the next page according to the above order of the pages that were in the cache initially, which leads to

$Mark_1$: | p_8 | p_9 | p_3 | p_4 | p_5 | p_6 | p_7 |

$Mark_2$: | p_1 | p_8 | p_9 | p_4 | p_5 | p_6 | p_7 |

$Mark_3$: | p_1 | p_2 | p_8 | p_9 | p_5 | p_6 | p_7 |

$Mark_4$: | p_1 | p_2 | p_3 | p_8 | p_9 | p_6 | p_7 |

as a result.

The idea is that if, for instance, the page p_2 is now requested, this page has only been removed from the cache by some algorithms; in this case $Mark_1$ and $Mark_2$. If one of these four algorithms is chosen uniformly at random, the page p_2 is still in the cache with a probability of $1/2$. However, we run into problems if we continue with this strategy. It can happen that some algorithms act identically after some time step. Suppose the "old" page p_1 is requested. Then we get the following situation.

$Mark_1$: | p_8 | p_9 | p_1 | p_4 | p_5 | p_6 | p_7 |

$Mark_2$: | p_1 | p_8 | p_9 | p_4 | p_5 | p_6 | p_7 |

$Mark_3$: | p_1 | p_2 | p_8 | p_9 | p_5 | p_6 | p_7 |

$Mark_4$: | p_1 | p_2 | p_3 | p_8 | p_9 | p_6 | p_7 |

We note that the algorithms $Mark_1$ and $Mark_2$ now have the same marked and unmarked pages in their caches. From this point on, these two algorithms behave the same until the end of the current phase. Clearly, we want to avoid such situations whenever possible. A way out is to make sure that $Mark_1$ does not remove the page p_3, but some other page which no other algorithm removed so far; an example is p_7, which leads to the following result.

$Mark_1$: | p_8 | p_9 | p_3 | p_4 | p_5 | p_6 | p_1 |

$Mark_2$: | p_1 | p_8 | p_9 | p_4 | p_5 | p_6 | p_7 |

$Mark_3$: | p_1 | p_2 | p_8 | p_9 | p_5 | p_6 | p_7 |

$Mark_4$: | p_1 | p_2 | p_3 | p_8 | p_9 | p_6 | p_7 |

Suppose page p_3 is requested next. Again, if all algorithms follow our original idea, two algorithms have the same cache content afterwards; this time these are $Mark_3$ and $Mark_4$, and the cache contents look as follows.

$Mark_1$: | p_8 | p_9 | p_3 | p_4 | p_5 | p_6 | p_1 |

$Mark_2$: | p_1 | p_8 | p_9 | p_3 | p_5 | p_6 | p_7 |

$Mark_3$: | p_1 | p_2 | p_8 | p_9 | p_3 | p_6 | p_7 |

$Mark_4$: | p_1 | p_2 | p_3 | p_8 | p_9 | p_6 | p_7 |

This problem can also be fixed by making $Mark_3$ remove the page p_6 instead of p_5; as a consequence, we get the following situation.

$Mark_1$: | p_8 | p_9 | p_3 | p_4 | p_5 | p_6 | p_1 |

$Mark_2$: | p_1 | p_8 | p_9 | p_3 | p_5 | p_6 | p_7 |

$Mark_3$: | p_1 | p_2 | p_8 | p_9 | p_5 | p_3 | p_7 |

$Mark_4$: | p_1 | p_2 | p_3 | p_8 | p_9 | p_6 | p_7 |

So far, so good, but now we encounter a point where we cannot use this strategy again. The problem is that there is no page left to remove from the cache that was not yet removed by any algorithm.   ◇

To analyze RMARKBARELY, we again consider the k-phase partition of the input according to Definition 1.8. Moreover, we use the notion of "old" and "new" pages as in the proof of Theorem 2.2, where we showed that RMARK is $2H_k$-competitive in expectation. Now suppose that, at the beginning, three new pages are requested. Every algorithm from strat(RMARKBARELY) removes pages using the principle from Example 2.6. Afterwards, every algorithm is assigned a sequence of three removed unmarked old pages; for instance, $Mark_3$ used (p_3, p_4, p_5). This is done by ordering the pages that are in the cache at the beginning in some way (for instance, by their indices) and make every algorithm replace a unique subsequence as long as this is possible; see Figure 2.4. As the computation continues, we want to ensure that these subsequences stay unique for every algorithm, such that no two of them act identically. Since marked pages do not get evicted in the current phase, they need to be removed from these subsequences.

If a new page is requested in some time step, the subsequences are extended by one page, which means that this unmarked old page is removed to load the new page into the cache. However, if an unmarked old page p is requested, the situation is more complex. After this request, p is not unmarked anymore and therefore has to be removed from every subsequence including it. Algorithms that already removed

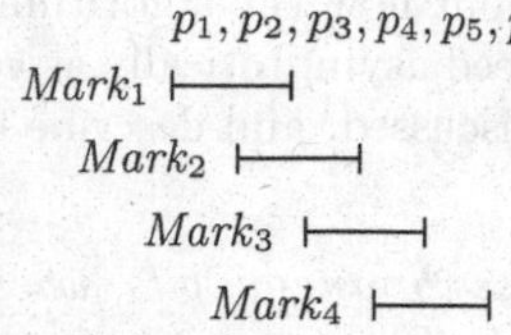

$$p_1, p_2, p_3, p_4, p_5, p_6, p_7, p_8, \ldots$$

$Mark_1$ ⊢――――⊣

$Mark_2$ ⊢――――⊣

$Mark_3$ ⊢――――⊣

$Mark_4$ ⊢――――⊣

Figure 2.4. The pages that are in the cache at the beginning of a phase and the first two pages that are replaced by the deterministic strategies RMARKBARELY chooses from.

p are now not allowed to remove the page p' that would be next according to the ordering. As we have seen in Example 2.6, we could not guarantee that all algorithms act differently afterwards. Instead, these algorithms use a page p'' which, so far, is in the cache of all algorithms, that is, it was not removed yet by any algorithm. We will soon investigate under what circumstances such a page exists, but for now just assume that it does. Then, we add p'' to all subsequences of all algorithms that do not have p in their caches, which means that in their caches p'' is replaced by p.

Example 2.7. We now take a closer look at the situation described in Example 2.6. The subsequence (p_1, p_2) was assigned to $Mark_1$ and (p_2, p_3) was assigned to $Mark_2$ after the first two requests p_8 and p_9. If p_1 is requested after that, the subsequence of $Mark_2$ is unchanged, since it has p_1 in its cache, and simply needs to mark it. The situation is different for $Mark_1$; here, p_1 is removed from the subsequence since the page is now marked. If now the page p_3 is removed to load p_1, both subsequences are (p_2, p_3). Thus, $Mark_1$ removes the unmarked page p_7 instead, which leads to a subsequence (p_2, p_7). Consequently, the two algorithms have different unmarked pages in their caches after this request. ◇

In general, after this strategy is repeated for some number of times, we will get to a point where we do not have any free (that is, unmarked old) pages left, and the adversary can force some of the algorithms to have the same marked and unmarked pages in their caches. RMARKBARELY therefore works in rounds in which it partitions the algorithms into groups. In every round, two algorithms from different groups replace different pages. The idea is that the unavoidable problem of some algorithms acting the same from some point on is somewhat "controlled" by building these groups. Note that RMARKBARELY must simulate all deterministic algorithms $Mark_1, Mark_2, \ldots, Mark_{2^b}$ at once in order to know how the randomly chosen one replaces pages.

Exercise 2.7. The instance in Example 2.6 is (p_8, p_9, p_1, p_3). It is easy to see that, after a fifth page is requested, the deterministic algorithms can still choose pages in their caches to replace such that all caches stay pairwise different.

For $b = 2$ and $k = 7$, give an instance of length 5 such that the last request forces two algorithms from strat(RMARKBARELY) to have the same cache content afterwards.

Now that we have a rough idea about how the algorithm works, in what follows, we prove that RMARKBARELY is indeed asymptotically as good as RMARK. To this end, we formalize the ideas we just discussed, and describe the algorithm's behavior in more detail.

Theorem 2.12. RMARKBARELY *uses b random bits, where $2^b < k$, and is strictly*

$$\left(3b + \frac{2(k+1)}{2^b}\right)\text{-}competitive$$

in expectation for paging.

Proof. Consider the deterministic algorithms $Mark_1, Mark_2, \ldots, Mark_{2^b}$ and the k-phase partition as given by Definition 1.8. The algorithms follow different strategies to remove unmarked pages. However, the set of marked pages is the same for every algorithm at any point in time, and thus all algorithms have the same pages in their caches at the beginning of any phase.

Let there be N phases in total, let P_j with $1 \leq j \leq N$ be an arbitrary phase, and let us denote pages by "new" and "old" as in the proof of Theorem 2.2; that is, all pages that are in the cache at the beginning of P_j are called old, and all pages that are not old and that are requested during P_j are called new. Moreover, we ignore all requests to pages that were already requested during P_j since they do not cause page faults for any of the considered marking algorithms. Recall that, during any phase, at least one new page is requested. For the sake of a simple notation, we assume that P_j consists of k requests $x_1, x_2, \ldots, x_k$ to unmarked old or new pages. These k requests are now processed in $b + 1$ rounds that are defined as follows.

- Round R_0 starts with request x_1 and takes until request x_{k-2^b+1} is processed.
- For $z \geq 1$, round R_z consists of the $2^b/2^z$ requests $x_{k-2^b-(z-1)+2}$ to x_{k-2^b-z+1}.

In every round, the 2^b algorithms are divided into $2^b/2^z$ groups $\mathcal{G}_1, \mathcal{G}_2, \ldots, \mathcal{G}_{2^{b-z}}$ each of size 2^z. In round R_0, every such group consists of one unique algorithm, that is, $\mathcal{G}_i = \{Mark_i\}$. At the beginning of round R_z with $z \geq 1$, the two groups $\mathcal{G}_i$ and $\mathcal{G}_{i+2^{b-z}}$ are merged into a single group $\mathcal{G}_i$; for instance, if there are eight algorithms in total, $\mathcal{G}_1$ and $\mathcal{G}_5$ are merged to $\mathcal{G}_1$, $\mathcal{G}_2$ and $\mathcal{G}_6$ are merged to $\mathcal{G}_2$, and so on, right before round R_1.

Now consider a request x_{t+1} processed in round R_z, and denote the number of new pages that are requested during $x_1, x_2, \ldots, x_t$ by l_t. Then there are $t - l_t$ old pages that were requested before and that are already marked in this time step. Conversely, there are

$$k - t + l_t \tag{2.18}$$

unmarked old pages, and, for every algorithm, some of them are in the cache and some are not. We denote these pages by $\overline{p}_1, \overline{p}_2, \ldots, \overline{p}_{k-t+l_t}$, and set

$$S_t := (\overline{p}_1, \overline{p}_2, \ldots, \overline{p}_{k-t+l_t}).$$

In other words, S_t is a sequence of old pages that remain unmarked until the tth time step of P_j; right before the first time step of P_j, these are all pages that are in the cache at the beginning of this phase.

As already stated, every group $\mathcal{G}_i$ replaces pages following a certain strategy. More specifically, in the tth time step of P_j, every $\mathcal{G}_i$ is assigned a set of l_t unmarked old pages (determined by the ordering that is given by S_t). This set is

$$E_{i,t} := \{\overline{p}_i, \overline{p}_{i+1}, \ldots, \overline{p}_{i+l_t-1}\} \, ,$$

for $l_t \geq 1$ and $E_{i,t} = \emptyset$ for $l_t = 0$. Algorithms in $\mathcal{G}_i$ only replace pages in their caches that are in this set in the corresponding time step. Note that every unmarked old page is in at most l_t different sets $E_{i,t}$ since $|E_{i,t}| = l_t$ and by the construction of the sets. We first have to show that there are always enough unmarked old pages. By the definition of the sets $E_{i,t}$ with $1 \leq i \leq 2^b/2^z$, the unmarked old pages assigned to groups are

$$\overline{p}_1, \overline{p}_2, \ldots, \overline{p}_{2^b/2^z+l_t-1} \, ,$$

which amounts to $2^b/2^z + l_t - 1$ pages. As noted in (2.18), there are $k - t + l_t$ unmarked old pages in total. Thus, there are

$$(k - t + l_t) - \left(\frac{2^b}{2^z} + l_t - 1\right) = k - t - \frac{2^b}{2^z} + 1 \tag{2.19}$$

unmarked old pages left. Next, we bound t from above. To this end, recall that round R_z with $z \geq 0$ of P_j ends after the $(k - 2^{b-z} + 1)$th time step of P_j. Consequently, we have

$$t + 1 \leq k - \frac{2^b}{2^z} + 1 \, . \tag{2.20}$$

From (2.19) and (2.20), it follows that the number of pages that are left is at least

$$k - \left(k - \frac{2^b}{2^z}\right) - \frac{2^b}{2^z} + 1 = 1 \, , \tag{2.21}$$

and thus the sets $E_{i,t}$ are well defined.

Now we describe how the sequences S_t are modified. As we assume that only unmarked pages are requested, we can simply distinguish the following two cases.

Case 1. Suppose x_{t+1} is a new page. In this case, we set $S_{t+1} = S_t$ (note that both t and l_t increase by one). Moreover, we add another element to all sets, that is, $E_{i,t+1} = E_{i,t} \cup \{\overline{p}_{i+l_t}\}$. This simply means that the page $\overline{p}_{i+l_t}$ gets replaced by x_{t+1} in the caches of the corresponding algorithms, which is always possible due to (2.21).

Case 2. Now suppose x_{t+1} is an unmarked old page. Then x_{t+1} is removed from S_t and replaced by some other page that is so far not assigned to any group.

Due to (2.21), there is at least one page that can take the place of x_{t+1}. Furthermore, since every unmarked old page is in at most l_t sets $E_{i,t}$, at most l_t sets $E_{i,t+1}$ are different from $E_{i,t}$.

We have just shown how the sets $E_{i,t}$, which are used to keep track of which pages are replaced when a page fault occurs, are created and maintained. Now let $Mark_q$ with $1 \leq q \leq 2^b$ be some algorithm from a group $\mathcal{G}_i$, and let x_{t+1} be a request that causes a page fault. Then $Mark_q$ loads this page into the cache by replacing a page from $E_{i,t+1}$. We show that such a page always exists. $Mark_q$ has $k - t$ unmarked old pages in its cache so far. By definition, there are l_{t+1} unmarked old pages in the set $E_{i,t+1}$. In total (see (2.18)), after x_{t+1} is processed, there are $k + l_{t+1} - (t+1)$ unmarked old pages. Consequently, there are only $k - t - 1$ unmarked old pages that are not in $E_{i,t+1}$, and hence the cache of $Mark_q$ must contain at least one page from $E_{i,t+1}$. The algorithms are therefore consistent for paging, that is, they always produce a feasible output.

It remains to bound the expected number of page faults that are caused by R.MARKBARELY. This is done by bounding the average number of page faults made by the algorithms $Mark_q$. We begin with the total number of page faults of all algorithms combined. To this end, let l'_j denote the number of new pages that are requested during phase P_j.

- Every new page that is requested obviously causes one page fault for every algorithm, which sums up to

$$l'_j 2^b \tag{2.22}$$

  page faults in total.

- It gets a little more tricky for unmarked old pages that are requested. As we have seen above, such a request x_{t+1} forces the algorithms of at most $l_t \leq l'_j$ groups to cause a page fault. Round R_0 consists of $k - 2^b + 1$ time steps, and since every group includes one single algorithm, this leads to at most $l'_j(k - 2^b + 1)$ page faults. In round R_z with $z \geq 1$, every group consists of 2^z algorithms and R_z consists of at most $2^b/2^z$ time steps; for each such round, at most l'_j groups are affected by this page fault. Since there are b such rounds in total, we get a maximum number of page faults of

$$l'_j \frac{2^b}{2^z} 2^z b .$$

All in all, the number of page faults in phase P_j due to unmarked old pages sums up to at most

$$l'_j(k - 2^b + 1) + l'_j 2^b b . \tag{2.23}$$

- Last, we bound the number of page faults that are due to the merging of groups. When the algorithms from group $\mathcal{G}_{i+2^{b-z}}$ with $1 \leq i \leq 2^b/2^z$ are added to the ones from $\mathcal{G}_i$, we assume that, afterwards, they only replace pages according to the strategy of $\mathcal{G}_i$. However, it may be the case that the former algorithms replaced unmarked old pages that are still in the caches of the algorithms from group $\mathcal{G}_i$. For the sake of an easier analysis, we thus assume that the algorithms from $\mathcal{G}_{i+2^{b-z}}$ simply load the corresponding unmarked old pages into their caches without marking them; after that, all algorithms from $\mathcal{G}_i$ are assigned the same group $E_{i,t}$. For any affected algorithm, this causes an additional cost of at most $l_t \leq l'_j$. Every merging, independent of both the preceding and succeeding round, affects exactly half of the algorithms, that is, 2^{b-1} many; this happens exactly b times. Therefore, in the sum, this causes at most another

$$l'_j 2^{b-1} b \qquad (2.24)$$

page faults.

As a direct consequence of (2.22) to (2.24), all algorithms in strat(RMARKBARELY) together have at most a cost of

$$l'_j 2^b + l'_j (k - 2^b + 1) + l'_j 2^b b + l'_j 2^{b-1} b = l'_j \left(k + 1 + \frac{3}{2} 2^b b \right)$$

in each phase. This leads to an average cost of

$$l'_j \left(\frac{k+1}{2^b} + \frac{3}{2} b \right)$$

of a single algorithm per phase. Finally, as in the proof of Theorem 2.2, we can sum over all N phases and argue that OPT has to make at least

$$\sum_{j=1}^{N} \frac{1}{2} l'_j$$

page faults in total; furthermore, we can assume that all phases are complete. With this, we can bound the strict expected competitive ratio of RMARKBARELY from above by

$$3b + \frac{2(k+1)}{2^b}$$

as we claimed. $\qquad \square$

Now we can use Theorem 2.12 with $b = \lfloor \log_2 k \rfloor - 1$. It follows that RMARKBARELY obtains a strict expected competitive ratio of at most

$$3 \lfloor \log_2 k \rfloor - 3 + \frac{2(k+1)}{2^{\lfloor \log_2 k \rfloor - 1}} = 3 \log_2 k + \mathcal{O}(1) \in \mathcal{O}(\log k).$$

Let us briefly interpret these results. No deterministic online algorithm can be better than k-competitive. However, this can be improved exponentially by picking a strategy uniformly at random from a set of constantly many ones. Such phenomena motivate the study of *advice complexity*, which we will introduce in the next chapter and which will subsequently accompany us throughout this book.

$\star$2.7 Bounds with Probability Tending to One

So far, we always measured the quality of randomized online algorithms by means of the expected competitive ratio. In Section 2.1, we mentioned that, for offline problems, one is usually more interested in the concrete probabilities with which "good" or "bad" output is created. For a broad class of offline algorithms, statements about the expected value allow for statements about the concrete probability of success by using the amplification technique. For online algorithms, this argumentation does not work in general since they cannot repeat their computation.

However, for some online algorithms for paging, we can make statements that speak about the concrete probabilities of creating a good output. As for offline optimization problems, "good" means that the gain or cost of the computed solution is very close to the expected gain or cost. A desirable result would be that the probability that this happens is large. But what does "large" mean in this context? Preferably, it means "not constant," and we would be happy if the probability tends to 1, for instance, with increasing input length. In the following, we show that such a statement is not possible in general by using the fact that any input of length n can be extended to an input of length dn by repeating every request d times. The following theorem only speaks about strict competitiveness; a general statement is given in Exercise 2.8.

Theorem 2.13. *Let $f\colon \mathbb{N} \to \mathbb{R}^+$ be some unbounded increasing function. There is no randomized online algorithm for paging that is strictly c-competitive for inputs of length n with a probability of $1 - 1/f(n)$, where $c < k$.*

Proof. Let $c < k$, and suppose there is some $n_0 \in \mathbb{N}^+$ such that there is a randomized online algorithm RAND that, for any instance I of paging with $|I| = n \geq n_0$ is strictly c-competitive with a probability of $1 - 1/f(n)$, for some function f that tends to infinity with growing n. Without loss of generality, we assume that RAND is a demand paging algorithm (see Exercises 1.5 and 1.6).

Now let $n' \geq n_0$ be an arbitrary natural number that is a large multiple of k such that

$$\frac{1}{k^{k-1}} > \frac{1}{f(n')} . \tag{2.25}$$

We design a randomized online algorithm RAND$'$ that has a strict performance of c with a probability of $1 - 1/f(n')$ on inputs of length k. To this end, RAND$'$

simulates RAND on an input that is obtained by repeating every request n'/k times. By definition, RAND has a strict performance of c on this input with a probability of $1 - 1/f(n')$. Since RAND$'$ replaces the same pages as RAND, RAND$'$ also has a strict performance of c on the original instance of length k with a probability of $1 - 1/f(n')$.

Next, we show that the existence of RAND$'$ and thus RAND leads to a contradiction. Again, let there be $k + 1$ pages in total. Now consider the following instance I' of paging of length k. First, the page p_{k+1} is requested, and then some sequence of $k - 1$ pages such that the same page is never requested in two consecutive time steps. We already know that there is an optimal solution for I' that only makes a page fault in the first time step.

Now consider the solution of RAND$'$ for I'. In every time step in which the algorithm causes a page fault, RAND$'$ randomly chooses a page to replace in its cache. There is always a page that is chosen with probability at least $1/k$, and the advesary requests this page in the next time step. Thus, there is a sequence $p_{i_1}, p_{i_2}, \ldots, p_{i_{k-1}}$ of "bad" choices that causes RAND$'$ to have cost k. In the first time step, RAND$'$ chooses the bad page (that is, the page that is requested right after that) with probability at least $1/k$; with probability at least $1/k^2$, it chooses the bad pages in the first and the second time step, and so on. Clearly, the probability that it chooses the bad sequence is at least $1/k^{k-1}$. Thus, RAND$'$ has a strict performance of k on I' with at least this probability; but together with (2.25), this immediately contradicts our assumption that RAND$'$ has a strict performance of c on I' with a probability of $1 - 1/f(n')$. As a consequence, RAND$'$ cannot be strictly c-competitive with a probability of $1 - 1/f(n)$ for inputs of length n; thus, RAND cannot exist. $\qquad\square$

Exercise 2.8.* For Theorem 2.13, we assume that RAND is strictly c-competitive with the given probability, and from this conclude that RAND$'$ cannot be strictly c-competitive with this probability on short instances. Prove this result for the case that the additive constant α from Definition 2.2 is allowed to be positive.

Hint. Consider an input length that depends on α.

A consequence of Theorem 2.13 (and Exercise 2.8) is that we cannot hope for a randomized online algorithm that is better than (strictly) k-competitive with a probability that tends to 1 with growing n. As we know that there are deterministic online algorithms that reach this bound, this seems disappointing. Then again, the instances we used in the proof of this theorem appeared to be rather artificial, as they basically consist of a linear number of requests for the same page, and the optimal cost is always one. For paging, instances are of interest for which also the cost of an optimal solution grows with the input length.

In what follows, we therefore measure the probability of being as good as the expected value in the number N of phases according to the k-phase partition from Definition 1.8. Our goal is to again study the randomized marking algorithm RMARK, which was introduced in Section 2.2, and to show that it achieves a competitive ratio that is close to its expected value $2H_k$ with a probability that tends to 1 as N increases. To prove this claim, we need the following technical lemma, which we state without a proof. Let $\exp \colon \mathbb{R} \to \mathbb{R}^+$ be the natural exponential function, that is, $\exp(x) = \mathrm{e}^x$ where $\mathrm{e} = 2.718\ldots$ is Euler's number.

Lemma 2.4 (Hoeffding's Inequality). *Let $X_1, X_2, \ldots, X_N$ be independent random variables such that $a_i \leq X_i - \mathbb{E}[X_i] \leq b_i$, for all i with $1 \leq i \leq N$. Then*

$$\Pr\left[\sum_{i=1}^{N}(X_i - \mathbb{E}[X_i]) \geq t\right] \leq \exp\left(-\frac{2t^2}{\sum_{i=1}^{N}(b_i - a_i)^2}\right),$$

for any $t > 0$. □

To prove the following theorem, we treat the cost of single phases as random variables. Note that the number of phases does not simply increase with the input length.

Theorem 2.14. *Let $\varepsilon > 0$. The probability that the competitive ratio of RMARK is at least $2H_k + \varepsilon$ tends to 0 as the number of phases tends to infinity.*

Proof. Let I be any instance of paging, and let RMARK be the randomized marking algorithm defined in Section 2.2; we consider the k-phase partition according to Definition 1.8. As in the proofs of Theorems 2.2 and 2.11, for any phase P_i, we denote the cost of RMARK on I during P_i by $\mathrm{cost}(\mathrm{RMARK}(P_i))$ and set

$$C_i := \mathrm{cost}(\mathrm{RMARK}(P_i)),$$

for every i with $1 \leq i \leq N$, to get an easier notation. Consequently, we have

$$\mathrm{cost}(\mathrm{RMARK}(I)) = \sum_{i=1}^{N} C_i. \tag{2.26}$$

Note that the C_i are independent random variables since the cache content at the beginning and the end of any phase does not depend on the random decisions made in any of the previous phases; indeed, it only depends on I, which is chosen deterministically.

Since at most k different pages are requested in one phase, we can trivially bound every random variable C_i by

$$0 \leq C_i \leq k,$$

and thus

$$\underbrace{-\mathbb{E}[C_i]}_{a_i} \leq C_i - \mathbb{E}[C_i] \leq \underbrace{k - \mathbb{E}[C_i]}_{b_i}. \tag{2.27}$$

Theorem 2.2 states that RMARK is strictly $2H_k$-competitive in expectation, which means that

$$\mathbb{E}[\text{cost}(\text{RMARK}(I))] \leq 2H_k \cdot \text{cost}(\text{OPT}(I)) . \tag{2.28}$$

Now we are interested in the probability that the cost of RMARK is at least $(2H_k + \varepsilon) \cdot \text{cost}(\text{OPT}(I))$, for any $\varepsilon > 0$. Using (2.28), (2.26), and linearity of expectation in this order, we obtain

$$\Pr[\text{cost}(\text{RMARK}(I)) \geq (2H_k + \varepsilon) \cdot \text{cost}(\text{OPT}(I))]$$

$$\leq \Pr\left[\text{cost}(\text{RMARK}(I)) \geq \frac{(2H_k + \varepsilon) \cdot \mathbb{E}[\text{cost}(\text{RMARK}(I))]}{2H_k}\right]$$

$$= \Pr\left[\text{cost}(\text{RMARK}(I)) - \mathbb{E}[\text{cost}(\text{RMARK}(I))] \geq \frac{\varepsilon \cdot \mathbb{E}[\text{cost}(\text{RMARK}(I))]}{2H_k}\right]$$

$$= \Pr\left[\sum_{i=1}^{N} C_i - \mathbb{E}\left[\sum_{i=1}^{N} C_i\right] \geq \frac{\varepsilon \cdot \mathbb{E}[\text{cost}(\text{RMARK}(I))]}{2H_k}\right]$$

$$= \Pr\left[\sum_{i=1}^{N} (C_i - \mathbb{E}[C_i]) \geq \frac{\varepsilon \cdot \mathbb{E}[\text{cost}(\text{RMARK}(I))]}{2H_k}\right] .$$

We now apply Hoeffding's inequality and obtain

$$\Pr\left[\sum_{i=1}^{N} (C_i - \mathbb{E}[C_i]) \geq \frac{\varepsilon \cdot \mathbb{E}[\text{cost}(\text{RMARK}(I))]}{2H_k}\right]$$

$$\leq \exp\left(-\frac{(\varepsilon \cdot \mathbb{E}[\text{cost}(\text{RMARK}(I))])^2}{2H_k^2 \sum_{i=1}^{N}(b_i - a_i)^2}\right) .$$

Recall that every phase contains at least one request for a new page. Thus, RMARK makes at least one page fault per phase, and we have

$$\mathbb{E}[\text{cost}(\text{RMARK}(I))] \geq N .$$

Moreover, due to (2.27), we have

$$\sum_{i=1}^{N} (b_i - a_i)^2 = Nk^2 .$$

With this, we finally get

$$\Pr\left[\sum_{i=1}^{N} (C_i - \mathbb{E}[C_i]) \geq \frac{\varepsilon \cdot \mathbb{E}[\text{cost}(\text{RMARK}(I))]}{2H_k}\right] \leq \exp\left(-\frac{\varepsilon^2}{2H_k^2 k^2} N\right) .$$

Since both ε and k are constant, this upper bound is monotonically decreasing in the number of phases N. To conclude, the probability that the actual cost of RMARK on I is at most $(2H_k + \varepsilon) \cdot \text{cost}(\text{OPT}(I))$ is at least

$$1 - \frac{1}{e^{\Omega(N)}},$$

which tends to 1 as we claimed. □

Unfortunately, this approach does not work in general. The proof of Theorem 2.14 only works since we have independent phases induced by RMARK.

Exercise 2.9. In the proof of Theorem 2.14, we also made use of the fact that RMARK is strictly $2H_k$-competitive in expectation. Does the proof still work if we also assume that the additive constant α from Definition 2.2 is positive?

2.8 The Ski Rental Problem

In this section, we study a very simple online problem that is met in disguise in various situations in everyday life, namely the *ski rental problem*. The idea is simple and captures the dilemma we are facing when we need to decide whether it is cheaper to rent some resource on demand again and again for small cost or to buy it at once, without knowing how often we need to use it.

Suppose you want to go skiing for as long as possible, but you do not own any skis. You have two choices. Either you rent skis for a small amount, say, EUR 1, or you buy the skis for EUR k, where k is some natural number larger than 1. To simplify things, assume that the only thing that would prevent you from skiing is the weather, so you are in excellent shape and highly motivated. The problem is, however, that you only get a reliable weather forecast on the morning of the current day. Thus, at the beginning of every day with good weather, you have to decide whether you rent skis or buy them. In the latter case, you probably assume that buying pays off later as you expect there will be many more days with good weather. Let us model this situation as an online problem to see what can be achieved in terms of competitive analysis.

Definition 2.3 (Ski Rental Problem). The *ski rental problem* is an online minimization problem. An input consists of a sequence of n requests, where each request is either "good" or "bad," and the ith request represents whether it is possible to ski on the ith day. If the request is "bad," the output is always "$\langle \text{null} \rangle$." If the request is "good," an online algorithm must either output "rent" or "buy." If an online algorithm answers "buy" in some time step, it can only answer "$\langle \text{null} \rangle$" in all subsequent time steps. Let $k \in \mathbb{N}^+$ with $k \geq 2$; the cost of an output is the number of "rent" answers, plus k if there was a "buy" answer.

Definition 2.3 implies that, for any online algorithm for the ski rental problem, we simply need to specify what it does on days with good weather. Let us start with deterministic strategies. First of all, we note that it is a bad strategy to never buy the skis at all. If some algorithm never buys the skis no matter how many days with good weather there are, an adversary can easily force it to have an unbounded cost, namely n. But when should the skis be bought? To buy on the first day with good weather also seems to be a bad idea, because then the adversary will make all subsequent days have bad weather, and the online algorithm pays k times as much as is necessary.

Let us try another strategy, namely "break even." This strategy is to rent the skis for the first $k-1$ days with good weather and to buy them on the kth day with good weather. It turns out that this is the best deterministic strategy we can follow in such a situation; we denote the corresponding online algorithm by BREAKEVEN.

Theorem 2.15. BREAKEVEN *is strictly* $(2-1/k)$*-competitive for the ski rental problem and no deterministic online algorithm is better than strictly* $(2-1/k)$*-competitive.*

Proof. Let us first prove the lower bound. We consider an adversary that always starts with a sequence of "good" requests, and possibly switches to "bad" at some point; after such a switch, it never switches back to "good." As we have just discussed, never buying the skis is not a promising idea. So we simply distinguish between three cases depending on when the skis are bought by some online algorithm ALG; say, this happens on the ith day with good weather if such a day exists.

Case 1. Suppose $1 \le i < k$. The adversary constructs the input such that, after the ith day, all days have bad weather and therefore an optimal strategy rents the skis for all i days with good weather. We can immediately bound the competitive ratio from below by

$$\frac{k+i-1}{i} > \frac{2k-1}{k}$$

in this case.

Case 2. Now suppose $i > k$. Again, the adversary causes all days after the ith to have bad weather. An optimal strategy in such a case is to buy the skis at the first day with good weather. We get a bound of

$$\frac{k+i-1}{k} > \frac{2k-1}{k}$$

on the competitive ratio also in the second case.

So far, we have basically covered all algorithms that have a strategy which deviates from that of BREAKEVEN. Now we study what happens in this case. Of course, we now consider an arbitrary adversary.

Case 3. So finally, suppose $i = k$. If there are at least k days of good weather, ALG (more specifically, BREAKEVEN) pays exactly $2k - 1$. In this case, an optimal algorithm pays at least k, no matter whether the skis are rented or bought. Therefore, the (strict) performance is

$$\frac{2k-1}{k} = 2 - \frac{1}{k}\,.$$

On the other hand, if there are fewer than k days with good weather, ALG is even optimal.

Summing up, no online algorithm can be better than strictly $(2-1/k)$-competitive, and only BREAKEVEN achieves this competitive ratio. □

According to Definition 1.6, BREAKEVEN is *strongly* strictly competitive. We chose to formulate the claim in terms of *strict* competitiveness, because the cost k of buying the skis is a fixed parameter of the problem. Indeed, BREAKEVEN's cost is never larger than $2k-1$ and therefore, for any I, if we plug

$$\text{cost}(\text{BREAKEVEN}(I)) \le 2k-1, \quad \text{cost}(\text{OPT}(I)) \ge 1, \quad \text{and } c = 1$$

into

$$\text{cost}(\text{BREAKEVEN}(I)) \le c \cdot \text{cost}(\text{OPT}(I)) + \alpha\,,$$

we get

$$2k - 1 \le 1 + \alpha\,.$$

Hence, for $\alpha = 2(k-1)$, BREAKEVEN is 1-competitive. Although there do exist online algorithms that are not competitive for the ski rental problem at all, it seems to be the case that all somewhat "serious" online algorithms are 1-competitive, but only for a value for α that depends on k. As a consequence, the interesting case is to consider strict competitiveness. As we have seen, we cannot be better than strictly $(2 - 1/k)$-competitive in a deterministic setting; with increasing k, this lower bound tends to 2.

Exercise 2.10. Suppose the cost of buying skis is not a parameter known to any online algorithm in advance, but is given with the first request; the subsequent requests are either "good" or "bad" as defined in Definition 2.3. What follows for the non-strict competitive ratio of BREAKEVEN?

Now we ask how much randomization helps for ski rental. In Section 2.2, we have seen that randomization allows for a rather drastic, namely exponential (with respect to the cache size), improvement for paging. As BREAKEVEN already has a competitive ratio that is better than 2, the improvement for ski rental has to be less significant. But does randomization help at all? From Theorem 2.1, we already know that there is no such thing as an optimal randomized online algorithm for this problem.

In the following, we describe the randomized online algorithm RSKI that chooses deterministic strategies according to some probability distribution Pr_{RSKI}. These strategies are defined as follows; for every i with $1 \leq i \leq k$, let Buy_i be the deterministic online algorithm that rents skis until day $i-1$ of good weather and buys them on the ith such day (if it exists). We set

$$\text{strat}(\text{RSKI}) := \{Buy_1, Buy_2, \ldots, Buy_k\}$$

and define a probability distribution $\text{Pr}_{\text{RSKI}} \colon \text{RSKI} \to [0,1]$ in what follows. To this end, let

$$\delta := \frac{k}{k-1}$$

and

$$\gamma := \frac{\delta - 1}{\delta^k - 1} .$$

The probability that RSKI chooses the strategy Buy_i is given by

$$\text{Pr}_{\text{RSKI}}[Buy_i] := \gamma \delta^{i-1} .$$

We immediately verify that

$$\sum_{i=1}^{k} \text{Pr}_{\text{RSKI}}[Buy_i] = \sum_{i=1}^{k} \gamma \delta^{i-1} = \gamma \sum_{i=0}^{k-1} \delta^i = \left(\frac{\delta - 1}{\delta^k - 1} \right) \left(\frac{\delta^k - 1}{\delta - 1} \right) = 1 ,$$

thus RSKI is well defined. Now we compute an upper bound on its expected competitive ratio.

Theorem 2.16. RSKI *is strictly*

$$\left(\frac{\delta^k}{\delta^k - 1} \right)\text{-competitive}$$

in expectation for the ski rental problem.

Proof. At first, we can apply two simplifications that allow us to ignore some instances that might be created by the adversary.

1. Since every deterministic online algorithm from $\text{strat}(\text{RSKI})$ buys the skis at the latest on the kth day with good weather, we only need to consider inputs that contain at most k such days.

2. Moreover, we may neglect days with bad weather that lie between days with good weather, because they do not change the achieved competitive ratio. This is due to the fact that RSKI's behavior does not depend on them (and neither does an optimal solution).

In other words, we can assume that all instances consist of j days with good weather and after that, there are only days with bad weather for $1 \leq j \leq k$. For such an instance, an optimal solution always has cost j. If there are j days with good weather, the online algorithm Buy_i has cost $i - 1 + k$ if $i \leq j$; conversely, it has cost j whenever $i > j$.

Therefore, the expected cost of RSKI on such an instance I, which has exactly j days with good weather, is

$$\mathbb{E}[\text{cost}(\text{RSKI}(I))]$$

$$= \sum_{i=1}^{j} (i - 1 + k) \cdot \text{Pr}_{\text{RSKI}}[Buy_i] + \sum_{i=j+1}^{k} j \cdot \text{Pr}_{\text{RSKI}}[Buy_i]$$

$$= \sum_{i=1}^{j} (i - 1) \cdot \text{Pr}_{\text{RSKI}}[Buy_i] + \sum_{i=1}^{j} k \cdot \text{Pr}_{\text{RSKI}}[Buy_i] + \sum_{i=j+1}^{k} j \cdot \text{Pr}_{\text{RSKI}}[Buy_i] \, .$$

By the definition of Pr_{RSKI}, we get

$$\mathbb{E}[\text{cost}(\text{RSKI}(I))] = \gamma \sum_{i=1}^{j} (i - 1)\delta^{i-1} + \gamma k \sum_{i=1}^{j} \delta^{i-1} + \gamma j \sum_{i=j+1}^{k} \delta^{i-1}$$

$$= \gamma \sum_{i=0}^{j-1} i\delta^{i} + \gamma k \sum_{i=0}^{j-1} \delta^{i} + \gamma j \sum_{i=j}^{k-1} \delta^{i}$$

$$= \gamma \sum_{i=0}^{j-1} i\delta^{i} + \gamma k \sum_{i=0}^{j-1} \delta^{i} + \gamma j \sum_{i=0}^{k-1} \delta^{i} - \gamma j \sum_{i=0}^{j-1} \delta^{i} \, .$$

We can now use the closed forms of these geometric series together with

$$\delta = \frac{k}{k-1} \iff k = \frac{\delta}{\delta - 1} \, ,$$

and get

$$\mathbb{E}[\text{cost}(\text{RSKI}(I))]$$

$$= \gamma \frac{(j-1)\delta^{j+1} - j\delta^{j} + \delta}{(\delta - 1)^2} + \gamma k \frac{\delta^{j} - 1}{\delta - 1} + \gamma j \frac{\delta^{k} - 1}{\delta - 1} - \gamma j \frac{\delta^{j} - 1}{\delta - 1}$$

$$= \frac{\gamma}{\delta - 1} \left(\frac{(j-1)\delta^{j+1} - j\delta^{j} + \delta}{\delta - 1} + k(\delta^{j} - 1) + j(\delta^{k} - \delta^{j}) \right)$$

$$= \frac{\gamma}{\delta - 1} \left(k(j-1)\delta^{j} - kj\delta^{j-1} + k + k(\delta^{j} - 1) + j(\delta^{k} - \delta^{j}) \right)$$

$$= \frac{\gamma}{\delta - 1} \left(jk\delta^{j} - kj\delta^{j-1} + j\delta^{k} - j\delta^{j} \right)$$

$$= \frac{\gamma}{\delta - 1} \left(\delta^{j} \underbrace{\left(k - \frac{k}{\delta} - 1 \right)}_{0} + \delta^{k} \right) j$$

$$= \frac{\delta^k \gamma}{\delta - 1} j \, .$$

We plug in $\mathrm{cost}(\mathrm{OPT}(I)) = j$ and $\gamma = (\delta - 1)/(\delta^k - 1)$, finally obtaining

$$\mathbb{E}[\mathrm{cost}(\mathrm{RSKI}(I))] = \frac{\delta^k(\delta - 1)}{(\delta - 1)(\delta^k - 1)} \cdot \mathrm{cost}(\mathrm{OPT}(I))$$

$$= \frac{\delta^k}{\delta^k - 1} \cdot \mathrm{cost}(\mathrm{OPT}(I))$$

as claimed.   □

We are now interested in the asymptotic behavior of the expected competitive ratio of RSKI if k tends to infinity. Thus, we consider

$$\lim_{k \to \infty} \delta^k = \lim_{k \to \infty} \left(\frac{k}{k-1} \right)^k = \mathrm{e} \, ,$$

where as before $\mathrm{e} = 2.718\ldots$ denotes Euler's number, and obtain

$$\lim_{k \to \infty} \frac{\delta^k}{\delta^k - 1} = \frac{\mathrm{e}}{\mathrm{e} - 1} = 1.582\ldots \, .$$

So, under which conditions is RSKI better in expectation than BREAKEVEN? To answer this question, we note that

$$\frac{\delta^k}{\delta^k - 1} < 2 - \frac{1}{k} \tag{2.29}$$

$$\Longleftrightarrow \qquad \delta^k < \left(2 - \frac{1}{k} \right) \delta^k - 2 + \frac{1}{k}$$

$$\Longleftrightarrow -\left(1 + \frac{1}{k} \right) \delta^k < -\left(2 - \frac{1}{k} \right)$$

$$\Longleftrightarrow \qquad \left(\frac{k}{k-1} \right)^k > \frac{2k - 1}{k + 1} \, ,$$

(by the definition of δ)

which holds whenever

$$\left(\frac{k}{k-1} \right)^k \geq 2 \, . \tag{2.30}$$

Since $(2/(2-1))^2 = 4$ and $(k/(k-1))^k$ is monotonically decreasing and tends to e for $k \geq 2$, (2.30) and thus (2.29) is true for any $k \geq 2$. We conclude that, already for $k \geq 2$ (which is always satisfied since k is a natural number larger than 1), the randomized online algorithm RSKI is better than any deterministic online algorithm; see Figure 2.5.

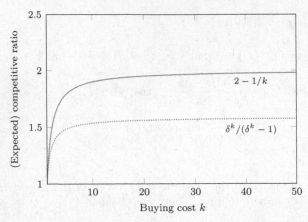

Figure 2.5. Comparison of the competitive ratios of BREAKEVEN and RSKI.

2.9 Historical and Bibliographical Notes

Introductions to randomized algorithms are given by, for instance, Hromkovič [81], Mitzenmacher and Upfal [118], and Motwani and Raghavan [120]. Also the textbook by Borodin and El-Yaniv [34] spends many chapters on randomized online algorithms. Knuth and Yao [96] discuss how to generate random numbers using random bits and remark "... we shall use the word 'algorithm' for such possibly infinite procedures, although strictly speaking we should be calling them 'computational methods' since algorithms are traditionally supposed to be finite in their worst case."

The Solovay-Strassen algorithm was published in 1977 by Solovay and Strassen [133]. A comprehensive analysis is, for instance, given in the aforementioned book by Hromkovič [81]. Note that this algorithm is a *one-sided-error Monte Carlo algorithm* for the inverse problem of deciding whether a given number is composite.

Yao's principle was first applied by Yao [145] in 1977. Since then, it was used for a large number of different online problems. The formulation and proof presented in this chapter follow the textbook by Borodin and El-Yaniv [34].

An introduction to game theory, including zero-sum games, is given by Straffin [136]. The minimax theorem is due to von Neumann [140]. Later, Nash [121] showed that all games with a finite number of strategies have equilibria in mixed strategies (they are therefore called *Nash equilibria*). Loomis' lemma was proven in 1946 by Loomis [111]. The application of games to online algorithms is discussed in detail by Borodin and El-Yaniv [35].

The randomized online algorithm RMARK is from Fiat et al. [61]. The lower bound for randomized paging algorithms is also due to Fiat et al. [61]; the proof presented here is taken from Motwani and Raghavan [120]. Actually, the lower bound of H_k is not just asymptotically tight; McGeoch and Sleator [116] designed a randomized paging algorithm that is H_k-competitive in expectation. The barely random algorithm RMARKBARELY and its analysis are due to Böckenhauer et al. [30] and Komm and Královič [101, 102].

Hoeffding's inequality was first proven by Hoeffding [77]. Komm et al. [100] proved that if a given online problem satisfies some natural conditions, a similar statement to Theorem 2.14 is possible. In this analysis, the random variables are not independent, but form a bounded supermartingale. Instead of Hoeffding's inequality, the Azuma-Hoeffding inequality [12] is used to bound the cost of any randomized online algorithm.

The upper bound of RSKI for the ski rental problem (see Theorem 2.16) is due to Karlin et al. [91], who also presented a matching lower bound. The presentation given in Section 2.8 follows Krumke and Thielen [109].

Advice Complexity

3

In this chapter, we introduce another important class of online algorithms. So far, we have considered deterministic and randomized approaches. For paging and the ski rental problem, randomization enables us to construct more powerful algorithms. More specifically, we are able to design randomized online algorithms that are a lot better in terms of their expected competitive ratio; for paging, we even have an exponential improvement. The third model, *online algorithms with advice*, is even more powerful. We introduce this concept and, as in the two preceding chapters, use paging as an example to illustrate the basic ideas. The main motivation to study this model is mostly a theoretical one; it gives us a very intuitive formalization of the notion of "hardness" in the context of online computation. The idea is to measure the amount of information about the yet unknown parts of the input that an online algorithm needs to know in order to achieve some particular output quality. To have a formal framework, we introduce an *oracle* which sees the whole input in advance and may encode any binary information about this input onto a so-called *advice tape*. An online algorithm can then use this tape as a resource during computation. We then ask for the number of bits of advice the online algorithm needs to be, say, c-competitive, for some specific constant c. The number of advice bits used is given by a function of the input length n, similar to the number of random bits, which we studied in the preceding chapter; this number is called the *advice complexity* of the algorithm.

We first introduce the model of advice formally. Next, to be able to prove upper bounds on the advice complexity, we describe the concept of *self-delimiting strings*; these allow an online algorithm to read a number of bits from the advice tape in a situation where it does not have any information about the length of this string. We continue by explaining how to prove lower bounds on the advice complexity; for this reason, we introduce so-called *partition trees*. After that, we study the advice complexity of paging (that is, the advice complexity of online algorithms for paging) both for obtaining optimal solutions and for using only a small number of advice bits.

© Springer International Publishing Switzerland 2016
D. Komm, *An Introduction to Online Computation*,
Texts in Theoretical Computer Science. An EATCS Series,
DOI 10.1007/978-3-319-42749-2_3

Finally, we make some interesting observations on the connection between advice and randomization.

3.1 Introduction

Before we designed the randomized online algorithm RSKI for the ski rental problem, we saw that deterministic online algorithms are almost twice as bad as an optimal offline algorithm. We want to have a closer look at this fact. More specifically, we want to answer the question

Why are they twice as bad?

To phrase the question even more exactly, we ask

What are they missing?

It is tempting to give a simple answer. What they miss is the complete input. Sure, if we had a complete and accurate weather forecast, we could simply compute an optimal solution for any instance of the ski rental problem; count the number of days with good weather, and check whether it is at least k. If it is, we buy the skis, otherwise we rent them. But is it really necessary to know the whole input to be optimal? If we think about it, all that we need is to be able to make a simple "yes"/"no" decision, namely, whether to buy the skis on the first day with good weather or to rent them again and again. So what we are missing is basically the smallest amount of information there is; one single bit.

As discussed in Chapter 1, the competitive ratio tells us how much we pay if we work on a specific online problem. The *advice complexity*, on the other hand, tells us what we pay for. For the ski rental problem, every deterministic online algorithm is almost 100% worse than the optimal solution in the worst case, and the "why" can be answered with "because we don't know this single bit." However, of course, in general the question "why" or "what" cannot be answered this easily; for instance, a single bit of information will probably not enable us to get an optimal solution for the paging problem (but surprisingly, later in this chapter, we will see that a constant amount of additional information does help quite a lot). As a matter of fact, different online problems behave very differently when we investigate them with respect to the information that is necessary to obtain some good solution quality. As mentioned above, we can always say that knowing the whole input in advance helps to create an optimal solution, but for some problems we may be able to compress some critical property of the input that already enables us to improve a lot over deterministic or randomized strategies. In a way, we ask about the *information content* of the problems, that is, the information that is hidden in the instances and that needs to be extracted; here, the advice complexity is a powerful tool.

To be able to measure this amount of information, we use a model where an *oracle* is introduced that knows the whole input I of a given online problem in advance. This oracle can write binary information about I on a so-called *advice tape* that can afterwards be used by an online algorithm that works on I. Informally, we can describe this model as follows.

- We do not simply design online algorithms, but an online algorithm ALG is always created together with an oracle. We call ALG an *online algorithm with advice*.

- For every input, the oracle writes some so-called *advice bits* on the advice tape.

- The adversary knows both ALG and the oracle; in particular, it knows which advice the oracle writes on the tape, given a specific input.

In the classical model, the adversary inspects ALG and then constructs an input that causes ALG to perform as badly as possible. Now, there is a third party, which is essentially an all-knowing counselor working for the algorithm. Note that the third bullet point suggests that, in the model of computing with advice, we have an extremely powerful adversary. However, if we take a closer look, this is not the case; it is sufficient if the adversary merely knows ALG, and, as a consequence, an upper bound $b(n)$ on the number of advice bits that the algorithm reads for a given input length n. For any n and $b(n)$, the adversary can simply simulate ALG on every possible advice string ϕ of length $b(n)$ and therefore find the best advice. It can then choose an instance I' of length n of the given online problem Π such that

$$I' := \arg\max_I \left\{ \min_\phi \left\{ \frac{\text{gain}(\text{OPT}(I))}{\text{gain}(\text{ALG}^\phi(I))} \right\} \right\}$$

if Π is a maximization problem, or

$$I' := \arg\max_I \left\{ \min_\phi \left\{ \frac{\text{cost}(\text{ALG}^\phi(I))}{\text{cost}(\text{OPT}(I))} \right\} \right\}$$

if Π is a minimization problem. If possible, the adversary will additionally try to make sure that, for the set of instances it constructs in the above way, the optimal cost (gain, respectively) increases unboundedly with the input length, such that a lower bound on the non-strict competitive ratio is obtained.

The above formula reminds us of the minimax theorem from Section 2.4. However, both the adversary and the algorithm pick pure strategies. The important thing is that no matter which strategy the adversary decides to use, ALG will *always* pick a best of its strategies as a response. Now let us describe the steps that are made in the model of computing with advice.

Step 1. The adversary constructs an input I of length n such that the competitive ratio of ALG using the advice tape is maximized; the adversary knows the number $b(n)$ of advice bits ALG reads at most.

Step 2. After that, the oracle inspects I and writes an advice string ϕ on the advice tape which depends on I.

Step 3. ALG reads the input I and computes an output O while using the advice tape; ALG reads at most a prefix of length $b(n)$ from the tape.

Step 4. If ALG obtains a competitive ratio of at most c, we say that ALG is c-competitive with *advice complexity* $b(n)$ or that ALG needs at most $b(n)$ advice bits to be c-competitive.

A crucial property of this model is that the advice tape has infinite length. This is important to prevent any situations in which information may be encoded into the length of the advice. On first sight, it seems redundant since the oracle and ALG are designed in such a way that the online algorithm never uses more than $b(n)$ advice bits in total anyway; but if we take a closer look, without this property, we could design an online algorithm with advice and an oracle that work as follows. Suppose that, for some input of length n, the oracle writes $b(n) = n$ advice bits on the tape. At the beginning, the online algorithm reads all the $b(n)$ bits until the end, and thus knows the length of the input. In a way, it gets this knowledge for free since it is only implicitly communicated by the advice length but not by its content. Of course, it is perfectly fine if the oracle writes the input length on the advice tape explicitly. The difference is that, in this case, this information is part of the advice and therefore accounted for.

Moreover, the tape is accessed sequentially (similar to the random tape of a randomized algorithm).

Example 3.1. Summarizing what we just learned, we can state that there is an optimal online algorithm with advice for the ski rental problem which uses 1 bit of advice. An oracle first reads the whole input and computes whether there are more than k days with good weather. If there are, it writes a 1 at the first position of the advice tape; else it writes a 0 at this position. In the first time step, the corresponding algorithm reads the first bit. If it is 1, the algorithm buys the skis at the first day with good weather; otherwise it rents them at every such day. Clearly, this algorithm always has the smallest cost possible. ◇

Now we are going to formally define online algorithms with advice. Following the preceding discussion, it seems to make sense to have a definition analogous to Definition 2.1 for randomized online algorithms.

Definition 3.1 (Online Algorithm with Advice). Let Π be an online problem and let $I = (x_1, x_2, \ldots, x_n)$ be an instance of Π. An *online algorithm* ALG *with advice* for Π computes the output $\text{ALG}^{\phi}(I) = (y_1, y_2, \ldots, y_n)$, where y_i depends on $\phi, x_1, x_2, \ldots, x_i$ and $y_1, y_2, \ldots, y_{i-1}$; ϕ denotes a *binary advice string*.

The essential difference between randomized online computation and online computation with advice comes into play when we define the competitive ratio for online algorithms with advice.

Definition 3.2 (Competitive Ratio with Advice). Let Π be an online problem, let ALG be a consistent online algorithm with advice for Π, and let OPT be an optimal offline algorithm for Π. For $c \geq 1$, ALG is *c-competitive with advice complexity* $b(n)$ for Π if there is a non-negative constant α such that, for every instance $I \in \mathcal{I}$, there is an advice string ϕ such that

$$\text{gain}(\text{OPT}(I)) \leq c \cdot \text{gain}\big(\text{ALG}^{\phi}(I)\big) + \alpha$$

if Π is a maximization problem, or

$$\text{cost}\big(\text{ALG}^{\phi}(I)\big) \leq c \cdot \text{cost}(\text{OPT}(I)) + \alpha$$

if Π is a minimization problem, and ALG uses at most the first $b(n)$ bits of ϕ. If the above inequality holds for $\alpha = 0$, ALG is called *strictly c-competitive with advice complexity* $b(n)$; ALG is called *optimal with advice complexity* $b(n)$ if it is strictly 1-competitive with advice complexity $b(n)$. The *competitive ratio* of an online algorithm ALG with advice complexity $b(n)$ is defined as

$$c_{\text{ALG}} := \inf\{c \geq 1 \mid \text{ALG is } c\text{-competitive for } \Pi$$
$$\text{with advice complexity } b(n)\}\,.$$

For such an online algorithm ALG, we thus require that, for every input, there is some advice string that allows ALG to obtain the given competitive ratio; we do not care whether this particular advice string is extremely bad for all other instances. This is the crucial difference when comparing this model to that of randomized online computation. The oracle deduces the advice string from the concrete input and does not use any randomness in the process. Still, the models share a common property, namely a binary tape that allows us to treat them as a collection of deterministic algorithms. We can thus formulate an analogous statement to Observation 2.2 (see also Exercise 2.2).

Observation 3.1. *Every online algorithm* ALG *with advice that uses at most* $b(n)$ *advice bits for inputs of length* n *can be viewed as a set* $\text{strat}(\text{ALG}, n) = \{A_1, A_2, \ldots, A_{2^{b(n)}}\}$ *of* $2^{b(n)}$ *deterministic online algorithms on inputs of length* n, *from which* ALG *always chooses one with the best performance for the given instance.*

For every given randomized online algorithm RAND, we can design an online algorithm ALG with advice that uses its advice tape the same way RAND uses its random tape. Accompanying ALG, we create an oracle that, for every instance, writes a "best" string on the advice tape; following this idea, we can state the following observation.

Observation 3.2. *For any online problem* Π, *the following two implications hold.*

(i) *If there is a randomized online algorithm for* Π *that is c-competitive in expectation and uses at most* $b(n)$ *random bits, then there is also an online algorithm with advice for* Π *that is c-competitive and that uses at most* $b(n)$ *advice bits.*

(ii) *Conversely, if there is provably no online algorithm with advice that is c-competitive while using at most* $b(n)$ *advice bits for* Π, *then there is also no randomized online algorithm for* Π *that is c-competitive in expectation and that uses at most* $b(n)$ *random bits.*

In Section 3.5, we will revisit the relation between advice and randomization and show some non-trivial connections.

3.2 Self-Delimiting Encoding of Strings

In this section, we focus on how to concretely encode information onto the advice tape, and especially on one particular problem that arises when there are multiple pieces of information that need to be delimited when using a binary alphabet.

Let d be some natural number. We know that we can encode 2^d different numbers in binary with d bits. To encode an arbitrary natural number m in binary, we need $\lceil \log_2(m+1) \rceil$ bits. If m is always at least 1, we only need $\lceil \log_2 m \rceil$ bits; this can be done by writing $m-1$ on the advice tape in binary. In the following considerations, we always assume that this is true for m.

It gets more difficult if we think about the special kind of resource we are dealing with in this setting. In particular, as already discussed in the previous section, we are facing the fact that the advice tape we are using has an infinite length; behind the actual advice, there is an infinite undefined suffix. The alphabet that the oracle uses to write on the advice tape is binary, and thus we do not have any *delimiter* to mark where the encoding of some binary substring (encoding, for instance, the length of the input) ends. Moreover, in general, we cannot use any special sequence of bits like, for instance, "111" as a delimiter since the same sequence might also be part of the advice (see Exercise 3.3).

What can we do about this? To answer this question, *self-delimiting encodings* come into play. The idea is to augment the advice with some *control bits* that allow the algorithm to decode the advice itself. Again, let m be a positive number that we want to encode. The idea is to tell the algorithm how many bits (from the infinite advice tape) belong to the binary representation of $m-1$.

First, we need at most $\lceil \log_2 m \rceil$ bits to encode $m-1$ on the tape. Then, we can use an additional $\lceil \log_2 m \rceil$ bits to tell the algorithm which bits belong to the string of length $\lceil \log_2 m \rceil$ as follows. We write the binary representation of $m-1$ on odd positions of the advice tape. On even positions, we write a 1 if the next bit still belongs to the binary representation of $m-1$, and a 0 otherwise. Thus, if $b_1 b_2 \ldots b_{\lceil \log_2 m \rceil}$ is the binary representation of $m-1$, the content of the advice tape starts with

$$b_1 \, 1 \, b_2 \, 1 \ldots b_{\lceil \log_2 m \rceil - 1} \, 1 \, b_{\lceil \log_2 m \rceil} \, 0 \, .$$

As a consequence, we need to use $2\lceil\log_2 m\rceil$ advice bits instead of $\lceil\log_2 m\rceil$ bits; we call this a *self-delimiting encoding* of m.

With another simple idea, we can improve this approach and use a smaller number of bits. For small values of m, we use the encoding

$$1:\boxed{0\;\;0}\lessgtr\ldots \quad\text{and}\quad 2:\boxed{0\;\;1}\lessgtr\ldots\;.$$

If m is at least 3, at the beginning of the advice tape, we tell the algorithm how many bits are used to encode $m-1$, that is, we write the number $\lceil\log_2 m\rceil$. This can be done using at most $\lceil\log_2(\lceil\log_2 m\rceil)\rceil$ additional bits since m is at least 3 and thus $\lceil\log_2 m\rceil$ is at least 2; hence, we can write $\lceil\log_2 m\rceil - 1$ on the tape. Now we are left with marking where these first $\lceil\log_2(\lceil\log_2 m\rceil)\rceil$ bits end and the binary representation of $m-1$ starts. To this end, we can use exactly the same idea as above and thus we need at most

$$2\lceil\log_2(\lceil\log_2 m\rceil)\rceil + \lceil\log_2 m\rceil$$

bits to encode m in a self-delimiting way. Note that, this way, the string always starts with a 1; hence, the cases where m is 1 or 2 can be distinguished from the case that m is at least 3 without any further information. The algorithm can now start reading until it encounters a 0 at an even position. Then, it computes the number of bits it needs to read afterwards to obtain m. We trade the multiplicative constant 2 for an additive term that is asymptotically smaller. Sample encodings are shown in the following table.

m	$m-1$	$\lceil\log_2 m\rceil - 1$	$\lceil\log_2(\lceil\log_2 m\rceil)\rceil$	self-delimiting string
1	0	–	–	0 0
2	1	–	–	0 1
3	2	1	1	1 0 1 0
4	3	1	1	1 0 1 1
5	4	2	2	1 1 0 0 1 0 0
6	5	2	2	1 1 0 0 1 0 1
7	6	2	2	1 1 0 0 1 1 0
8	7	2	2	1 1 0 0 1 1 1
9	8	3	2	1 1 1 0 1 0 0 0
10	9	3	2	1 1 1 0 1 0 0 1
⋮	⋮	⋮	⋮	⋮
256	255	7	3	1 1 1 1 1 0 1 1 1 1 1 1 1 1
				$\underbrace{\hspace{3cm}}_{2\lceil\log_2(\lceil\log_2 m\rceil)\rceil\text{ bits}}\;\underbrace{\hspace{2.5cm}}_{\lceil\log_2 m\rceil\text{ bits}}$
⋮	⋮	⋮	⋮	⋮

Example 3.2. Suppose we want to encode the number 43 onto the advice tape; moreover, it is known that the encoded number is not 0. Thus, we write 42 on the tape. If we simply encode it in binary, we get a prefix

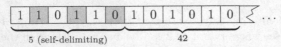

of the advice string; but if we only see this string, we cannot at all decode it in a unique way. It could, for instance, also be interpreted as

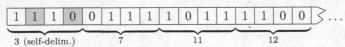

by an online algorithm assuming that the last two depicted bits already belong to the undefined part of the tape. Now let us make use of self-delimiting encodings. We realize that we need $\lceil \log_2 42 \rceil = 6$ bits to encode 42 in binary. Therefore, we first write the number 5 in a self-delimiting way on the advice tape (using $2\lceil \log_2 5 \rceil = 6$ additional bits) followed by the number 42 and obtain a prefix

1	1	0	1	1	0	1	0	1	0	1	0	...

5 (self-delimiting) 42

of the tape content. Now an online algorithm with advice is able to decode the advice without further knowledge. ◇

At times, we want to encode multiple numbers, and we know that they have some common upper bound.

Example 3.3. Suppose we want to encode the numbers 8, 12, and 13. Furthermore, we know that there are three numbers in total and none of them are 0 or larger than 16, that is, they can all be written in binary using at most four bits. We can encode them as

1	1	1	0	0	1	1	1	1	0	1	1	1	1	0	0	...

3 (self-delim.) 7 11 12

and again, an algorithm is able to unambiguously decode the string. ◇

We will use self-delimiting strings on several occasions. One application is immediate, namely this enables us to let some online algorithm know the input length n. Intuitively, this already might be a great advantage in some applications. The input length is never 0. Furthermore, we ignore the special cases that n is 1 or 2 to keep the formulas simple. Therefore, to encode n in a self-delimiting way, we usually need an additional

$$2\lceil \log_2(\lceil \log_2 n \rceil) \rceil + \lceil \log_2 n \rceil$$

advice bits.

Exercise 3.1. Describe alternative ways to obtain self-delimiting encodings of a natural number m that use roughly $2\lceil \log_2 m \rceil$ bits. Again, assume that m is at least 1.

Exercise 3.2. Improve the upper bound on how many bits must be used to encode a number m in a self-delimiting way by iterating the above strategy. Informally discuss the limitations of this approach.

Exercise 3.3. Consider the following idea. No single bit is interpreted as a letter, but three consecutive bits, and the information is encoded using this larger alphabet. The sequence "111" marks the end of the current string. Argue why this strategy is not superior to the one we introduced above; here, we are interested in the case that the length of the string we want to encode tends to infinity.

Of course, there are situations where we do not need a self-delimiting encoding of the advice. Similarly to barely random algorithms, we can design online algorithms with advice that read a constant number of advice bits, which is fixed from the beginning; an extreme case was the simple algorithm for the ski rental problem from Example 3.1. Moreover, we could think of algorithms that read a fixed number of advice bits in every time step. In this case, the algorithm knows how much advice to use as it realizes when the input ends.

3.3 Proving Lower Bounds

Proving the existence of some object is usually a lot simpler than proving its non-existence. To show that an object with some given property (for instance, an online algorithm with advice that uses a certain number of advice bits) exists, it suffices to construct such an object; therefore, such proofs are usually *constructive*. Showing that such an object does not exist may generally be more difficult. What we need to do is to prove that all possible objects do not have the given property. In our case, how do we prove that there is no online algorithm with advice that reads at most a given number of advice bits and achieves a given output quality? For such hardness results, we often use combinatorial arguments that, on a high level, work as follows.

1. For infinitely many $n \in \mathbb{N}^+$, construct sets of instances of length n that have unique and pairwise different optimal solutions.

2. If an algorithm has to make different decisions for, say, two different instances in some time step T_i with $1 \leq i \leq n$, the common prefix of length i of these instances is the same. In other words, a deterministic online algorithm cannot tell which of the two instances it is dealing with until after T_i.

3. From Observation 3.1, we know that an online algorithm with advice that uses $b(n)$ advice bits can be seen as picking one from $2^{b(n)}$ deterministic algorithms. Thus, for each of the instances, one of these algorithms is chosen. If the set of instances of length n is larger than $2^{b(n)}$, some instances must be processed by the same deterministic algorithm; we do not know which, but we can still

argue why this implies that this particular algorithm cannot be optimal on all of these instances (or is even unable to achieve some particular competitive ratio).

This idea behind this is formalized by so-called "partition trees." These are used to structure a set of instances according to common prefixes. In what follows, for every instance I of the given online problem, let $[I]_{n'}$ denote the prefix of length n' of I; likewise $[O]_{n'}$ denotes the prefix of length n' of a solution $O \in \mathrm{sol}(I)$. For every instance I, let $\mathrm{solOpt}(I) \subseteq \mathrm{sol}(I)$ denote the set of optimal solutions for I.

Definition 3.3 (Partition Tree). Let $\mathcal{I}$ be a set of instances of some online problem Π. A *partition tree* $\widehat{\mathcal{T}}$ of $\mathcal{I}$ is a tree with the following properties.

  (i) Every vertex $\hat{v}$ of $\widehat{\mathcal{T}}$ is labeled by a set $\mathcal{I}_{\hat{v}} \subseteq \mathcal{I}$ of instances and a natural number $\rho_{\hat{v}}$ such that all instances in $\mathcal{I}_{\hat{v}}$ have a common prefix of length at least $\rho_{\hat{v}}$.

 (ii) For every inner vertex $\hat{v}$ of $\widehat{\mathcal{T}}$, the set of instances of its children form a partition of the instances of $\mathcal{I}_{\hat{v}}$.

(iii) For the root $\hat{r}$, we have $\mathcal{I}_{\hat{r}} = \mathcal{I}$.

The set of instances $\mathcal{I}$ does not necessarily only include instances of the same length (see Theorem 8.13). The usual way to define partition trees, however, is to construct sets $\mathcal{I}^{(n)}$ of instances of length n for infinitely many n together with partition trees for every $\mathcal{I}^{(n)}$. The key to using partition trees to prove lower bounds on the advice complexity of optimal online algorithms with advice is formalized by the next lemma.

Lemma 3.1. *Let $\mathcal{I}$ be a set of instances of some online problem Π with a partition tree $\widehat{\mathcal{T}}$ of $\mathcal{I}$. Let $\hat{v}_1$ and $\hat{v}_2$ be two vertices from $\widehat{\mathcal{T}}$ such that neither one is an ancestor of the other one, let $I_1 \in \mathcal{I}_{\hat{v}_1}$ and $I_2 \in \mathcal{I}_{\hat{v}_2}$ be any two instances of Π, and let $\hat{v}$ be the lowest common ancestor of both $\hat{v}_1$ and $\hat{v}_2$. If*

$$[O_1]_{\rho_{\hat{v}}} \neq [O_2]_{\rho_{\hat{v}}},$$

for every $O_1 \in \mathrm{solOpt}(I_1)$ and $O_2 \in \mathrm{solOpt}(I_2)$, then every optimal online algorithm with advice has to use different advice strings for I_1 and I_2.

Proof. Since $\hat{v}$ is an ancestor of both $\hat{v}_1$ and $\hat{v}_2$, we have both $I_1 \in \mathcal{I}_{\hat{v}}$ and $I_2 \in \mathcal{I}_{\hat{v}}$, for all $I_1 \in \mathcal{I}_{\hat{v}_1}$ and $I_2 \in \mathcal{I}_{\hat{v}_2}$. Due to Definition 3.3, we have $[I_1]_{\rho_{\hat{v}}} = [I_2]_{\rho_{\hat{v}}}$, but due to the assumption of the lemma, $[O_1]_{\rho_{\hat{v}}} \neq [O_2]_{\rho_{\hat{v}}}$ for every $O_1 \in \mathrm{solOpt}(I_1)$ and $O_2 \in \mathrm{solOpt}(I_2)$. In other words, the instances have the same prefix of length $\rho_{\hat{v}}$, but their optimal solutions differ in the first $\rho_{\hat{v}}$ answers.

Now let ALG be any optimal online algorithm with advice for Π, and assume that ALG reads the same advice for I_1 and I_2, which means that it chooses the same deterministic algorithm A for both instances. Since I_1 and I_2 have the same prefix of length $\rho_{\hat{v}}$, that is, they look identical to A up to time step $T_{\rho_{\hat{v}}}$, A produces the same output on this prefix. However, by the assumption of the lemma, some of the first $\rho_{\hat{v}}$ optimal answers must be different for I_1 and I_2, and therefore A and thus ALG cannot compute optimal solutions for both of them. $\qquad\square$

Finally, we can use Lemma 3.1 to prove the following theorem.

Theorem 3.1. *Let $\mathcal{I}$ be a set of instances of some online problem Π with a partition tree $\widehat{\mathcal{T}}$ of $\mathcal{I}$ with w leaves, such that the conditions of Lemma 3.1 are satisfied. Then every optimal online algorithm with advice for Π has to use at least $\log_2 w$ advice bits.*

Proof. It follows from Lemma 3.1 that, under the given conditions, every optimal online algorithm with advice needs to use two different advice strings for any two instances that correspond to different vertices in $\widehat{\mathcal{T}}$ with neither one being an ancestor of the other. Thus, such an algorithm needs to use a different advice string for every leaf. Since, when reading at most b bits, there are 2^b different advice strings, it follows that $2^b \geq w$ must be satisfied, and thus $b \geq \log_2 w$. $\qquad\square$

In order to keep our arguments simple, we will usually try to construct the set $\mathcal{I}$ such that all instances have unique optimal solutions that are only optimal for this one instance. Moreover, the leaves of the partition tree are such that they only contain (a set with) a single instance each. In many of the subsequent lower-bound proofs, we will not explicitly construct partition trees, but incorporate the above ideas in our direct arguments. Learning about this general idea is important if one is to see the bigger picture of what is happening. Sometimes, however, there will be alternative proofs that explicitly use partition trees.

The arguments for lower bounds can also be used in another way. Suppose that we can show that every deterministic online algorithm can only be optimal (c-competitive, respectively) for, say, at most δn instances of length n of some online problem Π. The best case for an online algorithm ALG with advice is met if all these sets of instances are disjoint. Suppose ALG uses at most $b(n)$ advice bits for inputs of length n. If we are able, for infinitely many n, to construct a set of instances of Π of size $\mu(n)$ with $\mu(n) > 2^{b(n)} \cdot \delta n$, then we know that ALG cannot be optimal (c-competitive, respectively).

3.4 The Advice Complexity of Paging

We are now ready to study the advice complexity of the paging problem, which we used before to illustrate the concepts of deterministic and randomized online computation.

3.4.1 Optimality

We start by describing three different approaches to design optimal online algorithms with advice that have linear advice complexity.

Example 3.4. We design a simple online algorithm PLIN1 with advice and an oracle for paging that work as follows. The oracle inspects the input I, which consists of a sequence of pages that have indices between 1 and m (where m is the number of pages in total). The most straightforward strategy would be to communicate the whole instance I by encoding the indices. Note that, for any I with $|I| = n$, there are obviously m^n different instances. Clearly, if PLIN1 knows the complete instance in advance, it can be optimal. A number between 1 and m can be encoded with $\lceil \log_2 m \rceil$ bits, thus we need a total of $n \lceil \log_2 m \rceil$ advice bits for this strategy.

However, we are not done yet. PLIN1 needs to compute an optimal solution in advance; but it does not know the length of the input and the advice tape has infinite length. Thus, we can use self-delimiting strings as described in Section 3.2. PLIN1 knows the number of different pages m in advance and it can thus compute $\lceil \log_2 m \rceil$; so the oracle "only" needs to tell the algorithm the concrete input length n. As we know from Section 3.2, writing it down in a self-delimiting way can be done with $2 \lceil \log_2(\lceil \log_2 n \rceil) \rceil + \lceil \log_2 n \rceil$ bits.

PLIN1 now proceeds as follows. It starts reading the advice tape until it finds a 0 at an even position. After that, it computes $\lceil \log_2 n \rceil$ from the first $\lceil \log_2(\lceil \log_2 n \rceil) \rceil$ bits it found at odd positions. Then it reads the next $\lceil \log_2 n \rceil$ bits and computes n. Now knowing n and m, it reads the next $n \lceil \log_2 m \rceil$ advice bits and interprets them as a sequence of length n of numbers between 1 and m. For this instance, it computes an optimal solution and acts according to it. All in all, we have thus created an optimal online algorithm with advice that uses

$$2 \lceil \log_2(\lceil \log_2 n \rceil) \rceil + \lceil \log_2 n \rceil + n \lceil \log_2 m \rceil$$

advice bits. $\diamond$

This was probably the easiest approach one could come up with. However, in general, we think of m as a very large constant, especially with respect to the cache size k. With an approach that is almost as simple as the one from Example 3.4, we now design an online algorithm with advice that has an advice complexity that does not depend on m at all. The only thing that is required is a little more work for the oracle.

Example 3.5. How about not encoding the input, but the optimal output? Again, we design an online algorithm PLIN2 with advice and an oracle. For a given instance I, the oracle computes an optimal solution $\text{OPT}(I)$ where OPT is some arbitrary but fixed optimal algorithm. This solution is uniquely defined by a sequence of length at most n of numbers between 1 and k. Each number simply represents the position of the cache cell that OPT uses on a page fault. Thus, in every time step where the requested page is not in PLIN2's cache, it reads the next $\lceil \log_2 k \rceil$ bits from the advice tape and removes the corresponding page. Clearly, both algorithms compute the same solution. Moreover, since no algorithm can make more than n page faults in total, PLIN2 never uses more than $n\lceil\log_2 k\rceil$ advice bits.

There is a nice detail about this strategy. Since the oracle already computed the optimal solution for us, we do not need to communicate n to the algorithm. PLIN2 can just read exactly $\lceil\log_2 k\rceil$ bits in every time step where it causes a page fault, and k is known in advance. ◇

Both PLIN1 and PLIN2 are optimal online algorithms for paging with linear advice complexity. However, their advice complexities differ in the multiplicative constant. We now prove that it is even possible to be optimal without using any multiplicative constant.

Theorem 3.2. *There is an optimal online algorithm* PLIN3 *with advice for paging that uses at most* $n + k$ *advice bits.*

Proof. Let OPT be an optimal offline algorithm for paging. We call a page in the cache of OPT *active* if it is requested once more before OPT removes it from the cache. PLIN3 is designed such that it also has every active page in its cache in the corresponding time step. To this end, the algorithm has a flag for every cache cell that marks the page it contains as either active or *passive*. Note that passive pages do not necessarily correspond to the pages in OPT's cache that are not active.

For every request that causes a page fault, PLIN3 removes an arbitrary page that is passive. So, if a page p is requested that causes a page fault for PLIN3, this cannot be an active page as PLIN3 has all active pages in its cache in every time step. Furthermore, p cannot be a passive page that is in OPT's cache at this point in time since this immediately contradicts the definition of passive pages. Thus, p also causes OPT to make a page fault in this time step. OPT now removes a page p' that is not active. In this case, there is always a passive page in PLIN3's cache, which may be different from p'. It follows that PLIN3 does not cause more page faults than OPT; but then PLIN3 must be optimal as well.

Now let us bound the number of advice bits from above. For every request, PLIN3 reads a bit from the advice tape that indicates whether the requested page is active or passive (if the page is already in the cache, its flag is updated). For PLIN3 to be optimal, the k pages that are in the cache at the beginning need to be marked active or passive before the input is processed. It follows that PLIN3 uses $n + k$ advice bits in total. □

Especially the difference between Example 3.5 and Theorem 3.2 gives us an idea about what *advice complexity* is all about. In the former case, we basically encode a complete optimal solution. Thus, PLIN2 really knows exactly what it has to do when a page fault occurs, that is, which page must be replaced. But this full knowledge is not necessary; what needs to be "extracted" from this information is just which pages may be removed and which must not be removed. Which concrete page is then chosen from the ones that are allowed to be removed is not important in computing an optimal solution.

Exercise 3.4. Prove that there is a 1-competitive online algorithm with advice for paging that uses at most n advice bits.

Exercise 3.5. Suppose that we change the definition of paging such that the cache of any online algorithm is empty at the beginning. Does this affect the upper bound of Theorem 3.2? What happens if the optimal algorithm starts with a different cache content?

Exercise 3.6. Prove that if $m = k + 1$, then there is an optimal online algorithm PLIN4 with advice for paging that uses $\lceil n/k \rceil \cdot \lceil \log_2 k \rceil$ advice bits.

Next, we complement the upper bound with some lower bounds. In this context, this means that we need to show that there is no optimal online algorithm with advice that uses fewer than a given number of advice bits. As mentioned in the previous section, such a proof is in many cases harder than the above constructive proofs. We now use one of the approaches described to give a linear lower bound on the advice complexity of any optimal online algorithm with advice for paging.

Theorem 3.3. *Every optimal online algorithm with advice for paging has to use at least $(\log_2 k/k)n$ advice bits if the total number of pages m may depend on n.*

Proof. Let n be a multiple of k. We construct a set $\mathcal{I}^{(n)}$ that contains instances of length n of the following form. Every instance is again divided into N phases; each phase consists of exactly k requests for different pages. We also design an optimal algorithm OPT that replaces exactly one page in every phase. Any algorithm that diverges from OPT at some point cannot be optimal, as we show in the following.

Let $p_{j_1}, p_{j_2}, \ldots, p_{j_k}$ denote the pages that are in the cache of OPT at the beginning of some phase P_j with $1 \leq j \leq N$. In P_j, first a page $\overline{p}_j$ is requested that is different from all these pages and that was never requested before. This causes a page fault for any demand paging algorithm. Next, $k - 1$ of the k pages that were in OPT's cache at the beginning of P_j are requested. This means that there is some page $p'_j \in \{p_{j_1}, p_{j_2}, \ldots, p_{j_k}\}$ that OPT can replace in the first time step $T_{(j-1)k+1}$ of P_j without causing an additional page fault during P_j. The important point is that, due to the new page $\overline{p}_j$, every demand paging algorithm must make one page fault in every phase. If, in some phase, a second page fault is caused, this cannot be compensated afterwards.

Now we show that the optimal solution for any given instance from $\mathcal{I}^{(n)}$ is unique. For a contradiction, suppose there is a different optimal solution. Thus, in some phase, the two corresponding solutions for the first time replace different pages in the first time step of this phase (if both solutions replace the same page, they both do not make page faults in the remainder of this phase). However, this immediately implies that one of them makes two page faults during this phase and therefore cannot be optimal. Moreover, any two different instances have different optimal solutions, because they need to replace different pages at least once to make only one page fault in each phase.

Next, we calculate how many instances there are in total for inputs of length n. There are $N = n/k$ phases in total. In every phase P_j, exactly one page p'_j, which is one of the k pages $p_{j_1}, p_{j_2}, \ldots, p_{j_k}$, is not requested. Since the page $\overline{p}_j$ that is requested first is the same for every instance, there are k different possibilities for a request sequence in one phase (the order of the other pages does not matter as it does not influence the optimal solution). It follows that

$$|\mathcal{I}^{(n)}| = k^{n/k} \, ,$$

and as a result of the observations we just made, each instance has a unique optimal solution that is only optimal for this particular instance.

Thus, every online algorithm ALG with advice that reads fewer than

$$\log_2\big(k^{n/k}\big) = \frac{n}{k} \cdot \log_2 k$$

advice bits uses one deterministic strategy $A \in \mathrm{strat}(\text{ALG}, n)$ for two different instances from $\mathcal{I}^{(n)}$. Let these two instances be I_1 and I_2. There is a phase P_i in which for the first time two different pages $p'_{i,1}$ and $p'_{i,2}$ for I_1 and I_2 are replaced by $\overline{p}_i$ in the corresponding optimal solutions $\mathrm{OPT}(I_1)$ and $\mathrm{OPT}(I_2)$, respectively. However, the prefixes of I_1 and I_2 that include the request $x_{(i-1)k+1} = \overline{p}_i$ are identical, and thus A replaces the same page for both instances; it immediately follows that A causes one additional page fault for one of the two instances. As a result, A cannot be optimal for both I_1 and I_2; and therefore ALG cannot be optimal for them as well. $\qquad \square$

Exercise 3.7. Give an alternative proof of Theorem 3.3 using partition trees (see Definition 3.3).

The arguments used in the proof of Theorem 3.3 rely on the fact that m is unbounded, that is, the number of pages requested in total grows with the input length n. It is preferable to get rid of this undesired requirement while maintaining that every input has one unique optimal solution. A naive approach that simply uses the same idea as above with a constant number of pages does not seem very promising, as the following example suggests.

Example 3.6. Let $k = 5$, $m = 6$, and suppose that the caches of ALG and OPT are, as always, initialized with the first five pages, that is, we have

$$\text{OPT:} \boxed{p_1 \mid p_2 \mid p_3 \mid p_4 \mid p_5} \quad \text{and} \quad \text{ALG:} \boxed{p_1 \mid p_2 \mid p_3 \mid p_4 \mid p_5} \, .$$

Assume that we follow the same strategy as we used in the proof of Theorem 3.3. The first phase starts by requesting p_6 and four of the other pages. In our example, the instance I starts with p_6, p_3, p_4, p_5, p_2. After the first request, OPT replaces the page p_1 with p_6, and therefore causes one page fault. Now let us assume that ALG replaces p_2 instead, which leads to the situation

$$\text{OPT:} \boxed{p_6 \mid p_2 \mid p_3 \mid p_4 \mid p_5} \quad \text{and} \quad \text{ALG:} \boxed{p_1 \mid p_6 \mid p_3 \mid p_4 \mid p_5} \, .$$

The subsequent requests of P_1 do not cause a page fault for OPT, but clearly, ALG causes a page fault when p_2 is requested in T_5. ALG may replace any page with p_2; let us assume it chooses p_3, which leads to

OPT: | p_6 | p_2 | p_3 | p_4 | p_5 | and   ALG: | p_1 | p_6 | p_2 | p_4 | p_5 |

when P_1 is over.

Now P_2 starts by requesting the unique page that is not in the cache of OPT, that is, p_1; the next four requests could be p_2, p_4, p_5, p_6. In this case, OPT replaces p_3 with p_1 in T_6, which causes one page fault. However, ALG does not induce any page fault in P_2. Therefore, after P_2, both algorithms made two page faults in total and we have

OPT: | p_6 | p_2 | p_1 | p_4 | p_5 | and   ALG: | p_1 | p_6 | p_2 | p_4 | p_5 | ,

that is, both caches have the same content.   ◇

We need to enlarge the phases so that there is still only one unique optimal solution for any instance we construct. Then, it is possible to give a proof for $m = k + 1$ that still shows a linear lower bound (with a constant that is two times worse).

Example 3.7. Again, let $k = 5$ and $m = 6$. Since the straightforward approach of Example 3.6 does not work, we now repeat each phase a second time right after the k different pages of this phase were requested. In this context, we speak of the first and second "iteration" of the phase. So this time, the instance starts with a phase P_1, which is, for instance, given by

$$\underbrace{(p_6, p_2, p_3, p_4, p_5,}_{\text{iteration 1}} \underbrace{p_6, p_2, p_3, p_4, p_5)}_{\text{iteration 2}} .$$

OPT again replaces p_1 with p_6 in T_1 and has cost 1 in P_1. If ALG again decides to replace another page with p_6 instead, for instance, p_5, this leads to a second page fault in the first iteration, because p_5 is requested again. We distinguish two cases depending on what ALG does when p_5 is requested during the first iteration of P_1.

Case 1. Assume that ALG replaces p_1 with p_5. The cache content is then

| p_2 | p_6 | p_3 | p_4 | p_5 | ,

which corresponds to the cache content of OPT after P_1. However, ALG made one additional page fault so far, and enters the next phase without any advantage compared to OPT.

Case 2. Assume that ALG replaces a page with p_5 such that its cache remains different from that of OPT, for instance, ALG removes p_4. This leads to

| p_1 | p_6 | p_3 | p_5 | p_2 | ,

which implies a third page fault in the second iteration of P_1 when p_4 is requested. Again, ALG may replace a page that leads to a cache content different from OPT, and it may be the case that ALG has cost 0 in the next phase P_2 as a consequence. However, we can show that this does not give ALG an advantage with respect to the whole instance since it now caused two more page faults than OPT.

In both cases, ALG is worse than OPT.   ◇

We generalize this idea to prove the following theorem.

Theorem 3.4. *Every optimal online algorithm with advice for paging has to use at least* $(\log_2 k/(2k))n$ *advice bits.*

Proof. Let there be $m = k+1$ pages in total; let n be a multiple of $2k$. We construct a set $\mathcal{I}^{(n)}$ of instances in the following way. Again, every input $I \in \mathcal{I}^{(n)}$ is divided into N phases, this time of length $2k$ each. Every phase P_j with $1 \le j \le N$ starts by requesting page $\overline{p}_j$, which is currently not in the cache of OPT. Then, as in the proof of Theorem 3.3, $k-1$ pages are requested that are all in the cache of OPT when P_j begins. These k different pages are then requested in the same order one more time. As in Example 3.7, we refer to these two sequences of k requests as the first and second iteration, respectively.

First, we prove that OPT is both optimal and unique. To this end, we show that, for all $I \in \mathcal{I}^{(n)}$, any solution that deviates from $\text{OPT}(I)$ is worse than OPT on I. Let ALG be some algorithm such that $\text{ALG}(I)$ and $\text{OPT}(I)$ differ; as before, we assume that ALG is a demand paging algorithm. Let P_j with $1 \le j \le N$ be the first phase in which ALG replaces a different page than OPT. This must happen at the beginning of P_j, that is, in time step $T_{(j-1)2k+1}$, because, if both algorithms replace the same page in such a time step, they act identically in the rest of the phase (since they both do not cause additional page faults during this phase).

As P_j is the first phase in which the algorithms differ, they have the same cache content at the beginning of P_j, and thus requesting $\overline{p}_j$ causes a page fault for both ALG and OPT. Since OPT removes the unique page p'_j that is not requested during P_j (note that $p'_j = \overline{p}_{j+1}$, for $1 \le j \le N-1$), ALG causes one additional page fault in this first iteration of P_j. This happens when the page $p''_j \ne p'_j$ is requested, which ALG replaced with $\overline{p}_j$ at the beginning. If $j = N$, it immediately follows that ALG is worse than OPT. Thus, in what follows, we assume that $1 \le j \le N-1$. We now distinguish two cases depending on ALG's action when p''_j is requested.

Case 1. If ALG replaces p'_j with p''_j, then the two algorithms end phase P_j with the same cache content, but ALG caused an additional page fault.

Case 2. If ALG replaces some page $p'''_j \ne p'_j$ with p''_j, then it will have another page fault in the second iteration, when p'''_j is requested again. On this request, ALG can again replace p'_j with p'''_j, which again leads to a cache content identical to that of OPT. If ALG chooses another page to replace with p'''_j, the two algorithms enter P_{j+1} with different cache contents.

If $j + 1 = N$, we are again done. So suppose $j + 1 < N$; then there is a (possibly empty) sequence of phases such that the cache content of ALG differs from that of OPT at the end of each phase. For any such phase, ALG makes at least one page fault (since exactly the pages in OPT's cache were requested), and thus the distance between the two algorithms stays the same. If this is true for all remaining phases, we are again done. Conversely, suppose there is a phase $P_{j'}$ in which ALG causes no page fault. Then, it still caused one more page fault than OPT, but has the same cache content as OPT at the end of $P_{j'}$.

In any case, either the input ends with ALG having a larger cost than OPT, or both algorithms end up in a situation in which they start the next phase with the same pages in their caches, but ALG made at least one more page fault than OPT. Thus, we can apply the above arguments inductively for the remainder of the input. Since ALG is worse than OPT on I, it follows that the solution computed by OPT is indeed unique and optimal.

By the same reasoning as in the proof of Theorem 3.3, an optimal online algorithm with advice needs to use two different advice strings for any two instances from $\mathcal{I}^{(n)}$. Consequently, it needs to use

$$\log_2\big(k^{n/(2k)}\big) = \frac{n}{2k} \cdot \log_2 k$$

advice bits. □

In conclusion, a linear number of advice bits is both necessary and sufficient to compute an optimal output for any paging instance.

3.4.2 Small Competitive Ratio

We continue with studying how much a small amount of advice can help when dealing with the paging problem. In particular, suppose an online algorithm is only allowed to read a constant number of advice bits that does not depend on the input length n. Actually, we already know that we can achieve quite a lot with a constant number of advice bits. We designed a barely random algorithm for paging in Section 2.6 that is $(3b + 2(k + 1)/2^b)$-competitive in expectation when using b random bits; in the first section of this chapter (see Observation 3.2(i)), we have seen that this enables us to construct an online algorithm with advice that uses b advice bits and is as good. We can therefore derive the following theorem.

Theorem 3.5. *There is an online algorithm with advice for paging that uses b advice bits, where $2^b < k$, and is strictly*

$$\left(3b + \frac{2(k + 1)}{2^b}\right)\text{-competitive.}$$

Proof. This is a direct consequence of Theorem 2.12 and Observation 3.2. □

Next, we complement this upper bound with a lower bound for a constant number of advice bits which is very close to it.

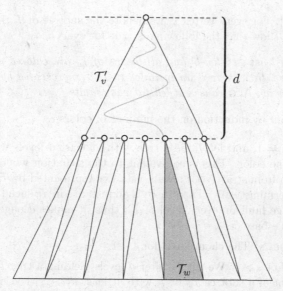

Figure 3.1. The tree $\mathcal{T}_v$ that represents some instances from $\mathcal{I}^{(n)}$.

Theorem 3.6. *Let $\varepsilon > 0$. No online algorithm with advice for paging that uses b advice bits, where $2^b < k$, is*

$$\left(\frac{k}{2^b} - \varepsilon\right)\text{-competitive.}$$

Proof. Let $\varepsilon > 0$, and let ALG be some online algorithm with advice for paging that uses a constant number b of advice bits. For the proof, it is again sufficient to consider instances with a total of $m = k + 1$ pages. Let n be a multiple of k. We now construct a set $\mathcal{I}^{(n)}$ of instances of length n that we can represent by a special kind of tree. All instances start by requesting the page p_{k+1}, which is not in the cache. Now we arrange all instances in a k-ary tree $\mathcal{T}$ that has n levels, that is, $\mathcal{T}$ is of height $n - 1$. The leaves represent the complete instances from $\mathcal{I}^{(n)}$ of length n. In general, every vertex v corresponds to a prefix of exactly those instances that are leaves in the subtree rooted at v. Every inner vertex in the tree has exactly k children, which represent the k possible pages that can be requested in the following time step. Of course, the same page is never requested twice in two consecutive time steps. It follows that the root of the tree corresponds to the first request p_{k+1}, which is a prefix of every instance that is represented by the tree.

For every instance, ALG chooses one out of 2^b online algorithms from strat(ALG); thus, every instance from $\mathcal{I}^{(n)}$ is processed by one of these algorithms. We are now going to color the leaves of $\mathcal{T}$ depending on which algorithm processes them; so every leaf gets a color between 1 and 2^b.

Let $d := \lfloor n/2^b \rfloor$. For every vertex v, we denote the subtree of $\mathcal{T}$ that has the root v by $\mathcal{T}_v$. We now show that the following is true for every v.

> *If $\mathcal{T}_v$ has at least $d \cdot i$ levels and all leaves of $\mathcal{T}_v$ are colored with at most i colors, then there is an instance in $\mathcal{I}^{(n)}$ (represented by a leaf of $\mathcal{T}_v$) for which ALG causes at least d page faults.*   (3.1)

We prove the claim by induction on the number of colors i.

Base Case. Let $i = 1$, and let $\mathcal{T}_v$ be a tree with at least d levels whose leaves are colored with one color. This is equivalent to the situation where ALG uses the same algorithm from strat(ALG) for all instances represented by $\mathcal{T}_v$, and therefore works fully deterministically. Then there is an instance in $\mathcal{T}_v$ such that ALG causes exactly one page fault on every level of $\mathcal{T}_v$; thus, it makes d page faults in total, which covers the base case.

Induction Hypothesis. The claim holds for $i - 1$.

Induction Step. Let $i > 1$. We cut T_v after d levels yielding a tree $\mathcal{T}_v'$. Every leaf w of $\mathcal{T}_v'$ is the root of a subtree $\mathcal{T}_w$ of $\mathcal{T}$ with at least $d(i - 1)$ levels; see Figure 3.1. We now distinguish two cases depending on the number of colors that are used in the trees $\mathcal{T}_w$.

Case 1. If there is a tree $\mathcal{T}_w$ whose leaves are colored with at most $i - 1$ different colors, then, by the induction hypothesis, it follows that ALG causes d page faults on some instance that is represented by a leaf of $\mathcal{T}_w$. Obviously, then there is also such an instance that is represented by a leaf of $\mathcal{T}_v$.

Case 2. Conversely, if such a tree does not exist, since all leaves of $\mathcal{T}_v$ are colored with i colors, we know that there is a color z such that every subtree $\mathcal{T}_w$ has a leaf that is colored with z. If we take these leaves from every subtree, the corresponding instances are again processed by the same algorithm, that is, the same advice is used for each of them.

Due to the construction of $\mathcal{T}$, the request sequences that lead to the corresponding trees $\mathcal{T}_w$ are all possible request sequences of length d (where the same page is never requested in two consecutive time steps). Hence, there is an instance such that ALG causes a page fault on all levels of $\mathcal{T}_v'$; therefore, it makes d page faults in total.

Now we can use (3.1) for $i = 2^b$ and conclude that ALG causes at least

$$\left\lfloor \frac{n}{2^b} \right\rfloor$$

page faults on inputs that are represented by a tree with $\lfloor n/2^b \rfloor \cdot 2^b \leq n$ levels, and thus have length at most n. On the other hand, we know that there is an optimal algorithm that makes a page fault at most every k requests. Since n is a multiple of k, it follows that the optimal cost for instances of length n is at most n/k.

To finish the proof, we plug these two bounds into Definition 3.2, that is, the definition of the competitive ratio, yielding

$$\frac{n}{2^b} - 1 \le \left\lfloor \frac{n}{2^b} \right\rfloor \le c \cdot \frac{n}{k} + \alpha \,,$$

which is why the competitive ratio of ALG can be bounded from below by

$$c \ge \frac{k}{2^b} - \frac{(\alpha + 1)k}{n} \,,$$

which is larger than $k/2^b - \varepsilon$ for infinitely many n. □

3.5 Advice and Randomization

If we follow our intuition, advice bits seem to be a lot more powerful than random bits. After all, we compare a situation where we always pick a best strategy for the given instance to a situation where we pick strategies with a fixed distribution; in essence, we compare "the best" with "the average." It is therefore natural to ask whether there exists a scenario in which it is possible to save some bits if they are supplied by an oracle and not a random source. In what follows, we give a positive answer to this question. More specifically, we show that if there is some randomized online algorithm RAND for some online minimization problem Π, then there is also some online algorithm with advice that is almost as good while using a number of advice bits which (and this is the interesting part) does not depend on the number of random bits RAND uses. However, the bound does depend on the number of possible instances of Π of the given length. The proof uses some ideas that are similar to the proof of Yao's principle, which we have introduced in Sections 2.3 and 2.4.

Theorem 3.7. *Let Π be an online minimization problem with $\mu(n)$ different instances of length n. Suppose there is a randomized online algorithm for Π that is c-competitive in expectation. Then, for any $\varepsilon > 0$, there is a $(1 + \varepsilon)c$-competitive online algorithm with advice for Π that uses at most*

$$2\lceil \log_2(\lceil \log_2 n \rceil) \rceil + \lceil \log_2 n \rceil + \log_2 \left(\left\lfloor \frac{\log_2(\mu(n))}{\log_2(1 + \varepsilon)} \right\rfloor + 1 \right)$$

advice bits.

Proof. Let RAND be a randomized online algorithm for Π that uses $b(n)$ random bits for any input length n. Due to Observation 2.2, this is equivalent to choosing uniformly at random a deterministic strategy from a set $\text{strat}(\text{RAND}, n) = \{A_1, A_2, \ldots, A_{2^{b(n)}}\}$. We design an online algorithm ALG with advice for Π in the following way. Since RAND is c-competitive in expectation, according to Definition 2.2, there is a constant α such that, for every instance I of Π, we have

$$\mathbb{E}[\text{cost}(\text{RAND}(I))] \le c \cdot \text{cost}(\text{OPT}(I)) + \alpha$$

or, equivalently,

$$\frac{\mathbb{E}[\text{cost}(\text{Rand}(I))] - \alpha}{\text{cost}(\text{Opt}(I))} \le c \,.$$

Now, for each deterministic strategy A_j and each instance I_i of length n, for $1 \le j \le 2^{b(n)}$ and $1 \le i \le \mu(n)$, we set

$$c_{i,j} := \frac{\text{cost}(A_j(I_i)) - \alpha}{\text{cost}(\text{Opt}(I_i))} \,;$$

recall that $c_{i,j}$ is called the *performance* of A_j on I_i. As a next step, we construct a $(\mu(n) \times 2^{b(n)})$-matrix $\mathcal{M}$ that we fill with these entries similarly to Section 2.4.

	A_1	A_2	A_3	$\cdots$
I_1	$c_{1,1}$	$c_{1,2}$	$c_{1,3}$	$\cdots$
I_2	$c_{2,1}$	$c_{2,2}$	$c_{2,3}$	
I_3	$c_{3,1}$	$c_{3,2}$	$c_{3,3}$	
$\vdots$	$\vdots$		$\ddots$	

As a result, the entry in the ith row and the jth column gives the performance of Rand on the input I_i if Rand chooses the deterministic strategy A_j. The central idea of the proof is to show that we are able to cleverly choose a small number of columns of $\mathcal{M}$ such that the performances of the corresponding deterministic strategies are good for many instances, and the chosen strategies cover all input instances. We collect these deterministic algorithms in a set $\mathcal{A}$, and Alg gets as advice the index of the algorithm from $\mathcal{A}$ that should be used for the input at hand (and some additional information we will describe later); the "index" can, for instance, refer to the canonical order of the binary random strings to which the algorithms correspond.

One row i of $\mathcal{M}$ corresponds to exactly one input I_i. Thus, by the definition of $c_{i,j}$ and the expected competitive ratio of Rand, for every i with $1 \le i \le \mu(n)$, we get

$$\begin{aligned}
\frac{1}{2^{b(n)}} \sum_{j=1}^{2^{b(n)}} c_{i,j} &= \frac{1}{2^{b(n)}} \sum_{j=1}^{2^{b(n)}} \frac{\text{cost}(A_j(I_i)) - \alpha}{\text{cost}(\text{Opt}(I_i))} \\
&= \frac{\frac{1}{2^{b(n)}} \sum_{j=1}^{2^{b(n)}} (\text{cost}(A_j(I_i)) - \alpha)}{\text{cost}(\text{Opt}(I_i))} \\
&= \frac{\mathbb{E}[\text{cost}(\text{Rand}(I_i))] - \alpha}{\text{cost}(\text{Opt}(I_i))} \\
&\le c
\end{aligned}$$

or, equivalently,

$$\sum_{j=1}^{2^{b(n)}} c_{i,j} \le c \cdot 2^{b(n)} \,.$$

For the sum of all entries in all cells of $\mathcal{M}$, we get

$$\sum_{i=1}^{\mu(n)} \sum_{j=1}^{2^{b(n)}} c_{i,j} \leq \sum_{i=1}^{\mu(n)} c \cdot 2^{b(n)} \leq c \cdot 2^{b(n)} \cdot \mu(n) \ .$$

Since there are $2^{b(n)}$ columns in $\mathcal{M}$, there is one column (deterministic strategy) j' such that

$$\sum_{i=1}^{\mu(n)} c_{i,j'} \leq c \cdot \mu(n) \ . \tag{3.2}$$

The corresponding online algorithm $A_{j'}$ is then included in $\mathcal{A}$ and it is used for any instance I_i, for which $c_{i,j'} \leq (1 + \varepsilon)c$. Let $s = s(j')$ denote the number of these instances. In what follows, we want to estimate the size of s, that is, for how many instances ALG can use $A_{j'}$. Clearly, the performance of $A_{j'}$ is worse than $(1 + \varepsilon)c$ on $\mu(n) - s$ instances.

Summing up, this gives a total of more than $(\mu(n)-s)(1+\varepsilon)c$ for the corresponding rows and we have

$$\sum_{i=1}^{\mu(n)} c_{i,j'} > (\mu(n) - s)(1 + \varepsilon)c \ .$$

Together with (3.2), it follows that $(\mu(n) - s)(1 + \varepsilon)c < \mu(n)c$ and therefore

$$s > \left(\frac{\varepsilon}{1 + \varepsilon} \right) \mu(n) \ ,$$

which means we can use the deterministic strategy $A_{j'}$ for a fraction $\varepsilon/(1 + \varepsilon)$ of the instances as we know that on these its performance is not worse than $(1 + \varepsilon)c$.

After $A_{j'}$ is put into the set $\mathcal{A}$, we remove the column j' from $\mathcal{M}$ together with all rows that correspond to inputs on which $A_{j'}$ achieves a sufficiently good performance. There remain

$$\left(1 - \frac{\varepsilon}{1 + \varepsilon} \right) \mu(n) = \left(\frac{1}{1 + \varepsilon} \right) \mu(n)$$

rows for which we need to find another algorithm from strat(RAND, n). For every remaining row, the removed entry in column j' was larger than c. It follows that, after removing this column, the average over all entries of the remaining rows is still not larger than c. Therefore, we can repeat the aforementioned procedure with the remaining $1/(1 + \varepsilon)\mu(n)$ rows of $\mathcal{M}$. This way, we find another deterministic online algorithm $A_{j''}$, which has a sufficiently good performance on a fraction $\varepsilon/(1 + \varepsilon)$ of the remaining instances.

Now we compute how often we have to iterate this procedure until we have found an algorithm for every input; this means we want to find a natural number r such that

$$\left(\frac{1}{1+\varepsilon}\right)^r \mu(n) < 1 \, .$$

We get

$$\left(\frac{1}{1+\varepsilon}\right)^r < \frac{1}{\mu(n)} \iff (1+\varepsilon)^r > \mu(n) \iff r > \log_{1+\varepsilon}(\mu(n)) \, ,$$

which means that we have to make at most

$$\left\lfloor \frac{\log_2(\mu(n))}{\log_2(1+\varepsilon)} \right\rfloor + 1$$

iterations, that is, we need that many deterministic algorithms from strat(RAND, n). This immediately gives an upper bound on the size of $\mathcal{A}$.

Finally, we calculate the number of advice bits needed for this approach.

1. First, ALG needs to know the input length n, which can be encoded on the advice tape using $\lceil \log_2 n \rceil$ bits. However, this must be done in a self-delimiting fashion (as described in Section 3.2), summing up to a total of $2\lceil \log_2(\lceil \log_2 n \rceil) \rceil + \lceil \log_2 n \rceil$ advice bits.

2. Knowing n, ALG constructs $\mathcal{M}$ by simulating the randomized online algorithm RAND on every possible input of length n and every possible "random" string of length $b(n)$. Then, ALG constructs $\mathcal{A}$ and enumerates all algorithms from $\mathcal{A}$ in, for instance, canonical order. After reading another

$$\log_2\left(\left\lfloor \frac{\log_2(\mu(n))}{\log_2(1+\varepsilon)} \right\rfloor + 1\right)$$

advice bits, ALG can pick one algorithm from $\mathcal{A}$, which is then simulated for the input at hand.

It follows that the performance of ALG on any instance is at most $(1+\varepsilon)c$ and ALG uses as much advice as claimed by the theorem. $\qquad\square$

Exercise 3.8. Explain where the argumentation in the proof of Theorem 3.7 does not work if we use Observation 2.1 instead of Observation 2.2, and specifically assume that $\ell(n) < 2^{b(n)}$?

The following example illustrates how the deterministic strategies are chosen in the proof of Theorem 3.7.

Example 3.8. Suppose we are given a randomized online algorithm RAND that uses three random bits for the given input length n; thus, we have strat$(\text{RAND}, n) = \{A_1, A_2, \ldots, A_8\}$. As described above, the online algorithm with advice knows n, computes $b(n)$, and finally simulates RAND on every input of length n and every "random" string of length $b(n)$.

Moreover, assume there are nine inputs of length n, and that RAND is 3-competitive in expectation. Then ALG obtains the following matrix $\mathcal{M}$.

	A_1	A_2	A_3	A_4	A_5	A_6	A_7	A_8	Average
I_1	5	4	4	2	3	1	4	1	3
I_2	3	1	1	3	5	5	2	4	3
I_3	4	6	4	1	2	4	1	2	3
I_4	1	1	5	5	4	2	3	3	3
I_5	2	2	4	2	5	2	2	5	3
I_6	1	5	1	8	1	2	4	2	3
I_7	2	1	4	1	4	3	5	4	3
I_8	1	3	1	7	2	2	3	5	3
I_9	3	3	6	2	1	4	1	4	3

As marked in $\mathcal{M}$, the deterministic strategy A_2 has a performance that is better than $(1 + \varepsilon) \cdot 3$ (even 3 in this simple example) on the six inputs I_2, I_4, I_5, I_7, I_8, and I_9. A_2 is included in $\mathcal{A}$, and the second column is removed from $\mathcal{M}$ together with the rows that correspond to the above inputs. This results in the following matrix with decreased average values for every row.

	A_1	A_3	A_4	A_5	A_6	A_7	A_8	Average
I_1	5	4	2	3	1	4	1	2.86
I_2								
I_3	4	4	1	2	4	1	2	2.58
I_4								
I_5								
I_6	1	1	8	1	2	4	2	2.72
I_7								
I_8								
I_9								

Finally, there are even two algorithms, namely A_5 and A_8, that perform well for all remaining instances. Thus, $\mathcal{A}$ has size 2. $\diamond$

At this point, one might wonder whether the factor of $1 + \varepsilon$ is unavoidable, or whether it is possible to design an online algorithm with advice from any randomized online algorithm that is as good. The answer is that the latter is not possible, as the following online problem shows.

Example 3.9. Consider the following online minimization problem. The input $I = (x_1, x_2, \ldots, x_n)$ starts with the request $x_1 = 0$. All other requests are bits, that is, $x_i \in \{0,1\}$ with $2 \leq i \leq n$; as answers, also bits must be given, that is, $y_i \in \{0,1\}$ with $1 \leq i \leq n$.

Now, if $y_i = x_{i+1}$ for all i with $1 \leq i \leq n-1$, then the total cost is 1, otherwise, it is n (the last answer y_n is ignored). In other words, an optimal algorithm has cost 1, and any other solution has cost n. Obviously, a best randomized online algorithm chooses every answer such that it is 0 or 1 with probability $1/2$ each. This algorithm uses $n-1$ random bits and its expected competitive ratio is

$$\frac{\frac{2^{n-1}-1}{2^{n-1}} \cdot n + \frac{1}{2^{n-1}} \cdot 1}{1} = n - \frac{n+1}{2^{n-1}} \ .$$

On the other hand, no online algorithm ALG with advice that uses fewer than $n-1$ advice bits is better than n-competitive. This is due to the fact that there are at most 2^{n-2} deterministic strategies ALG chooses from if it uses at most $n-2$ advice bits. Therefore, there are at least two different instances that get the same advice string. Let these two instances be I_1 and I_2, and let $A \in \text{strat}(\text{ALG})$ be the deterministic algorithm that is chosen for both of them. I_1 and I_2 differ for the first time in time step T_i with $2 \leq i \leq n$; but they have the same prefix of length $i-1$. Therefore, A outputs the same bit in T_{i-1}, and consequently has cost n on one of the two instances. $\diamond$

In Chapter 7, we will return to such problems where bits need to be guessed; however, there we will consider different cost functions. It follows that there exist online problems for which an online algorithm with advice that is equally good as a best randomized online algorithm in expectation needs as many advice bits as the latter uses random bits.

We have now introduced the three models of online computation that we will study in the following chapters. It will turn out that the relationship between them varies heavily with the problem we are considering.

3.6 Historical and Bibliographical Notes

The advice complexity of online problems was introduced by Dobrev et al. [53] in 2008 as a new measurement for online algorithms addressing the aforementioned pessimistic view of competitive analysis. In particular, the authors investigated paging and the problem of *differentiated services*; see, for instance, Lotker and Patt-Shamir [112]. Originally, two different "modes of operation" were proposed and studied, which allow different ways of communication between the oracle and the online algorithm. The following description is taken from Komm [97].

- *The helper model.* Here, we think of an oracle that oversees ALG's actions during runtime. The oracle may interact with the algorithm by giving some bits of advice in every time step; this is done without a request for help by ALG. The crucial observation is that the advice may be empty, which can also carry some piece of information and thus may be exploited by the algorithm.

- *The answerer model.* The second model is more restrictive in some sense as the algorithm ALG has to explicitly ask the oracle for advice in some time step. The oracle then has to respond with some advice string, that is, it is not allowed to send an empty string, but still may encode some extra information into the length of its answer.

In both models, it is assumed that ALG knows the length of the input in advance. A more detailed and formal description is given by Dobrev et al. [53,54].

The problem with the above model (and both modes of operation) is that some information can be encoded into the lengths of the advice strings. Moreover, it is desirable to stick to a scenario where the input length of the current instance is not known in advance, because this is exactly one of the properties that define the nature of computing online. Of course, it is possible that the input length is communicated to the algorithm, but we demand that this is accounted for in a clean way and it is not possible to do such a thing implicitly.

Addressing these issues, two different refined models were suggested in 2009. Emek et al. [58] proposed a model in which the number of advice bits supplied is fixed in every time step. Note that it is therefore impossible to study sublinear advice as we did, for example, in Theorem 3.5. Emek et al. applied this model to metrical task systems and the k-server problem (which we will investigate in Chapter 4). Böckenhauer et al. [30] and Hromkovič et al. [82] proposed the model that is used throughout this book. Hromkovič et al. suggested using this approach to quantify the information content of the given online problem. Böckenhauer et al. first applied it to paging (obtaining some of the results given in Section 3.4), the disjoint path allocation problem (which will be described in Subsection 7.4.3), and the job shop scheduling problem (which we will study in Chapter 5); for more details, we refer to the technical report [31].

It is noteworthy that this model is equivalent to a variant of the answerer model where the input length is unknown and the online algorithm with advice specifies the number of bits it wants to get as an answer (it may ask multiple times in one time step); the oracle is not allowed to answer with any other number of advice bits (in particular, it is also not allowed to give an empty answer).

The self-delimiting encoding of binary strings that we introduced in Section 3.2 is strongly related to *Elias coding*, which was developed by Elias [57].

The concept of partition trees was implicitly used in many publications. It was first formalized (see Definition 3.3, Lemma 3.1, and Theorem 3.1) by Barhum et al. [16]; see also Steffen [135].

The problem-independent construction of an online algorithm with advice from a randomized online algorithm for online minimization problems was shown by Böckenhauer et al. [24,29]. An analogous theorem for online maximization problems was later proven by Selečéniová [129].

Emek et al. [58,60] proved a lower bound on the advice complexity of an online algorithm that also uses randomness for metrical task systems. Böckenhauer et al. [25] introduced the so-called boxes problem to further study the collaboration between advice and randomization. More non-trivial connections between randomization and advice were observed by Komm [97], Mikkelsen [117], and Böckenhauer et al. [23].

The k-Server Problem

4

In this chapter, we learn about another online problem that is among the most studied, and that is especially interesting from a theoretical point of view. The *k-server problem* is concerned with moving k objects (called "servers") in a metric space to points that are requested in consecutive time steps. We show that this problem, although it may not seem obvious, is actually a generalization of paging, which we studied in the first three chapters. However, the k-server problem is less well understood, and we introduce both the *k-server conjecture* and the *randomized k-server conjecture*, which are two of the most famous open problems in online computation. We define a very natural class of algorithms for k-server called *lazy algorithms*. Basically, these algorithms are the counterparts of demand paging algorithms for paging. Since the k-server problem is rather difficult to get a grip on in a general setting, that is, if the metric space is arbitrary, we will first restrict ourselves to specific settings such as a line segment and tree graphs. We show that greedy algorithms are not competitive for k-server even on a very simple metric space. The best competitive ratio that can be reached by deterministic online algorithms is k for any metric space that has more than k points. To be able to show an upper bound on the competitive ratio of deterministic online algorithms for k-server, we introduce *potential functions* that allow us to bound the amortized cost of an online algorithm. We use such functions subsequently to analyze online algorithms that work on the abovementioned special metric spaces, and that have competitive ratios of k; these algorithms are therefore strongly competitive.

Next, we focus on the advice complexity of the k-server problem starting with the number of advice bits that are necessary and sufficient to produce an optimal output. While it is rather straightforward to prove an upper bound, establishing a lower bound needs a more careful analysis. We show that there are instances where computing an optimal solution basically reduces to guessing a permutation. Next, we construct online algorithms with advice for the line segment (again using a potential function) and the Euclidean plane. For the former case, the constructed algorithm

© Springer International Publishing Switzerland 2016
D. Komm, *An Introduction to Online Computation*,
Texts in Theoretical Computer Science. An EATCS Series,
DOI 10.1007/978-3-319-42749-2_4

is optimal and uses one bit of advice per time step. The algorithm for the plane has a small competitive ratio and reads a constant number of advice bits in every time step; here, "constant" means independent of both k and n. The last online algorithm with advice works for general metric spaces. It uses a greedy approach in some time steps while cleverly using the advice to bound the additional cost that is induced by the greedy moves. At the end of this chapter, we discuss the impact of the connection between advice and randomization stated in Theorem 3.7 on the randomized k-server conjecture.

4.1 Introduction

Suppose you want to navigate a number of k police cars through a traffic network. In every time step, a crime is committed, and a police car needs to be specified to move to the crime scene. Assume that the police car arrives at this crime scene in the next time step, when the next crime scene is revealed. Of course, an optimal strategy to navigate the cars is not obvious at the beginning. Maybe, a police car will be moved away from a position that is the site of a crime in the next time step. Thus, such a problem is intrinsically online. In the k-server problem, this scenario is generalized and put into a theoretical framework. Here, servers (police cars) are moved in a *metric space* (traffic network) to requested points (crime scenes). An example is given in Figure 4.1, where servers are depicted as squares and requests as crosses (we will stick to these symbols). To give a formal definition, we first need to define the notion of a metric space.

Definition 4.1 (Metric Space). Let P denote a set of *points* and dist: $P \times P \to \mathbb{R}$ a *distance function*. $\mathcal{M} = (P, \text{dist})$ is a *metric space* if the following constraints are satisfied.

Identity of Indiscernibles and Non-Negativity. All distances are non-negative and we do not have to pay to stay at a point, that is, $\text{dist}(p_i, p_i) = 0$, for all $p_i \in P$, and $\text{dist}(p_i, p_j) > 0$, for all $p_i \neq p_j$ and $p_i, p_j \in P$.

Symmetry. The way back is as expensive as the way there, that is, $\text{dist}(p_i, p_j) = \text{dist}(p_j, p_i)$, for all $p_i, p_j \in P$.

Triangle Inequality. The direct connection is never more expensive than taking a detour, that is, $\text{dist}(p_i, p_j) \leq \text{dist}(p_i, p_k) + \text{dist}(p_k, p_j)$, for all $p_i, p_j, p_k \in P$.

An example of a subclass of metric spaces is the class of complete undirected graphs that have edge weights that satisfy the triangle inequality. In Chapter 1, we briefly discussed the traveling salesman problem. In this context, we mentioned that there is a 3/2-approximation algorithm if "certain natural conditions" are met; such *metric graphs* are exactly what we referred to. For convenience, we will also denote vertices in a graph by p_i. In the following, for two given vertices of a graph p_1 and p_2

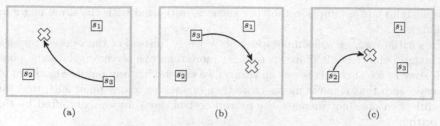

Figure 4.1. An example of k-server with three servers.

that are connected by an edge $\{p_1, p_2\}$, we write $\mathrm{dist}(p_1, p_2)$ instead of $\mathrm{dist}(\{p_1, p_2\})$ to get an easier notation that is also consistent with the distance function of other metric spaces; $\mathrm{dist}(p_1, p_2)$ is then referred to as the *weight of the edge* $\{p_1, p_2\}$. We can make an easy observation about another class of graphs.

Observation 4.1. *All complete undirected graphs that only have edge weights of 1 and 2 satisfy the triangle inequality.*

Exercise 4.1. Prove Observation 4.1.

We now formalize our intuition by formally defining the k-server problem on arbitrary metric spaces.

> **Definition 4.2 (k-Server).** The k-*server problem* is an online minimization problem. Let $\mathcal{M} = (P, \mathrm{dist})$ be a metric space with m points according to Definition 4.1; we allow $m = \infty$, that is, the metric space may have an unbounded size. Furthermore, we are given k *servers* $s_1, s_2, \ldots, s_k$, which are positioned on some of the points of P. A *configuration* $C_i \subseteq P$, $|C_i| = k$, is a multiset of points that describes the positions of the servers in time step T_i. The configuration C_1 that describes where the servers are positioned at the beginning is called the *initial configuration*. An input $I = (x_1, x_2, \ldots, x_n)$ consists of n requests, and each one is a point from P. If, in time step T_i, a point x_i is requested and there is no server positioned on x_i, a server must be moved to x_i to *serve* this request (it is also allowed to move servers to other points); this leads to a new configuration C_{i+1}. The *distance* between two configurations C_j and $C_{j'}$ is given by the cost of a minimum-weight matching between C_j and $C_{j'}$. The aim is to serve all requests while minimizing the sum of the distances between all pairs of consecutive configurations.

Definition 4.2 does not make any assumption on C_1, that is, the points on which the servers are positioned initially. However, we always assume that, for any online algorithm, these initial positions are the same as for the optimal offline algorithm (similarly to our assumption that the cache is initialized with the same pages for paging).

In what follows, we will simply speak of "k-server" instead of the k-server problem. Although Definition 4.2 allows us to place more than one server on the same point, it is easy to see that this is not necessary; we can modify any online algorithm for k-server such that it never moves more than one server to one point such that this modification does not increase the overall cost of any solution computed by this algorithm.

We can further restrict algorithms for k-server, which will prove useful later. A solution for an instance of k-server is a sequence of configurations, and, between two configurations, an arbitrary number of servers can be moved. However, sometimes it is convenient to restrict ourselves to so-called *lazy algorithms* that move at most one server in response to each request. Due to the triangle inequality, this can be done without loss of generality, as any algorithm for k-server can be transformed into a lazy one without increasing the cost of any solution it produces. It is easy to see that, for the case of lazy algorithms, the solutions can be uniquely described as a sequence of servers used to serve individual requests.

Definition 4.3 (Lazy Online Algorithm). An online algorithm for k-server is called *lazy* if it only moves a server in time steps where there is not yet a server located at the requested position. Moreover, such an algorithm never moves more than one server in one time step.

Note that lazy algorithms only act if this is necessary in the corresponding time step, which resembles the concept of demand paging algorithms for paging from Section 1.2. We leave the proof that Definition 4.3 does not cause any restriction as an exercise for the reader.

Theorem 4.1. *Every c-competitive online algorithm for k-server can be transformed into a lazy online algorithm for k-server that is also c-competitive.*

Exercise 4.2. Prove Theorem 4.1.

Exercise 4.3. Suppose we are dealing with a modified version of the k-server problem where the distance function does not have to satisfy the triangle inequality. Discuss the problems that come up when proving Theorem 4.1 for this setting.

When proving lower bounds, we will sometimes assume that all algorithms we deal with are lazy to simplify our arguments. However, later in this chapter, we will design online algorithms that are not lazy; also, we will study algorithms that are consistent with the above definition of laziness, but that may move the unique server used in one time step back to its original position afterwards.

Now let us study a first approach to deal with k-server by considering a simple greedy algorithm KSGREEDY. Such an algorithm always moves the closest server to

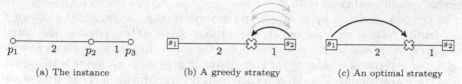

(a) The instance   (b) A greedy strategy   (c) An optimal strategy

Figure 4.2. A hard instance for KSGREEDY of k-server on the line.

any requested point. If there is not one unique closest server, it picks one among the closest ones arbitrarily. It turns out that this algorithm is not competitive, that is, it is arbitrarily bad already for the case of 2-server on a very simple metric space.

Theorem 4.2. KSGREEDY *is not competitive for k-server.*

Proof. Consider the following instance I that is defined on a graph with three vertices p_1, p_2, and p_3. The edge weights are given by

$$\text{dist}(p_1, p_2) = 2 \quad \text{and} \quad \text{dist}(p_2, p_3) = 1.$$

Moreover, we are given two servers s_1 and s_2 that are positioned on the vertices p_1 and p_3 at the beginning. The instance I consists of n requests that are alternatingly p_2 and p_3. The first request p_2 must be answered by either moving s_1 or s_2 to this vertex. Due to $\text{dist}(p_2, p_3) < \text{dist}(p_1, p_2)$, KSGREEDY uses s_2, which leads to a cost of 1. After that, p_3 is requested, and again s_2 is the server that is closer; thus, KSGREEDY also has a cost of 1 in the second time step. This is repeated $n/2$ times, and as a result KSGREEDY pays n in total. On the other hand, there is an optimal algorithm OPT that uses s_1, has a cost of 2 in the first time step, and no further cost in any subsequent time step; this is shown in Figure 4.2. It follows that $\text{cost}(\text{KSGREEDY}(I))/\text{cost}(\text{OPT}(I)) = n/2$, and thus there is no constant c such that KSGREEDY is c-competitive. $\square$

Nevertheless, later in this chapter, we will design an algorithm that partially follows the greedy approach and, making use of the advice supplied, is able to restrict the harm done by greedy moves.

Exercise 4.4. The analysis of KSGREEDY shows a lower bound of $n/2$. How much can you improve this lower bound when sticking to three vertices on a line?

4.2 A Lower Bound for Deterministic Algorithms

So, following a greedy strategy is a bad idea for this problem, but what about online algorithms for k-server in general? To give a first answer, we realize that k-server is actually a generalization of paging. To see this, let I be any instance of paging, where as always k is the cache size and m is the total number of pages. We construct a complete undirected graph with m vertices $p_1, p_2, \ldots, p_m$ and set all edge weights to 1; we position all servers $s_1, s_2, \ldots, s_k$ on the vertices $p_1, p_2, \ldots, p_k$. In the following, we identify vertices with pages. These positions of the servers (that is, the initial configuration) symbolize the initial content of the cache. Requesting a vertex p_i with $1 \le i \le m$ represents requesting the corresponding page p_i. If no server is located at p_i in the corresponding time step, a page fault occurs. Moving a server from some vertex p_j with $1 \le j \le m$ to p_i induces cost 1. In the corresponding paging instance, this means that p_j is replaced by p_i in the cache.

Theorem 4.3. *There is a metric space such that no deterministic online algorithm for k-server is better than k-competitive.*

Proof. This is a direct consequence of Theorem 1.5. $\qquad \square$

We can even prove a far more general statement that speaks about every metric space with a least $k + 1$ points.

Theorem 4.4. *Let $\varepsilon > 0$. No deterministic online algorithm for k-server is $(k - \varepsilon)$-competitive on any metric space with at least $k + 1$ points.*

Proof. Let $\mathcal{M} = (S, \text{dist})$ be any metric space with $m \ge k + 1$ points; for the proof, we only need to consider the first $k + 1$ points $p_1, p_2, \ldots, p_{k+1}$. Again, the servers are initially positioned on $p_1, p_2, \ldots, p_k$. Let ALG be any deterministic online algorithm for k-server. We construct an instance I of length n in the following way. As the discussion preceding Theorem 4.3 suggests, $I = (x_1, x_2, \ldots, x_n)$ is created by requesting in every time step T_i the one point on which ALG has not placed a server (we assume that ALG is lazy, so there is exactly one such point). In time step T_1, the point $x_1 := p_{k+1}$ is requested and ALG moves some server that is located at, say, point p to x_1. After that, in T_2, the point $x_2 := p$ is requested by the adversary. It follows that the cost of ALG in T_1 can be written as $\text{dist}(x_2, x_1)$. ALG moves a server that is located at some point p' to x_2 as a response. The adversary then requests $x_3 := p'$, and thus the cost of ALG in T_2 is $\text{dist}(x_3, x_2)$. Let x_{n+1} denote the last point from which ALG moves a server to serve the request x_n; then

$$\text{cost}(\text{ALG}(I)) = \sum_{i=1}^{n} \text{dist}(x_{i+1}, x_i) . \qquad (4.1)$$

In order to prove that there is some algorithm that is k times better than ALG (minus some constant α), we consider k algorithms $\text{ALG}_1, \text{ALG}_2, \ldots, \text{ALG}_k$ that work as follows. To make the arguments simple, we assume that every such algorithm starts with a non-lazy move such that the algorithm ALG_j moves the server located at p_j to the point p_{k+1}. Therefore, before the first request is served, ALG_j has no server positioned on p_j. All subsequent moves are lazy. If, in any time step T_i, any algorithm ALG_j has to move a server to x_i, it uses the server located at x_{i-1}; note that no such algorithm has to move a server in T_1 after it made the initial move since $x_1 = p_{k+1}$.

We now claim that, after the initial moves in T_1, there are never two algorithms that have the same uncovered point. The proof is done by induction on T_i.

Base Case. Since every algorithm ALG_j moves the server from the distinct point p_j to p_{k+1} at the beginning, the base case is covered.

Induction Hypothesis. The claim holds for T_{i-1}.

Induction Step. Consider any two algorithms $\text{ALG}_{j'}$ and $\text{ALG}_{j''}$ in some time step T_i with $i \geq 2$. We distinguish two cases depending on whether the point x_i is covered by both of them or not; it follows from the induction hypothesis that the case that both algorithms have the same point uncovered cannot occur.

Case 1. If the requested point x_i is covered by both algorithms, they both do not have to move any server and the claim follows.

Case 2. Without loss of generality, assume that x_i is not covered by $\text{ALG}_{j'}$. By construction, $\text{ALG}_{j'}$ moves the server located at x_{i-1} to x_i. Thus, after this move, $\text{ALG}_{j'}$ has placed servers on all points of P except for x_{i-1}. At the beginning of T_i, both $\text{ALG}_{j'}$ and $\text{ALG}_{j''}$ covered x_{i-1}. Therefore, $\text{ALG}_{j''}$ still has a server placed on this point. As a result, $\text{ALG}_{j'}$ and $\text{ALG}_{j''}$ still cover different sets of points.

It follows that at most one algorithm has a requested point uncovered in any time step. Thus, in every time step T_i, at most one algorithm moves a server by a distance of $\text{dist}(x_{i-1}, x_i)$. An exception is the first time step, in which every algorithm ALG_j moves one server by a distance of exactly $\text{dist}(p_j, p_{k+1})$. In other words, we have

$$\sum_{j=1}^{k} \text{cost}(\text{ALG}_j(I)) = \sum_{j=1}^{k} \text{dist}(p_j, p_{k+1}) + \sum_{i=2}^{n} \text{dist}(x_{i-1}, x_i)$$

$$= \sum_{j=1}^{k} \text{dist}(p_j, p_{k+1}) + \sum_{i=2}^{n} \text{dist}(x_i, x_{i-1})$$

(due to the symmetry of $\mathcal{M}$)

$$= \sum_{j=1}^{k} \text{dist}(p_j, p_{k+1}) + \sum_{i=1}^{n-1} \text{dist}(x_{i+1}, x_i)$$

$$= \sum_{j=1}^{k} \text{dist}(p_j, p_{k+1}) + \sum_{i=1}^{n} \text{dist}(x_{i+1}, x_i) - \text{dist}(x_n, x_{n+1})$$

$$\leq \sum_{j=1}^{k} \text{dist}(p_j, p_{k+1}) + \text{cost}(\text{ALG}(I))$$

(as a consequence of (4.1))

Therefore, the average cost of an algorithm ALG_j is bounded from above by

$$\frac{1}{k} \cdot \text{cost}(\text{ALG}(I)) + \frac{1}{k} \sum_{j=1}^{k} \text{dist}(p_j, p_{k+1}) \,,$$

and consequently there must be at least one algorithm among them that has at most this cost on I. Thus,

$$\text{cost}(\text{OPT}(I)) \leq \frac{1}{k} \cdot \text{cost}(\text{ALG}(I)) + \underbrace{\frac{1}{k} \sum_{j=1}^{k} \text{dist}(p_j, p_{k+1})}_{\beta} \,, \tag{4.2}$$

where β is constant with respect to n. For a contradiction, assume that ALG is $(k - \varepsilon)$-competitive, for some $\varepsilon > 0$. Hence, there is a constant α such that

$$\text{cost}(\text{ALG}(I)) \leq (k - \varepsilon) \cdot \text{cost}(\text{OPT}(I)) + \alpha \,,$$

and, together with (4.2), it follows that

$$\text{cost}(\text{ALG}(I)) \leq (k - \varepsilon) \cdot \frac{1}{k} \cdot \text{cost}(\text{ALG}(I)) + (k - \varepsilon)\beta + \alpha$$

$$\Longleftrightarrow \text{cost}(\text{ALG}(I)) \leq \frac{k((k - \varepsilon)\beta + \alpha)}{\varepsilon} \,. \tag{4.3}$$

However, the cost of ALG cannot be bounded from above by a constant since it grows with the input length. Thus, there are infinitely many instances for which (4.3) leads to a contradiction. It follows that there is no deterministic online algorithm that achieves a competitive ratio of $k - \varepsilon$. $\qquad\square$

Exercise 4.5. Suppose that we are dealing with a resource-augmented version of k-server, where any online algorithm has k servers and OPT has h servers where $h \leq k$; we call this problem (h, k)-*server*. Generalize Theorem 4.4 for (h, k)-server by proving that no deterministic online algorithm is $(k/(k - h + 1) - \varepsilon)$-competitive, for any $\varepsilon > 0$.

Hint. The proof can be done using the same input as in the original proof.

Exercise 4.6. Consider k-server with lookahead ℓ. Does this help?

From Section 1.4, we know that the lower bound of k is tight for paging; in other words, there are (strictly) k-competitive deterministic online algorithms for paging. Whether this also holds for k-server is one of the most famous open problems in online computation.

Conjecture 4.1 (k-Server Conjecture). *There is a k-competitive deterministic online algorithm for k-server.*

If the k-server conjecture were true, this would mean that paging is as hard as k-server from a deterministic point of view. This would certainly be an interesting insight, as we saw that the latter is quite a large generalization of the former; nevertheless, so far, the best known online algorithm for arbitrary metric spaces achieves a competitive ratio of $2k - 1$. In what follows, we will discuss special metric spaces where we are able to achieve better results.

We have already seen that "a little bit" of randomization helps a lot when dealing with paging. Therefore, it seems justified to ask what we can do for k-server if we allow an online algorithm to use randomness. For this question, there is also no answer given yet; in fact, the best-known upper bound is also just that of $2k - 1$, which is trivially implied by the deterministic setting. Whether this bound can be improved (maybe even exponentially as for paging) is also open to this day.

Conjecture 4.2 (Randomized k-Server Conjecture). *There is a randomized online algorithm for k-server that is $\Theta(\log k)$-competitive in expectation.*

There is an interesting connection between online algorithms with advice and the randomized k-server conjecture, which is a consequence of Theorem 3.7; we will return to this in Subsection 4.6.5.

4.3 Potential Functions

To prove upper bounds on the competitive ratios of online algorithms for minimization problems, we now study a technique that helps us to bound the *amortized cost*, that is, the average cost per request that is caused by processing some instance, of an online algorithm. This tool sometimes allows us to do a clever analysis of the competitive ratio of a given algorithm. In what follows, we consider online minimization problems and deterministic online algorithms.

We make the following observations. If we want to show that some online algorithm ALG achieves a competitive ratio c, for some constant α, the inequality

$$\text{cost}(\text{ALG}(I)) \leq c \cdot \text{cost}(\text{OPT}(I)) + \alpha$$

must hold for every instance $I = (x_1, x_2, \ldots, x_n)$ of the given online minimization problem Π. Recall that we denote the cost of ALG on a request x_i with $1 \leq i \leq n$ by $\text{cost}(\text{ALG}(x_i))$. Obviously, we would be done if we could show

$$\text{cost}(\text{ALG}(x_i)) \leq c \cdot \text{cost}(\text{OPT}(x_i))$$

for $1 \leq i \leq n$. However, things are not so easy in general, which is why we analyzed phases and not single requests when dealing with paging. The idea is that it is sufficient to show that the cost of the solution computed by ALG is at most c times larger on average over all requests than the cost of an optimal solution. In other words, ALG may pay more in some time steps if it compensates for this in other steps. If such time steps even out, ALG is still c-competitive.

Now we want to formalize this simple idea by looking at how much "too much" or "too little" ALG pays for every request. For this purpose, we need the notion of a *configuration* of an online algorithm. Formalizing this term is tricky and we will thus stay on an intuitive level. The configuration of a paging algorithm, for instance, is the content of the cache, for k-server it is the positions of the k servers in the metric space; for the latter, we even used the notion in the definition. Note that this configuration is different from the "internal configuration" of an algorithm; if we use the formalization of Turing machines, such a configuration is given by the current state, the head positions, and the content of its tape or tapes. In this context, a configuration is basically the observable state of the algorithm.

Now let $\mathcal{C}_{\mathrm{ALG}}$ denote the set of all configurations of an online algorithm ALG, and let $\mathcal{C}_{\mathrm{OPT}}$ denote the set of configurations of an arbitrary but fixed optimal algorithm OPT. An *initial configuration* is a configuration of some algorithm before any part of the input is processed, such as the initial server positions for k-server or the initial cache content for paging. A *potential function* Φ is a function

$$\Phi \colon \mathcal{C}_{\mathrm{ALG}} \times \mathcal{C}_{\mathrm{OPT}} \to \mathbb{R} \,.$$

The computation of a fixed deterministic online algorithm can be described by a sequence of configurations that are uniquely determined by the requests of the input. Therefore, if ALG and OPT are clear from context, Φ can also be regarded as a function on requests. In what follows, we will use both views to have an easier notation. We call $\Phi(x_i)$ the *potential* of ALG in time step T_i; $\Phi(x_0)$ is the potential before the first request. For an instance $I = (x_1, x_2, \ldots, x_n)$, we thus have a sequence $\Phi(x_0), \Phi(x_1), \ldots, \Phi(x_n)$ of potentials. The potential is therefore a value that changes during the run of ALG depending on the configurations of ALG and OPT; in time step T_i it changes by $\Phi(x_i) - \Phi(x_{i-1})$.

We now define the *amortized cost* of ALG on the request x_i as

$$\mathrm{amcost}(\mathrm{ALG}(x_i)) := \mathrm{cost}(\mathrm{ALG}(x_i)) + \Phi(x_i) - \Phi(x_{i-1}) \,. \tag{4.4}$$

These are the costs that we want to guarantee for ALG on average; conversely, $\mathrm{cost}(\mathrm{ALG}(x_i))$ denotes the *real cost* of ALG on x_i. Let us stay on an intuitive level. In what follows, we want to show that

$$\mathrm{amcost}(\mathrm{ALG}(x_i)) \leq c \cdot \mathrm{cost}(\mathrm{OPT}(x_i))$$

and thus

$$\mathrm{cost}(\mathrm{ALG}(x_i)) \leq c \cdot \mathrm{cost}(\mathrm{OPT}(x_i)) - (\Phi(x_i) - \Phi(x_{i-1}))$$

holds in every time step T_i. If we now pay too much in some time step, that is, more than $c \cdot \mathrm{cost}(\mathrm{OPT}(x_i))$, we can compensate for this by decreasing the potential by the corresponding value. We demand, however, that the potential must not be negative (for now, see Exercise 4.8 for an extension to negative values). On the other hand, the potential may also increase, which allows us to pay more in some subsequent time step. Our goal is to find some potential function and some c so that we are able to guarantee these properties. Let us now express this formally.

Theorem 4.5. *Let Π be an online minimization problem, let $I = (x_1, x_2, \ldots, x_n)$ be an instance of Π, and let Φ be a potential function. For any online algorithm ALG, we define the amortized cost of ALG on I as in (4.4). If*

(i) $\Phi(x_i) \geq 0$, for all i with $1 \leq i \leq n$, and

(ii) $\mathrm{amcost}(\mathrm{ALG}(x_i)) \leq c \cdot \mathrm{cost}(\mathrm{OPT}(x_i))$, for all i with $1 \leq i \leq n$,

then ALG is c-competitive for Π.

Proof. Note that $\Phi(x_0)$ only depends on the initial configurations and is therefore constant, say, $\Phi(x_0) = \beta$, for some $\beta \in \mathbb{R}$. The proof is very simple; we basically only plug in the definitions from above together with the assumptions of the theorem, and observe that we are dealing with an easy telescoping series when summing the potentials. For the cost of ALG on I, it immediately follows that

$$
\begin{aligned}
\mathrm{cost}(\mathrm{ALG}(I)) &= \sum_{i=1}^{n} \mathrm{cost}(\mathrm{ALG}(x_i)) \\
&= \sum_{i=1}^{n} (\mathrm{amcost}(\mathrm{ALG}(x_i)) + \Phi(x_{i-1}) - \Phi(x_i)) \\
&= \Phi(x_0) - \Phi(x_n) + \sum_{i=1}^{n} \mathrm{amcost}(\mathrm{ALG}(x_i)) \\
&\leq \Phi(x_0) - \Phi(x_n) + \sum_{i=1}^{n} c \cdot \mathrm{cost}(\mathrm{OPT}(x_i)) \\
&\qquad \textit{(due to condition (ii))} \\
&= \Phi(x_0) - \Phi(x_n) + c \cdot \mathrm{cost}(\mathrm{OPT}(I)) \\
&\leq \Phi(x_0) + c \cdot \mathrm{cost}(\mathrm{OPT}(I)) \\
&\qquad \textit{(since $\Phi(x_n)$ is non-negative due to condition (i))} \\
&= c \cdot \mathrm{cost}(\mathrm{OPT}(I)) + \beta \, ,
\end{aligned}
$$

and consequently ALG is c-competitive, where we set $\alpha := \beta$ for the additive constant α of Definition 1.6; note that, in principle, β might even be negative. $\qquad \square$

If we want to show a strict competitive ratio, we can ask for a potential function that fulfills the same conditions as in Theorem 4.5, but additionally demand that the initial potential $\Phi(x_0)$ is 0. In this case, the above calculation easily holds for $\alpha = 0$ in Definition 1.6.

Corollary 4.1. *Let Π, I, and Φ be as defined in Theorem 4.5. For any online algorithm ALG, we define the amortized cost of ALG on I as above. If the two conditions (i) and (ii) of Theorem 4.5 hold and*

(iii) $\Phi(x_0) = 0$,

then ALG is strictly c-competitive for Π.

So much for the theory of what can be shown using a potential function. The difficult part is now to find a potential function for a given problem that satisfies the above conditions. In the next section, we will show an application for a subclass of k-server instances.

Exercise 4.7. How many possible configurations does a paging algorithm have? How about algorithms for k-server?

Exercise 4.8. Generalize Theorem 4.5 such that the potential is also allowed to be negative in some of the time steps.

Exercise 4.9. Generalize the idea of potential functions such that it works for randomized online algorithms for online minimization problems.

4.4 k-Server on the Line

In Section 4.1, we showed that a very simple class of instances on three points on a line is hard for the greedy strategy for k-server. Now we look at a related class of instances, namely instances on the real interval between 0 and 1; formally, we are dealing with the metric space $\mathcal{M}_{[0,1]} = ([0, 1], \text{dist})$ where $\text{dist}(x, y) = |x - y|$ for any two points x and y. It immediately follows that KSGREEDY is also not competitive for this metric space. Therefore, we now study a more clever online algorithm named DCOV (short for "double coverage") that obtains good results for such instances.

---

for every request x **do**
    $s_{\text{right}} := \langle \text{null} \rangle$;   // Initialize for this time step
    $s_{\text{left}} := \langle \text{null} \rangle$;
    $s_{\text{right}} := $ Closest server right of x;
    $s_{\text{left}} := $ Closest server left of x;
    if $s_{\text{right}} = \langle \text{null} \rangle$
        output "Move s_{left} to x";
    else if $s_{\text{left}} = \langle \text{null} \rangle$
        output "Move s_{right} to x";
    else
        $d := \min\{\text{dist}(s_{\text{right}}, x), \text{dist}(s_{\text{left}}, x)\}$;
        output "Move s_{right} d to the left and s_{left} d to the right";
end

Algorithm 4.1. The algorithm DCOV for k-server on the metric space $\mathcal{M}_{[0,1]}$.

DCOV uses a simple greedy strategy when all servers are positioned on the same side of the requested point. However, if there are servers both to the left and to the right of the requested point, DCOV moves both the closest server to the left and the closest server to the right towards the requested point until at least one of them is

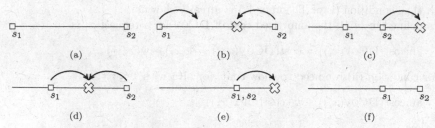

Figure 4.3. The algorithm DCov on the hard instance for KSGreedy.

positioned on it; the idea is formalized in Algorithm 4.1. In both cases, if there is more than one server positioned on the same point that is closest to the requested one, DCov picks one of them arbitrarily. Note that DCov is not a lazy algorithm.

First, we observe that the hard example for KSGreedy does not lead to an arbitrarily bad performance (on $\mathcal{M}_{[0,1]}$). Indeed, the solution DCov computes has constant cost, but it is not optimal; see Figure 4.3. More precisely, the cost is 6, which means it is three times larger than the optimal cost. Now we prove an upper bound of k for any instance on the metric space $\mathcal{M}_{[0,1]}$.

Theorem 4.6. *DCov is k-competitive for k-server on $\mathcal{M}_{[0,1]}$.*

Proof. We define a potential function Φ for which conditions (i) and (ii) of Theorem 4.5 are satisfied. As already mentioned above, a configuration of an (online) algorithm for k-server is given by all the positions of the servers. Hence, the set $\mathcal{C}_{\mathrm{DCov}}$ contains all possible configurations

$$C_{\mathrm{DCov}} = \{p_{\mathrm{DCov},1}, p_{\mathrm{DCov},2}, \ldots, p_{\mathrm{DCov},k}\}$$

that describe the server positions of DCov in the current time step; for $\mathcal{C}_{\mathrm{OPT}}$, we analogously define

$$C_{\mathrm{OPT}} = \{p_{\mathrm{OPT},1}, p_{\mathrm{OPT},2}, \ldots, p_{\mathrm{OPT},k}\}.$$

Recall that both C_{DCov} and C_{OPT} are multisets. The potential function Φ is composed of two parts. The first part is the weight of a minimum-weight matching between the server positions of the two algorithms multiplied by k; for two configurations C_{DCov} and C_{OPT}, we denote the weight of the matching by $M_{\min}(C_{\mathrm{DCov}}, C_{\mathrm{OPT}})$. The second part is the sum of the distances between all pairs of servers of DCov, and we denote this value by $D_{\mathrm{DCov}}(C_{\mathrm{DCov}})$. Then we set

$$\Phi(C_{\mathrm{DCov}}, C_{\mathrm{OPT}}) := k \cdot M_{\min}(C_{\mathrm{DCov}}, C_{\mathrm{OPT}}) + D_{\mathrm{DCov}}(C_{\mathrm{DCov}}).$$

Obviously, the value of Φ is never negative, that is, for all configurations of DCov and OPT, we have

$$\Phi(C_{\mathrm{DCov}}, C_{\mathrm{OPT}}) \geq 0.$$

With this, condition (i) of Theorem 4.5 is already shown.

As defined in (4.4), the amortized cost of DCov for a request x_i is

$$\mathrm{amcost}(\mathrm{DCov}(x_i)) = \mathrm{cost}(\mathrm{DCov}(x_i)) + \Phi(x_i) - \Phi(x_{i-1}) \;.$$

For condition (ii), we need to show that, for all i with $1 \le i \le n$,

$$\mathrm{amcost}(\mathrm{DCov}(x_i)) \le k \cdot \mathrm{cost}(\mathrm{OPT}(x_i)) \;,$$

and thus

$$\Phi(x_i) - \Phi(x_{i-1}) \le k \cdot \mathrm{cost}(\mathrm{OPT}(x_i)) - \mathrm{cost}(\mathrm{DCov}(x_i)) \;. \tag{4.5}$$

To this end, we have to consider the movements of both OPT and DCov since both cause a change of the potential. Following Theorem 4.1, without loss of generality, we assume that OPT is lazy. DCov is not lazy, as already observed.

We now investigate what happens when DCov and OPT change their configuration in a time step. For the analysis, we assume that the two algorithms make their moves alternatingly. First, OPT changes its configuration, and then DCov. In both cases, we bound the change of the potential; we start with the one OPT causes. Since OPT is lazy, it moves at most one server s per request. Clearly, this movement does not affect the term D_{DCov}, but only the weight of the minimum-weight matching $M_{\min}$. In the matching before moving s, s was matched to some server s'. After OPT moved s, the distance between s and s' changed by at most the distance that s traveled, that is, $\mathrm{cost}(\mathrm{OPT}(x_i))$. Thus, there now is a new matching that has a weight that is at most $\mathrm{cost}(\mathrm{OPT}(x_i))$ larger than the weight of the old one. Clearly, the minimum-weight matching $M_{\min}$ after moving s may even be cheaper. Hence, the potential increases by at most

$$k \cdot \mathrm{cost}(\mathrm{OPT}(x_i)) \;. \tag{4.6}$$

Next, we look at the change in potential that is caused by the change of DCov to another configuration after OPT already changed its configuration. We distinguish two cases that depend on whether DCov moves one or two servers.

Case 1. First, we assume that the algorithm only moves a single server; without loss of generality, let there be no server positioned to the left of the request, and DCov therefore moves s_{right}. The server s_{right} increases its distance to all other servers from DCov by $\mathrm{cost}(\mathrm{DCov}(x_i))$; thus the second term D_{DCov} of the potential increases by

$$(k-1) \cdot \mathrm{cost}(\mathrm{DCov}(x_i)) \;. \tag{4.7}$$

Now we want to bound how much the first term changes, that is, the weight of the minimum-weight matching. Note that we are now interested in the matching before and after DCov moves s_{right}, and that OPT already moved the server s

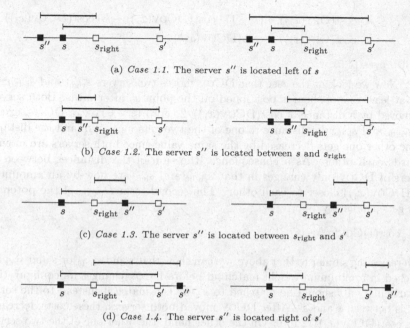

(a) *Case 1.1.* The server s'' is located left of s

(b) *Case 1.2.* The server s'' is located between s and s_{right}

(c) *Case 1.3.* The server s'' is located between s_{right} and s'

(d) *Case 1.4.* The server s'' is located right of s'

Figure 4.4. The different cases regarding the positions of s''; the servers of OPT are filled squares, those of DCOV are not filled. In every case, there is a matching that is not more expensive and in which s and s_{right} are matched. It is easy to see that the argument also works when s' and s_{right} are positioned on the same point.

which is now positioned on the requested point x_i. We claim that, before DCOV moves the server s_{right}, there is a minimum-weight matching in which s_{right} and s are matched.

For a contradiction, suppose this is not the case. Then s is matched with some other server s' of DCOV and s' is further to the right of s than s_{right}. Conversely, s_{right} is matched with a server s'' from OPT. We can now make a case distinction regarding the position of s''. For each of the four possible cases, we immediately see that there is a matching that is not more expensive and in which s and s_{right} are matched; these cases are shown in Figure 4.4. After DCOV answered the request x_i, the two servers s and s_{right} are positioned on the same point, and s_{right} was moved by $\text{cost}(\text{DCOV}(x_i))$. Therefore, there is now a matching that is as expensive as the latter one minus this cost; we conclude that the first term $k \cdot M_{\min}$ of the potential decreases by

$$k \cdot \text{cost}(\text{DCOV}(x_i)) . \tag{4.8}$$

With (4.6) to (4.8), it follows that

$$\Phi(x_i) - \Phi(x_{i-1})$$

127

$$\leq k \cdot \text{cost}(\text{OPT}(x_i)) + (k-1) \cdot \text{cost}(\text{DCOV}(x_i)) - k \cdot \text{cost}(\text{DCOV}(x_i))$$
$$= k \cdot \text{cost}(\text{OPT}(x_i)) - \text{cost}(\text{DCOV}(x_i)) ,$$

which proves (4.5).

Case 2. Now we look at the case that DCOV moves two servers s_{right} and s_{left} such that at least one of them is positioned on the point x_i afterwards. Both servers are moved by a distance of $\text{cost}(\text{DCOV}(x_i))/2$. For every server of DCOV, except for s_{right} and s_{left}, the distance to one of the two gets increased, and the distance to the other one gets decreased by the same value since both servers are moving towards each other. As a consequence, the sum of the distances between all servers of DCOV only changes in that s_{right} and s_{left} are now by an amount of $\text{cost}(\text{DCOV}(x_i))$ closer to each other. The second term D_{DCOV} of the potential thus gets smaller by

$$\text{cost}(\text{DCOV}(x_i)) . \tag{4.9}$$

With reasoning similar to that above, we can show that s and s_{right} or s and s_{left} are matched in a minimum-weight matching before DCOV changes its configuration; in particular, if s should be matched to s', we can match it instead to the server that is between s and s'. After DCOV moved both servers, these costs decreased from $\text{cost}(\text{DCOV}(x_i))/2$ to 0. On the other hand, the other one of the two servers was matched with some server s'''; clearly, the distance between these servers can increase by at most $\text{cost}(\text{DCOV}(x_i))/2$. The weight of the minimum-weight matching therefore does not change in the worst case or even decreases. From (4.6) and (4.9), it follows that (4.5) is also true in this case.

We conclude that all conditions to apply Theorem 4.5 are met, and it immediately follows that DCOV is k-competitive. We can bound the additive constant α by the initial potential, which is at most k^2. To see this, note that M_{min} is 0 since the two algorithms have the servers positioned on the same points at the beginning. The sum D_{DCOV} of the distances between all servers of DCOV, on the other hand, cannot be larger than

$$\binom{k}{2} \leq k^2 ,$$

since the maximum distance between any two servers is at most 1 on $\mathcal{M}_{[0,1]}$. $\qquad\square$

Potential functions are widely applicable; for instance, it is possible to give an alternative proof of the k-competitiveness of LRU (see Exercise 1.7) using a potential function that imposes an ordering on the pages that are currently in the cache.

Exercise 4.10. In the proof of Theorem 4.6, we argued that, when there are two servers s_{left} and s_{right} next to s, one of them is matched to s after OPT made its move. Show that it matters which of the two is used. In particular, give an example where one of them is closer to s, but a minimum-weight matching matches the other one to s.

Exercise 4.11.* As already mentioned, the configurations $\mathcal{C}_{\mathrm{ALG}}$ of an (online) algorithm for paging are the pages that are currently in the cache of ALG. Consider the online algorithm LRU for paging, which we introduced in Section 1.2. We define a weight function $w\colon \mathcal{C}_{\mathrm{LRU}} \to \{1, 2, \ldots, k\}$ such that, for any two pages $p, p' \in C_{\mathrm{LRU}}$, we have $w(p) < w(p')$ if and only if the most recent request for p was earlier than that for p'. For $C_{\mathrm{LRU}} \in \mathcal{C}_{\mathrm{LRU}}$ and $C_{\mathrm{OPT}} \in \mathcal{C}_{\mathrm{OPT}}$, let $C := C_{\mathrm{LRU}} \setminus C_{\mathrm{OPT}}$. Use the potential function

$$\Phi(C_{\mathrm{LRU}}, C_{\mathrm{OPT}}) := \sum_{p \in C} w(p)$$

to prove that LRU is k-competitive for paging.

Does your proof show that LRU is strictly k-competitive?

4.5 *k*-Server on Trees

Now we modify the online algorithm DCOV to work on a rather large class of graphs. First, suppose that we are given a *path* graph, that is, a graph whose vertices all have degree 2 except two endpoints that have degree 1. We assume that all edges have weight 1. Consider the online algorithm DCOVP that is a straightforward adaptation of DCOV. The servers are positioned on some of the vertices of the given path, and every request is served greedily if all servers are located on the same side of the requested vertex. If however, there is one server to the left and one to the right, these move towards the request, one edge at a time, until at least one server is positioned on it. Using reasoning as in the proof of Theorem 4.6, it can be shown that DCOVP is k-competitive for such graphs.

Next, we generalize paths and consider *trees*, that is, connected graphs that do not contain cycles. For now, we assume that all edge weights are 1. We define the online algorithm DCOVT in the obvious fashion. More precisely, if a vertex is requested, all neighboring servers are moved towards this vertex until at least one of them is located on it. Formally, a *neighbor* of a request is a server for which there is no other server located on any vertex of the unique path between the requested vertex and the vertex this server is placed on. We have to be careful at this point, because during the movements of the servers, some of them might no longer be neighbors because another server "blocks" them. As an example, consider the tree shown in Figure 4.5. Here, initially s_3, s_5, and s_6 are the neighbors of the request; however, when s_6 moves one edge towards the requested vertex, s_5 is no longer a neighbor (hence, s_5 is only moved one edge in total).

We now show that, although trees are a lot more general than paths, following the double coverage[3] strategy again allows us to be k-competitive.

Theorem 4.7. DCOVT *is k-competitive for k-server on trees.*

---

[3]Speaking of a "double coverage" strategy in this context is a little misleading since, generally, more than two servers are moved. However, we will stick with the name "DCOVT" as it is commonly used in the literature.

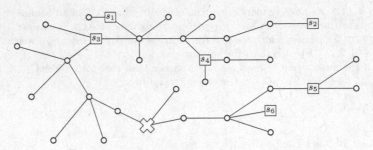

Figure 4.5. An example tree.

Proof. Let $\mathcal{C}_{\mathrm{DCovT}}$ and $\mathcal{C}_{\mathrm{OPT}}$ be defined according to the preceding section. Again, we assume that OPT is lazy. The proof is very similar to that of Theorem 4.6. We use the same potential function

$$\Phi(C_{\mathrm{DCovT}}, C_{\mathrm{OPT}}) := k \cdot M_{\min}(C_{\mathrm{DCovT}}, C_{\mathrm{OPT}}) + D_{\mathrm{DCovT}}(C_{\mathrm{DCovT}}),$$

for $C_{\mathrm{DCovT}} \in \mathcal{C}_{\mathrm{DCovT}}$ and $C_{\mathrm{OPT}} \in \mathcal{C}_{\mathrm{OPT}}$. Recall that $M_{\min}$ is a minimum-weight matching between the server positions of OPT and DCovT, and D_{DCovT} is the sum of the distances between all pairs of servers of DCovT. First, we note that the potential is again always positive, which means that condition (i) of Theorem 4.5 is satisfied.

For a given request x_i with $1 \leq i \leq n$, we again consider the movements of OPT and DCovT separately. First, OPT moves a server s, which causes an increase of the potential by at most

$$k \cdot \mathrm{cost}(\mathrm{OPT}(x_i)) \tag{4.10}$$

since s increases its distance to the server s' from DCovT it was matched to by at most $\mathrm{cost}(\mathrm{OPT}(x_i))$.

Now we consider the moves of DCovT. As described above, we have to be a little more careful than in the case of a line or path. While the servers are moving towards the requested vertex x_i, some of them might become *blocked*, that is, they were neighbors of x_i at the beginning, but then some other server got closer to the request. Moreover, there can be multiple servers positioned on the same vertex; in this case, DCovT moves one of them. We now subdivide the movement of the servers into N phases such that, during one phase $P_{\mathrm{DCovT},j}$, a fixed number of servers k_j is moved. If a server gets blocked or two servers get positioned on the same vertex, $P_{\mathrm{DCovT},j}$ ends, and the next phase $P_{\mathrm{DCovT},j+1}$ starts. The last phase ends when at least one server is positioned on x_i.

Let us bound the change in potential that is due to DCovT in a single phase $P_{\mathrm{DCovT},j}$. Let d_j denote the distance that every server travels in this phase; thus, the total cost of DCovT in $P_{\text{DCovT},j}$ is $k_j d_j$, and the total cost of DCovT in time step T_i with $1 \le i \le n$ is

$$\text{cost}(\text{DCovT}(x_i)) = \sum_{j=1}^{N} k_j d_j \,. \tag{4.11}$$

We first consider the change of $M_{\min}$. By the same arguments as in the proof of Theorem 4.6, one of the moving servers can be matched with the server s used by OPT, which is now positioned on x_i. This server decreases its distance to s by d_j, while the other $k_j - 1$ servers might increase the distances to the servers they were matched with before by d_j each. Therefore, $M_{\min}$ increases by at most

$$(k_j - 2)d_j \,. \tag{4.12}$$

Second, consider the change in D_{DCovT}. All servers that are moved within phase $P_{\text{DCovT},j}$ move a distance of d_j towards the same vertex x_i. Consequently, they decrease their distances to each other by $2d_j$, and there are exactly

$$\binom{k_j}{2} = \frac{k_j(k_j - 1)}{2}$$

pairs of servers that are affected by this. For all of the $k - k_j$ non-neighboring servers, one of the neighboring servers increases its distance d_j. Then again, all other neighboring servers decrease their distance by d_j, because they are located in different subtrees rooted in x_i. This leads to a decrease of

$$(k - k_j)(k_j - 2)d_j \,.$$

Therefore, D_{DCovT} decreases by

$$2d_j \frac{k_j(k_j - 1)}{2} + (k - k_j)(k_j - 2)d_j \,. \tag{4.13}$$

From (4.12) and (4.13), we obtain that the potential decreases by at least

$$d_j k_j (k_j - 1) + (k - k_j)(k_j - 2)d_j - k(k_j - 2)d_j = k_j d_j \tag{4.14}$$

in $P_{\text{DCovT},j}$, which is exactly the cost of DCovT in that phase. From (4.10), (4.11) and (4.14), we finally get

$$\Phi(x_i) - \Phi(x_{i-1}) \le k \cdot \text{cost}(\text{OPT}(x_i)) - \sum_{j=1}^{N} k_j d_j$$

$$= k \cdot \text{cost}(\text{OPT}(x_i)) - \text{cost}(\text{DCovT}(x_i)) \,,$$

as we claimed. We can again easily bound the additive constant α, which is now larger than for DCov. To this end, let $d_{\max}$ denote the length of a path of maximum length in $\mathcal{T}$. Then the sum of the distances between all servers D_{DCovT} is

$$\binom{k}{2} \cdot d_{\max} \le k^2 \cdot d_{\max} \,,$$

which is a constant since $d_{\max}$ does not depend on the input length. $\qquad \square$

Exercise 4.12. Modify DCovT to work on weighted trees as well. Assume that the weights are positive integers.

4.6 Advice Complexity

In the last chapter, we introduced advice complexity and studied how powerful additional information is for paging. In this section, we study the advice complexity of k-server; since this problem is a generalization of paging, advice will surely not prove to be more helpful. We start by analyzing the number of advice bits that allow us to compute an optimal solution.

4.6.1 Optimality for the General Case

First, we give an upper bound by describing a simple optimal online algorithm with advice for k-server. With a very simple argument similar to the one we used in Example 3.5, we can give an upper bound on the number of advice bits that guarantee to produce an optimal output for any given instance.

Theorem 4.8. *There is an optimal online algorithm with advice for k-server that uses $n\lceil\log_2 k\rceil$ advice bits.*

Proof. For any fixed lazy optimal algorithm OPT, the oracle simply specifies the server that is used in the ith time step using $\lceil\log_2 k\rceil$ bits. Then, on every request, the online algorithm reads the index of this server, serves the request accordingly, and is therefore optimal. □

For paging, we were able to improve the bound of Example 3.5 to $n + k$ in Theorem 3.2. Thus, the question naturally arises whether we can also decrease the bound of Theorem 4.8 and get rid of the $\lceil\log_2 k\rceil$ factor in exchange for an additive constant. As a matter of fact, we cannot. More specifically, we show that if an online algorithm with advice is optimal for every instance of k-server, it needs to use asymptotically $\log_2 k$ advice bits for every request. First, we give a bound for inputs with k requests, which we generalize for instances of arbitrary length afterwards. For the following construction, recall that any graph with a weight function that maps edges to values 1 and 2 only trivially obeys the triangle inequality and is therefore metric (see Observation 4.1).

Theorem 4.9. *For every optimal online algorithm ALG with advice for k-server, there exists an instance with k requests in total, such that ALG has to use at least $k(\log_2 k - \beta)$ advice bits, for a constant $\beta < 1.443$.*

Proof. Let $k \in \mathbb{N}$ and let $G = (U \cup W, E, \text{dist})$ be a complete bipartite graph with a metric cost function $\text{dist}\colon E \to \{1, 2\}$, where $U = \{u_1, u_2, \ldots, u_k\}$ and $W = \{w_1, w_2, \ldots, w_{2^k}\}$. Since $|W| = 2^k$, we can define a bijective function $\text{set}\colon W \to \mathcal{P}(U)$

that maps every vertex from W to a unique subset of vertices from U. We define the edge weights as follows. For $u \in U$ and $w \in W$, let

$$\text{dist}(u, w) := \begin{cases} 2 & \text{if } u \in \text{set}(w), \\ 1 & \text{otherwise}. \end{cases}$$

Additionally, since formally any instance of k-server has to be defined on a complete weighted graph, we define the weights of all edges from $(U \times U) \cup (W \times W)$ to be 2. We call edges of weight 1 *cheap* and edges of weight 2 *expensive*. A schematic view of the constructed graph for $k = 4$ is shown in Figure 4.6. We now partition the vertices from W into groups as follows. Let $\mathcal{G}_i \subseteq W$ denote the vertices from W that correspond to subsets of U with exactly i elements, that is,

$$\mathcal{G}_i = \{w \in W \mid |\text{set}(w)| = i\}.$$

It follows that

$$|\mathcal{G}_i| = \binom{k}{i}.$$

Since the group $\mathcal{G}_k$ is irrelevant for our subsequent arguments, we will ignore it in what follows.

Initially, every vertex of U is covered by a single server. We construct a set of instances $\mathcal{I}^{(k)}$ in the following way. An instance $I \in \mathcal{I}^{(k)}$ is a sequence $(x_1, x_2, \ldots, x_k)$ of requests such that, for every j with $1 \leq j \leq k$,

1. $x_j \in \mathcal{G}_{j-1}$ and
2. $\text{set}(x_j) \subseteq \text{set}(x_{j+1})$.

Note that all requests are from W. The first requested vertex is the unique vertex from W (namely the only vertex from $\mathcal{G}_0$) with only cheap edges to U. Every following request has exactly one more expensive edge than the one before; the requests are chosen in such a way that the set of expensively connected vertices from U is extended by one vertex in every time step.

In what follows, to get an easier notation, let us identify the vertices from U with their indices. We may represent I as a permutation π_I of $\{1, 2, \ldots, k\}$ in the following way.

$$\pi_I(j) := \text{set}(x_{j+1}) \setminus \text{set}(x_j), \text{ for } 1 \leq j \leq k - 1 \quad \text{and}$$
$$\pi_I(k) := U \setminus \{\pi_I(j) \mid 1 \leq j \leq k - 1\} = U \setminus \text{set}(x_k).$$

In other words, $\pi_I(j)$ denotes that vertex from U that is connected to the requested vertices via expensive edges from request x_j on. The unique optimal solution $\text{OPT}(I)$ for I has a cost of exactly k, and can also be described by π_I in the following way. For every j, $\text{OPT}(I)$ serves the jth request x_j by moving one server from some vertex from U, in particular from the vertex $\pi_I(j)$, to the requested vertex from W, via

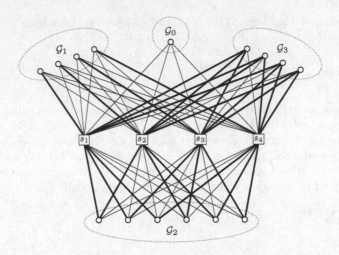

Figure 4.6. An example input of 4-server as used in the proof of Theorem 4.9 without $\mathcal{G}_4$. Note that, for ease of presentation, not all edges are shown.

a cheap edge. It is easy to see that there is no solution with a cost of less than k, since all the servers start in U, all requests are different vertices from W, and every edge has cost of at least 1.

To see that $\text{OPT}(I)$ is indeed the *unique* optimal solution, consider an offline environment where an optimal offline algorithm OFF receives the whole input at once and may serve the requests in an arbitrary order. It does so in the opposite order to the order in which the requests are made. The last vertex requested is from the group $\mathcal{G}_{k-1}$ and there is one unique vertex $\pi_I(k)$ connected to it with a cheap edge. The vertex that was requested before is from $\mathcal{G}_{k-2}$. Due to our construction, it also has a cheap edge to $\pi_I(k)$ and to a second vertex $\pi_I(k-1)$, so that OFF now uses this second edge. Following this strategy, OFF uses exactly k edges of weight 1; its strategy is the only one not more expensive than k.

As we may represent any instance from $\mathcal{I}^{(k)}$ by a unique permutation of $\{1, 2, \ldots, k\}$, the size of $\mathcal{I}^{(k)}$ is $k!$. It remains to show that we also need a unique advice string for every input to be solved optimally by any online algorithm ALG with advice. For a contradiction, let I_1 and I_2 be two different inputs from $\mathcal{I}^{(k)}$, and suppose that ALG is optimal for both of them. However, for the same advice string ϕ, the algorithm ALG behaves deterministically. Let us take the algorithm's point of view. In time step T_1, the only vertex from $\mathcal{G}_0$ is requested, and ALG uses some server to serve this request. Then, in time step T_2, it is revealed whether this was a good choice, that is, whether the server at $\pi_I(1)$ was used to serve the first request optimally. After that, the algorithm chooses a second server to move and again, in time step T_3, it is revealed whether this was a good choice, and so on.

Suppose that the corresponding permutations of I_1 and I_2 differ at position j for the first time. This means that, in time step T_{j-1}, the algorithm has to make two different choices for the different inputs. But since it reads the same prefix of the input up to this point and furthermore uses the same advice string, it has to behave in the same way. This directly implies that ALG cannot be optimal for both I_1 and I_2. We conclude that we need a different advice string for every instance and therefore $\log_2(k!)$ advice bits. Using Stirling's approximation, we get

$$\log_2(k!) \geq \log_2\left(\sqrt{2\pi k}\left(\frac{k}{e}\right)^k\right)$$

$$= \frac{1}{2}(\log_2(2\pi) + \log_2 k) + k(\log_2 k - \log_2 e)$$

$$\geq k(\log_2 k - \beta),$$

where $e = 2.718\ldots$ is Euler's number and $\beta = \log_2 e < 1.443$, which concludes our proof. □

From a formal point of view, Theorem 4.9 is sufficient to show a lower bound on the number of advice bits necessary to compute an optimal solution; but we are not very happy with the restriction to instances that have a constant length (namely k). Therefore, we now generalize this statement in the following theorem, where we deal with an arbitrary number of requests. First, we make an observation, which we need in what follows.

Observation 4.2. *Suppose that we are dealing with an instance as constructed in the proof of Theorem 4.9. Moreover, assume that a lazy online algorithm ALG uses $k' < k$ servers, which are initially positioned on some vertices of U. Recall that there are k requests that are each from a different group $\mathcal{G}_i$ with $0 \leq i \leq k-1$. For at least $k - k'$ of these requests, ALG needs to move a server between two groups. Since all groups are connected to each other by edges of weight 2, it follows that ALG has a cost of 2 in every such time step.*

The idea for the proof of the following theorem is to use $2k$ graphs of the type used in the proof of Theorem 4.9, and to connect them in a special manner. The optimal solution is forced to act in a unique way on each of them alternatingly, and any wrong move within any of them cannot be compensated later. We still only need edge weights of either 1 or 2.

Theorem 4.10. *Every optimal online algorithm with advice for k-server has to use at least $n(\log_2 k - \beta)/2$ advice bits, for a constant $\beta < 1.443$.*

Proof. We create a set $\mathcal{I}^{(n)}$ of instances as follows. We take $2k$ disjoint graphs $G_i = (U_i \cup W_i, E_i, \text{dist}_i)$, where $1 \leq i \leq 2k$, as used to construct instances from $\mathcal{I}^{(k)}$ in the proof of Theorem 4.9; the groups $\mathcal{G}_{i,j}$ with $1 \leq i \leq 2k$ and $0 \leq j \leq k$ are also defined as above. We then connect all vertices from W_i to the vertices from

$$U_{(i+1) \bmod (2k)} = \left\{u_{(i+1) \bmod (2k),1}, u_{(i+1) \bmod (2k),2}, \ldots, u_{(i+1) \bmod (2k),k}\right\}$$

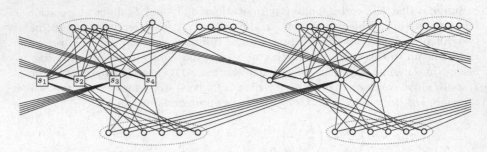

Figure 4.7. The graph used in the proof of Theorem 4.10; only cheap edges are shown. The two subgraphs are those from Figure 4.6.

such that the edges from $\mathcal{G}_{i,j}$ to $u_{(i+1) \bmod (2k),j+1}$ have weight 1. All other newly added edges are assigned weight 2. Formally, the complete input graph $G = (P, E, \text{dist})$ is defined by

$$P := \bigcup_{i=1}^{2k}(U_i \cup W_i)\,,$$

$$E := \{\{p, p'\} \mid p, p' \in P\}\,,$$

$$\text{dist}(p, p') := \begin{cases} \text{dist}_i(p, p') & \text{if } p, p' \in U_i \cup W_i\,, \\ 1 & \text{if } p \in \mathcal{G}_{i,j} \text{ and } p' = u_{(i+1) \bmod (2k),j+1}\,, \\ 2 & \text{else}\,. \end{cases}$$

At the beginning, the servers are located at the vertices of U_1. A scheme of a part of G is depicted in Figure 4.7.

There are n requests in total, where n is a multiple of $4k^2$. The instances are subdivided into phases that are further partitioned into rounds. One round consists of $2k$ requests, and one phase consists of $2k$ rounds. This leads to a length of $4k^2$ requests for each phase, and thus there are $n/(4k^2)$ phases in total. The first k requests of a round are defined analogously to the k requests from the proof of Theorem 4.10; the next k requests are called "resets" as their purpose is solely to place the servers on the starting positions of the next subgraph.

To describe the idea in more detail, let us consider a single phase P_i with $1 \le i \le n/(4k^2)$. The $2k$ rounds in P_i are denoted by $R_{i,1}, R_{i,2}, \dots, R_{i,2k}$. As in the proof of Theorem 4.10, let $\pi_{i,j}$ denote a permutation of $\{1, 2, \dots, k\}$ that corresponds to the first k requests of round $R_{i,j}$. Then, we can write

$$\begin{aligned} P_i = (&\pi_{i,1}(1), \pi_{i,1}(2), \dots, \pi_{i,1}(k), u_{2,1}, \dots, u_{2,k}, && \text{Round } R_{i,1}\\ &\pi_{i,2}(1), \pi_{i,2}(2), \dots, \pi_{i,2}(k), u_{3,1}, \dots, u_{3,k}, && \text{Round } R_{i,2}\\ &\dots, && \vdots\\ &\pi_{i,2k}(1), \pi_{i,2k}(2), \dots, \pi_{i,2k}(k), u_{1,1}, u_{1,2}, \dots, u_{1,k})\,. && \text{Round } R_{i,2k} \end{aligned}$$

All other phases are defined analogously. We observe that, for these instances, there is a solution that

1. acts according to the corresponding permutations $\pi_{i,j}$ whenever vertices from $W_{i,j}$ are requested (as in the proof of Theorem 4.9);

2. moves servers located at $\mathcal{G}_{i,j}$ to $u_{(i+1) \bmod (2k), j+1}$ whenever vertices from $U_{(i+1) \bmod (2k)}$ are requested.

Obviously, this solution has cost n in total as it uses an edge of weight 1 in every time step. We claim that this is indeed the unique optimal solution for any given instance $I \in \mathcal{I}^{(n)}$.

To give a proof, we first show that any algorithm ALG that has cost 0 in some time step is worse than OPT in total. Without loss of generality, we assume that ALG is lazy. Since all vertices that are requested in one phase are different, we make the following observation. If there is a time step in this phase in which ALG has cost 0, a server must already be placed on the vertex that is requested in this time step. Due to laziness, this server must be located at this vertex for the last $2k$ rounds or longer; we call such a server *parked*. In the following, we always assume that such a parking is successful, that is, the corresponding vertex is indeed requested in the subsequent phase.

Now let $T_{j'}$ denote any time step in which ALG parks a server s; in some subsequent time step $T_{j''}$, ALG has cost 0 as a consequence. In the time steps preceding $T_{j'}$, some other servers may have been parked, but at most $k - 2$. This follows immediately from

$$(j'' - 1) - j' = 4k^2 - 1 > k \,,$$

that is, ALG needs at least one server to serve the requests $x_{j'+1}, x_{j'+2}, \ldots, x_{j''-1}$. Therefore, ALG has parked at most $k - 1$ servers in time step $T_{j'}$, which means that it saves at most a cost of $k - 1$ while processing the requests $x_{j'+1}, x_{j'+2}, \ldots, x_{j''}$. Now we bound from below what ALG has to pay additionally due to having s parked. There are at least $2k - 1$ rounds between these two time steps, and each round takes place on a different subgraph. Thus, there must be at least

$$2k - 1 - (k - 1) = k$$

rounds in which no servers are parked between $x_{j'+1}$ and $x_{j''-1}$, and ALG has at most $k - 1$ servers available in them. Following Observation 4.2 for $k' = k - 1$, this means that ALG uses at most one edge of weight 2 in each of them, leading to an additional cost of $2k$. It follows that parking s in $T_{j'}$ caused an additional cost of $2k - (k - 1) = k + 1$ for ALG. This is independent of whether any servers were parked already in $T_{j'}$; indeed, we assumed that both a maximum number of $k - 1$ servers was parked and ALG had a maximum number of servers available to serve the subsequent requests.

Since there is no algorithm that is as good as OPT while inducing cost 0 in some time step, OPT must indeed be optimal. Now we can easily argue that $\mathrm{OPT}(I)$ is also unique. Whenever requests from $\mathcal{G}_{i,j}$ with $1 \leq i \leq 2k$ and $0 \leq j \leq k-1$ are made, we know from Theorem 4.9 that only acting according to $\pi_{i,j}$ allows us to serve all corresponding requests with cost 1 each. For the resets, there is also only one unique server that can be used in order to avoid cost 2.

Recall that there are $n/(4k^2)$ phases and each phase consists of $2k$ rounds; thus, there are $n/2k$ rounds in total. Summing up, since there is one unique optimal solution for every instance $I \in \mathcal{I}^{(n)}$ that needs to act according to the permutations

$$\pi_{1,1}, \pi_{1,2}, \ldots, \pi_{n/(4k^2),2k} \, ,$$

by the same argumentation as in the proof of Theorem 4.9, it directly follows that at least

$$\frac{n}{2k} \log_2(k!) \geq \frac{n}{2}(\log_2 k - \beta)$$

bits of advice are necessary in total to be optimal, for $\beta = \log_2 e$. □

An advantage of the proof of Theorem 4.10 is that it works on a finite metric space. Conversely, if we allow the graph to have unbounded size, which is in accordance with Definition 4.2, it is easy to prove the lower bounds by easier arguments. In this case, we can just define an infinite number of rounds, where each round is defined as above. For such a graph, the same vertex cannot be requested twice, and it is thus trivial that there is no solution that has cost 0 in any time step.

If we think about it, it is in this case even possible to give a lower bound of

$$n(\log_2 k - \log_2 e) \qquad \qquad .$$

by branching the graph infinitely often. If ALG served the first k requests according to the corresponding permutation π_1, all k servers are located at unique vertices that we use as the starting positions for the next k requests corresponding to a permutation π_2, and so on. To prevent ALG from being able to anticipate any requests by inspecting the graph, we need to do this construction for *any* possible set of starting positions, which causes an exponential branching with every additional k requests.

4.6.2 Optimality for the Line

We have just seen that an optimal online algorithm for k-server on general metric spaces needs roughly $\log_2 k$ advice bits in every time step. In contrast to paging, which we discussed in Subsection 3.4.1, we are not able to give an upper bound that solely depends on n. However, we have seen in Section 4.4 that k-server is easier for deterministic online algorithms when we restrict ourselves to simpler metric spaces. More specifically, DCOV achieves a competitive ratio of k on the line. It is therefore natural to ask how much advice helps for this particular metric space. One of the first ideas that come to our mind is to take DCOV and make it use advice in the obvious way. Instead of using the two closest servers (if there are two) to serve a request, simply use one of them; which one (the left one or the right one) is indicated by one advice bit. We call the corresponding online algorithm with advice CMP (short for "compliance"). Note that, in contrast to DCOV, CMP is lazy. We now show that CMP is optimal. The proof is very similar to that of Theorem 4.6, which showed that DCOV is k-competitive; in fact, most of the arguments are even simpler.

Theorem 4.11. CMP *is optimal for k-server on the line and uses n advice bits.*

Proof. Let I be any instance of k-server on the line and let $\text{OPT}(I)$ be some fixed optimal solution for I; once more, we assume that OPT is lazy. As in the proof of Theorem 4.6, we use a potential function Φ; however, this time, the potential function is only based on a minimum-weight matching $M_{\min}$ between the server positions of both algorithms. More specifically, for two configurations C_{CMP} and C_{OPT}, we denote the value of the matching by $M_{\min}(C_{\text{CMP}}, C_{\text{OPT}})$, and we set

$$\Phi(C_{\text{CMP}}, C_{\text{OPT}}) := M_{\min}(C_{\text{CMP}}, C_{\text{OPT}}) .$$

Again, we assume that the two algorithms make their moves alternatingly. This is when the advice comes into play. The oracle simulates OPT. From the proof of Theorem 4.6, we already know that, after OPT made its move, either s_{left} or s_{right} is matched with the server s that OPT uses to serve the given request; if only one of them exists, there is a minimum-weight matching where this distinct server is matched with s. After every move of OPT, the oracle computes $M_{\min}(C_{\text{CMP}}, C_{\text{OPT}})$ for the two current configurations C_{CMP} and C_{OPT}. Then, with one bit of advice, it tells CMP which of s_{left} or s_{right} is matched with s. CMP then uses this server to serve the current request.

The potential is clearly never negative, and thus condition (i) of Theorem 4.5 is satisfied. According to (ii), if we want to show that CMP is 1-competitive, we further need to show that, for all i with $1 \le i \le n$,

$$\Phi(x_i) - \Phi(x_{i-1}) \le \text{cost}(\text{OPT}(x_i)) - \text{cost}(\text{CMP}(x_i)) . \tag{4.15}$$

This means, we need to bound the change of $M_{\min}$ caused by OPT and CMP in every time step. First, OPT makes its move using some server s; this server was matched with some server in CMP's configuration. The distance between these two servers increases by at most

$$\text{cost}(\text{OPT}(x_i)) , \tag{4.16}$$

and therefore $M_{\min}$ (and thus Φ) increases by at most this value.

Now we consider the movement of CMP after OPT moved s to x_i. We can argue analogously to the proof of Theorem 4.6 and distinguish the following cases.

Case 1. Suppose CMP moves one server; without loss of generality, this is again s_{right} since there is no server positioned to the left of x_i. We already know from Theorem 4.6 that there is a minimum-weight matching, in which s_{right} and s were matched before CMP moves s_{right}. After CMP's move, the distance decreased to zero by exactly $\text{cost}(\text{CMP}(x_i))$.

Case 2. If there are both servers s_{left} and s_{right}, we know from the proof of Theorem 4.6 that one of them is matched with s before CMP makes its move. Due to the advice, CMP uses this server, without loss of generality, say, s_{right}, to serve x_i. After this, the weight of the matching again decreased by $\text{cost}(\text{CMP}(x_i))$.

Thus, in both cases, the potential decreases by

$$\text{cost}(\text{CMP}(x_i)) \,. \tag{4.17}$$

Due to (4.16) and (4.17), (4.15) is true in both cases, which proves that CMP is 1-competitive. Finally, we note that initially both algorithms have their servers positioned on the same points, which means that the potential is zero at the beginning, that is, $\Phi(x_0) = 0$. According to Corollary 4.1, CMP is therefore strictly 1-competitive, that is, optimal. $\square$

A particularly interesting point of the proof of Theorem 4.11 is that we use a tool that is designed to analyze a given algorithm (a potential function) to improve this algorithm.

4.6.3 An Upper Bound for the Euclidean Plane

In this subsection, we consider the subproblem of k-server where the underlying metric space is the Euclidean plane; that is, every point p of P has two coordinates p_x and p_y, and the distance between any two points p' and p'' is given by the Pythagorean theorem, that is,

$$\text{dist}(p', p'') := \sqrt{(p''_y - p'_y)^2 + (p''_x - p'_x)^2} \,.$$

For this case, we study a simple online algorithm SEG with advice that achieves a constant competitive ratio while using a linear number of advice bits; in particular, SEG reads a constant number of advice bits b' with $b' \geq 3$ in every time step. If the requested point is $p = (p_x, p_y)$, SEG divides the plane into $2^{b'}$ disjoint *segments* $S_1, S_2, \ldots, S_{2^{b'}}$ with their origin in p and with an angle of

$$\frac{2\pi}{2^{b'}} =: \gamma$$

each; note that $\gamma \leq \pi/4$. Then SEG reads b' bits of advice that identify some segment S_j with $1 \leq j \leq 2^{b'}$ and moves the closest server from S_j to p. The idea is shown in Figure 4.8a. In the following, let

$$r := \frac{1}{1 - 2\sin\left(\frac{\gamma}{2}\right)} \,. \tag{4.18}$$

Figure 4.8b shows the situation for the first time step T_1, where a point $x_1 = p$ is requested. SEG uses a server $\hat{s}$ (located at some point $\hat{p}$ in S_j), incurring a cost of a whereas some given solution uses a server s_1 (located at some point p_1) that causes

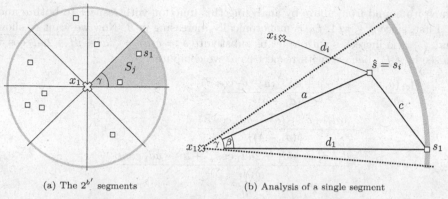

(a) The $2^{b'}$ segments   (b) Analysis of a single segment

Figure 4.8. The segments around the request x_1 used by SEG.

cost d_1 where $d_1 \geq a$. The initial distance between the locations of s_1 and $\hat{s}$, that is, p_1 and $\hat{p}$, is denoted by c. To show that SEG achieves a constant competitive ratio, we first prove a technical lemma that we need in the analysis. In the proof of this lemma, we use two trigonometric equalities; we leave their proofs to the reader as a warm-up.

Exercise 4.13. Prove the *law of cosines*, which is a generalization of the Pythagorean theorem and which states that

$$c^2 = a^2 + d^2 - 2ad\cos\beta$$

in the Euclidean plane, when a, c, and d are the sides of a possibly non-right triangle and β is the angle opposite to c, where $\beta \leq \pi$.

Exercise 4.14. Prove that for any angle ψ, we have $\cos(2\psi) = 1 - 2(\sin\psi)^2$.

Hint. Use the addition theorem, that is, $\cos(\sigma + \tau) = \cos\sigma \cdot \cos\tau - \sin\sigma \cdot \sin\tau$, for any angles σ and τ.

Lemma 4.1. *Let a, d_1, c, r, and γ be as defined above. If d_1 is fixed, we have $a/(d_1 - c) \leq r$.*

Proof. Let β denote the angle that is defined by x_1, s_1, and $\hat{s}$ as depicted in Figure 4.8b; then $\beta \leq \gamma \leq \pi/4$. Recall that $a \leq d_1$. Due to the law of cosines (see Exercise 4.13), we have

$$c = \sqrt{a^2 + d_1^2 - 2ad_1\cos\beta} \, .$$

As a consequence (recall that we consider d_1 to be fixed), we obtain

$$\frac{a}{d_1 - c} = \frac{a}{d_1 - \sqrt{a^2 + d_1^2 - 2ad_1\cos\beta}} =: f_{d_1}(a, \beta) \, ,$$

141

which we bound from above by analyzing this function with respect to both a and β. First, since $\beta \leq \pi/4$, f_{d_1} is monotonically increasing in β. Now we want to show that f_{d_1} also increases with a; let us substitute $\delta := \delta(a) = \sqrt{a^2 + d_1^2 - 2ad_1 \cos \beta}$. To see how f_{d_1} behaves with respect to a, we compute

$$\frac{\partial f_{d_1}(a, \beta)}{\partial a} = \frac{d_1 - \delta + a\delta^{-1}(a - d_1 \cos \beta)}{(d_1 - \delta)^2}$$

$$= \frac{\delta(d_1 - \delta) + (a^2 - ad_1 \cos \beta)}{\delta(d_1 - \delta)^2}$$

$$= \frac{d_1\delta - a^2 - d_1^2 + 2ad_1 \cos \beta + a^2 - ad_1 \cos \beta}{\delta(d_1 - \delta)^2}$$

$$\text{(by resubstituting } \delta^2)$$

$$= d_1 \frac{\delta - d_1 + a \cos \beta}{\delta(d_1 - \delta)^2} \, . \tag{4.19}$$

If we can show that (4.19) is always positive, then f_{d_1} is increasing in a. Since d_1 and the denominator of (4.19) are clearly always positive, it remains to show that $\delta + a \cos \beta$ is larger than d_1, which can be rewritten as

$$\sqrt{a^2 + d_1^2 - 2ad_1 \cos \beta} > d_1 - a \cos \beta \tag{4.20}$$

after resubstituting δ. Since $d_1 - a \cos \beta$ is always positive (as a consequence of $d_1 \geq a$ and $\cos \beta \leq 1$), we can square both sides of (4.20) and obtain

$$a^2 - a^2(\cos \beta)^2 > 0 \, ,$$

which is always true.

It follows that $a/(d_1 - c)$ is maximal for $a = d_1$ and $\beta = \gamma$, which means that

$$\frac{a}{d_1 - c} \leq \frac{d_1}{d_1 - \sqrt{d_1^2 + d_1^2 - 2d_1^2 \cos \gamma}} = \frac{1}{1 - \sqrt{2(1 - \cos \gamma)}} \, .$$

Finally, we use $\cos \gamma = 1 - 2(\sin(\gamma/2))^2$ (see Exercise 4.14) yielding

$$\frac{a}{d_1 - c} \leq \frac{1}{1 - \sqrt{2\left(1 - 1 + 2(\sin(\frac{\gamma}{2}))^2\right)}} = \frac{1}{1 - 2\sin(\frac{\gamma}{2})}$$

as we claimed. □

Now we are ready to analyze the competitive ratio of SEG. To this end, we need to take special care of the positions at which the servers are located at the beginning. As in Definition 4.2, a configuration C is a multiset of k points from P that are occupied by the servers. A configuration $C_{p \mapsto p'}$ is obtained from C by moving a server from $p \in C$ to p'. Recall that the *initial configuration* is the configuration at the beginning, that is, before any request is served. In the following, we will simply speak of the initial configuration of a given instance.

Theorem 4.12. SEG *is strictly*

$$\left(\frac{1}{1 - 2\sin\left(\frac{\pi}{2^{b'}}\right)}\right)\text{-competitive}$$

for k-server on the Euclidean plane and uses $b'n$ advice bits, where $b' \geq 3$.

Proof. Let $I = (x_1, x_2, \ldots, x_n)$ be any instance with an initial configuration C, and let S be any solution for I and C. We restrict ourselves to lazy algorithms; therefore, a solution of an instance is a sequence of servers. To describe a server that is used to serve a certain request, it is sufficient to specify the point occupied by this server; thus, the solution can be described by a sequence of points as well. Let S serve the ith request x_i using a server located at p_i, incurring a cost of $d_i = \|p_i - x_i\|$. Hence, we can describe S as

$$(p_1, p_2, \ldots, p_n) .$$

As described above, for the first request, SEG uses b' bits of advice to specify the segment S_j around x_1 in which the point p_1 is located. SEG moves the closest server $\hat{s}$ located at a point $\hat{p}$ in S_j to x_1, incurring a cost of $a \leq d_1$. Hence, after the first request x_1, S leads to a configuration $C_{p_1 \mapsto x_1}$, whereas SEG is in a configuration $C_{\hat{p} \mapsto x_1}$; this situation is illustrated in Figure 4.8b.

We prove that the cost of SEG on I with initial configuration C is at most $r \cdot \text{cost}(S)$, where r is defined as in (4.18). The proof is done by induction on the input length n.

Base Case. If $n = 1$, the cost of SEG is $a \leq d_1 = \text{cost}(S)$.

Induction Hypothesis. The claim holds for every instance of length $n - 1$ with any initial configuration.

Induction Step. Let $n \geq 2$, and let x_i be the first request that is served by $\hat{s}$ in S. Consider the instance $I' = (x_2, x_3, \ldots, x_n)$ of length $n - 1$ with initial configuration $C_{\hat{p} \mapsto x_1}$; the sequence

$$(p_2, p_3, \ldots, p_{i-1}, p_1, p_{i+1}, \ldots, p_n)$$

is a solution for I' with a cost of at most

$$c + \sum_{i=2}^{n} d_i ,$$

where c is the distance between s_1 and $\hat{s}$; see Figure 4.8b. By induction, the cost of SEG on I' is at most

$$r \cdot \left(c + \sum_{i=2}^{n} d_i\right) ,$$

and therefore the cost of SEG on I is at most

$$a + r \cdot \left(c + \sum_{i=2}^{n} d_i\right) .$$

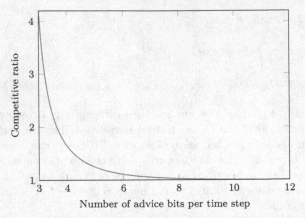

Figure 4.9. The competitive ratio of SEG depending on the number of advice bits b' per request.

Due to Lemma 4.1, we have that $a \leq r(d_1 - c)$ and thus the cost of SEG on I with initial configuration C is at most

$$r \cdot (d_1 - c) + r \cdot \left(c + \sum_{i=2}^{n} d_i \right) = r \cdot \sum_{i=1}^{n} d_i = r \cdot \text{cost}(\mathcal{S}) .$$

Since $\mathcal{S}$ is an arbitrary solution, the claim follows. $\qquad\square$

Note that, with b' tending to infinity, the upper bound on the competitive ratio of SEG converges to 1; see Figure 4.9.

⋆4.6.4 An Upper Bound for the General Case

We now focus on the tradeoff between the number of advice bits and the competitive ratio achievable in general metric spaces. As we have seen at the beginning of this chapter, a simple (deterministic) greedy strategy is very bad for k-server. In the previous two subsections, we have seen, for two special metric spaces, how advice can be used to somewhat restrict the greedy moves in order to improve the solution quality; both algorithms use a number of advice bits that is linear in the input length. In what follows, we design an algorithm CHASE with advice that follows a greedy strategy for some of the requests and that is again able to bound the harm done by these moves by using the advice tape. The algorithm also implements a kind of marking. In particular, CHASE reads, with every request x_i, two so-called *control bits* that trigger one of the following three actions.

1. If the control bits are 00, CHASE serves x_i greedily (ties are broken arbitrarily), and then returns the chosen server to its original position.

2. If they are 01, x_i is served by the closest unmarked server, which is not returned to its original position afterwards. Then, this server gets marked.

3. If they are 11, CHASE reads another $\lceil \log_2 k \rceil$ bits from the advice tape. These bits encode the index of a server that is then used to serve x_i; again, this server stays at x_i.

For the rest of this subsection, let

$$r := \left\lceil \frac{\lceil \log_2 k \rceil}{b' - 2} \right\rceil,$$

where b' is the number of advice bits CHASE reads per time step. Before we elaborate on the competitive ratio of CHASE, we need to describe the algorithm in more detail. In what follows, let $\text{OPT}(I)$ be a fixed optimal solution for some given instance I. We again assume that OPT is lazy; note, however, that CHASE is not. Now we take a closer look at OPT. For every i with $1 \leq i \leq k$, we denote by I_i the subsequence of I consisting of all requests for which OPT uses the server s_i. In other words, I_i corresponds to the *trajectory* of s_i with respect to OPT. Let us give an example.

Example 4.1. Suppose we are given an instance I of length 12 for 3-server, and an optimal algorithm uses the servers as follows.

	x_1	x_2	x_3	x_4	x_5	x_6	x_7	x_8	x_9	x_{10}	x_{11}	x_{12}
s_1	×			×				×				
s_2		×			×	×					×	
s_3			×				×		×	×		×

Then, the three subsequences are

$$I_1 = (x_1, x_4, x_8),$$
$$I_2 = (x_2, x_5, x_6, x_{11}),$$
$$I_3 = (x_3, x_7, x_9, x_{10}, x_{12}). \qquad \diamond$$

The idea behind CHASE is to consider all subsequences I_i separately. For every such sequence, the oracle will ensure that a "correct" server $\hat{s}_i$ (taking the role of s_i in OPT's solution) will be positioned on the "correct" point from time to time; this "correct" positioning is done using $\lceil \log_2 k \rceil$ advice bits that encode the index of $\hat{s}_i$; $\hat{s}_i$ can then be used for some of the subsequent requests within I_i. We will show that the total cost of CHASE is at most r times as large as that of OPT (plus some constant). As in the last subsection, we start with a technical lemma that we need in the analysis of the algorithm.

Lemma 4.2. *For some $r \in \mathbb{N}^+$, consider a sequence $a_1, a_2, \ldots, a_r$ with $a_l \in \mathbb{R}^+$, for $1 \leq l \leq r$. Then there is a natural number δ with $1 \leq \delta \leq r$ such that*

$$\sum_{l=1}^{r} (2(r + \delta - l) + 1)a_l - \sum_{l=1}^{\delta} 2ra_l \leq r \sum_{l=1}^{r} a_l. \qquad (4.21)$$

Proof. We prove the claim by computing the average value of the left-hand side of (4.21) over all possible values δ with $1 \leq \delta \leq r$. We start by summing over all such values, which yields

$$
\sum_{\delta=1}^{r} \left(\sum_{l=1}^{r} (2(r+\delta-l)+1)a_l - \sum_{l=1}^{\delta} 2ra_l \right)
$$

$$
= \sum_{\delta=1}^{r} \left(\sum_{l=1}^{r} (2(r+\delta)+1)a_l \right) - \sum_{\delta=1}^{r} \left(\sum_{l=1}^{r} 2la_l \right) - \sum_{\delta=1}^{r} \left(\sum_{l=1}^{\delta} 2ra_l \right)
$$

(by splitting the sum into a positive and a negative part)

$$
= \left(\sum_{\delta=1}^{r} (2(r+\delta)+1) \right) \cdot \sum_{l=1}^{r} a_l - 2r \sum_{l=1}^{r} la_l - 2r \sum_{\delta=1}^{r} \left(\sum_{l=1}^{\delta} a_l \right) . \tag{4.22}
$$

(since l, a_l, and r do not depend on δ)

Next, we simultaneously add and subtract

$$
\left(\sum_{\delta=1}^{r} 4\delta \right) \cdot \sum_{l=1}^{r} a_l , \tag{4.23}
$$

and then use that

$$
\sum_{\delta=1}^{r} (2(r-\delta)+1) = r + 2\sum_{\delta=1}^{r}(r-\delta) = r + 2\sum_{\delta=0}^{r-1}\delta = r^2 . \tag{4.24}
$$

As a result of adding and subtracting (4.23) and plugging (4.24) into (4.22), we obtain that the sum of the left-hand side of (4.21) over all δ is equal to

$$
r^2 \sum_{l=1}^{r} a_l + \left(\sum_{\delta=1}^{r} 4\delta \right) \sum_{l=1}^{r} a_l - 2r \left(\sum_{l=1}^{r} la_l + \sum_{\delta=1}^{r} \left(\sum_{l=1}^{\delta} a_l \right) \right)
$$

$$
= r^2 \sum_{l=1}^{r} a_l + (2r^2 + 2r) \sum_{l=1}^{r} a_l - 2r \left(\sum_{l=1}^{r} la_l + \sum_{\delta=1}^{r} \left(\sum_{l=1}^{\delta} a_l \right) \right) . \tag{4.25}
$$

Now note that

$$
\sum_{\delta=1}^{r} \left(\sum_{l=1}^{\delta} a_l \right) = a_1 + a_1 + a_2 + a_1 + a_2 + a_3 + \ldots + a_1 + a_2 + \ldots + a_r
$$

$$
= \underbrace{a_1 + a_1 + \ldots + a_1}_{r \text{ times}} + \underbrace{a_2 + a_2 + \ldots + a_2}_{r-1 \text{ times}} + \ldots + a_r
$$

$$
= \sum_{l=1}^{r} (r-l+1)a_l . \tag{4.26}
$$

146

From (4.25) and (4.26), we finally obtain

$$r^2 \sum_{l=1}^{r} a_l + (2r^2 + 2r) \sum_{l=1}^{r} a_l - 2r \left(\sum_{l=1}^{r} la_l + \sum_{l=1}^{r} (r - l + 1)a_l \right)$$

$$= r^2 \sum_{l=1}^{r} a_l + (2r^2 + 2r) \sum_{l=1}^{r} a_l - 2r \sum_{l=1}^{r} (r + 1)a_l$$

$$= r^2 \sum_{l=1}^{r} a_l + \underbrace{(2r^2 + 2r) \sum_{l=1}^{r} a_l - (2r^2 + 2r) \sum_{l=1}^{r} a_l}_{0}$$

$$= r^2 \sum_{l=1}^{r} a_l .$$

Since there are r possible values for δ, it follows that for at least one of them we have

$$\sum_{l=1}^{r} (2(r + \delta - l) + 1)a_l - \sum_{l=1}^{\delta} 2ra_l \leq r \sum_{l=1}^{r} a_l$$

as we claimed. $\qquad \square$

Now we are ready to compute an upper bound on the competitive ratio of CHASE.

Theorem 4.13. CHASE *is*

$$\left\lceil \frac{\lceil \log_2 k \rceil}{b' - 2} \right\rceil \text{-competitive}$$

for k-server and uses $b'n$ advice bits, where $b' \geq 3$.

Proof. For any instance I of k-server, let the subsequence I_i be as defined above, that is, OPT uses the server s_i for every request in I_i, for every i with $1 \leq i \leq k$. For every I_i, we fix a constant $\delta_i \leq r$, which we will determine later. Every I_i is further divided into N_i *phases* as follows.

- Phase $P_{i,1}$ (that is, the first phase of I_i) starts with the first request from I_i and ends with the δ_ith request from I_i.

- For $j \geq 2$, phase $P_{i,j}$ (that is, the jth phase of I_i) starts with the $(\delta_i + (j - 2)r + 1)$th request of I_i and ends with the $(\delta_i + (j - 1)r)$th request of I_i.

For the sake of an easier proof, we assume that the last phase P_{i,N_i} is padded by requesting the last request from P_{i,N_i} repeatedly such that it has a length of r. Note that all other phases also have a length of r with the sole exception of the first one, which has length δ_i; we may think of δ_i as an *offset* that specifies when the second phase starts. In the following, we denote the lth request of the jth phase $P_{i,j}$ of I_i by $x_{i,j,l}$.

The oracle inspects I and $\text{OPT}(I)$ and constructs the subsequences I_i as above. Then, it supplies the advice for every request x as follows.

1. If $x = x_{i,1,\delta_i}$, that is, x is the last request of the first phase of I_i, the oracle writes 01 on the advice tape. Since this situation occurs at most k times, there is always an unmarked server, which CHASE can use for the greedy move without moving the server back; for the rest of the proof, the unique server that CHASE uses is called $\hat{s}_i$.

2. If $x = x_{i,j,r}$, for $j \geq 2$, that is, x is the last request of any other phase, the oracle writes 11 on the advice tape, followed by the index of $\hat{s}_i$.

3. Else, the oracle writes 00 on the advice tape.

We now bound the cost of CHASE on a subsequence I_i from above. To this end, we analyze every phase of I_i separately. First, consider the jth phase $P_{i,j}$ with $j \geq 2$. $P_{i,j}$ starts with the request $x_{i,j,1}$. Due to the advice, CHASE positioned $\hat{s}_i$ on the last request of the previous phase $P_{i,j-1}$, that is, at the point $x_{i,j-1,z}$, where $z = \delta_i$ if $j = 2$ and $z = r$ if $j > 2$. After that, this server was marked (either right after that move if $j = 2$, or before if $j > 2$). Therefore, it was only used for greedy moves and returned to $x_{i,j-1,z}$ until the start of $P_{i,j}$. Since we are considering the subsequence I_i, for which OPT only uses the server s_i, it follows that OPT moved this server to $x_{i,j-1,z}$ and did not move it until $x_{i,j,1}$.

For an easier argument, let $x_{i,j,0} := x_{i,j-1,z}$. During $P_{i,j}$, CHASE has $\hat{s}_i$ positioned on $x_{i,j,0}$ at the beginning of every time step. For every request $x_{i,j,l}$ with $1 \leq l \leq r-1$, CHASE uses some server and moves it back to its original position. We have

$$\text{cost}(\text{CHASE}(x_{i,j,l})) \leq 2 \cdot \text{dist}(x_{i,j,0}, x_{i,j,l})$$

$$\leq 2 \sum_{t=1}^{l} \text{dist}(x_{i,j,t-1}, x_{i,j,t}) \,. \tag{4.27}$$

(due to the triangle inequality)

Now we consider the last request of $P_{i,j}$, that is, $x_{i,j,r}$. This request is also served by $\hat{s}_i$, which is then left at $x_{i,j,r}$. It follows that

$$\text{cost}(\text{CHASE}(x_{i,j,r})) \leq \text{dist}(x_{i,j,0}, x_{i,j,r})$$

$$\leq \sum_{t=1}^{r} \text{dist}(x_{i,j,t-1}, x_{i,j,t}) \,. \tag{4.28}$$

Next, let us consider OPT; since it uses the same server s_i for all requests in $P_{i,j}$, we easily have, for $1 \leq l \leq r$,

$$\text{cost}(\text{OPT}(x_{i,j,l})) = \text{dist}(x_{i,j,l-1}, x_{i,j,l}) \,. \tag{4.29}$$

Together with (4.27) and (4.28), we can now bound the cost of CHASE on $P_{i,j}$ as

$$\text{cost}(\text{CHASE}(P_{i,j})) = \sum_{l=1}^{r} \text{cost}(\text{CHASE}(x_{i,j,l}))$$

$$\leq \sum_{t=1}^{r} \text{dist}(x_{i,j,t-1}, x_{i,j,t}) + \sum_{l=1}^{r-1}\left(2\sum_{t=1}^{l}\text{dist}(x_{i,j,t-1}, x_{i,j,t})\right)$$

$$= \sum_{t=1}^{r} \text{cost}(\text{OPT}(x_{i,j,t})) + \sum_{l=1}^{r-1}\left(\sum_{t=1}^{l} 2 \cdot \text{cost}(\text{OPT}(x_{i,j,t}))\right)$$

(due to (4.29))

$$= \sum_{t=1}^{r} \text{cost}(\text{OPT}(x_{i,j,t})) + \sum_{l=1}^{r-1} 2(r-l) \cdot \text{cost}(\text{OPT}(x_{i,j,l}))$$

(by an argument similar to (4.26))

$$= \sum_{t=1}^{r} \text{cost}(\text{OPT}(x_{i,j,t})) + \sum_{l=1}^{r} 2(r-l) \cdot \text{cost}(\text{OPT}(x_{i,j,l}))$$

(since $r - r = 0$)

$$= \sum_{l=1}^{r}(2(r-l)+1) \cdot \text{cost}(\text{OPT}(x_{i,j,l})) . \tag{4.30}$$

Now we bound the cost of CHASE on the first phase $P_{i,1}$ of I_i. Essentially, we can argue in a similar way as for the phases $P_{i,j}$ with $j \geq 2$. However, in $P_{i,1}$, we cannot assume that CHASE has positioned a server on the same point where OPT has positioned s_i. CHASE may have marked and positioned s_i somewhere else; that is, $s_i = \hat{s}_{i'}$ with $i \neq i'$. Let p_i denote the initial position of s_i, and let D be the maximum distance between any two servers in the initial configuration. At the beginning of $P_{i,1}$, there is at least one unmarked server s left at its original position p. By the triangle inequality, for every request $x_{i,1,l}$ with $1 \leq l \leq \delta_i$ from $P_{i,1}$, we have

$$\text{dist}(p, x_{i,1,l}) \leq \text{dist}(p, p_i) + \text{dist}(p_i, x_{i,1,l}) \leq D + \text{dist}(p, p_i) . \tag{4.31}$$

This time, for an easier argument, let $x_{i,1,0} := p_i$, that is, $x_{i,1,0}$ denotes the initial position of s_i. For every request $x_{i,1,l}$ with $1 \leq l \leq \delta_i - 1$, due to (4.31), we have

$$\text{cost}(\text{CHASE}(x_{i,1,l})) \leq 2(D + \text{dist}(p_i, x_{i,1,l}))$$

$$\leq 2\left(D + \sum_{t=1}^{l}(\text{dist}(x_{i,1,t-1}, x_{i,1,t}))\right), \tag{4.32}$$

analogously to (4.27). For the last request $x_{i,1,\delta_i}$ of $P_{i,1}$, we get

$$\text{cost}(\text{CHASE}(x_{i,1,\delta_i})) \leq (D + \text{dist}(p_i, x_{i,1,\delta_i}))$$

$$\leq D + \sum_{t=1}^{\delta_i} \text{dist}(x_{i,1,t-1}, x_{i,1,t}) \ . \tag{4.33}$$

Adding (4.32) and (4.33), we can use (4.29) for $j = 1$ and do a calculation similar to (4.30) yielding

$$\begin{aligned}
&\text{cost}(\text{Chase}(P_{i,1})) \\
&= \sum_{l=1}^{\delta_i} \text{cost}(\text{Chase}(x_{i,1,l})) \\
&\leq \sum_{t=1}^{\delta_i} \text{dist}(x_{i,1,t-1}, x_{i,1,t}) + \sum_{l=1}^{\delta_i-1} \left(2 \sum_{t=1}^{l} \text{dist}(x_{i,1,t-1}, x_{i,1,t}) \right) + 2\delta_i D \\
&= \sum_{l=1}^{\delta_i} (2(\delta_i - l) + 1) \cdot \text{cost}(\text{Opt}(x_{i,1,l})) + 2\delta_i D \tag{4.34}
\end{aligned}$$

as an upper bound on the cost of Chase in $P_{i,1}$, where $2\delta_i D$ is constant with respect to the input length. Note that the length δ_i of $P_{i,1}$ is possibly smaller than r, that is, the lengths of the other phases in I_i.

In order to make (4.30) and (4.34) more consistent, we do the following. We add r "dummy" requests at the beginning of I_i with non-positive indices that all induce cost 0 for both Chase and Opt. Then, we count $r - \delta_i$ of these dummy requests towards $P_{i,1}$. More specifically, we assume that $P_{i,1}$ also consists of r requests

$$\underbrace{x_{i,1,-r+\delta_i+1}, x_{i,1,-r+\delta_i+2}, \dots, x_{i,1,-r+\delta_i+(r-\delta_i-1)}, x_{i,1,0},}_{\text{new requests}} x_{i,1,1}, \dots, x_{i,1,\delta_i} \ ,$$

where the $r - \delta_i$ new requests at the beginning are dummy requests.

Now let $x_{i,\delta_i+(j-2)r+l}$ denote the $(\delta_i + (j-2)r + l)$th request of the ith subsequence I_i. For $j \geq 2$, we have $x_{i,j,l} = x_{i,\delta_i+(j-2)r+l}$, and can thus rewrite (4.30) as

$$\text{cost}(\text{Chase}(P_{i,j})) \leq \sum_{l=1}^{r} (2(r - l) + 1) \cdot \text{cost}\big(\text{Opt}(x_{i,(j-2)r+\delta_i+l})\big) \ . \tag{4.35}$$

Moreover, for $j = 1$, we can rewrite (4.34) as

$$\begin{aligned}
&\text{cost}(\text{Chase}(P_{i,1})) \\
&\leq 2\delta_i D + \sum_{l=1}^{r} (2(r - l) + 1) \cdot \text{cost}(\text{Opt}(x_{i,1,-r+\delta_i+l})) \\
&= 2\delta_i D + \sum_{l=1}^{r} (2(r - l) + 1) \cdot \text{cost}\big(\text{Opt}(x_{i,(j-2)r+\delta_i+l})\big) \ , \tag{4.36}
\end{aligned}$$

due to the dummy requests.

Recall that there are N_i phases in total within the subsequence I_i. We can give an upper bound on the cost of CHASE on I_i by simply summing (4.35) $N_i - 1$ times and adding (4.36), which yields

$$\text{cost}(\text{CHASE}(I_i))$$

$$\leq 2\delta_i D + \sum_{j=1}^{N_i} \left(\sum_{l=1}^{r} (2(r-l)+1) \cdot \text{cost}\big(\text{OPT}(x_{i,(j-2)r+\delta_i+l})\big) \right)$$

$$= 2\delta_i D + \sum_{l=1}^{r} \left((2(r-l)+1) \sum_{j=1}^{N_i} \text{cost}\big(\text{OPT}(x_{i,(j-2)r+\delta_i+l})\big) \right)$$

$$= 2\delta_i D + \sum_{l=-r+\delta_i+1}^{\delta_i} \left((2(\delta_i-l)+1) \sum_{j=1}^{N_i} \text{cost}\big(\text{OPT}(x_{i,(j-1)r+l})\big) \right). \qquad (4.37)$$

(by shifting the index of the outer sum by $-r + \delta_i$)

Next, we define

$$\text{opt}_{i,l} := \sum_{j=1}^{N_i} \text{cost}\big(\text{OPT}(x_{i,(j-1)r+l})\big),$$

that is, the sum of the costs of OPT on every rth request starting with the lth request in I_i (counting from $-r + \delta_i + 1$).

Then, (4.37) implies

$$\text{cost}(\text{CHASE}(I_i))$$

$$\leq 2\delta_i D + \sum_{l=-r+\delta_i+1}^{\delta_i} (2(\delta_i-l)+1) \cdot \text{opt}_{i,l}$$

$$= 2\delta_i D + \sum_{l=1}^{\delta_i} (2(\delta_i-l)+1) \cdot \text{opt}_{i,l} + \sum_{l=-r+\delta_i+1}^{0} (2(\delta_i-l)+1) \cdot \text{opt}_{i,l}$$

$$= 2\delta_i D + \sum_{l=1}^{\delta_i} (2(\delta_i-l)+1) \cdot \text{opt}_{i,l} + \sum_{l=\delta_i+1}^{r} (2(r+\delta_i-l)+1) \cdot \text{opt}_{i,l-r}$$

$$\leq 2\delta_i D + \sum_{l=1}^{\delta_i} (2(\delta_i-l)+1) \cdot \text{opt}_{i,l} + \sum_{l=\delta_i+1}^{r} (2(r+\delta_i-l)+1) \cdot \text{opt}_{i,l}$$

(since requests with non-positive index have cost 0)

$$= 2\delta_i D + \sum_{l=1}^{r} (2(r+\delta_i-l)+1) \cdot \text{opt}_{i,l} - \sum_{l=1}^{\delta_i} 2r \cdot \text{opt}_{i,l}.$$

It remains to define the length of the first phase, that is, δ_i; we do so separately for every i with $1 \leq i \leq k$. From Lemma 4.2, we know that we can always pick a δ_i with $1 \leq \delta_i \leq r$ such that

$$\text{cost}(\text{CHASE}(I_i)) \leq r \sum_{l=1}^{r} \text{opt}_{i,l} + 2\delta_i D = r \cdot \text{cost}(\text{OPT}(I_i)) + 2\delta_i D .$$

Now that we have an upper bound on the cost of CHASE in one subsequence, we can easily bound its cost on I with respect to the cost of OPT by

$$\text{cost}(\text{CHASE}(I)) = \sum_{i=1}^{k} \text{cost}(\text{CHASE}(I_i))$$

$$\leq \sum_{i=1}^{k} (r \cdot \text{cost}(\text{OPT}(I_i)) + 2\delta_i D)$$

$$\leq \sum_{i=1}^{k} (r \cdot \text{cost}(\text{OPT}(I_i)) + 2rD)$$

$$= r \cdot \text{OPT}(I) + 2krD ,$$

where $2krD$ is constant with respect to the input length. In other words, CHASE is r-competitive.

As a last step, we bound from above the number of advice bits CHASE uses.

- In every time step, CHASE reads two control bits.
- At the end of every first phase $P_{i,1}$, CHASE also only reads two bits. However, at the end of any phase $P_{i,j}$ with $j \geq 2$, the algorithm reads $\lceil \log_2 k \rceil$ additional bits that encode the index of the server $\hat{s}_i$; thus, it reads $2 + \lceil \log_2 k \rceil$ bits in every rth time step of I_i. This means that, for every time step in which CHASE reads $2 + \lceil \log_2 k \rceil$ advice bits, there are $r - 1$ preceding time steps of I_i in which only two advice bits are used.

The number of advice bits b' read per time step can therefore be bounded from above by

$$b' \leq \frac{2(r-1)}{r} + \frac{2 + \lceil \log_2 k \rceil}{r} = 2 + \frac{\lceil \log_2 k \rceil}{r} ,$$

which is ensured by

$$r \leq \frac{\lceil \log_2 k \rceil}{b' - 2} .$$

The claim follows. $\qquad\square$

This completes our study of concrete online algorithms with advice for the k-server problem. We conclude with a general remark.

4.6.5 Advice and the Randomized k-Server Conjecture

In Section 4.1, we introduced the randomized k-server conjecture, which states that there is a randomized online algorithm for this problem that is $\Theta(\log k)$-competitive in expectation. The next theorem shows how we could use the advice complexity as a technique to disprove the conjecture.

Theorem 4.14. *If every online algorithm with advice for k-server on metric spaces with at most 2^n points has to use $\omega(\log n)$ advice bits to be $\mathcal{O}(\log k)$-competitive, then the randomized k-server conjecture does not hold.*

Proof. Let $\mathcal{M}$ be a metric space with a size that is bounded from above by 2^n, where n is the length of the given instance. Again, let $\mu(n)$ denote the number of instances of length n. In every time step, one point of $\mathcal{M}$ is requested, and thus

$$\mu(n) \leq (2^n)^n .$$

If there is a randomized online algorithm RAND that is $\mathcal{O}(\log k)$-competitive in expectation on all such instances, then Theorem 3.7 implies that there is also an $\mathcal{O}(\log k)$-competitive online algorithm with advice that uses at most

$$2\lceil \log_2(\lceil \log_2 n \rceil) \rceil + \lceil \log_2 n \rceil + \log_2\left(\left\lfloor \frac{\log_2((2^n)^n)}{\log_2(1+\varepsilon)} \right\rfloor + 1 \right) \in \mathcal{O}(\log n)$$

advice bits. Note that this online algorithm with advice is worse than RAND by a factor of $1 + \varepsilon$, for any $\varepsilon > 0$, which is hidden in the $\mathcal{O}$-notation.

As a consequence, if we can show that any $\mathcal{O}(\log k)$-competitive online algorithm with advice for k-server on $\mathcal{M}$ needs to use asymptotically more advice bits, we have a contradiction to the existence of RAND. □

On the other hand, if the randomized k-server conjecture were true, CHASE could be improved exponentially for instances on at most 2^n points (so far, it uses a linear number of advice bits).

4.7 Historical and Bibliographical Remarks

The k-server problem is certainly one of the most generic and famous online problems; in the last couple of years, it has been repeatedly called "the holy grail" in the field of online computation [14, 42]. It was introduced by Manasse et al. in 1988 [114]. Since then, it has been thoroughly studied; for a survey we refer to Koutsoupias [104].

It has been conjectured that there exists a k-competitive deterministic online algorithm for k-server, which continues to be one of the most famous open problems in theoretical computer science (known as the aforementioned *k-server conjecture*, which was already posed by Manasse et al. [114]). So far, the best known deterministic algorithm is due to Koutsoupias and Papadimitriou, and it achieves a competitive ratio of $2k - 1$ [105] (and a strict competitive ratio of $4k - 2$ [59]). The algorithm

DCov is due to Chrobak et al. [45], and its generalization DCovT was given by Chrobak and Larmore [46]. In the original publication, the authors already showed that there is a k-competitive online algorithm for metric spaces with $k+1$ points [114]. In 1996, Koutsoupias and Papadimitriou showed that this is also true for $k+2$ points [106].

As for employing randomization, Bansal et al. [13] showed in 2011 that there is a randomized online algorithm that is $\mathcal{O}((\log k)^2 (\log m)^3 \log \log m)$-competitive in expectation; recall that m denotes the number of points of the metric space at hand. This algorithm thus obtains a competitive ratio bounded by a function that is polylogarithmic in k if m is polynomial in k. Intriguingly, before that, no randomized online algorithm was known that is better than the deterministic one from Koutsoupias and Papadimitriou [105]; and if we speak about arbitrary (possibly even infinite) metric spaces, this is still the case up to today.

The proof that Lru is k-competitive for paging using a potential function (Exercise 4.11) is taken from Albers [4].

Online algorithms with advice for the k-server problem were first investigated by Emek et al. [60]. In this publication, a different model of advice was used, which we described in Section 3.6. They gave an online algorithm that reads b' bits per time step and achieves a competitive ratio of $k^{\mathcal{O}(1/b')}$. Böckenhauer et al. [29] exponentially improved this result by showing the existence of a

$$2 \left\lceil \frac{\lceil \log_2 k \rceil}{b' - 1} \right\rceil \text{-competitive}$$

online algorithm with advice for k-server; for details, see the technical report [28]. Renault and Rosén [125] enhanced both the algorithm and analysis, obtaining the online algorithm Chase with advice, which we presented in Subsection 4.6.4. The optimal online algorithm with advice for the line Cmp is also due to Renault and Rosén [125]. The online algorithm with advice for the Euclidean plane Seg is due to Böckenhauer et al. [29], as well as the lower bound presented for optimal online algorithms with advice (see Theorems 4.9 and 4.10). The upper bound of $n\lceil \log_2 k \rceil$ (see Theorem 4.8) was already noted by Emek et al. [60].

Renault and Rosén [125] also studied online algorithms with advice on trees. They gave a 1-competitive online algorithm with advice that uses a number of advice bits that grows logarithmically with the tree's caterpillar dimension. Gupta et al. [69] studied k-server on special metric spaces with, for instance, bounded treewidth. For this large subclass of k-server instances, the authors gave both well-performing online algorithms with advice and hardness results. Among other results, they showed that there is a 3-competitive online algorithm with advice for planar graphs that uses $\mathcal{O}(n \log \log m)$ bits, where m again denotes the number of vertices of the graph.

Job Shop Scheduling

5

A typical setting in which problems are often intrinsically online is that of scheduling problems. Here, we are given a number of *machines*, which are abstractions of certain resources, for instance, CPUs. Additionally, there is a number of *jobs* that we want to assign to these machines in a particular way; we say that we want to *schedule* the jobs on the machines. The *load* of a machine depends on how long it needs to process all the jobs that are scheduled on it. There are many different kinds of such problems, for instance, depending on whether the jobs all need the same processing time, and whether the machines are all equally fast. Also, there are different optimization goals; as an example, one could ask for a schedule that is as balanced as possible, that is, where all machines have roughly the same load (if possible). In our case, we deal with minimizing the so-called *makespan*, which is the time until the last job is processed.

This chapter studies a very simple variant of the scheduling problem, namely the so-called *job shop scheduling with unit-length tasks* (JSS for short). We assume there are only two jobs and a fixed number of machines; every job needs each machine exactly once for one time unit. Thus, the load of every machine is exactly two. More specifically, each job consists of a number of tasks, and each task requires one particular machine. These tasks are revealed online while the number of machines (and thus tasks) is known in advance. First, we analyze deterministic online algorithms for the problem. Using some very easy arguments, it turns out that no such algorithm is worse than 2-competitive, and so we need to pay special attention to small values of the competitive ratio. A more careful analysis then yields a tight bound of 4/3. Next, we construct a class of randomized online algorithms for the problem. Using a number of random bits that grows logarithmically with the input length, we show that it is possible to obtain an expected competitive ratio that tends to 1 with increasing input length. This algorithm also obtains this solution quality with a probability that tends to 1. After that, we give barely random algorithms for the problem. Last, we discuss the advice complexity of JSS by giving both upper

© Springer International Publishing Switzerland 2016
D. Komm, *An Introduction to Online Computation*,
Texts in Theoretical Computer Science. An EATCS Series,
DOI 10.1007/978-3-319-42749-2_5

and lower bounds on the number of advice bits of optimal online algorithms with advice. We then turn to algorithms with a constant number of advice bits. An upper bound is implied by the existence of the aforementioned barely random algorithms, and an almost matching lower bound concludes the chapter.

5.1 Introduction

We are given two *jobs* that each need to use some given *machines* for one time unit (time step) each in some specific order. The goal is to schedule the jobs on the machines while minimizing the processing time of the job that needs longest to be processed, by parallelizing as much of the work as possible. The difficult part is that the order in which the machines need to be used is revealed in an online fashion. Let the two jobs be denoted by A and B, each of which consists of m tasks. These tasks must be executed in sequential order, and each task needs to be processed on a specific machine. There are exactly m such machines, identified by their indices $1, 2, \ldots, m$, and each job has exactly one task for every machine. Processing a task takes exactly one time unit, and, since both jobs need every machine exactly once, we may represent them as permutations π_A and π_B of the set $\{1, 2, \ldots, m\}$. The meaning of such a permutation is that the tasks must be performed in the order specified by it and, for every machine, the ith task must be finished before task $i + 1$ can be processed. If, in some time step, both jobs A and B ask for the same machine, one of them has to be delayed. The cost of a solution is given by the total time needed to finish all tasks of both jobs. As mentioned above, the goal is to minimize this time (the *makespan*). Let us continue with a formal definition.

Definition 5.1 (Job Shop Scheduling). *Job shop scheduling of two jobs with unit-length tasks* (job shop scheduling or JSS for short) is an online minimization problem. The input is given by two permutations π_A and π_B, which correspond to the indices $1, 2, \ldots, m$ of the machines that are requested by the jobs A and B, respectively. In every time step, an online algorithm for JSS outputs a pair (run, delay), (delay, run), or (run, run). The entry $\pi_A(i + 1)$ ($\pi_B(i + 1)$, respectively) is revealed in the time step after which "run" appeared i times as the first (second, respectively) entry of a pair, for $1 \leq i \leq m - 1$. If "run" appeared m times as one of the entries, all following entries at this position must be "delay." The output (run, run) is only allowed if the most recently revealed entries of π_A and π_B are different. The aim is to minimize the *makespan*, that is, the last time step in which "run" appears.

Note that JSS has a characteristic which is very important for its theoretical analysis; the length of the permutations m is known in advance as it is a parameter of the problem. Strictly formally, we should thus be speaking of m-JSS or even

(d, m)-JSS as the number of jobs d is also fixed from the start (although we only consider $d = 2$ here). To make the notation easier, we will stick to JSS in this book.

There is another special property of this problem; formally, it is not consistent with the definition of online problems (see Definition 1.4) since the next part of the input depends on the algorithm's answer to the current one. Indeed, in Definition 5.1, we did not assign the requests to time steps, but they are revealed only after the preceding ones are processed. Conversely, if the algorithm delays a job, the next task of this job will not be revealed in the subsequent time step. Of course, in our model of online computation, the adversary always reacts to the previous answers of the algorithm; but for this problem, it is not allowed to give certain requests depending on what the algorithm does. Consequently, the length of the input depends on the output of the algorithm. If we had allowed the answer (delay, delay), an online algorithm could even delay every instance an arbitrary number of time steps by delaying both jobs again and again; of course, this would only increase its cost. We will treat JSS like any other online problem presented in this book, which will not cause any formal problems; the only difference is that m plays the role of n.

Note that Definition 5.1 implicitly assumes that every algorithm is done after $2m$ time steps, which easily implies that every online algorithm is 2-competitive (or better) for JSS. All online algorithms presented in this chapter are strictly competitive. The lower bounds hold for the case where the additive constant α is allowed to be positive since the optimal cost grows with m.[4]

Theorem 5.1. *Every deterministic online algorithm for JSS is strictly 2-competitive.*

Proof. In every time step, one task is scheduled. Therefore, scheduling both jobs cannot take longer than $2m$ time steps. On the other hand, every solution has a cost of at least m. $\square$

Before we start a formal analysis of the problem, let us give a small example of an instance of JSS.

Example 5.1. Suppose there are five machines; thus, we know that we will be given two permutations of length 5 each, which represent the machine indices $1, 2, 3, 4, 5$. Consider an instance I where, in the first time step, a pair $(4, 1)$ is given, which means that the first job requests machine 4 and the second one requests machine 1. Since these are two different machines, the two tasks can be scheduled in parallel, and the output (run, run) is created by some online algorithm ALG. In the next time step, both jobs request machine 2, that is, the pair $(2, 2)$ is given. Thus, ALG must delay one of them, say job B, which corresponds to the output (run, delay). Since the second task of B is not yet processed after that, only the third part of A, requesting machine 5, is revealed in the next time step; the corresponding part of the input is therefore $(5, \langle \text{null} \rangle)$. Hence, B still requests machine 2 while A requests

---

[4]More formally, we construct sets of instances that always contain infinitely many instances with an increasing optimal cost.

5, which means that the third task of A and the second task of B can be parallelized, leading to the output (run, run), and so on.

Suppose the complete permutations are given by

$$\pi_A = (4, 2, 5, 3, 1) \quad \text{and} \quad \pi_B = (1, 2, 3, 5, 4) \,,$$

and the complete output of ALG is given by

$$\begin{aligned} \text{ALG}(I) = (&(\text{run}, \text{run}), (\text{run}, \text{delay}), (\text{run}, \text{run}), (\text{run}, \text{delay}), (\text{run}, \text{run}), \\ &(\text{delay}, \text{run}), (\text{delay}, \text{run})) \,. \end{aligned}$$

This representation of the output is not well suited to give us a good intuition about the computed solution; a more intuitive representation is given by

$$\begin{aligned} \text{Schedule}_{\text{ALG}}(\pi_A) &= (4, 2, 5, 3, 1, -, -) \,, \\ \text{Schedule}_{\text{ALG}}(\pi_B) &= (1, -, 2, -, 3, 5, 4) \,, \end{aligned}$$

and we see that the makespan is 7. This is not optimal; an optimal solution for this instance is

$$\begin{aligned} \text{Schedule}_{\text{OPT}}(\pi_A) &= (4, 2, 5, -, 3, 1) \,, \\ \text{Schedule}_{\text{OPT}}(\pi_B) &= (1, -, 2, 3, 5, 4) \end{aligned}$$

and has a delay of 1 instead of 2. $\diamond$

To get an even more intuitive view of instances and solutions of JSS, we use the following graphical representation. Consider an $(m \times m)$-grid where we label the x-axis with π_A and the y-axis with π_B. The cell in the ith column and the jth row is simply called "cell (i, j)." A feasible schedule for the induced instance of JSS is a path that starts at the upper left-hand corner of the grid (that is, the upper left-hand corner of $(1, 1)$) and ends at the lower right-hand corner (that is, the lower right-hand corner of (m, m)). In every time step, where it is initially located at a cell (i, j) and $\pi_A(i) \neq \pi_B(j)$, it may make a diagonal move. In this case, the first $i - 1$ tasks of A and the first $j - 1$ tasks of B have already been processed, and the two jobs request different machines. However, if $\pi_A(i) = \pi_B(j)$, both A and B ask for the same machine at the same time, and therefore one of them has to be delayed. In this case, we say that A and B *collide*, and we call the corresponding cells in the grid *obstacles*; see Figure 5.1. If some algorithm has to delay a job, we say that it *hits an obstacle* and therefore cannot make a diagonal move, but makes either a horizontal or a vertical one. In the first case, B gets delayed; in the second case, A gets delayed.

Example 5.2. Let us revisit both the instance and the schedule from Example 5.1. Since $m = 5$, we draw a grid of size 5×5 using the graphical representation, which is shown in Figure 5.1a. The x-axis is labeled with π_A, that is, $4, 2, 5, 3, 1$, and the

(a) ALG's solution   (b) An optimal solution

Figure 5.1. Example of an instance of JSS together with the schedule produced by the online algorithm ALG from Example 5.1 and an optimal schedule.

y-axis is labeled with π_B, that is, $1, 2, 3, 5, 4$. The gray squares mark the obstacles, that is, the positions in which both jobs request the same machine. In the first time step, machines 1 and 4 are requested simultaneously, thus a diagonal move can be made. After that, however, machine 2 is requested by both A and B; as a result, one of the jobs has to be delayed. The online algorithm ALG we study in this example decides to delay B, and thus there is a horizontal line shown in the graphical representation. Then it is revealed that A requests machine 5, and thus a diagonal move is made, meaning that the work is parallelized because now A requests machine 5 while B still requests machine 2. Right after that, another obstacle is hit. Eventually, ALG arrives at the lower right-hand corner of the grid, and it makes three diagonal, two horizontal, and two vertical moves in total. An optimal schedule makes four diagonal moves and only one horizontal and one vertical move; see Figure 5.1b. ◊

We will use the graphical representation of instances in all of the subsequent proofs. Before that, however, we make the following observations, which will be of great help.

Observation 5.1. *For every instance of JSS, the following is true.*

(i) *We can always assume that one of the two permutations is the identity by relabeling the machines; in our case, this will be π_A.*

(ii) *Since π_A and π_B are permutations, there is exactly one obstacle per row and exactly one obstacle per column.*

(iii) *It follows that there are exactly m obstacles in the whole grid.*

(iv) *Every feasible solution makes exactly as many horizontal moves as it makes vertical ones. We call the number of horizontal (or, alternatively, vertical) moves the* delay *of the solution.*

(v) *The cost of a solution is equal to m plus the delay of the solution. It follows that every solution has a cost of at least m.*

Exercise 5.1. Prove Observation 5.1(v).

For any online algorithm ALG, we denote the number of diagonal moves ALG makes on the grid induced by I by d_{ALG}; h_{ALG} and v_{ALG} are defined analogously as shorthands for the number of horizontal and vertical moves, respectively. Moreover, we denote the delay of ALG on I by $\text{delay}(\text{ALG}(I))$. From Observation 5.1(iv) and Observation 5.1(v), we conclude

$$\text{delay}(\text{ALG}(I)) = h_{\text{ALG}} = v_{\text{ALG}}$$

and

$$\text{cost}(\text{ALG}(I)) = m + \text{delay}(\text{ALG}(I)) = m + h_{\text{ALG}} = m + v_{\text{ALG}} \,.$$

Exercise 5.2. As suggested in Observation 5.1(i), relabel the instance

$$\pi_A = (14, 4,\ 6\ , 10, 7, 2, 11, 12, 16, 17,\ 5\ , 13,\ 1\ , 8, 15,\ 3\ ,\ 9\ , 19, 20, 18) \,,$$
$$\pi_B = (\ 1\ , 6, 17, 19, 8, 9,\ 2\ ,\ 5\ ,\ 4\ , 13, 12, 11, 15, 7, 20, 16, 18, 10, 14,\ 3\ ) \,.$$

Exercise 5.3. Find an optimal solution for the instance

$$\pi_A = (1, 2, 3, 4, 5, 6, 7, 8,\ 9\ , 10, 11, 12, 13, 14, 15) \,,$$
$$\pi_B = (1, 2, 3, 4, 5, 7, 8, 9, 10, 11, 12, 13, 14, 15,\ 6\ ) \,.$$

First, try to figure it out using the permutations only. Then use the graphical representation to verify your solution.

5.2 Deterministic Algorithms

In this section, we study what can be done by a deterministic online algorithm for JSS. We have learned in Theorem 5.1 that no algorithm for JSS is worse than 2-competitive. Thus, there is rather small room for improvement. Before we have a look at what we can do, we define a special class of algorithms. Similarly to demand paging algorithms for paging and lazy algorithms for k-server, it will sometimes come in handy to restrict ourselves to such algorithms. Basically, these algorithms are greedy ones, but to emphasize the context, we give them a special name.

> **Definition 5.2 (Ambitious Online Algorithm).** An online algorithm for JSS is called *ambitious* if it makes a diagonal move whenever possible; that is, as long as it does not arrive at the right or bottom border of the grid, it always moves diagonally if no obstacle is in its way.

Considering ambitious algorithms (for lower-bound proofs) is no restriction of generality similarly to the cases of the aforementioned demand paging and lazy algorithms. The proof is left to the reader as an exercise.

Theorem 5.2. *Every online algorithm for JSS with delay d can be transformed into an ambitious online algorithm for JSS that also has delay d.*

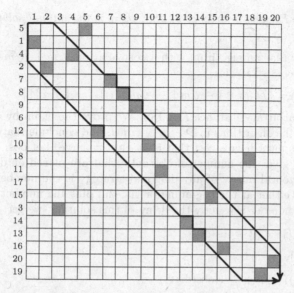

Figure 5.2. An example input with two jobs each of size 20 and the strategies D_{-3} and D_2; obstacles are marked by filled cells.

Exercise 5.4. Prove Theorem 5.2.

Next, we introduce a class of solutions that allows us to bound the optimal cost from above (and which we will use later when considering randomized online algorithms in Section 5.3 and online algorithms with advice in Section 5.4). Let diag_0 denote the main diagonal from $(1,1)$ to (m,m) in the given grid. The diagonal that has a distance of i from diag_0 and lies below (above, respectively) it is denoted by diag_{-i} (diag_i, respectively). For any odd d that may depend on m, we consider a certain set of *diagonal strategies*

$$\mathcal{D}_d := \left\{ D_i \ \middle| \ i \in \left\{ -\frac{d-1}{2}, -\frac{d-3}{2}, \dots, \frac{d-1}{2} \right\} \right\},$$

where D_j is the strategy to move to the starting point of diag_j with $|j|$ moves, to follow diag_j when possible, and to avoid any obstacle by making a horizontal move directly followed by a vertical one (thus returning to diag_j). We have, for instance, $\mathcal{D}_7 = \{D_{-3}, D_{-2}, D_{-1}, D_0, D_1, D_2, D_3\}$; examples of the diagonal strategies D_{-3} and D_2 are shown in Figure 5.2.

Note that it is crucial for our analysis that the strategy returns to the diagonal even though there might be situations where it is an advantage not to take the vertical move after the horizontal one; by definition, online algorithms that follow diagonal strategies are not ambitious algorithms. Now we show that, for any given instance, there is at least one diagonal strategy that has a rather small cost.

Theorem 5.3. *For every instance of JSS, there is an optimal solution that has a cost of at most $m + \lceil \sqrt{m} \rceil$.*

Proof. We show that an algorithm with a cost of at most $m + \lceil \sqrt{m} \rceil$ can be found among the diagonal strategies

$$\mathcal{D}_{2\lceil \sqrt{m} \rceil + 1} = \left\{ D_i \mid i \in \{ -\lceil \sqrt{m} \rceil, -\lceil \sqrt{m} \rceil + 1, \ldots, \lceil \sqrt{m} \rceil \} \right\} .$$

Consider an arbitrary instance I of JSS. We prove the claim by computing the average cost of the algorithms in $\mathcal{D}_{2\lceil \sqrt{m} \rceil + 1}$ on I, and conclude that at least one of these algorithms must have a cost that is at most as large. Let obs: $\mathbb{Z} \to \mathbb{N}$ denote a function that gives the number of obstacles that are placed on diag_i in I. The number of horizontal moves of any diagonal strategy is the number of horizontal moves it makes either at the beginning or the end plus the number of obstacles it hits. Since this number is exactly the delay of this solution, we get

$$\mathrm{delay}(D_i(I)) = |i| + \mathrm{obs}(\mathrm{diag}_i) \tag{5.1}$$

and consequently

$$\mathrm{cost}(D_i(I)) = m + |i| + \mathrm{obs}(\mathrm{diag}_i) .$$

Following Observation 5.1(iii), there cannot be more than m obstacles in total, which implies

$$\sum_{i=-\lceil \sqrt{m} \rceil}^{\lceil \sqrt{m} \rceil} \mathrm{obs}(\mathrm{diag}_i) \le m . \tag{5.2}$$

If we sum over all i, for $-\lceil \sqrt{m} \rceil \le i \le \lceil \sqrt{m} \rceil$, using (5.1) and (5.2) we obtain

$$\sum_{i=-\lceil \sqrt{m} \rceil}^{\lceil \sqrt{m} \rceil} \mathrm{delay}(D_i(I)) = \sum_{i=-\lceil \sqrt{m} \rceil}^{\lceil \sqrt{m} \rceil} \left(|i| + \mathrm{obs}(\mathrm{diag}_i) \right)$$

$$\le m + 2 \sum_{i=1}^{\lceil \sqrt{m} \rceil} i$$

$$= m + \lceil \sqrt{m} \rceil (\lceil \sqrt{m} \rceil + 1) .$$

The average delay of the strategies in $\mathcal{D}_{2\lceil \sqrt{m} \rceil + 1}$ is therefore at most

$$\frac{m + \lceil \sqrt{m} \rceil (\lceil \sqrt{m} \rceil + 1)}{2\lceil \sqrt{m} \rceil + 1} \le \frac{\lceil \sqrt{m} \rceil^2 + \lceil \sqrt{m} \rceil (\lceil \sqrt{m} \rceil + 1)}{2\lceil \sqrt{m} \rceil + 1}$$

$$= \frac{\lceil \sqrt{m} \rceil (2\lceil \sqrt{m} \rceil + 1)}{2\lceil \sqrt{m} \rceil + 1}$$

$$= \lceil \sqrt{m} \rceil ,$$

which implies that there has to be at least one deterministic strategy in $\mathcal{D}_{2\lceil \sqrt{m} \rceil + 1}$ with at most this delay and therefore a cost of at most $m + \lceil \sqrt{m} \rceil$ on I. $\qquad \square$

Now that we have an upper bound on the cost of an optimal algorithm for JSS on any instance, we bound the cost of any deterministic online algorithm from below. The key idea is that the adversary can always make sure that, after a diagonal move, any online algorithm has to make a non-diagonal move. In other words, we show that the adversary can ensure that every second move of a given online algorithm is non-diagonal.

Theorem 5.4. *No deterministic online algorithm for JSS has a cost less than $4/3m$.*

Proof. Let ALG be any deterministic online algorithm for JSS, and let I denote the instance we describe in what follows. As a consequence of Theorem 5.2, we assume without loss of generality that ALG is ambitious, that is, it makes a diagonal move whenever possible. We now show that, as long as ALG did not hit a border, we have that, for every time step T_i,

- if either $i = 1$ or ALG made a diagonal move in T_{i-1}, the adversary can force ALG to make a non-diagonal move in T_i, and

- if ALG made a non-diagonal move in T_{i-1}, the adversary can assign the tasks such that this does not prevent it from placing any necessary obstacle later.

Let (x_i, y_i) with $1 \le x_i, y_i \le m$ and $1 \le i \le n$ denote the position of the cell at whose upper left-hand corner ALG is located at the beginning of time step T_i. Then the x_ith task of job A and the y_ith task of B have to be assigned (possibly, one of them was already assigned earlier). In order to show how the adversary places the obstacles, we prove that the following is true for every i.

$$\text{At most the first } \max\{x_i, y_i\} \text{ machines are used in } T_1, T_2, \ldots, T_i \text{ for} \tag{5.3}$$
$$\text{each of the two jobs.}$$

We prove the claims by induction on T_i; an example is shown in Figures 5.3 and 5.4.

Base Case. At the beginning of T_1, ALG is at the upper left-hand corner of the cell $(1, 1)$. It is easy to see that the adversary can force it to make a non-diagonal move by placing an obstacle at $(1, 1)$, that is, setting $\pi_A(1) = \pi_B(1) = 1$. After that, the two first tasks have been assigned, and thus (5.3) holds; see Figure 5.3a.

Induction Hypothesis. The claim holds for T_{i-1}.

Induction Step. Consider time step T_i. We make a case distinction depending on ALG's past and present behavior.

Case 1. Suppose ALG made a diagonal move in T_{i-1} (and thus $x_i = x_{i-1} + 1$ and $y_i = y_{i-1} + 1$). Then, ALG now enters both a new row and a new column, and the adversary is able to place a new obstacle as follows. Without loss of generality, assume $x_{i-1} \ge y_{i-1}$ (and thus $x_i \ge y_i$), that is, ALG made at least as many horizontal moves as vertical ones so far. By the induction hypothesis, at most the first $\max\{x_{i-1}, y_{i-1}\} = x_{i-1}$ machines have been assigned so far. Then the adversary sets $\pi_A(x_i) = \pi_B(y_i) = x_{i-1} + 1 = x_i$, hence creating an obstacle at (x_i, y_i). Clearly, (5.3) still holds after this; see Figure 5.3c.

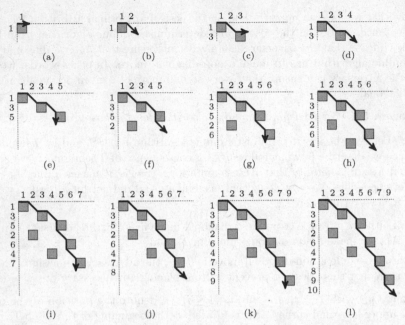

Figure 5.3. The first 12 time steps of an instance created by the adversary in the proof of Theorem 5.4.

Case 2. Suppose ALG made a non-diagonal move in T_{i-1}. In this case, the adversary cannot force ALG to make another non-diagonal move in T_i since there can only be one obstacle per column and one obstacle per row, and ALG is still either in the same column or the same row as right before T_{i-1}. Due to Theorem 5.2, we assume that ALG makes a diagonal move. In such a case, the adversary needs to reveal the next value of either π_A or π_B. Without loss of generality, assume again that $x_{i-1} \geq y_{i-1}$. Recall that, by the induction hypothesis, at most the first $\max\{x_{i-1}, y_{i-1}\} = x_{i-1}$ machines have been assigned so far. We need to distinguish two cases depending on the previous move of ALG.

Case 2.1. Suppose ALG made a horizontal move in T_{i-1} (and thus $x_i = x_{i-1} + 1$ and $y_i = y_{i-1}$). Then the adversary sets $\pi_A(x_i) = x_{i-1} + 1 = x_i$; see Figure 5.3d.

Case 2.2. Suppose ALG made a vertical move in T_{i-1} (and thus $x_i = x_{i-1}$ and $y_i = y_{i-1} + 1$). If $x_{i-1} = y_{i-1}$, the adversary sets $\pi_B(y_i) = x_{i-1} + 1 = y_i$; see Figure 5.3j. Conversely, if $x_{i-1} > y_{i-1}$, then the adversary assigns $\pi_B(y_i) = j$, where j with $j < x_{i-1}$ is the smallest index of some machine that is not yet assigned for B; see Figure 5.3f for $x_i > y_i$ and Figure 5.3h for $x_i = y_i$.

In both cases, (5.3) holds after assigning the task in T_i.

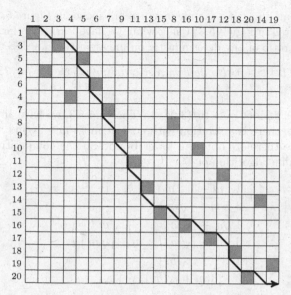

Figure 5.4. An example of how to place the obstacles in such a way that any deterministic algorithm cannot make two consecutive diagonal moves.

If ALG hits a border, the adversary simply assigns the remaining jobs in any way. Now we bound the cost of ALG on I from below. Recall that $\text{delay}(\text{ALG}(I)) = h_{\text{ALG}} = v_{\text{ALG}}$. We have

$$m = d_{\text{ALG}} + h_{\text{ALG}} \iff \text{delay}(\text{ALG}(I)) = m - d_{\text{ALG}} , \tag{5.4}$$

which means that the delay of ALG decreases as d_{ALG} increases.

Thus, what remains to be done is to bound d_{ALG} from above. To this end, consider the time step right after which ALG hits one of the borders (possibly arriving at the lower right-hand corner of the grid). After that, ALG cannot make any additional diagonal move. For a contradiction, assume that $d_{\text{ALG}} \geq 2m/3 + 1$. Since, after every such move, ALG made a non-diagonal move, ALG made more than $2m/3$ non-diagonal moves (recall that ALG starts with a non-diagonal move). Thus, so far, ALG made more than $m/3$ horizontal moves or more than $m/3$ vertical moves. However, this implies that ALG made more than $m/3 + 2m/3 + 1 > m$ moves to the right or to the bottom, which would lead it outside the grid; a contradiction.

It follows that

$$d_{\text{ALG}} \leq \frac{2}{3}m ,$$

and thus, due to (5.4), the delay of ALG is at least $m/3$, which leads to a cost of $4m/3$ on I. $\qquad\square$

165

The first 12 time steps of a sample instance are shown in Figure 5.3; the complete instance is depicted in Figure 5.4. Using what we have learned so far, we can bound the competitive ratio of any deterministic online algorithm for JSS as follows.

Theorem 5.5. *Let $\varepsilon > 0$. No deterministic online algorithm for JSS is $(4/3 - \varepsilon)$-competitive.*

Proof. Let $\varepsilon > 0$, and let $m > 16/(3\varepsilon)^2$. In Theorem 5.3, we have already seen that, for any instance, there is a solution with cost at most $m + \lceil \sqrt{m} \rceil$. Together with Theorem 5.4, we therefore obtain a lower bound on the competitive ratio of any deterministic online algorithm of

$$
\begin{aligned}
\frac{m + 1/3m}{m + \lceil \sqrt{m} \rceil} &= 1 + \frac{1}{3} \cdot \frac{m - 3\lceil \sqrt{m} \rceil}{m + \lceil \sqrt{m} \rceil} \\
&= 1 + \frac{1}{3} \left(\frac{m + \lceil \sqrt{m} \rceil}{m + \lceil \sqrt{m} \rceil} - \frac{4\lceil \sqrt{m} \rceil}{m + \lceil \sqrt{m} \rceil} \right) \\
&= 1 + \frac{1}{3} - \frac{4\lceil \sqrt{m} \rceil}{3(m + \lceil \sqrt{m} \rceil)} \\
&\geq 1 + \frac{1}{3} - \frac{4(\sqrt{m} + 1)}{3(m + \sqrt{m})} \\
&= 1 + \frac{1}{3} - \frac{4}{3\sqrt{m}} \\
&> 1 + \frac{1}{3} - \varepsilon,
\end{aligned}
$$

$$(\text{since } m > 16/(3\varepsilon)^2)$$

which proves the claim. $\qquad\square$

To complement this lower bound, we now prove the existence of a deterministic online algorithm for JSS that is $4/3$-competitive. Most of the ideas we need have already been presented. Let MDIAG be an online algorithm that follows the main diagonal diag_0 at the beginning. If it hits an obstacle, it makes a horizontal move and continues on diag_1. Conversely, if it encounters an obstacle on diag_1, it makes a vertical move, thus returning to diag_0. This way, MDIAG moves between these two diagonals while making a diagonal move whenever possible. Thus, the main difference between MDIAG and the algorithms from $\mathcal{D}_d$ is that MDIAG does not immediately return to its assigned diagonal (that is, diag_0) after it hits an obstacle.

In a nutshell, the idea of MDIAG is to maximize the number of diagonal moves due to (5.4).

Theorem 5.6. *MDIAG is strictly $4/3$-competitive for JSS.*

Proof. Let I be any instance of JSS. As in the proof of Theorem 5.4, we note that right after any non-diagonal move due to an obstacle, the adversary cannot force

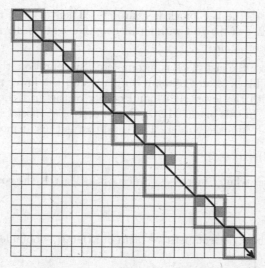

Figure 5.5. A solution computed by MDIAG and the blocks used in its analysis.

another delay. Let us first speak about time steps in which MDIAG does not hit a border. Consider any such step in which MDIAG starts on the main diagonal, and in which it hits an obstacle (for instance, T_1). Then, MDIAG makes a horizontal move. In the next time step, MDIAG can make a diagonal move. Then, a possibly empty sequence of diagonal moves follows. If MDIAG hits another obstacle, it makes a vertical move, thus returning to diag_0. This is followed by another diagonal move, and another possibly empty sequence of diagonal moves.

We subdivide the grid into *blocks* such that every block is a subgrid of maximum size containing exactly one horizontal move of MDIAG. Every block contains exactly one horizontal and one vertical move; see Figure 5.5. Note that the last block may not be complete. In the worst case, all blocks (except possibly the last one) have a size of 3×3 and, in every block, MDIAG advances three cells on the main diagonal while making four moves in the worst case. Indeed, if MDIAG made more than one diagonal move after the horizontal move, this ratio would only change in its favor. Likewise, we can assume that the adversary places another obstacle in the cell that is entered by the algorithm right after the diagonal move that follows the vertical move. We distinguish the following cases.

Case 1. Suppose there is no obstacle on the main diagonal. Then MDIAG is optimal as it never leaves this diagonal.

Case 2. Suppose there is at least one obstacle on the main diagonal. In this case, the optimal solution has to make at least one horizontal move; thus, its cost on I is at least $m + 1$.

Case 2.1. Suppose the last block is complete. Then MDIAG reaches the lower right-hand corner of the grid without hitting the right border first. Then, it has a cost of at most $4/3m$.

Case 2.2. Suppose the last block is incomplete. By definition, the upper left-hand corner of this block is on the main diagonal and the lower right-hand corner is identical with the lower right-hand corner of the grid. Let the size of this block be $l \times l$. In this block, MDIAG has a cost of at most $l + 1$ since it moves to diag_1 until it hits the border. The total cost is thus at most

$$\frac{4}{3}(m - l) + (l + 1),$$

which decreases when l increases. Since l is at least 1, the cost is at most

$$\frac{4}{3}m + 1.$$

It follows that the strict competitive ratio of MDIAG is bounded from above by

$$\frac{4m/3 + 1}{m + 1} \leq \frac{4}{3}$$

as we claimed. □

Exercise 5.5. Give a lower bound on the competitive ratio of any deterministic online algorithm for JSS that follows a fixed diagonal strategy from $\mathcal{D}_{2\lceil \sqrt{m} \rceil + 1}$.

Exercise 5.6. How does your bound of Exercise 5.5 change if the algorithm returns to its diagonal only after it hits another obstacle and not right after the non-diagonal move?

Exercise 5.7. So far, we assumed that both jobs need to use the same number of machines. Now consider the case where one of the two needs twice as many as the other one. What can you say about the competitiveness of deterministic online algorithms in this case?

5.3 Randomized Algorithms

We now have tight bounds on the competitive ratio of deterministic online algorithms for JSS. More specifically, we found out that such an algorithm is always worse by a factor of at least roughly $4/3$ compared to the optimal solution. In this section, we once more want to find out how much randomization may help us. To this end, again consider the class $\mathcal{D}_d$ of diagonal strategies, for some odd $d \geq 1$; d may depend on m. Let RDIAG$_d$ be a randomized online algorithm that chooses a strategy from this class uniformly at random using at most $\Theta(\log d)$ random bits.[5] We start with a general result that proves an upper bound on the expected competitive ratio that depends on d.

---

[5]Recall our discussion from Section 2.1; since d is odd and therefore not a power of 2, there are some issues with choosing a strategy uniformly at random.

Theorem 5.7. RDIAG$_d$ *is strictly*

$$\left(1 + \frac{1}{d} + \frac{d^2 - 1}{4dm}\right)\text{-competitive}$$

in expectation for JSS.

Proof. For every odd d, consider the random variables $X_1, X_2, X, Y : \mathcal{D}_d \to \mathbb{N}$, where $X_1(D_i)$ is the delay caused by the initial horizontal (vertical, respectively) moves made by the strategy D_i, $X_2(D_i)$ is the delay caused by D_i due to hitting obstacles,

$$X(D_i) := X_1(D_i) + X_2(D_i)$$

is D_i's overall delay, and

$$Y(D_i) := m + X(D_i)$$

is D_i's overall cost. Recall that D_{-j} and D_j make the same number of non-diagonal (vertical or horizontal, respectively) moves at the beginning. Since there are exactly m obstacles in total for every instance, we get

$$\mathbb{E}[X_2] = \frac{1}{d}\left(X_2(D_0) + 2\sum_{i=1}^{(d-1)/2} X_2(D_i)\right) \leq \frac{m}{d},$$

and since $X_1(D_0) = 0$, we get

$$\mathbb{E}[X_1] = \frac{1}{d}\left(X_1(D_0) + 2\sum_{i=1}^{(d-1)/2} X_1(D_i)\right) = \frac{2}{d}\sum_{i=1}^{(d-1)/2} i = \frac{d^2 - 1}{4d}.$$

Due to the linearity of expectation, it follows that

$$\mathbb{E}[Y] = m + \mathbb{E}[X] = m + \mathbb{E}[X_2] + \mathbb{E}[X_1] \leq m + \frac{m}{d} + \frac{d^2 - 1}{4d}.$$

As a result, the expected competitive ratio of RDIAG$_d$ is at most

$$\left(\frac{(d+1)m}{d} + \frac{d^2 - 1}{4d}\right)\frac{1}{m} = 1 + \frac{1}{d} + \frac{d^2 - 1}{4dm},$$

as we claimed. □

The above class of algorithms proves to be very useful for JSS. In the following three subsections, we analyze different aspects.

5.3.1 A One-Competitive Randomized Algorithm

First, we consider a randomized online algorithm that chooses between a number of diagonals that depends on the number of machines m. More specifically, as in Section 5.2, let $d = 2\lceil \sqrt{m} \rceil + 1$. Let $\text{RDIAG} = \text{RDIAG}_{2\lceil \sqrt{m} \rceil + 1}$ be a randomized online algorithm that chooses a number i uniformly at random, for $-\lceil \sqrt{m} \rceil \leq i \leq \lceil \sqrt{m} \rceil$, at the beginning (it can do so since m is known) and follows the corresponding diagonal strategy D_i, that is, for a fixed m,

$$\text{strat}(\text{RDIAG}) = \mathcal{D}_{2\lceil \sqrt{m} \rceil + 1} := \left\{ D_{-\lceil \sqrt{m} \rceil}, D_{-\lceil \sqrt{m} \rceil + 1}, \dots, D_{\lceil \sqrt{m} \rceil} \right\}.$$

We show that this algorithm achieves an expected competitive ratio that is asymptotically the best possible.

Theorem 5.8. *RDIAG has a strict expected competitive ratio with an upper bound that tends to 1 as m tends to infinity for JSS.*

Proof. RDIAG chooses between exactly $2\lceil \sqrt{m} \rceil + 1$ diagonal strategies. As a direct consequence of Theorem 5.7, RDIAG therefore has a strict expected competitive ratio of at most

$$1 + \frac{1}{2\lceil \sqrt{m} \rceil + 1} + \frac{(2\lceil \sqrt{m} \rceil + 1)^2 - 1}{4m(2\lceil \sqrt{m} \rceil + 1)} \leq 1 + \frac{1}{2\sqrt{m}} + \frac{(2\lceil \sqrt{m} \rceil + 1)^2}{4m(2\lceil \sqrt{m} \rceil + 1)}$$

$$= 1 + \frac{1}{2\sqrt{m}} + \frac{2\lceil \sqrt{m} \rceil + 1}{4m},$$

which tends to 1 as m tends to infinity. $\qquad \square$

5.3.2 Bounds with Probability Tending to One

In Section 2.2, we have studied the randomized online algorithm RMARK for paging and showed that it is $2H_k$-competitive in expectation. Surprisingly, in Section 2.7 we could also prove that this algorithm achieves this bound with a probability that tends to 1. In this subsection, we prove a similar statement for RDIAG. In other words, we want to show that this algorithm is also 1-competitive with a probability that tends to 1 with an increasing number of jobs m.

Theorem 5.9. *Let $f \colon \mathbb{N} \to \mathbb{R}^+$ be some decreasing function with $1/f(m) \in o(\sqrt{m})$. RDIAG is strictly $(1 + f(m))$-competitive with a probability that tends to 1 as m tends to infinity for JSS.*

Proof. Recall that Observation 5.1(v) states that any optimal solution has a cost of at least m. Let l be the number of considered diagonals that cause RDIAG to have a cost of more than $m(1 + f(m))$. Then, the probability that the computed solution has a cost of more than $m(1 + f(m))$ is

$$q := \frac{l}{2\lceil \sqrt{m} \rceil + 1}. \tag{5.5}$$

Let us have a closer look at RDIAG. The delay of any solution it computes is caused by two things; the number i of horizontal (vertical, respectively) moves the algorithm makes at the beginning to reach a diagonal with distance i (that is, diag_i or diag_{-i}) from the main diagonal, and the number of obstacles hit. Since every obstacle that is hit is evaded by exactly one horizontal and one vertical move, this causes an additional cost of exactly 1. Note that i is at most $\lceil \sqrt{m} \rceil$ in any case.

Let l' denote the number of diagonals that contain more than $mf(m) - \lceil \sqrt{m} \rceil$ obstacles; we call such diagonals *expensive*. By the above observation, any diagonal that causes a cost of more than $m + mf(m)$ must have more than $mf(m) - \lceil \sqrt{m} \rceil$ obstacles on it. It follows that $l \leq l'$ and hence (5.5) implies

$$q \leq \frac{l'}{2\lceil \sqrt{m} \rceil + 1} .$$

We can now bound l' from above as follows. It is easy to see that if l' is maximally large, all of the m obstacles are distributed on the expensive diagonals. Conversely, since there cannot be more than m obstacles for any instance, we have $m \geq l'(mf(m) - \lceil \sqrt{m} \rceil)$ and therefore

$$l' \leq \frac{m}{mf(m) - \lceil \sqrt{m} \rceil} .$$

As a result, we get

$$\begin{aligned}
q &\leq \frac{m}{mf(m) - \lceil \sqrt{m} \rceil} \cdot \frac{1}{(2\lceil \sqrt{m} \rceil + 1)} \\
&= \frac{m}{(2\lceil \sqrt{m} \rceil + 1)(mf(m) - \lceil \sqrt{m} \rceil)} \\
&\leq \frac{m}{(2\sqrt{m} + 1)(mf(m) - 2\sqrt{m})} \\
&\quad \text{(since } \lceil \sqrt{m} \rceil \leq 2\sqrt{m} \text{ for every } m \geq 1) \\
&= \frac{1}{(2\sqrt{m} + 1)(f(m) - 2/\sqrt{m})} \\
&\leq \frac{1}{f(m)(2\sqrt{m} + 1) - 6} .
\end{aligned}$$

(using that $2/\sqrt{m} \leq 2$ for every $m \geq 1$)

Finally, since $1/f(m) \in o(\sqrt{m})$, for instance, $f(m) = 1/\log_2 m$, it immediately follows that q tends to 0 as m tends to infinity, which finishes the proof. $\qquad \square$

5.3.3 A Barely Random Algorithm

Now consider the randomized online algorithm RDIAG_d as defined above, but this time, let d be constant. Note that, in this case, the bound given by Theorem 5.7 tends to $1 + 1/d$ as m tends to infinity. Moreover, as already discussed, RDIAG_d uses $\Theta(\log d)$ random bits. Therefore, RDIAG_d is a barely random algorithm for JSS.

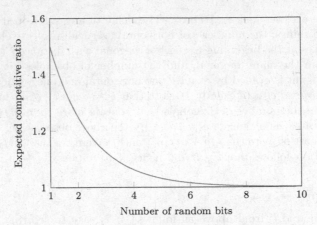

Figure 5.6. The strict expected competitive ratio of RDIAG_d depending on $\log_2 d$ as m tends to infinity.

Theorem 5.10. RDIAG_d *has a strict expected competitive ratio with an upper bound that tends to $1 + 1/d$ as m tends to infinity for JSS.* □

The strict expected competitive ratio is shown in Figure 5.6 (to reflect the asymptotic behavior, the plot assumes that $\log_2 d$ random bits are used and that d can also be even). Later in this chapter, we will complement this bound with a lower bound using results we obtain for the advice complexity of JSS.

5.4 Advice Complexity

Now that we have a good overview of what is and what is not possible deterministically and with the help of randomness, we elaborate on the power of advice for JSS. To this end, we use some of the results from previous sections. It is important to recall that any online algorithm for this problem already knows m from the start.

5.4.1 Optimality

First, let us discuss the amount of information that is both sufficient and necessary for an online algorithm to produce an optimal solution for JSS. We start with a straightforward upper bound.

Theorem 5.11. *There is an optimal online algorithm with advice for JSS that uses at most $2\lceil \sqrt{m} \rceil$ advice bits.*

Proof. The idea is to construct an online algorithm with advice that uses one bit of advice for every obstacle that is hit, indicating whether to move horizontally or vertically to bypass it. Since we know from Theorems 5.2 and 5.3 that there is an ambitious optimal algorithm which makes at most $\lceil\sqrt{m}\,\rceil$ vertical and $\lceil\sqrt{m}\,\rceil$ horizontal moves, and thus hits at most $2\lceil\sqrt{m}\,\rceil$ obstacles, the claim follows. $\qquad\square$

It is possible to improve this upper bound by compressing the advice strings. The proof is left as an exercise for the reader.

Theorem 5.12. *There is an optimal online algorithm with advice for JSS that uses at most* $2\lceil\sqrt{m}\,\rceil - (\log_2 m)/4$ *advice bits.*

Exercise 5.8. Prove Theorem 5.12.

Hint. Use that every solution makes the same number of horizontal and vertical moves.

Next, we give a lower bound on the advice complexity of any optimal online algorithm with advice for JSS, which asymptotically matches the upper bound of Theorems 5.11 and 5.12.

Theorem 5.13. *Let* $\varepsilon > 0$. *Every optimal online algorithm with advice for JSS has to use at least* $(1 - \varepsilon)\sqrt{m/2}$ *advice bits.*

Proof. Let $\varepsilon > 0$, let k be a positive integer, and let m be a multiple of $4k + 13$ such that $m \geq 145(1 - \varepsilon)^2/\varepsilon^2$. Consider the instance shown in Figure 5.7 that consists of three *levels* that are of sizes $2k + 1$, 11, and $2k$. Additionally, we need one more row and one more column to place spare obstacles. Suppose that exactly one of the two black obstacles b_1 and b_2 is not present. This instance has a size of $(4k + 13) \times (4k + 13)$.

Obviously, there is an optimal solution that starts at the upper left-hand corner and follows the main diagonal until it hits the first obstacle c that is in its way. Depending on which one of the next two obstacles b_1 and b_2 is not present, it makes a horizontal or a vertical move to avoid the present one. It then follows diag_1 (diag_{-1}, respectively) for exactly five moves after which it hits another obstacle, which it bypasses by returning to the main diagonal. Thereafter, it does not hit any other obstacle until it reaches the lower right-hand corner. In total, the number of non-diagonal moves is exactly two (one horizontal and one vertical move as shown in Figure 5.7).

We now construct an instance I that consists of

$$s := \frac{m}{4k + 13}$$

such sub-instances, which we call *widgets* in what follows. All these widgets are placed consecutively on the main diagonal (that is, for every widget, its main diagonal is a part of the main diagonal of I) such that they do not overlap. For now, suppose that no optimal solution can diverge from the main diagonal by more than $2k$ moves (which means it cannot leave the gray field in Figure 5.7, which we call the *active zone*). An optimal solution $\text{OPT}(I)$ for I enters every widget at its upper left-hand

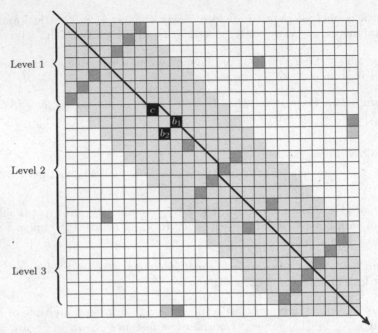

Figure 5.7. The widget of size $(4k + 13) \times (4k + 13)$ used to prove Theorem 5.13 and an optimal solution (in the absence of b_1) making one horizontal and one vertical move.

corner and leaves it at its lower right-hand corner, acting as described above in between. This solution has a delay of exactly s.

We now show that $\text{OPT}(I)$ is unique for every I. To this end, consider a feasible solution $\mathcal{S}$ that is different from $\text{OPT}(I)$; without loss of generality, $\mathcal{S}$ is computed by an ambitious algorithm. $\mathcal{S}$ acts like $\text{OPT}(I)$ in the first i widgets $W_1, W_2, \ldots, W_i$ after which, in W_{i+1}, it hits, without loss of generality, b_1. This means that $\mathcal{S}$ has to make at least four non-diagonal moves in this widget. If $i + 1 = s$, we are done. Thus, assume $i + 1 < s$. Recall that $\mathcal{S}$ is not allowed to leave the active zone. It is easy to see that the following invariant holds for all W_j with $j \geq i + 2$ as long as $\mathcal{S}$ does not enter W_j on the main diagonal diag_0 (recall that, after leaving W_{i+1}, $\mathcal{S}$ made two more non-diagonal moves than $\text{OPT}(I)$ so far).

- If $\mathcal{S}$ both enters and leaves W_j on a diagonal with an even index, it makes at least two non-diagonal moves in W_j.

- Likewise, if $\mathcal{S}$ both enters and leaves W_j on a diagonal with an odd index, it makes at least two non-diagonal moves in W_j.

- If $\mathcal{S}$ enters W_j on a diagonal with an even index and leaves W_j on a diagonal with an odd index, it makes at least three non-diagonal moves in W_j.

174

- If $\mathcal{S}$ enters W_j on a diagonal with an odd index and leaves W_j on a diagonal with an even index, it makes a least one non-diagonal move in W_j. If this happens for the first time, then, after leaving W_j, $\mathcal{S}$ still made more than two non-diagonal moves on average per widget $W_{i+1}, W_{i+2}, \ldots, W_j$. If this happened before, then $\mathcal{S}$ entered a widget $W_{j'}$ with $i+1 < j' < j$ on a diagonal with an even index and left it on a diagonal with an odd index. As seen above, this caused at least three non-diagonal moves. Hence, $\mathcal{S}$ again made more than two non-diagonal moves on average in every widget.

Finally, if $\mathcal{S}$ enters any widget W_j with $j \geq i+2$ on diag_0, it cannot be optimal since it made more non-diagonal moves than $\mathrm{OPT}(I)$ so far.

It remains to choose k such that if any solution leaves the active zone, it cannot be optimal, that is, it has a cost larger than s. Leaving the active zone means making at least either $2k+1$ horizontal or $2k+1$ vertical moves. Hence, we get

$$\frac{m}{4k+13} + 1 \leq 2k+1 \iff m \leq 8k^2 + 26k \,,$$

which is ensured if

$$k \geq \sqrt{\frac{m}{8} + \left(\frac{13}{8}\right)^2} - \frac{13}{8} \,.$$

Since k must be a natural number, we can safely set

$$k := \left\lceil \sqrt{\frac{m}{8} + \left(\frac{13}{8}\right)^2} - \frac{13}{8} \right\rceil \,.$$

Now we are ready to compute s for this value of k. We get

$$\begin{aligned}
s &= \frac{m}{4\left\lceil \sqrt{\frac{m}{8} + \left(\frac{13}{8}\right)^2} - \frac{13}{8} \right\rceil + 13} \\
&\geq \frac{m}{4\left(\sqrt{\frac{m}{8} + \left(\frac{13}{8}\right)^2} - \frac{5}{8}\right) + 13} \\
&\geq \frac{m}{4\sqrt{\frac{m}{8}} + 4\sqrt{\left(\frac{13}{8}\right)^2} - \frac{5}{2} + 13} \\
&\quad \text{(since, for any } a, b \in \mathbb{R}^+, \sqrt{a+b} \leq \sqrt{a} + \sqrt{b}) \\
&= \frac{m}{\sqrt{2m} + \frac{13}{2} - \frac{5}{2} + 13} \\
&= \frac{m}{\sqrt{2m} + 17} \,.
\end{aligned}$$

Finally, we must show that

$$\frac{m}{\sqrt{2m} + 17} \geq (1-\varepsilon)\sqrt{\frac{m}{2}} \,,$$

which follows from $m \geq 145(1-\varepsilon)^2/\varepsilon^2$.

Until now, we did not speak about algorithms with advice. To this end, suppose that we consider the set $\mathcal{I}$ of all possible inputs as constructed in the above way. Since, for every widget, there are two possibilities (either b_1 or b_2 is missing), it follows that $|\mathcal{I}| = 2^s$. Furthermore, for every $I \in \mathcal{I}$, there is one unique optimal solution, and, for every two different $I, I' \in \mathcal{I}$, the corresponding optimal solutions are never the same. Moreover, a fixed deterministic online algorithm cannot be optimal for I and I', because for one of them some obstacle c needs to be evaded by a horizontal move, and for the other one a vertical move is necessary. This has to be done (for the first time) in a time step where I and I' cannot be distinguished.

Therefore, as a direct consequence of the pigeonhole principle, an optimal online algorithm needs to read s bits of advice at least. $\qquad\square$

We conclude that a rather large amount of advice, namely $\Theta(\sqrt{m})$ advice bits, is necessary to perform optimally for JSS.

5.4.2 Small Competitive Ratio

Now we are interested in the question of what is possible with a constant number of advice bits, that is, an advice complexity that does not depend on m. An upper bound can easily be given since we already know what can be done with a constant number of random bits for JSS. To this end, consider the online algorithm ADIAG_d with advice, which is the counterpart of the randomized online algorithm RDIAG_d introduced in Section 5.3, that is, ADIAG_d reads $\lceil \log_2 d \rceil$ advice bits to choose a diagonal from $\mathcal{D}_d$.

Theorem 5.14. ADIAG_d *has a strict competitive ratio with an upper bound that tends to $1 + 1/d$ as m tends to infinity for JSS.*

Proof. This is a direct consequence of Observation 3.2(i) and Theorem 5.10. $\qquad\square$

Intuitively speaking, Theorem 5.14 implies that there is always a cheap solution close to the main diagonal diag_0, which is why ADIAG_d only needs a few bits to achieve a good result. Using this idea, it is possible to give an alternative proof of the upper bound that does not depend on the existence of a randomized online algorithm. We leave this task as an exercise for the reader.

Exercise 5.9. Prove that there is at least one diagonal strategy in $\mathcal{D}_d$ that has a delay of at most

$$\left\lceil \left(\frac{d^2}{4} - d + m \right) \frac{1}{d} \right\rceil .$$

Exercise 5.10. Using your result from Exercise 5.9, prove that, for every odd d, ADIAG_d uses $\lceil \log_2 d \rceil$ advice bits and achieves a competitive ratio of at most

$$1 + \frac{1}{d} + \frac{d}{4(m+1)} - \frac{d+1}{d(m+1)} .$$

Figure 5.6 shows how the competitive ratio of ADIAG_d behaves depending on the number of advice bits (assuming that $\log_2 d$ bits are read instead of $\lceil \log_2 d \rceil$ and that d can also be even). From Theorem 5.5, we know that, for any $\varepsilon > 0$, no deterministic online algorithm without advice is $(4/3 - \varepsilon)$-competitive. On the other hand, the bound on the competitive ratio of ADIAG_d tends to $1 + 1/7$ (recall that d is odd) with only three bits of advice, for m tending to infinity. Hence, we can beat deterministic strategies with only very little additional information.

It is not difficult to see that the analysis of ADIAG_d is almost tight for every d. Since we will prove a more general result soon, we leave to the reader the proof that this particular algorithm cannot obtain a competitive ratio that is better when m tends to infinity.

Exercise 5.11. Show that, for any odd d and any $\varepsilon > 0$, ADIAG_d is not $(1 + 1/d - \varepsilon)$-competitive.

So far, we did not care about the uniformity of ADIAG_d for different values of d. It is, however, not difficult to avoid the non-uniformity, that is, to define a single algorithm ADIAG that reaches a competitive ratio tending to $1 + 1/d$, for any odd d. To do so, the oracle first encodes the number $\lceil \log_2 d \rceil$ on the advice tape; this has to be done in a self-delimiting way. From Section 3.2, we know that at most $2\lceil \log_2(\lceil \log_2 d \rceil) \rceil$ additional advice bits are sufficient to do so.

Corollary 5.1. *There is an online algorithm ADIAG with advice for JSS that has a strict competitive ratio with an upper bound that tends to $1 + 1/d$ as m tends to infinity, and that uses $2\lceil \log_2(\lceil \log_2 d \rceil) \rceil + \lceil \log_2 d \rceil$ advice bits.* □

Up to this point, we have shown that, with a small constant number of advice bits, it is possible to perform very well. Additionally, in Theorem 5.13, we have proven that, for any arbitrarily small $\varepsilon > 0$, $(1 - \varepsilon)\sqrt{m/2}$ advice bits are necessary to create an optimal output.

This poses the question of whether we can be $(1 + o(1))$-competitive by reading a constant number of advice bits, that is, whether it suffices to use a constant number of bits to get arbitrarily close to the optimal solution. In the following, we disprove this.

Theorem 5.15. *Let $\varepsilon > 0$. No online algorithm with advice for JSS that uses b advice bits is*

$$\left(1 + \frac{1}{3 \cdot 2^b} - \varepsilon\right)\text{-competitive.}$$

Proof. In the proof of Theorem 5.4, we have seen that there is an adversary that can make sure that, while some online algorithm ALG' has not yet hit a border, every second move of ALG' is not a diagonal one, which results in a delay of at least $m/3$;

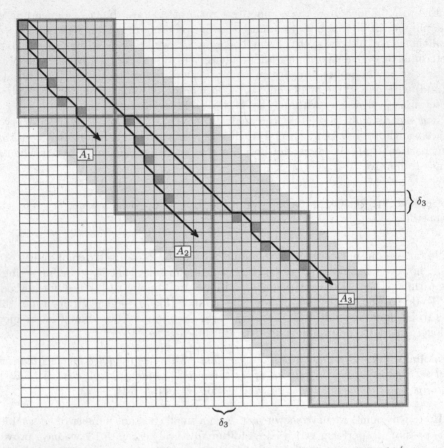

Figure 5.8. A hard instance for ALG as used in the proof of Theorem 5.15, which uses the construction from the proof of Theorem 5.4 (see Figure 5.4) 2^b times.

see Figure 5.4. Furthermore, we know from Theorem 5.3 that, for every instance of JSS, there is an optimal solution with a cost of at most $m + \lceil \sqrt{m} \rceil$.

Let $\varepsilon > 0$, and let ALG be some online algorithm with advice that reads b advice bits. In the following, let m be a multiple of 2^b such that $m > ((6 \cdot 2^b + 2)/(3 \cdot 2^b \cdot \varepsilon))^2$. We construct an instance of size $m \times m$ such that ALG has a delay of at least

$$\frac{m}{3 \cdot 2^b} \, .$$

We impose another virtual grid on the $(m \times m)$-grid, where each virtual cell consists of $m' \times m'$ original cells with

$$m' := \frac{m}{2^b} \, .$$

Let us now consider the 2^b virtual cells on the main diagonal (as shown in Figure 5.8). We call these cells *blocks* and label them $S_1, S_2, \ldots, S_{2^b}$.

Furthermore, similarly to the proof of Theorem 5.13, we call all original cells that have a deviation of at most m' from the main diagonal the *active zone* (marked gray in Figure 5.8). Any algorithm that leaves this zone at any point makes at least m' horizontal (vertical, respectively) moves and thus has a delay of at least $m' > m/(3 \cdot 2^b)$. We may therefore assume that the given algorithm never leaves the active zone.

Following Observation 3.1, we may think of ALG as a set strat(ALG) of 2^b deterministic algorithms $A_1, A_2, \ldots, A_{2^b}$ we have to deal with. Without loss of generality, we may assume that each of these algorithms is ambitious. We assign each deterministic algorithm $A_i \in$ strat(ALG) to exactly one block S_i. Now we construct the input instance sequentially in a way such that all obstacles are located in some block. Note that S_i spans the columns and the rows $m'i + 1, m'i + 2, \ldots, m'i + m'$. We thus construct the input such that both

$$\pi_A(m'i + 1), \pi_A(m'i + 2), \ldots, \pi_A(m'i + m')$$

and

$$\pi_B(m'i + 1), \pi_B(m'i + 2), \ldots, \pi_B(m'i + m')$$

are permutations of the numbers $m'i + 1, m'i + 2, \ldots, m'i + m'$.

Assume that, so far, we have constructed the blocks $S_1, S_2, \ldots, S_{i-1}$. We define the block S_i such that A_i has a delay of at least $m/(3 \cdot 2^b)$, regardless of the content of any block S_j, for $j > i$. Without loss of generality, assume that A_i reaches the right border of S_{i-1} at distance δ_i above the main diagonal; the case that A_i reaches the bottom border of S_{i-1} is analogous. Moreover, we define $\delta_1 := 0$, since the first algorithm A_1 starts at the top-left point of the main diagonal. In the following, we show how to ensure that A_i has a delay that is sufficiently large in block S_i.

Since there are no obstacles outside the blocks and we assume that A_i makes a diagonal move whenever possible, A_i makes δ_i diagonal moves after leaving S_{i-1} until it reaches the top border of S_i, that is, the upper left-hand corner of the cell $(m'i + \delta_i + 1, m'i + 1)$. We assign the first δ_i tasks to the first job sequentially, that is,

$$\pi_A(m'i + j) := m'i + j \,,$$

for all j with $1 \leq j \leq \delta_i$.

After A_i reaches the upper left-hand corner of the cell $(m'i + x, m'i + y)$, the first $m'i + x$ tasks of the first job and the first $m'i + y$ tasks of the second job must be assigned. Similarly to the proof of Theorem 5.4, we maintain the invariant that, in such a situation, only the numbers (that is, machines) up to $m'i + \max\{x, y\}$ are used for both jobs.

When A_i reaches S_i, we employ the strategy of the proof of Theorem 5.4 to ensure that every second move of A_i is non-diagonal. At first, we assign

$$\pi_A(m'i + \delta_i + 1) = \pi_B(m'i + 1) := m'i + \delta_i + 1 \,,$$

thus creating an obstacle; therefore, the next move of A_i will be a non-diagonal one. Whenever A_i makes a horizontal (vertical, respectively) move, we assign the smallest possible number as the next task of the first (second, respectively) job. When A_i makes a diagonal move in cell $(m'i + x, m'i + y)$, thus reaching the upper left-hand corner of cell $(m'i + x + 1, m'i + y + 1)$, we assign

$$\pi_A(m'i + x + 1) = \pi_B(m'i + y + 1) := m'i + \max\{x, y\} + 1 .$$

Hence, we create an obstacle and force A_i to make another non-diagonal move. We use this strategy until A_i reaches the right or bottom border of S_i. Assume that A_i makes h_i horizontal moves, v_i vertical moves, and d_i diagonal moves in this part of the computation (that is, in block S_i). Since every diagonal move is followed by a non-diagonal one and the first move is non-diagonal, we have $h_i + v_i \geq d_i$. We now give a lower bound on delay$(A_i(I))$ on the constructed instance. As already stated, even though we have not yet constructed S_j, for $j > i$, we can proceed, because our bound will not depend on them. Recall that the total number of horizontal and vertical moves of A_i over the whole input must be equal, and delay$(A_i(I))$ is defined as exactly this number; see Observation 5.1(iv). We distinguish two cases depending on the relation between h_i and v_i.

Case 1. Suppose that $h_i \geq v_i$. In this case, A_i reaches the right border of S_i (possibly at the lower right-hand corner of S_i). Since A_i entered S_i in column $m'i + \delta_i + 1$, there were $m' - \delta_i$ non-vertical moves, hence

$$m' - \delta_i = h_i + d_i \leq 2h_i + v_i \leq 3h_i .$$

Therefore, $h_i \geq (m' - \delta_i)/3$. Since A_i leaves S_{i-1} at distance δ_i above the main diagonal, it made at least δ_i horizontal moves before it entered S_i. Thus, we can bound the total number of horizontal moves of A_i, which is equal to delay$(A_i(I))$, by

$$\delta_i + h_i \geq \frac{m' + 2\delta_i}{3} \geq \frac{m'}{3} .$$

Case 2. Suppose that $h_i < v_i$. Assume that A_i leaves S_i at distance δ'_i above the bottom border of S_i; if A_i reaches the bottom border (and again possibly the lower right-hand corner of S_i), $\delta'_i = 0$. Since A_i made $m' - \delta'_i$ non-horizontal moves in S_i, we have

$$m' - \delta'_i = v_i + d_i \leq 2v_i + h_i \leq 3v_i ,$$

and thus $v_i \geq (m' - \delta'_i)/3$. After leaving S_i, A_i must make at least δ'_i vertical moves to end up at the main diagonal. Hence, the total number of vertical moves of A_i, which is equal to delay$(A_i(I))$, can be bounded by

$$\delta'_i + v_i \geq \frac{m' + 2\delta'_i}{3} \geq \frac{m'}{3} .$$

In both cases, A_i has a delay of at least $m'/3$. Therefore, after constructing all blocks S_i in the described way, we obtain an instance for which every $A_j \in \text{strat}(\text{ALG})$ has a cost of at least $m + m/(3 \cdot 2^b)$ as we claimed.

Hence, the makespan of this algorithm is at least

$$m\left(1 + \frac{1}{3 \cdot 2^b}\right).$$

Since any optimal solution has a cost of at most $m + \lceil \sqrt{m} \rceil$, it remains to show that

$$\frac{m\left(1 + \frac{1}{3 \cdot 2^b}\right)}{m + \lceil \sqrt{m} \rceil} > 1 + \frac{1}{3 \cdot 2^b} - \varepsilon,$$

which holds if

$$1 + \frac{1}{3 \cdot 2^b} > \left(1 + \frac{1}{3 \cdot 2^b} - \varepsilon\right)\left(1 + \frac{\sqrt{m} + 1}{m}\right),$$

which is equivalent to

$$\frac{m}{\sqrt{m} + 1} > \frac{1}{\varepsilon} + \frac{1}{3 \cdot 2^b \cdot \varepsilon} - 1.$$

This is implied by

$$\frac{m}{2\sqrt{m}} > \frac{3 \cdot 2^b + 1}{3 \cdot 2^b \cdot \varepsilon},$$

which follows from $m > ((6 \cdot 2^b + 2)/(3 \cdot 2^b \cdot \varepsilon))^2$. $\qquad\qquad \square$

Using this result, an easy calculation shows that the bound of Theorem 5.14 (and Exercise 5.10) is tight up to a multiplicative constant of roughly

$$\frac{3 \cdot 2^b + 3}{3 \cdot 2^b + 1},$$

which tends to 1 for increasing b.

5.5 Historical and Bibliographical Notes

Scheduling problems form a huge and important class of problems in computer science and operations research, and we only dealt with a very special one in this chapter. There is a lot of literature on scheduling, for instance, the textbooks of Brucker [40], Pinedo [124], and Conway et al. [48]. The textbook of Hromkovič [81] also gives a more detailed introduction to the variant that we studied here.

While the general offline job shop scheduling problem is well known to be $\mathcal{NP}$-hard (shown by Garey et al. [66]), it is obvious that the considered special case is efficiently solvable in an offline scenario; indeed, we simply need to calculate a shortest path on a sparse, directed, acyclic graph, which can be done in linear time [49]. The graphical representation that we used to visualize instances of JSS is due to Akers [2], and it was used since in many other publications [30, 39, 76, 81, 83, 137].

The results on deterministic online algorithms and the randomized online algorithm RDIAG were introduced by Hromkovič et al. [83] together with an analysis of the more general problem where the number of jobs is arbitrary. This generalization leads to graphical representations of the instances that correspond to higher-dimensional grids. Akveld and Bernhard [3] improved the randomized online algorithm from Hromkovič et al. [83] for the case of three jobs; in this paper, the authors also answer Exercise 5.7. Mömke [119] considered the case where the tasks may each have lengths up to k units, where $k \in \mathbb{N}^+$. The observation that RDIAG also performs well with a probability that tends to 1 was first made by Komm [97]. Komm et al. [100] later gave a similar result for an arbitrary number of jobs.

JSS was among the very first problems studied in the model of advice complexity. Böckenhauer et al. [30] proved the upper bound on optimality from Theorem 5.11 together with an asymptotically matching lower bound; more details are found in the technical report [31]. Komm [97] improved this lower bound by a factor of roughly $\sqrt{2}$ (see Theorem 5.13), and also showed the upper bound of Theorem 5.12. Komm and Královič [101, 102] studied the connection between barely random algorithms and online algorithms with small advice for both paging (see Section 2.6) and JSS. In this paper, they proved Exercises 5.9 and 5.10, and they established the lower bounds from Theorem 5.15 and Exercise 5.11. Wehner [141] showed that the lower bound of Theorem 5.13 can also be adapted to JSS with three jobs. Theorem 5.2 was proven by Böckenhauer et al. [30], and Theorem 5.12 was proven by Komm [97]. Wehner [142] studied the advice complexity of job shop scheduling with two jobs against a more powerful adversary that is allowed to randomly choose between different instances. Besides that, Wehner [143] considered an alternative cost measure, namely the delay of a given solution instead of the makespan.

There has also been research on online algorithms with advice for online makespan scheduling. Dohrau [55] focused on what can be done for makespan scheduling where only a sublinear number of advice bits are allowed. He showed that, surprisingly, even a constant number of advice bits is sufficient to obtain a competitive ratio that is arbitrarily close to 1. Renault et al. [126] considered scheduling problems with advice where the objective is to minimize the makespan, to maximize the load of the machine with smallest load (machine cover), or to minimize the ℓ_p-norm of the loads; they gave a general framework that allows us to obtain online algorithms with advice that use a linear number of advice bits and achieve a competitive ratio that is also arbitrarily close to 1. Albers and Hellwig [7] followed a similar approach by allowing an online algorithm to produce parallel schedules. The goal is that, for any instance, at least one of these schedules performs well while minimizing their total number; this can be seen as minimizing $|\mathrm{strat}(\mathrm{ALG}, n)|$ for a given online algorithm ALG with advice instead of its advice complexity, that is, $\log_2(|\mathrm{strat}(\mathrm{ALG}, n)|)$.

The Knapsack Problem

6

This chapter revisits a maximization problem that we already briefly studied in Chapter 1 in the context of approximation algorithms. We are given a knapsack of fixed capacity and we want to pack a number of objects into it; each object has both a weight and a value (we start by assuming that both are the same, and speak of the *simple knapsack problem* as we did before). The main difference is that this time the objects are not known in advance, but arrive gradually in consecutive time steps. In every such step, an online algorithm gets offered an object, and it must decide whether to pack it into the knapsack; this decision is final.

We study this problem thoroughly, that is, we analyze what can and cannot be done deterministically, randomized, or with advice. Our aim is to get a full picture. An intriguing property of the simple knapsack problem is its threshold behavior with respect to both advice and randomization. We start with an easy proof that shows that any deterministic online algorithm has an arbitrarily bad competitive ratio. Then we show that a linear number of advice bits is both sufficient and necessary to obtain an optimal result. Next, using arguments that basically make use of cleverly applying a greedy strategy, we prove that one advice bit allows for a 2-competitive online algorithm. After that, we show that any increase does not help until a number of advice bits is supplied that grows logarithmically with the input length. With this many advice bits, we can even design an online algorithm that is $(1 + \varepsilon)$-competitive, for any $\varepsilon > 0$. However, to be "truly optimal" and not just "almost optimal," we need a further increase of the number of advice bits; specifically, as mentioned above, we need a number that is linear in the input length. It turns out that, for the simple knapsack problem, one single random bit is in expectation as powerful as one advice bit. In other words, there is a randomized online algorithm (a barely random algorithm) that uses only one random bit and achieves an expected competitive ratio of 2. Surprisingly, this is where the power of randomness ends for this problem. We prove that no number of random bits allows for a better algorithm; thus, a logarithmic, linear, or even exponential number of random bits are as powerful as a

© Springer International Publishing Switzerland 2016
D. Komm, *An Introduction to Online Computation*,
Texts in Theoretical Computer Science. An EATCS Series,
DOI 10.1007/978-3-319-42749-2_6

single one. Next, we turn to resource augmentation, which means that we allow the online algorithm to use a knapsack that is a little larger than the one the optimal solution uses.

Last, we study the general online knapsack problem, where the weights and values of the offered objects are different values in general. We prove that if the values of the objects are not too large, there is an online algorithm with logarithmic advice that also computes a solution that is almost optimal; however, the advice complexity here is larger than for the simple variant of the problem. Moreover, we use Yao's principle (see Theorem 2.6 and the preceding discussion) to show that there is no competitive randomized online algorithm at all for the general problem.

6.1 Introduction

As in Definition 1.3, we denote the capacity of the knapsack by a natural number B. In our online setting, this parameter is known to any online algorithm in advance. Note that, for any given B, we can scale down all weights of given objects by dividing them by B, and set $B := 1$. To make things easier, we will thus assume that we deal with a class of online knapsack problems where the capacity is 1 without any loss of generality. In contrast to Definition 1.3, the weights and values of the objects are thus real numbers. We now define the general knapsack problem where the weights and values of objects may be different. However, we start by studying the simple version of the problem.

Definition 6.1 (Online Knapsack Problem). The *online knapsack problem* is an online maximization problem. An instance $I = ((w_1, v_1), (w_2, v_2), \ldots, (w_n, v_n))$ consists of a sequence of n pairs, where we call $w_i \leq 1$ the *weight* and v_i the *value* of the ith object, where $1 \leq i \leq n$. A feasible solution is a set of indices $O \subseteq \{1, 2, \ldots, n\}$ such that

$$\sum_{i \in O} w_i \leq 1 .$$

The objective is to choose O such that

$$\sum_{i \in O} v_i$$

is maximized. The objects are offered to an online algorithm one after another, one in every time step. In the corresponding time step, the algorithm must decide whether to pack the object into the knapsack or not. This decision cannot be changed afterwards.

Throughout this chapter, we simply speak of the "(simple) knapsack problem" instead of the "online (simple) knapsack problem." For the simple version of the

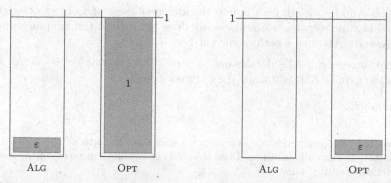

(a) *Case 1.* Object of weight 1 is offered   (b) *Case 2.* No further object is offered

Figure 6.1. An adversary for the simple knapsack problem.

problem, we see that the gain of any solution is bounded from above by the knapsack capacity 1. This implies that any online algorithm (even one that never chooses to pack any object into the knapsack) is 1-competitive since we can always choose the additive constant from Definition 1.6 to be 1. We therefore only speak about the strict competitive ratio when dealing with the simple knapsack problem. Still the situation is somewhat different to that of the job shop scheduling problem, which we studied in Chapter 5; for the simple knapsack problem, no online algorithm knows an upper bound on the length of the input in advance.

6.2 Deterministic Algorithms

We now investigate the strict competitive ratio of deterministic online algorithms for the simple knapsack problem. First, we observe that the greedy algorithm we studied in Chapter 1 for the offline version first sorted the objects. Obviously, we cannot follow such a strategy in the online version since we never know which objects are yet to be offered, and we need to make a definite decision in every time step. This is bad news; and the following theorem formalizes this dilemma by showing that every online algorithm has a strict competitive ratio that is arbitrarily large.

Theorem 6.1. *Let $\varepsilon > 0$. No deterministic online algorithm for the simple knapsack problem is better than strictly $1/\varepsilon$-competitive.*

Proof. Let ALG be any deterministic online algorithm for the simple knapsack problem. We construct an adversary that first offers an object w with a weight of ε. We can make a simple case distinction depending on whether ALG decides to pack w into the knapsack or not; both cases are shown in Figure 6.1.

Case 1. If ALG decides to pack w into the knapsack, a second object of weight 1 is offered in time step T_2, which obviously does not fit into the knapsack anymore. In this case, ALG has a performance of $1/\varepsilon$.

Case 2. Conversely, if ALG decides not to pack w, no other object is offered. In this case, the gain of ALG is 0 while the optimal gain is ε.

The claim follows. □

Exercise 6.1. Suppose we change Definition 6.1 such that the capacity B is some arbitrary positive integer known in advance. Does this change anything in terms of the reachable non-strict competitive ratio?

Exercise 6.2. Suppose B becomes a part of the input and is given as the first request, as it is in Definition 1.3. Does this change anything compared to Exercise 6.1?

Exercise 6.3.⋆ Again, suppose B becomes a part of the input as in Definition 1.3. Prove that, defined this way, the simple knapsack problem becomes a so-called *scalable problem*. This means that if there is some c-competitive online algorithm with some additive constant α, then there also is a c-competitive online algorithm where the additive constant is arbitrarily small (but positive).

Exercise 6.4. Suppose we consider an adversary that is not allowed to end the input after at most two requests, but that is required to give an arbitrarily long sequence of objects, where the weight of every object must be positive. More precisely, it must construct an input of length n, for any $n \in \mathbb{N}^+$. What is the best lower bound you can prove now?

Exercise 6.5. Consider the following variant of the problem, which we call the *simple removable knapsack problem*. Here, an online algorithm is allowed to remove objects it already packed into the knapsack. However, once an object is removed, it cannot be packed again. We see that there is a simple online algorithm for this problem that is optimal on the instances from the proof of Theorem 6.1. Show that this does not hold in general. More precisely, prove that any online algorithm for the simple removable knapsack problem has a strict competitive ratio of at least $3/2$.

We have just seen that every deterministic online algorithm performs very poorly and this of course includes the greedy algorithm KNGREEDY. However, this strategy is not that bad if we restrict ourselves to a specific subclass of instances.

Theorem 6.2. *For every instance of the simple knapsack problem for which all objects have a weight of at most β, KNGREEDY obtains a gain of at least $1 - \beta$ or it is optimal.*

Proof. We distinguish two cases depending on the total weight of all objects in the given instance.

Case 1. If the total weight is at most 1, KNGREEDY is optimal as it packs every object into the knapsack.

Case 2. If the total weight is larger, the space that is unused in KNGREEDY's solution must be smaller than β. Otherwise, there would be space for another object. Thus, the knapsack is filled up to a fraction that is larger than $1 - \beta$.

The claim follows. □

For another subclass, KNGREEDY is even optimal.

Theorem 6.3. *For every instance of the simple knapsack problem for which an optimal solution has a gain of at most $1/2$, KNGREEDY is optimal.*

Proof. Let I be such an instance. If $\text{gain}(\text{OPT}(I)) \leq 1/2$, we clearly also have $\text{gain}(\text{KNGREEDY}(I)) \leq 1/2$. Now, if $\text{gain}(\text{KNGREEDY}(I)) < \text{gain}(\text{OPT}(I))$, this must be due to the fact that KNGREEDY did not pack an object into the knapsack that has a weight larger than $1/2$. But this is a direct contradiction as it implies the existence of an optimal solution with a gain that is larger than $1/2$. □

In the following section, we will design online algorithms with advice for the simple knapsack problem, and (to this end) we will make use of Theorems 6.2 and 6.3.

6.3 Advice Complexity

Now that we have seen that deterministic online algorithms for the simple knapsack problem perform very badly, we want to investigate what can be done with advice.

6.3.1 Optimality

We start with the number of advice bits that are sufficient and necessary to compute an optimal solution. The following upper bound is easy to prove.

Theorem 6.4. *There is an optimal online algorithm with advice for the simple knapsack problem that uses n advice bits.*

Proof. For each of the n objects the algorithm gets offered, it reads a bit from the advice tape that tells it whether the current object is part of an arbitrary fixed optimal solution. As a consequence, the algorithm computes this solution. □

Things get more interesting if we complement this result with the following theorem, which shows that the upper bound is essentially tight. The central idea of the following proof is that no power of 2 is the sum of any other distinct powers of 2.

Theorem 6.5. *Every optimal online algorithm with advice for the simple knapsack problem has to use at least $n - 1$ advice bits.*

Proof. For every $n \geq 2$, we construct a set $\mathcal{I}^{(n)}$ of instances of the simple knapsack problem as follows. Consider an instance that consists of the requests

$$\frac{1}{2}, \frac{1}{4}, \ldots, \frac{1}{2^{n-1}}, w_s,$$

where w_s is defined as

$$w_s := 1 - \sum_{i=1}^{n-1} s_i 2^{-i},$$

for a binary string $s = s_1 s_2 \ldots s_{n-1}$; see Example 6.1. Now consider the first $n - 1$ objects, which are the same for any fixed n. Two different subsets of these objects obviously lead to two different partial weights. Thus, for every value of w_s (equivalently, s), there is a unique optimal solution. To be able to compute this solution, an online algorithm must accept the correct objects in the first $n - 1$ time steps. Only then packing the object w_s into the knapsack fills it up to 1.

If some online algorithm uses fewer than $n - 1$ advice bits, it can only distinguish between fewer than 2^{n-1} different instances. Thus, following the pigeonhole principle, it behaves identically on two of them and cannot be optimal for both since these two instances have different optimal solutions. □

Example 6.1. For an input length $n = 8$ and a binary string $s = 1101101$, we get an instance I that consists of the requests

$$\frac{1}{2}, \frac{1}{4}, \frac{1}{8}, \frac{1}{16}, \frac{1}{32}, \frac{1}{64}, \frac{1}{128}, \text{ and } w_s = 1 - \left(\frac{1}{2} + \frac{1}{4} + \frac{1}{16} + \frac{1}{32} + \frac{1}{128} \right) = \frac{109}{128},$$

in this order. I has a unique optimal solution

$$\frac{1}{2}, \frac{1}{4}, \frac{1}{16}, \frac{1}{32}, \frac{1}{128}, w_s$$

of gain 1. ◇

Exercise 6.6. Give an alternative proof of Theorem 6.5 using partition trees (see Definition 3.3).

6.3.2 Small Advice

It follows that we need a lot of additional information to be optimal for the simple knapsack problem. On the other hand, as we have seen before, we are arbitrarily bad without any advice. What happens between these two extrema? Surprisingly, even one bit of information enables us to design a 2-competitive online algorithm. Consider the online algorithm KNONE with advice that reads one advice bit at the beginning; depending on its value the algorithm either follows a greedy strategy or waits for an object with a weight of more than $1/2$.

Theorem 6.6. KNONE *is strictly 2-competitive for the simple knapsack problem.*

Proof. Again, we make an easy case distinction; this time depending on whether there is an object with a weight of more than $1/2$ in the input.

Case 1. If such an object exists, the oracle tells KNONE by setting the first bit on the advice tape to 1. Then the first object with a weight of more than $1/2$ gets packed into the knapsack. Since any optimal algorithm has a gain of at most 1, KNONE's gain is at least half as good as the optimal one.

Case 2. If there is no such object in the input, the first bit on the advice tape is set to zero. In this case, KNONE follows a greedy strategy, and the claim follows immediately from Theorem 6.2.

In both cases, the optimal gain is at most twice as large as that of KNONE. $\qquad\square$

6.3.3 Logarithmic Advice

So one bit is all that is missing to get from an arbitrarily bad solution to a 2-competitive one. The next question we should try to answer is how much it helps to slightly increase the number of advice bits. Are two bits more powerful than one? How about three, 10, or 100? Almost as surprising as the preceding result is the following theorem, which basically states that it does not help at all to further increase the number of advice bits until a logarithmic number is reached.

Theorem 6.7. *Let $\varepsilon > 0$. No online algorithm with advice for the simple knapsack problem that uses fewer than $\log_2(n-1)$ advice bits is better than strictly $(2-\varepsilon)$-competitive.*

Proof. In what follows, let

$$\delta := \frac{\varepsilon}{4-2\varepsilon} \, ,$$

and let ALG be some online algorithm with advice for the simple knapsack problem that reads $b(n) < \log_2(n-1)$ advice bits for inputs of length n. We construct a set $\mathcal{I}^{(n)}$ that contains instances I_j with $1 \le j \le n-1$ that consist of the requests

$$\frac{1}{2}+\delta^2, \frac{1}{2}+\delta^3, \ldots, \frac{1}{2}+\delta^{j+1}, \frac{1}{2}-\delta^{j+1}, \underbrace{\frac{1}{2}+\delta, \ldots, \frac{1}{2}+\delta}_{n-j-1 \text{ times}} \, .$$

We immediately observe that

$$|\mathcal{I}^{(n)}| = n-1 = 2^{\log_2(n-1)} > 2^{b(n)} \, ,$$

which means that in $\mathcal{I}^{(n)}$ there are more instances than there are different advice strings for ALG. Now we can again use the pigeonhole principle and argue that there are two different instances for which ALG gets the same advice. To be optimal for an input I_j, ALG must pack exactly the jth and the $(j+1)$th object into the knapsack and this solution is unique. This is easy to see by the following case distinction.

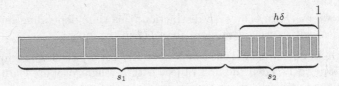

Figure 6.2. The knapsack as it is packed by an optimal solution using heavy and light objects.

Case 1. If ALG packs the ith object, where $i < j$, then no other object can be packed into the knapsack afterwards; in particular, there is no space left in the knapsack for the $(j+1)$th object since

$$\frac{1}{2} + \delta^{i+1} + \frac{1}{2} - \delta^{j+1} > 1 .$$

Case 2. Conversely, if ALG packs the ith object, where $i > j$, then there is also no space for any of the subsequent objects, which all have a weight of $1/2 + \delta$.

It follows that if ALG gets the same advice for two different instances from $\mathcal{I}^{(n)}$, its gain on one of them is at most $1/2 + \delta$; therefore, the achievable strict competitive ratio is not better than

$$\frac{1}{\frac{1}{2} + \delta} = 2 - \varepsilon$$

as we claimed. □

Next, we prove an upper bound that asymptotically matches the preceding one with respect to the number of advice bits used. Even better, we show that with a number of advice bits that is logarithmic in the input length, we can get arbitrarily close to an optimal solution; this is rather surprising as in Theorem 6.5 we have already seen that we need a linear number of advice bits to be "really optimal" and not just "almost optimal." To prove the following theorem, we make use of self-delimiting strings, which we discussed in Chapter 3.

Theorem 6.8. *Let $\varepsilon > 0$. There is a strictly $(1 + \varepsilon)$-competitive online algorithm* KNLOG *with advice for the simple knapsack problem that uses $\mathcal{O}(\log n)$ advice bits.*

Proof. In the following, let

$$\delta := \frac{\varepsilon}{3 + 3\varepsilon} ,$$

and note that KNLOG can compute δ without any advice since it knows ε. Furthermore, let I be an arbitrary instance of the simple knapsack problem.

We make a case distinction depending on the objects that an arbitrary but fixed optimal solution OPT(I) for I packs into the knapsack.

Case 1. First, we assume that there is no object with a weight larger than δ in I; obviously, this can be communicated with one bit of advice at the beginning. In this case, KNLOG simply implements a greedy strategy; following Theorem 6.2, the algorithm achieves a strict competitive ratio of at most

$$\frac{1}{1-\delta} = 1 + \frac{\delta}{1-\delta} = 1 + \frac{\varepsilon}{3+2\varepsilon} \le 1 + \varepsilon$$

in this case and we are done.

Case 2. Now we suppose that there is at least one object with a weight larger than δ in I. As a consequence, OPT(I) consists of two disjoint sets of objects, say S_1 and S_2 (S_1 or S_2 may be empty). S_1 contains all objects with a weight of more than δ (we call these objects "heavy"), and S_2 contains objects that have a weight of at most δ (we call those objects "light"). Let $|S_1| = k$, and let s_1 denote the sum of all weights of objects in S_1; s_2 is defined analogously. The indices of the heavy objects (with respect to I) are written on the advice tape such that KNLOG packs all objects from S_1 into the knapsack when they are offered.

Next, we need to take care of the light objects, but we cannot spend as much advice as would be necessary to encode their positions. Instead, the idea is to encode a lower bound on the part of the knapsack that is filled in OPT(I) with light objects, and to make KNLOG pack light objects using the greedy strategy as long as their total weight is smaller than this bound. More precisely, the oracle writes a number h on the advice tape such that

$$h\delta \le s_2 < (h+1)\delta\,. \tag{6.1}$$

Obviously, $h \le 1/\delta$ since $s_2 \le 1$. KNLOG is then able to compute $h\delta$ as the abovementioned lower bound for the part of the knapsack that is filled with light objects in OPT(I). Therefore, every light object that is offered to the algorithm is packed into the knapsack as long as the total weight of all light objects that are already packed is at most $h\delta$; see Figure 6.2.

Now we make a further case distinction that again depends on OPT(I).

Case 2.1. If OPT does not pack any light objects into the knapsack, then KNLOG is clearly optimal, because it packs all heavy objects.

Case 2.2. Suppose that OPT packs at least one light object into the knapsack and has a gain smaller than $1 - \delta$. In this case, it follows that OPT packs all light objects into the knapsack. The oracle then simply writes $h = \lceil 1/\delta \rceil$ on the advice tape and KNLOG is again optimal.

Case 2.3. So suppose that OPT packs at least one light object and its solution has a gain of at least $1 - \delta$. Now we bound what we lose (compared to OPT(I)) due to the fact that KNLOG does not necessarily pack "the best selection" of light objects.

When restricting ourselves to light objects, we can think of KNLOG as a greedy algorithm that works on an instance $I_{h\delta}$ for a knapsack of capacity $h\delta$, where every object has a weight of at most δ. Again, we can make use of Theorem 6.2, which states that KNLOG has a gain of at least $h\delta - \delta$ on $I_{h\delta}$, or is even optimal. In the former case, (6.1) implies that the gain of KNLOG on $I_{h\delta}$ is at least $s_2 - 2\delta$.

To conclude, KNLOG has a gain of at least $s_1 + s_2 - 2\delta$ and OPT's gain is exactly $s_1 + s_2$, and is furthermore bounded by $1 - \delta \leq \text{gain}(\text{OPT}(I)) \leq 1$. For the strict competitive ratio of KNLOG we therefore get

$$\frac{s_1 + s_2}{s_1 + s_2 - 2\delta} \leq \frac{1}{1 - 3\delta} = 1 + \frac{3\delta}{1 - 3\delta} = 1 + \varepsilon$$

in this case.

To finish the proof, we bound the number of advice bits from above.

- First, KNLOG needs to read one bit that indicates whether I contains at least one heavy object.

- As already mentioned, $h \leq 1/\delta$ since $s_2 \leq 1$. Thus, h is a natural number between 0 and $\lceil 1/\delta \rceil$, which can be encoded with $\lceil \log_2(\lceil 1/\delta \rceil + 1) \rceil$ bits.

- Furthermore, we note that no solution can pack more than $1/\delta$ heavy objects since the total weight of these objects would be larger than 1. Thus, k is also a natural number between 0 and $\lceil 1/\delta \rceil$.

- Note that the encoding of k and h does not need to be self-delimiting since KNLOG knows δ and can therefore compute upper bounds on these values on its own. The actual encodings of these two numbers are padded with leading zeros by the oracle to obtain the correct length.

- The index of each of the k heavy objects is encoded using $\lceil \log_2 n \rceil$ bits.

- To be able to decode the advice, KNLOG has to know the number $\lceil \log_2 n \rceil$, which needs to be encoded in a self-delimiting form; according to the observations made in Section 3.2, this can be achieved using $2\lceil \log_2(\lceil \log_2 n \rceil) \rceil$ bits.

Altogether, we can bound the number of advice bits from above by

$$1 + 2 \cdot \left\lceil \log_2\left(\left\lceil \frac{1}{\delta} \right\rceil + 1\right) \right\rceil + k \cdot \lceil \log_2 n \rceil + 2 \cdot \lceil \log_2(\lceil \log_2 n \rceil) \rceil$$

$$\leq 1 + 2 \cdot \left\lceil \log_2\left(\left\lceil \frac{3\varepsilon + 3}{\varepsilon} \right\rceil + 1\right) \right\rceil + \left\lceil \frac{3\varepsilon + 3}{\varepsilon} \right\rceil \cdot \lceil \log_2 n \rceil + 2 \cdot \lceil \log_2(\lceil \log_2 n \rceil) \rceil ,$$

which is in $\mathcal{O}(\log n)$ since ε is constant. $\qquad\square$

Let us summarize what we have learned up to this point. Without advice, every online algorithm for the (simple) knapsack problem is arbitrarily bad. However, already one advice bit allows for a strict competitive ratio of 2. Every further advice bit, on the other hand, does not help to improve the strict competitive ratio until a

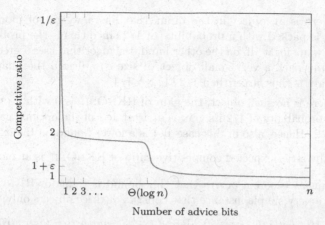

Figure 6.3. The schematic behavior of the advice complexity of the simple knapsack problem.

logarithmic number (with respect to the input length) is reached. If this threshold is crossed (asymptotically), we can design an online algorithm that is almost optimal. Then again, to be truly optimal and not just almost optimal, we need to increase the number of advice bits exponentially; a schematic view of this behavior is shown in Figure 6.3.

6.4 Randomized Algorithms

In this section, we investigate how powerful randomization is for the simple knapsack problem. Doing this, we will observe some more surprising characteristics of this knapsack problem; in particular, when comparing advice bits and random bits.

6.4.1 A Barely Random Algorithm

So far, we know that one advice bit is extremely powerful. Now we want to ask how much one random bit may help us. As we have already discussed in Section 2.6, we call a randomized online algorithm that uses a constant number of random bits a *barely random algorithm*. First, consider RKNONE′, which works analogously to the previously introduced online algorithm KNONE with advice, but guesses the bit that states whether to wait for an object with a weight of more than $1/2$ instead of having an oracle tell it.

Theorem 6.9. RKNONE′ *is strictly 4-competitive in expectation for the simple knapsack problem.*

Proof. We make a similar case distinction to the proof of Theorem 6.6.

193

Case 1. If there is an object in the input that has a weight of more than $1/2$, this object is packed with a probability of $1/2$ since this is the probability that RKnOne′ waits for it. If, on the other hand, the algorithm uses a greedy strategy, it might only pack a very small object of size $\varepsilon > 0$ into the knapsack. The expected gain is thus larger than $1/2 \cdot 1/2 = 1/4$.

Case 2. If there is no such object, the gain of RKnOne′ is 0 with a probability of $1/2$. With probability of $1/2$ its gain is at least $1/2$ of the optimal gain following Theorem 6.2. Hence, also in this case $1/4$ is a lower bound on the expected gain.

As a result, the strict expected competitive ratio of RKnOne′ is at most 4.   □

The subsequent theorem proves that this bound is tight for RKnOne′; in the proof we use a very simple instance that consists of three objects only.

Theorem 6.10. *Let $1/6 > \varepsilon > 0$. RKnOne′ is not better than strictly $(4 - \varepsilon)$-competitive in expectation for the simple knapsack problem.*

Proof. In what follows, let

$$\delta := \frac{\varepsilon}{4(6 - \varepsilon)} .$$

Consider the instance of the simple knapsack problem that consists of three objects of weights

$$\frac{1}{2} - \delta, \, 3\delta, \, \frac{1}{2} - \delta .$$

Clearly, a unique optimal solution is to pack the first and the third object into the knapsack; the gain is $1 - 2\delta$. Again, we distinguish two cases depending on which strategy RKnOne′ picks.

Case 1. A greedy strategy accepts the first two objects and, as a consequence, has a gain of $1/2 + 2\delta$.

Case 2. Since no object has a weight of more than $1/2$, the strategy to wait for an object of this weight leads to a gain of 0.

It follows that the strict expected competitive ratio of RKnOne′ is not better than

$$\frac{1 - 2\delta}{\frac{1}{2}\left(\frac{1}{2} + 2\delta\right) + \frac{1}{2} \cdot 0} = 4 \cdot \frac{1 - 2\delta}{1 + 4\delta} = 4 - \varepsilon .$$

□

Intuitively, this is what we expected. One advice bit that always tells us the best strategy is twice as powerful as a random bit that only allows for such a strategy with a probability of $1/2$; the next result is thus quite surprising. In the following, consider the randomized online algorithm RKnOne that chooses uniformly at random between the strategies from

$$\mathrm{strat}(\mathrm{RKnOne}) = \{ Greedy_1, \, Greedy_2 \} .$$

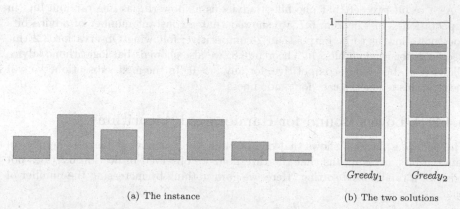

(a) The instance   (b) The two solutions

Figure 6.4. The two deterministic online algorithms $Greedy_1$ and $Greedy_2$.

Here, $Greedy_1$ is the straightforward greedy strategy. Conversely, $Greedy_2$ starts by simulating $Greedy_1$ without accepting any objects; but as soon as the algorithm realizes that the object offered in the current time step does not fit into the knapsack as $Greedy_1$ packed it, it starts accepting objects and again acts greedily from now on; see Figure 6.4.

Theorem 6.11. RKnOne *is strictly 2-competitive in expectation for the simple knapsack problem.*

Proof. We distinguish two cases depending on the total weight of the objects in the given input I.

Case 1. If the total weight of all objects that are offered is at most 1, $Greedy_1$ is clearly optimal (since it packs all objects), while $Greedy_2$ has a gain of 0. The expected gain of RKnOne is therefore $1/2 \cdot \mathrm{gain}(\mathrm{Opt}(I))$.

Case 2. If, on the other hand, the total weight is larger than 1, then the sum of the gains of both algorithms must also be larger than 1; therefore, the expected gain of RKnOne is

$$\frac{1}{2}\,\mathrm{gain}(Greedy_1(I)) + \frac{1}{2}\,\mathrm{gain}(Greedy_2(I))$$
$$= \frac{1}{2}\left(\mathrm{gain}(Greedy_1(I)) + \mathrm{gain}(Greedy_2(I))\right)$$
$$\geq \frac{1}{2}\,.$$

Since the gain of an optimal solution cannot be larger than 1, the expected gain of RKnOne is at least $1/2 \cdot \mathrm{gain}(\mathrm{Opt}(I))$.

Consequently, the strict expected competitive ratio of RKnOne is at most 2. □

As a result, we get that one bit of advice is as powerful as one random bit (in expectation). In Theorem 6.7, we showed that a constant number of advice bits does not allow us to be better than 2-competitive; following Observation 3.2 this also holds for random bits. In Theorem 6.8, we also showed that logarithmic advice allows us to be $(1 + \varepsilon)$-competitive, for any $\varepsilon > 0$. In the next subsection, we will see that this is not the case for randomness.

6.4.2 A Lower Bound for Randomized Algorithms

The following theorem shows that one random bit is as powerful as any number of random bits. This means that the threshold we observed in Section 6.3 does not exist for a randomized setting. Here, we gain nothing by increasing the number of bits.

Theorem 6.12. *Let $\varepsilon > 0$. No randomized online algorithm for the simple knapsack problem is better than strictly $(2 - \varepsilon)$-competitive in expectation.*

Proof. Consider the following set $\mathcal{I}$ that contains two instances. For both, first an object of weight ε is offered. After that, either nothing is offered or another object with a weight of 1 is offered. Now let RAND be any randomized online algorithm for the simple knapsack problem; RAND accepts the first object with some probability q. Obviously, q is not 0 since, otherwise, RAND has a gain of 0 on the instance that only consists of the first object. We now distinguish two cases depending on whether the second object is offered.

Case 1. If the second object is offered, this leads to an optimal gain of 1. If RAND accepts the first object, it does not have any space left in the knapsack for the second one. The strict expected competitive ratio of RAND is hence bounded by

$$\frac{1}{q \cdot \varepsilon + (1 - q) \cdot 1} = \frac{1}{(\varepsilon - 1) \cdot q + 1}.$$

Case 2. If the second object is not offered, an optimal solution has a gain of ε. In this case, RAND's gain is 0 if it does not accept the first object. Thus, the strict competitive ratio of RAND can be bounded by

$$\frac{\varepsilon}{q \cdot \varepsilon + (1 - q) \cdot 0} = \frac{1}{q}.$$

Through the concrete instance that is given, the adversary can always make sure that the strict expected competitive ratio of RAND is the maximum of these two values. Consequently, RAND wants to choose q such that this maximum is minimized. Since $((\varepsilon - 1)q + 1)^{-1}$ is monotonically increasing in q while $1/q$ is monotonically decreasing in q, the best strategy for RAND is to choose q such that the two strict competitive ratios are equal; this "equalizing of expectations" is shown in Figure 6.5.

We conclude that

$$\frac{1}{(\varepsilon - 1) \cdot q + 1} = \frac{1}{q} \iff q = \frac{1}{2 - \varepsilon},$$

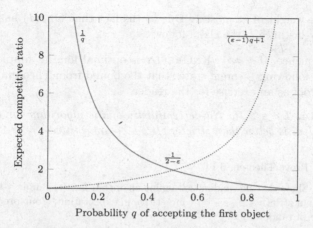

Figure 6.5. The two different strict expected competitive ratios for RAND depending on the probability that the first object is chosen.

and, if we plug this value into either of the formulas that bound the strict expected competitive ratio, we get that it is at least $2 - \varepsilon$. □

Exercise 6.7. The proof of Theorem 6.12 uses a direct argumentation over the probability distribution used by a given randomized online algorithm. Give an alternative proof using Yao's principle.

6.5 Resource Augmentation

In Section 1.6 and Exercise 4.5, we learned about *resource augmentation* as a possible way to give an online algorithm an advantage over the adversary; it turned out that this indeed helps for paging and k-server. In this section, we allow an online algorithm for the simple knapsack problem to use more resources. In this context, this means that the algorithm uses a knapsack that has a larger capacity than the one an optimal algorithm has available. Specifically, we consider an environment where the online algorithm uses a knapsack of capacity $1 + \gamma$ with $0 < \gamma \le 1$ and an optimal solution must use a knapsack with a capacity of 1. Furthermore, we still assume that all objects in the input have a weight (value) of at most 1. We call this problem the *simple γ-knapsack problem*. If we consider deterministic online algorithms, we note that a greedy strategy achieves a best possible result.

Theorem 6.13. KNGREEDY *is strictly $1/\gamma$-competitive for the simple γ-knapsack problem.*

Proof. If KNGREEDY has no space left in the knapsack to pack an object, this means that it is already filled with objects that have a total weight of at least γ since all objects have a weight of at most 1. Due to the fact that $\text{OPT}(I)$ has a gain of at most 1 for any instance I, the claim follows. □

As a consequence, if $\gamma = 1$, KNGREEDY is optimal for the simple γ-knapsack problem. The following theorem states that the bound from Theorem 6.13 is tight; we leave its proof as an exercise for the reader.

Theorem 6.14. *Let $\varepsilon > 0$. No deterministic online algorithm for the simple γ-knapsack problem is better than strictly $1/(\gamma + \varepsilon)$-competitive.*

Exercise 6.8. Prove Theorem 6.14.

Exercise 6.9. Show that no randomized online algorithm for the simple γ-knapsack problem is better than strictly $(2 - \varepsilon - \gamma)$-competitive in expectation. Your proof should work for any number of random bits.

As a consequence, for small values of γ resource augmentation does not help a lot in a deterministic or randomized setting. However, things change drastically if we consider online algorithms with advice instead. If we combine these two concepts, we are able to design an online algorithm with advice that uses a constant number (depending on γ) of advice bits, and that computes a solution with a gain that is very close to that of an optimal solution; the attainable competitive ratio also depends on γ.

Theorem 6.15. *Let $1/4 > \gamma > 0$. There is an online algorithm AUG with advice for the simple γ-knapsack problem that is strictly*

$$\left(1 + \frac{3\gamma}{1 - 4\gamma}\right)\text{-competitive}$$

and that uses at most

$$1 + \left\lceil \frac{1}{\gamma} \log_2\left(\left\lceil \frac{1}{\gamma^2} \right\rceil\right) \right\rceil + \left\lceil \log_2\left(\left\lceil \frac{1}{\gamma} \right\rceil + 1\right) \right\rceil$$

advice bits.

Proof. Let I be a fixed instance of the simple γ-knapsack problem. First, we bound the gain of an optimal solution $\text{OPT}(I)$ from below. Using Theorem 6.3, we assume that OPT's gain is at least $1/2$; otherwise, AUG follows a greedy approach and is optimal. This is communicated with the first bit on the advice tape.

As in the proof of Theorem 6.8, we subdivide the objects that OPT packs into the knapsack into "heavy" and "light" ones. The heavy objects are denoted by $x_1, x_2, \ldots, x_k$ and the light ones by $y_1, y_2, \ldots, y_m$. Objects are considered heavy if they have a weight of at least γ; if they have a weight smaller than γ, they are called light. For any instance I we thus have

$$\text{OPT}(I) = \{x_1, x_2, \ldots, x_k\} \,\dot\cup\, \{y_1, y_2, \ldots, y_m\} \,.$$

Clearly, for the number k of heavy objects, we have $k \leq 1/\gamma$.

We design AUG such that it works as follows. The algorithm knows γ and it computes the approximate weights of the heavy objects. The weights of these objects are rounded down to a multiple of γ^2. Apart from that, AUG computes a bound for the part of the knapsack that OPT fills with light objects. As long as this bound is not exceeded by the light objects packed by AUG so far, it accepts light objects following a greedy strategy.

Next, we need to show how the weights of the heavy objects are encoded. To this end, let

$$\overline{x}_i := j \in \mathbb{N}, \quad \text{such that } j\gamma^2 \leq x_i < (j+1)\gamma^2 \,, \tag{6.2}$$

for every heavy object x_i, where $1 \leq i \leq k$. All $\overline{x}_i$s are written on the advice tape and read by AUG at the beginning. Now, if an object w' is offered, AUG checks whether the corresponding $\overline{x}_i$ is part of the advice. In other words, the algorithm checks whether there is some $\overline{x}_i$ encoded on the advice tape such that

$$\overline{x}_i\gamma^2 \leq w' < (\overline{x}_i + 1)\gamma^2 \,. \tag{6.3}$$

If this is the case, w' is accepted; we denote this object by x_i' as it corresponds to x_i in OPT(I) (although x_i and x_i' may of course be different). Otherwise, w' is discarded.

Now if we compare x_i and x_i', we note that due to the rounding, we have from (6.2) and (6.3) that

$$x_i' < \overline{x}_i\gamma^2 + \gamma^2 \leq x_i + \gamma^2 \tag{6.4}$$

and

$$x_i - \gamma^2 < \overline{x}_i\gamma^2 \leq x_i' \,,$$

which together give

$$x_i - \gamma^2 < x_i' < x_i + \gamma^2 \,,$$

for all i with $1 \leq i \leq k$. If we add all these values using $k \leq 1/\gamma$, we get

$$\sum_{i=1}^{k} x_i' < \sum_{i=1}^{k}(x_i + \gamma^2) = \left(\sum_{i=1}^{k} x_i\right) + k\gamma^2 \leq \left(\sum_{i=1}^{k} x_i\right) + \gamma \tag{6.5}$$

and

$$\left(\sum_{i=1}^{k} x_i\right) - \gamma \leq \left(\sum_{i=1}^{k} x_i\right) - k\gamma^2 = \sum_{i=1}^{k}(x_i - \gamma^2) < \sum_{i=1}^{k} x_i' \,. \tag{6.6}$$

Intuitively, (6.5) means that, for every heavy object in OPT(I), AUG packs a (possibly different) object such that the sum of all weights of these objects needs

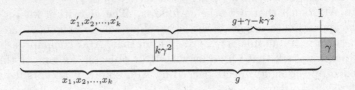

Figure 6.6. The knapsack as it is packed by AUG and OPT, respectively.

less than γ more capacity than the heavy objects in the knapsack packed by $\text{OPT}(I)$. Moreover, (6.6) states that not more than a space of γ stays unused in the computed solution compared to $\text{OPT}(I)$.

Next, we compare AUG and $\text{OPT}(I)$ with respect to the objects of weight less than γ. To this end, we distinguish two cases concerning the gain of $\text{OPT}(I)$.

Case 1. Assume that $\text{gain}(\text{OPT}(I)) < 1 - \gamma$. This means that $\text{OPT}(I)$ packs all objects with a weight of less than γ into the knapsack, because otherwise it would not be optimal. In (6.5), we just saw that by packing the x_i's AUG uses at most γ more space of the knapsack. Since we are dealing with the simple γ-knapsack problem, this means that AUG has at least as much space in the knapsack as $\text{OPT}(I)$, and therefore also packs all light objects due to the greedy strategy. On the other hand, due to (6.6) we know that the total gain of AUG on I is at least $\text{gain}(\text{OPT}(I)) - \gamma$. We conclude that

$$\frac{\text{gain}(\text{OPT}(I))}{\text{gain}(\text{OPT}(I)) - \gamma} = 1 + \frac{\gamma}{\text{gain}(\text{OPT}(I)) - \gamma} \leq 1 + \frac{2\gamma}{1 - 2\gamma} \leq 1 + \frac{3\gamma}{1 - 4\gamma} \,,$$

where we used $\text{gain}(\text{OPT}(I)) \geq 1/2$ for the first inequality.

Case 2. Now assume that $1 - \gamma \leq \text{gain}(\text{OPT}(I)) \leq 1$. Let

$$g := 1 - \sum_{i=1}^{k} x_i$$

denote the space in the knapsack that is left for objects with a weight less than γ in $\text{OPT}(I)$; see Figure 6.6. The ones that $\text{OPT}(I)$ packs into the knapsack become the light objects $y_1, y_2, \ldots, y_m$. AUG does not know g, but it can compute an approximation

$$g' := 1 - \sum_{i=1}^{k} (\overline{x}_i + 1)\gamma^2 \,.$$

Due to (6.4) and again using $k \leq 1/\gamma$, we have

$$g' \geq 1 - \sum_{i=1}^{k} (x_i + \gamma^2) = 1 - \left(\sum_{i=1}^{k} x_i\right) - k\gamma^2 \geq 1 - \left(\sum_{i=1}^{k} x_i\right) - \gamma \,,$$

and therefore

$$g - \gamma \leq g' \leq g \, . \tag{6.7}$$

Both AUG and OPT(I) have all objects with a weight less than γ available. Now let I_g be the instance I restricted to a knapsack of capacity g and only objects with a weight of less than γ. Furthermore, let OPT(I_g) be a fixed optimal solution for I_g. We define $I_{g'}$ and OPT$(I_{g'})$ analogously. Since AUG implements a greedy strategy on $I_{g'}$, following Theorem 6.2 it is either optimal or it has a gain of at least $g' - \gamma$. On the other hand, OPT(I) has a gain of gain$($OPT$(I_g)) \leq g$ on I_g. From this, we can finally bound the strict competitive ratio of AUG by

$$\frac{\text{gain}(\text{OPT}(I))}{\left(\sum_{i=1}^{k} x_i'\right) + g' - \gamma} \leq \frac{\text{gain}(\text{OPT}(I))}{\left(\sum_{i=1}^{k} x_i'\right) + g - 2\gamma}$$

(as a consequence of (6.7))

$$\leq \frac{\text{gain}(\text{OPT}(I))}{\left(\sum_{i=1}^{k} x_i\right) + g - 3\gamma}$$

(which follows from (6.6))

$$\leq \frac{\text{gain}(\text{OPT}(I))}{\left(\sum_{i=1}^{k} x_i\right) + \text{gain}(\text{OPT}(I_g)) - 3\gamma}$$

(since gain(OPT$(I_g)) \leq g$)

$$= \frac{\text{gain}(\text{OPT}(I))}{\text{gain}(\text{OPT}(I)) - 3\gamma}$$

(due to the definition of OPT(I))

$$\leq 1 + \frac{3\gamma}{1 - 4\gamma} \, .$$

To finish the proof, we bound the number of advice bits AUG reads from above.

- The first advice bit tells AUG whether gain$($OPT$(I)) \geq 1/2$ or not.

- There are at most k different $\overline{x}_i$s (namely as many as there are heavy objects in OPT(I)).

- Due to (6.2) and since every object in the input has a weight of at most 1, every $\overline{x}_i$ is at most $1/\gamma^2$.

- To encode all $\overline{x}_i$s on the advice tape, we thus need

$$k \log_2\left(\left\lceil \frac{1}{\gamma^2} \right\rceil\right) \leq \left\lceil \frac{1}{\gamma} \log_2\left(\left\lceil \frac{1}{\gamma^2} \right\rceil\right) \right\rceil$$

bits.

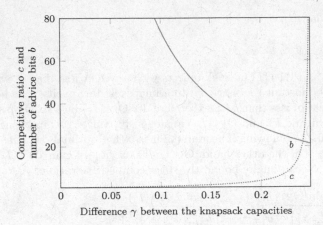

Figure 6.7. The strict competitive ratio of AUG and the number of advice bits depending on γ.

- To be able to decode the advice, AUG has to know k, which can be encoded using $\lceil \log_2(k+1) \rceil \leq \lceil \log_2(\lceil 1/\gamma \rceil + 1) \rceil$ advice bits.

- An upper bound on the length of the binary encoding of the $\overline{x}_i$s can be computed by AUG without any further information. Likewise, AUG can compute g' based on the $\overline{x}_i$s and γ.

Summing up, AUG uses at most

$$1 + \left\lceil \frac{1}{\gamma} \log_2 \left(\left\lceil \frac{1}{\gamma^2} \right\rceil \right) \right\rceil + \left\lceil \log_2 \left(\left\lceil \frac{1}{\gamma} \right\rceil + 1 \right) \right\rceil$$

advice bits as we claimed. $\qquad \square$

Note that the number of advice bits decreases monotonically in γ while the obtained strict competitive ratio grows in γ; this is shown in Figure 6.7. This concludes our study of the simple online knapsack problem. In the remainder of this chapter, we look at the general case, where the weights and the values of the objects that are offered are not necessarily equal.

6.6 The General Case

In this section, we now consider the general knapsack problem from Definition 6.1, where every object has both a weight and a value. This fact makes the situation a lot harder for an online algorithm. The next exercise shows that this is even the case if we change the problem definition in its favor.

Exercise 6.10. In Exercise 6.5, we introduced the simple removable knapsack problem, for which there is no deterministic online algorithm that is better than 3/2-competitive. Now consider the corresponding variant where the weights and values of objects may be different. Prove that no deterministic online algorithm is competitive for this *general removable knapsack problem*.

⋆6.6.1 Advice Complexity

The results presented in what follows only hold if we restrict ourselves to instances where the values and weights can be represented within polynomial space. More formally, recall that, for any object x_i with $1 \leq i \leq n$, w_i denotes the weight of x_i and v_i is the value of x_i; moreover, the knapsack's capacity is still 1, and also $w_i \leq 1$ is true for all objects. Later, we will sometimes use two functions w and v with $w(x_i) = w_i$ and $v(x_i) = v_i$ to have an easier notation. Throughout this subsection, let

$$r(x_i) := \frac{v_i}{w_i} = \frac{v(x_i)}{w(x_i)}$$

be the *value/weight ratio* of x_i. We assume that, for every x_i, both v_i and w_i are rational numbers, and their numerators and denominators are bounded by $2^{p(n)}$ for some fixed polynomial p, where n is the input length. We assume that p is known to any online algorithm for the problem.

First of all, we note that the lower bounds for the simple knapsack problem from Section 6.3 carry over immediately since we are now dealing with a generalization of the above problem. Indeed, we can always choose $v_i = w_i$, for all i with $1 \leq i \leq n$. Second, Theorem 6.4, which states that n advice bits allow for optimality, obviously also applies for the general knapsack problem. However, for this problem, small advice is a lot less powerful.

Theorem 6.16. *No online algorithm with advice for the knapsack problem that uses fewer than $\log_2 n$ advice bits is competitive.*

Proof. Let ALG be some online algorithm with advice that reads $b(n) < \log_2 n$ advice bits for inputs of length n, which allows it to distinguish at most $2^{b(n)}$ different inputs. For every n, we construct a set $\mathcal{I}^{(n)}$ of n different instances as follows. Let $\beta := 2^n$, and let

$$I_s = \left((1, \beta), (1, \beta^2), \ldots, (1, \beta^s), \underbrace{(1, 1), (1, 1), \ldots, (1, 1)}_{n-s \text{ times}}\right),$$

for every s with $1 \leq s \leq n$. We set $\mathcal{I}^{(n)} := \{I_s \mid 1 \leq s \leq n\}$. Since $|\mathcal{I}^{(n)}| = 2^{\log_2 n} > 2^{b(n)}$, there are more inputs than strategies to choose from, and thus there are at least two different inputs for one advice string. Let these two instances be I_i and I_j and assume, without loss of generality, that $i > j$. The unique optimal solution for I_i (I_j, respectively) packs the knapsack with the ith (jth, respectively) object, yielding a gain of β^i (β^j, respectively).

Clearly, if ALG does not choose the jth object when given the instance I_j, its gain is at least a factor of β away from gain($\text{OPT}(I_j)$). Since ALG cannot distinguish between I_j and I_i in the first j time steps (and it is given the same fixed advice string), it also packs the jth object when given I_i. This results in a competitive ratio of at least $\beta^i/\beta^j \geq \beta$. $\qquad\square$

It seems reasonable that, for the general knapsack problem, logarithmic advice is less powerful than for the simple one. The next question is whether we need much more advice to have any satisfying result; for instance, what do we need to get any constant competitive ratio? Surprisingly, logarithmic advice suffices (when obeying the restrictions on the value/weight ratio as described above). In the following, we even show how to solve the general knapsack problem almost optimally when using logarithmic advice. This implies that the bound of Theorem 6.16 is asymptotically tight.

The algorithm achieving this is called GLOG, and it works in a far more complex way than the ones presented so far for the simple knapsack problem. On an intuitive level, the strategy of GLOG can be outlined as follows. According to their values, some objects of a fixed optimal solution are called "expensive." The algorithm packs all the expensive objects that are part of a fixed optimal solution; other expensive objects are discarded. Moreover, GLOG uses all objects that have a large value/weight ratio as long as this ratio is larger than some lower bound. However, this lower bound cannot be communicated with absolute accuracy; objects that are part of the optimal solution, but whose ratio is too small, are explicitly communicated to GLOG if their weight is larger than some specific threshold. Finally, GLOG calculates a bound on the space that it fills greedily with objects that are not too heavy and that have a good value/weight ratio.

Theorem 6.17. *Let $\varepsilon > 0$. GLOG is strictly $(1 + \varepsilon)$-competitive for the knapsack problem and uses $\mathcal{O}(\log n)$ advice bits. Here, the $\mathcal{O}$-notation hides a multiplicative constant depending on ε and on the degree d of the polynomial $p(n)$.*

Proof. Let I be any instance of the knapsack problem, and let

$$\delta := \frac{\sqrt{1+\varepsilon}-1}{2\sqrt{1+\varepsilon}+1}.$$

Consider any optimal solution $\text{OPT}(I)$ for I, and let c' be such that

$$\frac{\text{gain}(\text{OPT}(I))}{1+\delta} < c' \leq \text{gain}(\text{OPT}(I)). \tag{6.8}$$

Next, let $x_1, x_2, \ldots, x_k$ be all objects in $\text{OPT}(I)$ with a value of at least $\delta c'$; we call these objects *expensive*. Since there are at most $\text{gain}(\text{OPT}(I))/(\delta c')$ such objects, we immediately get $k \leq (1 + \delta)/\delta$.

Let $\mathcal{S}_1$ be an (offline) solution for I constructed as follows. At first, all expensive objects $x_1, x_2, \ldots, x_k$ are packed; then, the rest of the knapsack is filled using objects that have values of less than $\delta c'$ greedily by their value/weight ratio in descending order. Consider $\mathcal{S}_1$ plus the object x that is the first one that did not fit into the knapsack in the greedy phase of $\mathcal{S}_1$'s construction. Clearly, we have

$$\text{gain}(\mathcal{S}_1) + v(x) \geq \text{gain}(\text{OPT}(I)) . \tag{6.9}$$

Since $v(x) \leq \delta c' \leq \delta \cdot \text{gain}(\text{OPT}(I))$, (6.9) implies

$$
\begin{aligned}
\text{gain}(\mathcal{S}_1) &\geq \text{gain}(\text{OPT}(I)) - v(x) \\
&\geq \text{gain}(\text{OPT}(I)) - \delta \cdot \text{gain}(\text{OPT}(I)) \\
&= (1 - \delta) \cdot \text{gain}(\text{OPT}(I)) .
\end{aligned}
$$

Let $y_1, y_2, \ldots, y_l$ denote the objects of $\mathcal{S}_1$ added in the greedy phase. Without loss of generality, assume that $r(y_1) \geq r(y_2) \geq \ldots \geq r(y_l)$, and let r' be such that

$$r(y_l) \leq r' < (1 + \delta) \cdot r(y_l) .$$

Let m be the largest number such that $r(y_m) \geq r'$, that is, the objects $y_1, y_2, \ldots, y_m$ have ratios of at least r' and all other objects $y_{m+1}, y_{m+2}, \ldots, y_l$ have ratios between r' and $r'/(1+\delta)$. Let g be the space not occupied by $x_1, x_2, \ldots, x_k, y_1, y_2, \ldots, y_m$ in $\mathcal{S}_1$, that is,

$$g := 1 - \sum_{i=1}^{k} w(x_i) - \sum_{i=1}^{m} w(y_i) .$$

Intuitively speaking, if we consider the part of the solution $\mathcal{S}_1$ that consists of the objects y_i with $i > m$, we see that this is a solution of an "almost simple" knapsack instance with knapsack capacity g. Therefore, we can approximate it by a solution for the simple knapsack problem without doing much harm. To this end, let g' be such that

$$\frac{g}{1+\delta} < g' \leq g . \tag{6.10}$$

Furthermore, let

$$\{z_1, z_2, \ldots, z_p\} := \{y_i \mid y_i \in \{y_{m+1}, y_{m+2}, \ldots, y_l\}, w(y_i) \geq \delta g'\} ,$$

that is, $z_1, z_2, \ldots, z_p$ are all objects from $\mathcal{S}_1$ that have a value/weight ratio of roughly r' and whose weights are at least a δ-fraction of g'. Due to (6.10), there are at most $(1+\delta)/\delta$ such objects.

Let

$$u := g - \sum_{i=1}^{p} w(z_i) , \tag{6.11}$$

that is, the space not occupied by $x_1, x_2, \ldots, x_k, y_1, y_2, \ldots, y_m, z_1, z_2, \ldots, z_p$, and let u' be such that

$$\frac{u}{1+\delta} < u' \leq u \, .$$

Again, we consider an (offline) solution $\mathcal{S}_2$ that is constructed as follows. At first, all objects $x_1, x_2, \ldots, x_k, y_1, y_2, \ldots, y_m, z_1, z_2, \ldots, z_p$ are packed. After that, we consider all remaining objects of weight less than $\delta g'$ and with a ratio of at least $r'/(1+\delta)$; each of these objects is added greedily to $\mathcal{S}_2$ if it fits into a reserved space of size u'. GLOG will compute $\mathcal{S}_2$.

We now show that

$$\text{gain}(\mathcal{S}_2) \geq \frac{1-2\delta}{(1+\delta)^2} \cdot \text{gain}(\mathcal{S}_1) \, . \tag{6.12}$$

To this end, consider two cases.

Case 1. Assume that the greedy construction of $\mathcal{S}_2$ packs all possible objects. In this case, $\mathcal{S}_2$ contains all objects included in $\mathcal{S}_1$, and therefore (6.12) follows trivially.

Case 2. Assume there is at least one object not packed by the greedy strategy. Since the objects $y_{m+1}, y_{m+2}, \ldots, y_l$ have a ratio of at most r' and weights of at most 1, it follows that the value of each such object is at most r' as well. Hence, due to (6.10), we get

$$\text{gain}(\mathcal{S}_1) \leq \sum_{i=1}^{k} v(x_i) + \sum_{i=1}^{m} v(y_i) + gr' \leq \sum_{i=1}^{k} v(x_i) + \sum_{i=1}^{m} v(y_i) + g'(1+\delta)r' \, .$$

Now we bound the gain of $\mathcal{S}_2$. To this end, note that, as a consequence of (6.11), the total weight of all z_is is $g - u$. Additionally, the greedy step packs objects of total weight at least $u' - \delta g'$. Together, this gives a space of at least

$$u' - \delta g' + g - u \geq (1-\delta)g' + u' - u \geq (1-2\delta)g' \, .$$

All the corresponding objects have a value/weight ratio of at least $r'/(1+\delta)$, and we therefore get

$$\text{gain}(\mathcal{S}_2) \geq \sum_{i=1}^{k} v(x_i) + \sum_{i=1}^{m} v(y_i) + g'(1-2\delta) \cdot \frac{r'}{1+\delta} \, .$$

Since the gains of $\mathcal{S}_1$ and $\mathcal{S}_2$ only differ in the last summand by at most $(1-2\delta)/(1+\delta)^2$, it follows that (6.12) also holds in this case.

Putting it all together, we finally get

$$\text{gain}(\mathcal{S}_2) \geq \frac{1-2\delta}{(1+\delta)^2} \cdot \text{gain}(\mathcal{S}_1) \geq \frac{(1-2\delta)^2}{(1+\delta)^2} \cdot \text{gain}(\text{OPT}(I)) = \frac{\text{gain}(\text{OPT}(I))}{1+\varepsilon}$$

as claimed.

It remains to bound the number of advice bits that are used by GLOG.

- At first, the oracle needs to encode n and k, which can be done using no more than $2\lceil \log_2 n \rceil + 2\lceil \log_2(\lceil \log_2 n \rceil) \rceil$ bits.

- The indices of the expensive objects $x_1, x_2, \ldots, x_k$ can be specified using $k\lceil \log_2 n \rceil \leq (1+\delta)/\delta \cdot \log_2 n + 1$ additional bits.

- Similarly, the indices of the objects z_i can be communicated using $p\lceil \log_2 n \rceil \leq (1+\delta)/\delta \log_2 n + 1$ bits.

- To make sure that (6.8) holds for c', we set
$$c' := (1+\delta)^{\lfloor \log_{1+\delta}(\mathrm{gain}(\mathrm{OPT}(I))) \rfloor}.$$

Since GLOG knows δ, only $\lfloor \log_{1+\delta}(\mathrm{gain}(\mathrm{OPT}(I))) \rfloor$ must be encoded on the advice tape. Recall that the value v_i of any object in the input is a rational number whose numerator and denominator are both at most $2^{p(n)}$, where p is a fixed polynomial with degree, say, d; recall that p is known to GLOG. Therefore, we have $1/2^{p(n)} \leq v_i \leq 2^{p(n)}$ for every i with $1 \leq i \leq n$. As there are n objects in the input, we obtain $n/2^{p(n)} \leq \mathrm{gain}(\mathrm{OPT}(I)) \leq n2^{p(n)}$. Note that $\lfloor \log_{1+\delta}(\mathrm{gain}(\mathrm{OPT}(I))) \rfloor$ may be negative if the optimal gain on I is smaller than 1.

So far, we did not have to deal with encoding negative numbers on the advice tape. We take an easy approach. The sign is communicated with one additional bit. If it is positive, $\lfloor \log_{1+\delta}(\mathrm{gain}(\mathrm{OPT}(I))) \rfloor$ is encoded onto the advice tape. Otherwise, $\lfloor \log_{1+\delta}(1/\mathrm{gain}(\mathrm{OPT}(I))) \rfloor$ is encoded instead, since $-\log_{1+\delta} x = \log_{1+\delta}(1/x)$ for any x. Using that $2^{p(n)}/n \leq n2^{p(n)}$, the number of advice bits needed is at most

$$\left\lceil \log_2\left(\left\lfloor \log_{1+\delta}\left(n2^{p(n)}\right) \right\rfloor\right) \right\rceil + 1 \leq \log_2\left(\frac{\log_2 n + \log_2\left(2^{p(n)}\right)}{\log_2(1+\delta)}\right) + 2$$

$$\leq \log_2\left(\frac{\log_2 n + n^d}{\log_2(1+\delta)}\right) + 2$$

$$\leq \log_2\left(\frac{n^{d+1}}{\log_2(1+\delta)}\right) + 2,$$

which is in $\mathcal{O}(\log(n^{d+1})) = \mathcal{O}(\log n)$.

- Likewise, we set
$$r' := (1+\delta)^{\lceil \log_{1+\delta}(r(y_l)) \rceil},$$
$$g' := (1+\delta)^{\lfloor \log_{1+\delta} g \rfloor}, \text{ and}$$
$$u' := (1+\delta)^{\lfloor \log_{1+\delta} u \rfloor},$$

and therefore $\lceil \log_{1+\delta}(r(y_l)) \rceil$, $\lfloor \log_{1+\delta} g \rfloor$, and $\lfloor \log_{1+\delta} u \rfloor$ must be written on the advice tape (note that the latter two will be negative). By similar arguments to those above, we verfiy that $\mathcal{O}(\log n)$ advice bits suffice to do that.

```
h := 0;                          // Initialize space that is filled greedily
for every request x do
    r(x) := v(x)/w(x);           // Compute value/weight ratio of x
    if x = x_i for some i        // v(x) ≥ δc' and OPT(I) packs x; thus, x is expensive
        pack x;
    elsif v(x) ≥ δc'             // v(x) ≥ δc', but OPT(I) does not pack x
        discard x;
    elsif r(x) ≥ r'              // x is one of y_1, y_2, ..., y_m
        pack x;
    elsif x = z_i for some i     // x is one of z_1, z_2, ..., z_p
        pack x;
    elsif r(x) < r'/(1 + δ) or w(x) ≥ δg'
        discard x;
    elsif h ≤ u'                 // Pack x greedily if there is space
        h := h + w(x);
        pack x;
    else
        discard x;
end
```

Algorithm 6.1. The algorithm GLOG for the (general) knapsack problem.

We conclude that at most $\mathcal{O}(\log(n^d)) = \mathcal{O}(\log n)$ bits are needed in total to communicate the x_is with $1 \leq i \leq k$, the z_is with $1 \leq i \leq p$, together with c', r', g', and u'. Using this knowledge, GLOG works as shown in Algorithm 6.1 to construct $\mathcal{S}_2$, and is therefore $(1 + \varepsilon)$-competitive. $\qquad\square$

6.6.2 Randomized Online Algorithms

Next, we show that no randomized online algorithm for the general knapsack problem, independent of the number of random bits it reads, is competitive. We will prove this claim using Yao's principle (see Exercise 6.7 for a warm-up).

Theorem 6.18. *No randomized online algorithm for the knapsack problem is competitive (independent of the number of random bits).*

Proof. We construct sets $\mathcal{I}_1, \mathcal{I}_2, \ldots$ of instances as follows. $\mathcal{I}_i$ consists of all instances

$$I_s = ((1, 2), (1, 2^2), \ldots, (1, 2^s), \underbrace{(1, 1), (1, 1), \ldots, (1, 1)}_{i+1-s \text{ times}})$$

of length $i + 1$, for every s with $1 \leq s \leq i + 1$. For each I_s, the optimal solution packs the last object with a value larger than 1, and therefore has a gain of 2^s; there is space for exactly one object in the knapsack.

Clearly, $\mathcal{I}_i$ is finite for any fixed i (more precisely, $|\mathcal{I}_i| = i + 1$). Now consider a probability distribution $\mathrm{Pr}_{\mathrm{ADV},i}$ over $\mathcal{I}_i$ such that each instance is drawn with probability $1/(i+1)$.

Moreover, for any fixed i, there is only a finite number of *generic algorithms* for $\mathcal{I}_i$. Any deterministic online algorithm that has any gain larger than 1 on these instances chooses exactly one object it packs into the knapsack (if it should be offered). Let ALG_k with $1 \le k \le i + 1$ denote such an algorithm that decides to wait until the kth object is offered and to pack it. We can thus apply Yao's principle for infinite maximization problems. In what follows, we will show that

$$\left(\mathbb{E}_{\mathrm{ADV},i} \left[\frac{\mathrm{gain}(\mathrm{ALG}_k(\mathcal{I}_i))}{\mathrm{gain}(\mathrm{OPT}(\mathcal{I}_i))} \right] \right)^{-1} \ge \frac{i+1}{3} . \tag{6.13}$$

Since the lower bound on the competitive ratio grows with the input length $i+1$, we do not need to show that the optimal gain increases unboundedly (see Exercise 2.4).

If the concrete input is I_k, the gain of ALG_k and the optimal gain are both 2^k, which happens with probability $1/(i+1)$. If the randomly chosen instance is I_j with $j < k$ (that is, if k is too large) ALG_k's gain is at most 1. Conversely, if the instance is I_j with $k < j$ (that is, if k is too small) ALG_k's gain is again 2^k while the optimal gain is 2^j. Summing up, we get

$$\mathbb{E}_{\mathrm{ADV},i} \left[\frac{\mathrm{gain}(\mathrm{ALG}_k(\mathcal{I}_i))}{\mathrm{gain}(\mathrm{OPT}(\mathcal{I}_i))} \right] \le \frac{1}{i+1} \sum_{j=1}^{k-1} \frac{1}{2^j} + \frac{1}{i+1} \cdot \frac{2^k}{2^k} + \frac{1}{i+1} \sum_{j=k+1}^{i+1} \frac{2^k}{2^j}$$

$$\le \frac{1}{i+1} + \frac{1}{i+1} \sum_{j=k}^{i+1} 2^{k-j} ,$$

for any fixed k, and hence the expected competitive ratio of ALG_k is at least

$$\frac{i+1}{1 + \sum_{j=k}^{i+1} 2^{k-j}} = \frac{i+1}{1 + 2^0 + 2^{-1} + \ldots + 2^{k-i-1}} \ge \frac{i+1}{3} ,$$

which proves (6.13). Therefore, (i) of Theorem 2.6 is satisfied. Consequently, no randomized online algorithm is competitive for the general knapsack problem. $\square$

6.6.3 Resource Augmentation

Note that all objects which we used in the proof of Theorem 6.18 have a weight of 1 each. It thus follows immediately that resource augmentation does not help at all for randomized online algorithms as long as $\delta < 1$. We call this problem the *γ-knapsack problem*.

Theorem 6.19. *No randomized online algorithm for the γ-knapsack problem is competitive (independent of the number of random bits).* $\square$

6.7 Historical and Bibliographical Notes

As already mentioned in the notes of Chapter 1, the offline version of the knapsack problem has both a long history and a rich literature [94]. The lower bound on the competitive ratio of deterministic online algorithms is due to Marchetti-Spaccamela and Vercellis [115], who were the first to study an online version of the knapsack problem. The results presented in this chapter about randomization and the advice complexity of the problem are from Böckenhauer et al. [32, 33].

The concept of scalable problems is described by Borodin and El-Yaniv [34]. Furrer [65] showed that the simple knapsack problem is scalable (see Exercise 6.3).

The simple removable knapsack problem, which was described in Exercise 6.5, was introduced by Iwama and Taketomi [87]; the authors showed a tight bound of $(1 + \sqrt{5})/2$ on the strict competitive ratio for deterministic online algorithms. Iwama and Zhang [88] proved that there is no competitive deterministic online algorithm for the general removable knapsack problem (see Exercise 6.10). Randomized online algorithms for the removable knapsack problem were studied by Han et al. [74].

It was also mentioned in the notes of Chapter 1 that resource augmentation was introduced by Kalyanasundaram and Pruhs [90]. This concept was used for the removable knapsack problem by Iwama and Zhang [88]. The latter authors also showed the bounds for deterministic online algorithms which are not allowed to remove objects in this setting (see Theorems 6.13 and 6.14). Han and Makino [75] studied resource augmentation for a variant of the problem where each object can be cut k times; the part that is cut off is then discarded. The presented results on using both resource augmentation and advice are also due to Böckenhauer et al. [33].

The advice complexity of the online bin packing problem, which is related to the knapsack problem, was investigated by Angelopoulos et al. [10], Boyar et al. [37], Renault et al. [126], and Zhao and Shen [146].

The Bit Guessing Problem

7

In this chapter, we describe a very generic online problem, called the *bit guessing problem*, which captures the very essence of online computation. This problem is of great importance for analyzing online algorithms with advice, in particular with respect to lower bounds. Essentially, in the bit guessing problem an online algorithm has to guess 0 or 1 in every time step. If the guess was incorrect, it pays a penalty of 1 in the corresponding time step; otherwise, it has no cost in this step. We define two versions of this problem. In the first one, the algorithm is not told whether its guesses were correct until the very end. In the second one, the algorithm gets feedback after every time step whether the preceding guess was correct or incorrect; we refer to this feedback as the *history* of the input. We are not interested in the competitive ratio that can be achieved for this problem, but in the solution quality in an absolute sense, that is, in the number of correct guesses that are obtained. We actually define the problem in a more general way such that the characters of a σ-ary string need to be guessed, where $\sigma \geq 2$. This problem is called the *string guessing problem over an alphabet of size σ*; however, we will mostly focus on a binary alphabet.

We first analyze the problem in both a deterministic and a randomized setting. While deterministic online algorithms perform extremely poorly for the problem with both known and unknown history, it turns out that one random bit is very powerful as it allows us to guess half of any instance correctly in expectation. Next, we study the advice complexity and prove lower bounds on the number of advice bits that are necessary in order to obtain a given number of correct guesses. We give two separate proofs for either knowing or not knowing the history, which follow different approaches and involve some arguments from coding theory. Moreover, we give an idea of how the known history can be exploited when using advice.

Then, we turn to our main reason for studying these problems. Since we can find the concept of guessing certain characters (in many cases, bits) in a large number of online problems, we can use the bounds on the advice complexity of the string

© Springer International Publishing Switzerland 2016
D. Komm, *An Introduction to Online Computation*,
Texts in Theoretical Computer Science. An EATCS Series,
DOI 10.1007/978-3-319-42749-2_7

guessing problem to obtain lower bounds for other online problems by using certain kinds of reductions. After describing this concept in more detail, we apply concrete reductions to three problems, namely the k-server problem, the online set cover problem, and the disjoint path allocation problem. By doing so, we get strong lower bounds on the number of advice bits necessary to achieve competitive ratios that are close to 1.

7.1 Introduction

On a very high level, an online algorithm has the task to output some answer to some request in every given time step. In some sense, these answers can be interpreted as natural numbers. For instance, according to Definition 1.7, in the paging problem, the algorithm needs either to output a 0 if no page fault occurs, or to specify which page in the current cache gets replaced; clearly, the latter operation is equivalent to specifying the index of that page. Likewise, in the k-server problem, in every time step, the index of a server is specified that is to be moved to the requested point in the metric space. Since, in a deterministic or randomized setting, these answers are given without knowing what comes next, we can call such an answer a "guess" of the algorithm. If we concatenate all the answers of an online algorithm, we obtain a string of length n over an alphabet (that is, a finite set) Σ, and may therefore speak of "string guessing."

Of course, an important point is how the cost or gain function of the given online problem is defined. We speak of the *string guessing problem* when we have a cost function where an incorrect guess induces a penalty of 1 for the current time step, while a correct guess leads to cost 0. Observe that an optimal solution for every given instance has cost 0 as a consequence. The overall cost is therefore the number of time steps in which the algorithm's guess is different from the optimal answer. For the formal definition of the problem we use the *Hamming distance* $\text{ham}(a, b)$ for two σ-ary strings $a_1 a_2 \ldots a_n$ and $b_1 b_2 \ldots b_n$. We define two versions that differ in whether the algorithm is given feedback (called the "history" of the instance).

Definition 7.1 (String Guessing, Known History). The *string guessing problem with known history over an alphabet Σ of size $\sigma \geq 2$* is an online minimization problem. The input $I = (n, s_1, s_2, \ldots, s_n)$ consists of a natural number n and the characters $s_1, s_2, \ldots, s_n$ with $s_i \in \Sigma$ for $1 \leq i \leq n$. The characters are revealed one by one. An online algorithm ALG for the problem computes the output sequence $\text{ALG}(I) = (y_1, y_2, \ldots, y_n)$ where $y_i \in \Sigma$. The algorithm is not required to respond with any output in the last time step. If $y_i = s_i$ with $1 \leq i \leq n$, then ALG made the *correct guess* in the corresponding time step; otherwise it made an *incorrect guess*. The cost of a solution $\text{ALG}(I)$ is the number of incorrectly guessed characters, that is, the Hamming distance $\text{ham}(s, \text{ALG}(I))$ between $s = s_1 s_2 \ldots s_n$ and $\text{ALG}(I)$.

Next, we give an analogous definition for the string guessing problem where the history is not known, which means that the algorithm is not supplied with any feedback until the very end.

Definition 7.2 (String Guessing, Unknown History). The *string guessing problem with unknown history over an alphabet* Σ *of size* $\sigma \geq 2$ is an online minimization problem. The input $I = (n, ?, ?, \ldots, ?, s)$ consists of the string length n in the first request, $n - 1$ subsequent requests "?" carrying no extra information, and the string $s = s_1 s_2 \ldots s_n \in \Sigma^n$. In each of the first n time steps, an online algorithm ALG for the problem is required to output one character from Σ, forming the output sequence $\text{ALG}(I) = (y_1, y_2, \ldots, y_n)$. As above, the algorithm is not required to respond with any output in the last time step, in which the string s is revealed. The cost of a solution $\text{ALG}(I)$ is again the Hamming distance between s and $\text{ALG}(I)$.

If an algorithm for the string guessing problem makes an incorrect guess in some time step, we will simply speak of it "making an error." Note that, for both problems, the input length is actually $n + 1$. For all of our subsequent investigations, however, we will take n as a measurement; we will interchangeably speak of "inputs of length $n + 1$" and "guessing a string of length n."

Most of the time, we will consider the string guessing problem with an alphabet size of 2 and the two letters 0 and 1, which is why we subsequently speak of the "bit guessing problem," or of "bit guessing," for simplicity. In other words, we consider the problem of guessing a binary string of length n. The results obtained in this chapter can easily be generalized to larger alphabets; we leave this to the reader.

7.2 Deterministic and Randomized Algorithms

If we think about deterministic online algorithms, it seems pretty obvious that there is no difference between knowing and not knowing the history; such an algorithm will make an error in every time step.

Theorem 7.1. *Every deterministic online algorithm has cost n for bit guessing with either known or unknown history.*

Proof. Let ALG be any online algorithm for the bit guessing problem with either known or unknown history. In every time step, the adversary knows the guess of ALG, no matter whether it is based on the history or not. Therefore, it can always choose the complement to be the correct answer, regardless of when this answer is supplied. $\square$

If we consider randomization, we can easily improve this bound by a factor of two. Let HALF be a randomized online algorithm that guesses 0 or 1 with probability $1/2$

each in every time step. In doing so, HALF ignores the history (if it is supplied), that is, which of its guesses were correct so far. Clearly, it guesses $n/2$ bits correctly in expectation, no matter which instance the adversary chooses. Moreover, HALF uses exactly n random bits. If we think about it, we can achieve the same result with one random bit, that is, there is a barely random algorithm BGRONE that has cost $n/2$ in expectation as well.

Theorem 7.2. BGRONE *has an expected cost of at most $n/2$ for bit guessing with both known and unknown history.*

Proof. BGRONE reads one random bit before processing the input. If this random bit is 1, it guesses 1 in every time step; otherwise, it guesses 0 in every time step. The important thing is that the adversary cannot foresee which of the two cases occurs (recall that we deal with an oblivious adversary). Therefore, no matter which input I the adversary chooses, at every position of I, BGRONE is correct with probability $1/2$, which leads to a total cost of $n/2$ in expectation. $\square$

Exercise 7.1. BGRONE outputs a string that consists of either 1s only or 0s only. Are there other strategies that also lead to a randomized online algorithm that has an expected cost of $n/2$ and uses one random bit?

Exercise 7.2. What can be achieved with one random bit when considering the general string guessing problem? In particular, what is doable for an alphabet size larger than 2?

Exercise 7.3. In Example 3.9, we defined a similar problem and designed a randomized online algorithm for it that uses $n-1$ random bits and is strictly $(2 - 1/(2^{n-1}))$-competitive in expectation. Is it possible to achieve this strict expected competitive ratio with fewer random bits?

BGRONE does not make use of the history. It is not difficult to prove that, for randomization, it also does not help to know the history, that is, the bound of Theorem 7.2 is tight independent of whether the history is known or not. We leave the proof as an exercise for the reader.

Theorem 7.3. *Every randomized online algorithm has an expected cost of at least $n/2$ for bit guessing with either known or unknown history.*

Exercise 7.4. Prove Theorem 7.3.

7.3 Advice Complexity

So far, it did not seem very meaningful to study bit guessing either with known or with unknown history; in general, the problem does not behave very surprisingly. Now what happens when advice comes into play? First off, it is straightforward to verify that there are optimal online algorithms with advice that use n advice bits; the advice simply encodes the input (more specifically, the string s). We do not need any self-delimiting strings; for every request, exactly one bit is read (and n is given as part of the input before any guess has to be made, anyway).

Theorem 7.4. *There are optimal online algorithms with advice for bit guessing with both known and unknown history that use n advice bits.* □

Next, we show that this bound is tight. The proof of the following theorem uses the pigeonhole principle as we usually do when proving lower bounds on the number of advice bits necessary to perform optimally.

Theorem 7.5. *Every optimal online algorithm with advice for bit guessing with either known or unknown history has to use at least n advice bits.*

Proof. For a contradiction, suppose there are optimal online algorithms with advice for the two problems that read at most $n - 1$ advice bits. Let ALG be such an algorithm for either of the two. Therefore, there are two instances I_1 and I_2 of length $n + 1$ (and therefore two strings of length n) for which ALG gets the same advice. Let i with $2 \leq i \leq n + 1$ denote the position at which I_1 and I_2 differ for the first time; this is equal to the $(i-1)$th bit of the string s, which must be guessed in time step T_{i-1}. We distinguish two cases depending on which of the two problem variants we are dealing with.

Case 1. If the history is unknown, ALG's guess in T_{i-1} can only be based on the advice, which is identical for both instances.

Case 2. If the history is known, ALG's guess can additionally depend on the feedback it received so far. However, I_1 and I_2 are not distinguishable in the first $i - 1$ time steps, because the feedback is the same up to this point.

As a result, ALG makes the same guess for both I_1 or I_2 in time step T_{i-1}, which means it cannot be optimal for both instances. □

Exercise 7.5. Give an alternative proof of Theorem 7.5 using partition trees (see Definition 3.3).

Again, this does not seem very surprising. Our next question is what can be done with very small advice. We already know from Theorem 7.2 that one random bit allows us to make at most $n/2$ errors in expectation. If we define a corresponding online algorithm BGONE with advice that outputs (based on one advice bit) in every time step the bit that appears in at least half of the positions of the string s, we immediately get the following result.

Theorem 7.6. BGONE *has a cost of at most $n/2$ for bit guessing with both known and unknown history.* □

Exercise 7.6. Prove an analogous result for the general string guessing problem when $\lceil \log_2 \sigma \rceil$ advice bits are used.

From Theorem 7.3 we know that we cannot guess more than $n/2$ bits correctly in expectation, no matter how much we increase the number of random bits. For advice, on the other hand, we know that we can be optimal with n advice bits.

While knowing the history (that is, getting feedback about the decisions made so far) does not help in purely deterministic and randomized settings, this knowledge might suddenly be of some help when advice comes into play. Let us give an example of how an online algorithm with advice can use this knowledge. More specifically, the following idea is to give advice only for the first $n - 4$ bits such that an incorrect bit is supplied on purpose at exactly one position; the position encodes the last four bits.

Example 7.1. Let I be an instance of the bit guessing problem with known history of length $n + 1$ (that is, there is a string s with n bits to be guessed). Assume that we allow our algorithm to make one error. Moreover, we want to do this while using at most $n - 4$ advice bits. If s is the 20-bit string given by the bits

$$1,0,0,1,1,0,1,0,1,0,1,0,0,0,1,1,1,1,0,1 \,,$$

the oracle reads the last four bits and interprets them as the binary representation of the number 13. This number will be communicated to the online algorithm with advice in the following way. The first $n - 4$ bits of s are copied to the advice tape. However, an incorrect bit is written at position 14 (since with four bits, we can encode the numbers from 0 to 15). This leads to an advice string

| 1 | 0 | 0 | 1 | 1 | 0 | 1 | 0 | 1 | 0 | 1 | 0 | 0 | 1 | 1 | 1 | $\lessgtr$ .... |

The online algorithm will then read these $n - 4$ bits, and guess accordingly. After it guessed the 14th bit, it will be told that it just made an error. It continues until $n - 4$ bits are guessed; then, the last four bits are guessed according to the binary representation (with four bits) of 13. Note that this strategy can always be followed for $n \geq 2^4 + 4$ (which gives enough space on the tape).

In general, for every $t \in \mathbb{N}^+$ and $n \geq 2^t + t$, we can follow the same approach and make at most one error while reading $n - t$ bits of advice.

We can even use this idea to save a number of bits that grows with n. Suppose that, instead of a constant number, we take the last $\lfloor \log_2 n \rfloor - 1$ bits of the string and encode them the way described above. Due to

$$2^{\lfloor \log_2 n \rfloor - 1} + \lfloor \log_2 n \rfloor - 1 \leq 2^{\log_2 n - 1} + \log_2 n = \frac{n}{2} + \log_2 n \,,$$

which is smaller than n for every $n \geq 4$, there is an online algorithm with advice for bit guessing with known history that makes one error and uses

$$n - \lfloor \log_2 n \rfloor + 1$$

advice bits to guess strings of length at least 4. $\diamondsuit$

Exercise 7.7. Now consider bit guessing with unknown history. Show that there is an online algorithm that makes at most one error but uses at most $n - 2$ advice bits.

Exercise 7.8. Generalize this idea to an arbitrary number of errors.

Next, we are interested in the number of advice bits that are necessary to guarantee that a specific number of errors is not exceeded. We start by analyzing the bit guessing problem with unknown history. If we allow errors, the arguments for lower bounds get more involved than for lower bounds on the number of advice bits necessary to compute optimal solutions. In the proof of Theorem 7.5, we used our standard approach involving the pigeonhole principle, which states that we need a unique advice string for every instance in order to make no errors. Now the situation changes. As an example, again suppose that one error is allowed (recall that Exercise 7.7 gives an upper bound of $n - 2$ for bit guessing with unknown history in this case). Then the advice may tell the online algorithm to guess 0 in every time step, thus "covering" $n + 1$ instances, namely every instance that consists of 0s only except for one 1 and of course the instance that consists of 0s only.

Generalizing this idea leads to the following situation. There are 2^n different strings, and the online algorithm can partition them into $2^{b(n)}$ groups $\mathcal{G}_1, \mathcal{G}_2, \ldots, \mathcal{G}_{2^{b(n)}}$; the adversary cannot influence this partitioning. For every group, there is a *center string* s_i, which is the string that the online algorithm outputs when the adversary picks an instance from the group $\mathcal{G}_i$ with $1 \leq i \leq 2^{b(n)}$. In general, of course, the center string is not necessarily within "its" group; if it is not, the algorithm always makes some errors when given an instance from the group. In what follows, however, we will assume that the center string is contained in its group. This way, if this string is the one to be guessed, the algorithm has no cost; clearly, this does not weaken the algorithm. The adversary then tries to pick a string s as the input string such that the Hamming distance between s and s_i is maximized. Therefore, the online algorithm tries to create the groups such that the Hamming distance from s_i to any string contained in $\mathcal{G}_i$ is minimized; an example of such a partitioning is shown in Figure 7.1.

The crucial thing is that, since we consider the bit guessing problem with unknown history (in which no feedback is supplied), the algorithm is completely "blind" with respect to which string is actually chosen by the adversary. The idea of the subsequent proof is therefore to analyze a best way of choosing the groups and center strings. Since guessing $n/2$ bits correctly can be done with one advice bit (see Theorem 7.6), we are only interested in how much information is needed to do better than that.

For the following analysis, we need the subsequent technical lemma, which involves the binary entropy function

$$\mathcal{H}_2(x) := -x \log_2 x - (1 - x) \log_2(1 - x),$$

which is depicted in Figure 7.2.

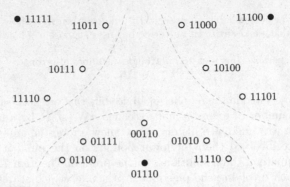

Figure 7.1. Example of groups that allow for a maximal error of 1.

Furthermore, we need the *binomial theorem*, which states that, for all $x, y \in \mathbb{R}$ and $m \in \mathbb{N}$, we have

$$\sum_{i=0}^{m} \binom{m}{i} x^i y^{m-i} = (x+y)^m .$$

Lemma 7.1. *For any $k \leq 1/2$, we have*

$$\sum_{i=0}^{kn} \binom{n}{i} \leq 2^{\mathcal{H}_2(k)n} .$$

Proof. To prove the claim, we need to show that

$$2^{-\mathcal{H}_2(k)n} \sum_{i=0}^{kn} \binom{n}{i} \leq 1 . \tag{7.1}$$

First, we rewrite the first factor of the left-hand side as

$$\begin{aligned}
2^{-\mathcal{H}_2(k)n} &= 2^{(k \log_2 k + (1-k) \log_2(1-k))n} \\
&= 2^{\log_2(k^{kn})} \cdot 2^{\log_2((1-k)^{(1-k)n})} \\
&= k^{kn} (1-k)^{(1-k)n} \\
&= \left(\frac{k}{1-k} \right)^{kn} (1-k)^n .
\end{aligned}$$

$$\text{(by multiplying by } (1-k)^{kn}/(1-k)^{kn})$$

With this, the left-hand side of (7.1) can be bounded by

$$2^{-\mathcal{H}_2(k)n} \sum_{i=0}^{kn} \binom{n}{i}$$

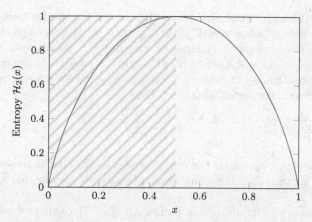

Figure 7.2. The binary entropy function. For us, this function is only interesting for $x \geq 1/2$ (that is, the part that is not hatched).

$$\leq \sum_{i=0}^{kn} \binom{n}{i} \left(\frac{k}{1-k} \right)^{kn} (1-k)^n$$

$$\leq \sum_{i=0}^{kn} \binom{n}{i} \left(\frac{k}{1-k} \right)^{i} (1-k)^n$$

(since $k/(1-k) \leq 1$ due to $k \leq 1-k$, which follows from $k \leq 1/2$)

$$= \sum_{i=0}^{kn} \binom{n}{i} k^i (1-k)^{n-i}$$

$$\leq \sum_{i=0}^{kn} \binom{n}{i} k^i (1-k)^{n-i} + \sum_{i=kn+1}^{n} \binom{n}{i} k^i (1-k)^{n-i}$$

$$= \sum_{i=0}^{n} \binom{n}{i} k^i (1-k)^{n-i}$$

$$= (k + (1-k))^n \,,$$

(using the binomial theorem)

which is equal to 1 and therefore proves the claim. $\qquad\square$

Now we are ready to prove the following theorem, which allows us to bound the number of advice bits necessary to guarantee we do not exceed a given fraction of errors.

Theorem 7.7. *Every online algorithm with advice that guesses at least γn bits correctly of every instance of bit guessing with unknown history has to use at least*

$$(1 + (1-\gamma)\log_2(1-\gamma) + \gamma \log_2 \gamma)n$$

advice bits, where $1/2 \leq \gamma \leq 1$.

Proof. Let ALG be an online algorithm with advice for the bit guessing problem with unknown history; we assume that ALG guesses γn bits correctly, that is, makes at most $(1 - \gamma)n$ errors on every input of length $n + 1$. As always, ALG uses $b(n)$ advice bits to guess strings of length n. Thus, by the pigeonhole principle, there are $2^n/2^{b(n)}$ instances that get the same advice. Let ϕ be one such advice string, and let $\mathcal{I}_\phi$ be the corresponding set of instances. Thus,

$$|\mathcal{I}_\phi| \geq \frac{2^n}{2^{b(n)}} . \tag{7.2}$$

There is one string s_ϕ, called the *center string*, for $\mathcal{I}_\phi$ that is the output of ALG whenever a string from $\mathcal{I}_\phi$ is the input; as noted above, we assume that s_ϕ is contained in $\mathcal{I}_\phi$.

Next, we want to give an upper bound on $|\mathcal{I}_\phi|$. To this end, we need some combinatorial ideas from coding theory. Consider a fixed binary string s' of length n. There are exactly

$$\binom{n}{i}$$

binary strings that are different from s' at exactly i positions, that is, that have Hamming distance i from s'. If we allow a maximum of $(1 - \gamma)n$ positions at which the strings are allowed to be different from s', we get a total of

$$\sum_{i=0}^{(1-\gamma)n} \binom{n}{i}$$

binary strings. This is exactly the maximum size that is allowed for a group of strings with center string s'.

In order to be able to guarantee that ALG makes at most $(1 - \gamma)n$ errors, it must therefore hold that

$$|\mathcal{I}_\phi| \leq \sum_{i=0}^{(1-\gamma)n} \binom{n}{i} \leq 2^{\mathcal{H}_2(1-\gamma)n} , \tag{7.3}$$

where we used Lemma 7.1 (note that $1 - \gamma \leq 1/2$ since $\gamma \geq 1/2$). Otherwise, there is at least one string contained in $\mathcal{I}_\phi$ that has a Hamming distance of more than $(1 - \gamma)n$ to s_ϕ. The adversary could choose this string as the input string and ALG would make more than $(1 - \gamma)n$ errors.

From (7.2) and (7.3), we obtain

$$\frac{2^n}{2^{b(n)}} \leq 2^{-\gamma n \log_2 \gamma - (1-\gamma)n \log_2(1-\gamma)}$$

$$\iff \quad 2^n \leq 2^{b(n)} \cdot 2^{\log_2(\gamma^{-\gamma n})} \cdot 2^{\log_2((1-\gamma)^{-(1-\gamma)n})}$$

$$\iff \quad 2^n \le 2^{b(n)} \cdot \left(\frac{1}{\gamma}\right)^{\gamma n} \cdot \left(\frac{1}{1-\gamma}\right)^{(1-\gamma)n}$$

$$\iff 2^{b(n)} \ge 2^n \cdot \gamma^{\gamma n} \cdot (1-\gamma)^{(1-\gamma)n}$$

$$\iff \quad b(n) \ge n + \gamma n \log_2 \gamma + (1-\gamma)n \log_2(1-\gamma)$$

$$\iff \quad b(n) \ge (1 + \gamma \log_2 \gamma + (1-\gamma) \log_2(1-\gamma))n \ ,$$

which proves the claim. $\qquad\qquad\qquad\qquad\qquad\qquad\qquad\qquad\qquad\qquad\square$

Note that the groups $\mathcal{G}_i$ with $1 \le i \le 2^{b(n)}$ are nothing else than so-called *Hamming balls* with radius $(1-\gamma)n$, and that the number of strings they maximally contain coincides with their volume.

Exercise 7.9. Prove the following generalization of Lemma 7.1. For every natural number $\sigma \ge 2$ and k with $k \le 1 - 1/\sigma$, we have

$$\sum_{i=0}^{kn} \binom{n}{i} (\sigma - 1)^i \le \sigma^{\mathcal{H}_\sigma(k)n} \ ,$$

where

$$\mathcal{H}_\sigma(x) = x \log_\sigma(\sigma - 1) - x \log_\sigma x - (1-x) \log_\sigma(1-x) \ .$$

is the σ-ary entropy function.

Exercise 7.10. Use the statement of Exercise 7.9 to prove the following generalization of Theorem 7.7. Every online algorithm with advice that guesses at least γn characters correctly of every instance of string guessing with unknown history with an alphabet size of $\sigma \ge 2$ has to use at least

$$\left(1 + (1-\gamma) \log_\sigma\left(\frac{1-\gamma}{\sigma - 1}\right) + \gamma \log_\sigma \gamma\right) n \log_2 \sigma$$

advice bits, where $1/\sigma \le \gamma \le 1$.

The proof of Theorem 7.7 uses the fact that, in the case of an unknown history, the online algorithm can only base its guesses on the advice. When the algorithm is provided with feedback, it may be able to single out some potential instances using what it knows about the history. Therefore, we need to be more careful when proving the subsequent theorem that bounds the number of advice bits for this version of the problem.

This time, let ALG be an online algorithm with advice for the bit guessing problem with known history; we again assume that ALG guesses γn bits correctly, where $1/2 \le \gamma \le 1$. We represent the 2^n different strings of length n by a binary tree $\mathcal{T} = (V, E)$ of height n (that is, with $n + 1$ levels). We label the vertices and edges of $\mathcal{T}$ as follows; see Figure 7.3 for an example with $n = 4$.

- For j with $1 \le j \le 2^n$, $v_{0,j}$ is the leaf that represents the jth binary string of length n in canonical order (all these strings are feasible inputs of length n).

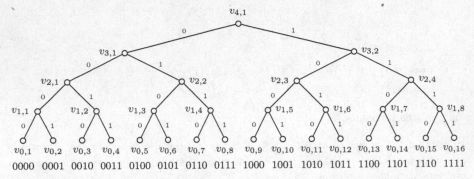

Figure 7.3. The binary tree $\mathcal{T}$ representing the strings of length 4 of bit guessing with known history.

- In general, the vertex $v_{i,j}$ with $0 \leq i \leq n$ and $1 \leq j \leq 2^{n-i}$ represents the string $s_{i,j}$, which is the jth binary string in canonical order of length $n - i$. Note that the index i increases from the bottom to the top; for instance, a vertex on level 0 is a leaf and the unique vertex $v_{n,1}$ on level n is the root of $\mathcal{T}$.

- We may think of the vertex $v_{i,j}$ as representing all instances that have the prefix $s_{i,j}$. Let $v_{i-1,j'}$ and $v_{i-1,j''}$ be the two children of $v_{i,j}$ with $1 \leq i \leq n$, $1 \leq j \leq 2^{n-i}$, and $1 \leq j', j'' \leq 2^{n-i-1}$. The strings $s_{i-1,j'}$ and $s_{i-1,j''}$ that are represented by these children have a common prefix, namely $s_{i,j}$. The edge from $v_{i,j}$ to $v_{i,j'}$ ($v_{i,j''}$, respectively) is labeled by the bit that extends $s_{i,j}$ to $s_{i,j'}$ ($s_{i,j''}$, respectively).

Without loss of generality, we assume that if $j' < j''$, $s_{i-1,j'}$ extends $s_{i,j}$ by appending a 0, and $s_{i-1,j''}$ extends $s_{i,j}$ by appending a 1.

Note that trees constructed this way are actually special kinds of partition trees, which we introduced in Section 3.3 (see also Exercise 7.5).[6] A similar idea was also followed in the proof of Theorem 3.6, where we gave a lower bound on the number of advice bits necessary to be c-competitive for paging.

Let us get back to the analysis of ALG. As always, due to the pigeonhole principle, there is an advice string that is used for at least $2^n/2^{b(n)}$ instances of length n; as above, let ϕ be one such advice string, and let $\mathcal{I}_\phi$ be the corresponding set of instances. We can view the computation of ALG when given an instance from $\mathcal{I}_\phi$ as traversing $\mathcal{T}$ as follows. ALG starts at the root vertex $v_{n,1}$. The instances from $\mathcal{I}_\phi$ correspond to some of the leaves; we assume that these leaves are known to ALG. However, the adversary can decide which instance from $\mathcal{I}_\phi$ is given, and thus which is the actual leaf. In T_1, ALG makes a guess, and corresponding to that guess chooses one of the two subtrees rooted at $v_{n-1,1}$ or $v_{n-1,2}$, respectively; for instance, if it

---

[6]However, the order of the levels is different from the one we sometimes use to describe partition trees, which makes the analysis easier.

guesses 0, it chooses the subtree rooted at $v_{n-1,1}$. After that, in T_2, the adversary must reveal which would have been the correct guess. If it says the correct bit is 1, ALG made an error, but now knows that the instance must correspond to a leaf that is rooted at $v_{n-1,2}$; it therefore continues the traversal of $\mathcal{T}$ from this vertex.

For ease of notation, if there is an instance $I \in \mathcal{I}_\phi$ in a subtree rooted at some inner vertex v such that, when given I, ALG makes m errors, we just say that the subtree rooted at v "contains m errors." Note that these errors are made in addition to the errors already made on the prefix of the input (on the path from $v_{n,1}$ to v).

In what follows, let the function size: $\mathbb{N} \times \mathbb{N} \to \mathbb{N}$ be defined such that $\text{size}(h, r)$ is equal to the maximum number of strings from $\mathcal{I}_\phi$ that can be represented by a vertex on level h in $\mathcal{T}$ such that ALG makes at most r errors on each of these instances. This bound is tight in the sense that increasing $\text{size}(h, r)$ by one enables the adversary to force ALG to make more than r errors.

Since the instances are represented by the leaves of $\mathcal{T}$, we are interested in $\text{size}(n, r)$, which tells us how many instances can maximally be contained in $\mathcal{I}_\phi$ such that ALG makes at most r errors. In what follows, we prove three technical lemmata; we start by showing how the maximum number of errors contained in a subtree can be computed recursively.

Lemma 7.2. *For every vertex u of $\mathcal{T}$, let* error: $V \to \mathbb{N}$ *be a function such that* $\text{error}(u)$ *is equal to the number of errors that are contained in the subtree rooted at u. Let v be any inner vertex of $\mathcal{T}$ such that the subtree rooted at v contains at least one leaf that represents an instance from $\mathcal{I}_\phi$, and let the children of v be v' and v''. Denoting*

$$m := \max\{\text{error}(v'), \text{error}(v'')\} ,$$

we have

$$\text{error}(v) \geq \begin{cases} m + 1 & \text{if } \text{error}(v') = \text{error}(v'') = m , \\ m & \text{else} . \end{cases}$$

Proof. We distinguish between the above two cases to prove the lemma.

Case 1. Suppose both the subtree rooted at v' and the one rooted at v'' contain m errors. In this case, the adversary can always choose the subtree that ALG did not choose, and therefore cause one error in the current time step and another m errors in the subtree that should have been entered.

Case 2. Without loss of generality, suppose the subtree rooted at v' contains m errors; the other subtree (rooted at v'') contains fewer errors. The adversary chooses the subtree rooted at v', and therefore ALG makes at least m errors in the subtree rooted at v. If ALG also chooses the subtree rooted at v', it does not make an error in the current time step; if it chooses the other one, it even makes an additional error.

This proves the claim. $\qquad\qquad\qquad\qquad\qquad\qquad\qquad\qquad\qquad\qquad\qquad\square$

Next, we show how size(n, r) can be computed recursively using Lemma 7.2.

Lemma 7.3. *For r and h with $r \leq h \leq n$, we have*

$$\text{size}(1, 0) = 1 \, , \tag{7.4}$$
$$\text{size}(1, 1) = 2 \, , \tag{7.5}$$
$$\text{size}(h, r) = \text{size}(h - 1, r) + \text{size}(h - 1, r - 1), \quad \textit{for } r \geq 2 \, . \tag{7.6}$$

Proof. We first prove (7.4) and (7.5). Note that both equations speak about vertices on level 1. In other words, ALG guesses the last position of the binary string on this level, and chooses one of the leaves. Clearly, if both instances are in $\mathcal{I}_\phi$, the adversary can always choose the leaf that ALG does not choose. Thus, there can only be one instance from $\mathcal{I}_\phi$ if ALG makes no error with this guess (that is, size$(1, 0) = 1$), and if the maximum number of errors is 1, then both leaves can represent instances (that is, size$(1, 1) = 2$).

It remains to prove (7.6); let $2 \leq r \leq h \leq n$. We know from Lemma 7.2 that if there is a subtree rooted at some vertex on level h that contains r errors, the maximum number of errors contained in each of the subtrees rooted at its two children cannot be larger than r. Moreover, we know that it cannot be the case that both these subtrees contain r errors. Since the function size clearly does not decrease with r, it is maximized if one subtree contains r errors and the other one contains $r - 1$ errors, which yields

$$\text{size}(h, r) = \text{size}(h - 1, r) + \text{size}(h - 1, r - 1)$$

as stated by (7.6). $\square$

Finally, we give a closed form for size(h, r), which seems familiar.

Lemma 7.4. *For r and h with $r \leq h \leq n$, we have*

$$\text{size}(h, r) = \sum_{i=0}^{r} \binom{h}{i} \, .$$

Proof. We prove the claim by induction on h.

Base Case. Let $h = 1$. Since $r \leq h$, it follows that either $r = 0$ or $r = 1$. Due to (7.4) and (7.5), we have

$$\text{size}(1, 0) = 1 = \sum_{i=0}^{0} \binom{1}{i} \quad \text{and} \quad \text{size}(1, 1) = 2 = \sum_{i=0}^{1} \binom{1}{i} \, ,$$

and thus the base case is covered.

Induction Hypothesis. The claim holds for every $h' \leq h$, that is,

$$\text{size}(h', r) = \sum_{i=0}^{r} \binom{h'}{i} \, .$$

Induction Step. We obtain

$$\text{size}(h+1,r) = \text{size}(h,r) + \text{size}(h,r-1)$$

(as a consequence of Lemma 7.3)

$$= \sum_{i=0}^{r} \binom{h}{i} + \sum_{i=0}^{r-1} \binom{h}{i}$$

(using the induction hypothesis)

$$= \binom{h}{0} + \sum_{i=1}^{r} \binom{h}{i} + \sum_{i=1}^{r} \binom{h}{i-1}$$

$$= \binom{h}{0} + \sum_{i=1}^{r} \left(\binom{h}{i} + \binom{h}{i-1} \right)$$

$$= \binom{h+1}{0} + \sum_{i=1}^{r} \binom{h+1}{i}$$

$$= \sum_{i=0}^{r} \binom{h+1}{i}.$$

The claim follows. □

Theorem 7.8. *Every online algorithm with advice that guesses at least γn bits correctly of every instance of bit guessing with known history has to use at least*

$$(1 + (1 - \gamma) \log_2(1 - \gamma) + \gamma \log_2 \gamma)n$$

advice bits, where $1/2 \leq \gamma \leq 1$.

Proof. With the above considerations, we get that

$$\frac{2^n}{2^{b(n)}} \leq \text{size}(n, (1-\gamma)n)$$

has to be true if ALG makes at most $(1-\gamma)n$ errors. Using Lemma 7.4 with $r = (1-\gamma)n$ and $h = n$, and then Lemma 7.1, yields

$$\frac{2^n}{2^{b(n)}} \leq \sum_{i=0}^{(1-\gamma)n} \binom{n}{i} \leq 2^{-\gamma n \log_2 \gamma - (1-\gamma)n \log_2(1-\gamma)}.$$

By the same calculations as in the proof of Theorem 7.7, we conclude that

$$b(n) \geq (1 + \gamma \log_2 \gamma + (1 - \gamma) \log_2(1 - \gamma))n,$$

which finishes the proof. □

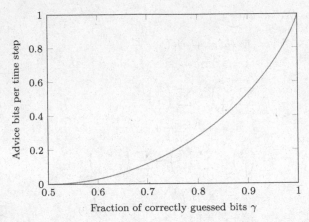

Figure 7.4. The average number of advice bits necessary per time step to guess a fraction γ of all bits correctly.

The number of advice bits necessary per time step on average to guess a fraction γ of all bits correctly is depicted in Figure 7.4. In this section, we gave two lower-bound proofs, which use different approaches; one for the case of unknown history (Theorem 7.7) and one for the case of known history (Theorem 7.8). However, note that a lower bound for the case with known history of course implies the same lower bound for the case of an unknown history.

Exercise 7.11.* Prove the following generalization of Theorem 7.8. Every online algorithm with advice that guesses at least γn bits correctly of every instance of string guessing with known history with an alphabet size of $\sigma \geq 2$ has to use at least

$$\left(1 + (1 - \gamma) \log_\sigma \left(\frac{1 - \gamma}{\sigma - 1}\right) + \gamma \log_\sigma \gamma\right) n \log_2 \sigma$$

advice bits, where $1/\sigma \leq \gamma \leq 1$.

7.4 Advice-Preserving Reductions

In many areas of theoretical computer science, we use the concept of *reductions* to show that a certain problem is hard (where the concept of "hardness" reflects what we are investigating) under the assumption that a second problem is hard. The two best-known examples are from the field of computability and classical complexity theory where we classify problems as $\mathcal{NP}$-hard (both of which we briefly mentioned in Section 1.1).

The bit guessing problem can be used to give lower bounds on the advice complexity of other online problems by means of a special kind of reduction. In doing so, we can use the lower bounds on the number of advice bits needed to guess a certain number of bits correctly (that is, Theorems 7.7 and 7.8) to obtain lower bounds on the number of advice bits needed to achieve some specific competitive ratio for the given problem; we call such a reduction an *advice-preserving reduction*. Our focus is not on formalizing this idea in every detail, but on describing this technique on an intuitive, yet precise level.

The general scheme is as follows. Consider some online problem Π, and assume there is some online algorithm BB ("black box") with advice for Π. Now we construct an online algorithm BGUESS with advice for the bit guessing problem that uses BB as follows. Let I' be an input of bit guessing with either known or unknown history; let n' denote the length of the string that is to be guessed (recall that the length of I' is actually $n' + 1$). BGUESS simulates BB, and thus creates its input I, may read its output, and is additionally able to write on its advice tape. BGUESS bases its own output on the output of BB. Whenever BB wants to read an advice bit, BGUESS copies a bit from its own tape and writes it to the corresponding position of BB's advice tape. As a result, the two algorithms use the same number of advice bits.[7] BGUESS creates the input for BB such that BB is forced to have a larger cost when the guess of BGUESS was incorrect. In the case of known history, this can be done right after the guess; for an unknown history, it is done at the end, when the correct bit string is revealed to BGUESS. This way, we get an equivalence of the type

BB's performance on I is c $\iff$ BGUESS guesses $\gamma n'$ bits correctly on I' .

Note that in essence all BGUESS does is to map its input to an input for BB, and map BB's output to its own output. Depending on the problem variant we consider, we know from Theorem 7.7 or 7.8, respectively, that any online algorithm for bit guessing needs to use at least

$$(1 + (1 - \gamma)\log_2(1 - \gamma) + \gamma\log_2\gamma)n'$$

advice bits to guess a fraction γ of all bits correctly. This implies that BB must use at least this many advice bits as well; otherwise, BGUESS would also use fewer advice bits, which is a direct contradiction.

In the three subsequent subsections, we will use reductions from bit guessing to give lower bounds for three different online problems. These reductions always follow the above idea. The challenge is usually to build independent *widgets* that form the input of BB, and that allow us to map a guess to a number of decisions of BB such that the above equivalence holds.

7.4.1 The k-Server Problem

We already studied the advice complexity of k-server in Section 4.6. So far, the only lower bound we gave dealt with the number of advice bits that are necessary to produce an optimal output. Now we want to use a reduction from the bit guessing

---

[7]In principle, we could allow BGUESS to read additional advice, but we will not need this for the examples presented in this chapter.

problem with known history to get a lower bound on the number of advice bits that are necessary to obtain a small competitive ratio. This time, we will consider 2-server on a path with three points p_1, p_2, and p_3 with $\text{dist}(p_1, p_2) = \text{dist}(p_2, p_3) = 1$. There are two servers s_1 and s_2. Initially, s_1 is positioned on p_1, and s_2 is positioned on p_3.

Following Theorem 4.1, we know that we can restrict ourselves to lazy algorithms for k-server. For the metric spaces we consider here, we can additionally assume that the initial order of the servers is never changed. Algorithms that follow this principle are called *non-swapping*.

Definition 7.3 (Non-Swapping Online Algorithm). An online algorithm for 2-server on the line is called *non-swapping* if it never positions the server s_2 to the left of s_1.

We leave the proof that Definition 7.3 does not cause any restriction (for paths of length 2) as an exercise for the reader.

Theorem 7.9. *Every c-competitive online algorithm for 2-server on a path of length 2 can be transformed into a lazy non-swapping online algorithm for 2-server on a path of length 2 that is also c-competitive.*

Exercise 7.12. Prove Theorem 7.9.

We now prove the following theorem by reducing the bit guessing problem with known history to k-server (more specifically, to 2-server on a path of length 2). The general idea is as described at the beginning of this section. We suppose we are given an online algorithm BBKS with advice for 2-server that achieves some specific competitive ratio. Then we show that BBKS needs to use at least a certain number of advice bits since otherwise it would allow us to design an online algorithm with advice for bit guessing that contradicts the lower bound of Theorem 7.8.

Theorem 7.10. *For every c with $c \leq 3/2$, every c-competitive online algorithm with advice for 2-server on a path of length 2 has to use at least*

$$\left(1 + (c - 1)\log_2(c - 1) + (2 - c)\log_2(2 - c)\right) \cdot \frac{n}{5}$$

advice bits.

Proof. We reduce bit guessing with known history to 2-server on a path of length 2. Let BBKS be some online algorithm with advice for 2-server. We construct an online algorithm BGUESS with advice for bit guessing with known history that uses BBKS as a black box. Whenever BBKS asks for advice, BGUESS simply copies it from its own tape. Due to Theorem 7.9, we assume without loss of generality that BBKS is a lazy non-swapping algorithm.

In the first time step T_1', BGUESS is given the length n' of the string it is supposed to guess as part of the input I'. BGUESS creates an input I for BBKS of length $n = 5n'$; in particular, BGUESS simulates the first five time steps $T_1, T_2, \ldots, T_5$ of BBKS as follows. Initially, BGUESS requests the point p_2, that is, the point in the middle that is not occupied by any server. BBKS has to answer this request by either moving s_1 to the right or s_2 to the left. If BBKS chooses s_1, BGUESS guesses the first bit to be 0; if BBKS chooses s_2, BGUESS outputs 1. After that, BGUESS is told whether its guess was correct in T_2'. Depending on this feedback, BGUESS extends the input that is given to BBKS. This is done before the next guess is made. We distinguish two cases; the corresponding sequences are depicted in Figure 7.5.

Case 1. Suppose the correct guess is 0. In this case, after the first request p_2 is sent in T_1, the points p_3, p_2, p_3, and p_1 are requested in this order. The five requests are shown in Figure 7.5a. We distinguish two subcases.

Case 1.1. Suppose BBKS uses s_1 to serve the first request p_2. Then it pays 1 in T_1. After that, the next three requests p_3, p_2, and p_3 do not require any movement. Finally, p_1 is requested. Since BBKS is non-swapping, it serves this request with s_1 and has cost 2 in total.

Since BGUESS guesses 0 in this case, it has cost 0 in T_1'.

Case 1.2. Suppose BBKS uses s_2 to serve p_2. Then it again pays 1 in T_1. After that, the second request p_3 must be served by moving s_2 (since BBKS is non-swapping). Next, p_2 is requested, and BBKS has to move one of the servers. No matter which one it picks, in the last two requests, this server has to be moved again. Therefore, it has cost 4 in total.

Since BGUESS guesses 1 in this case, it has cost 1 in T_1'.

Case 2. Suppose the correct guess is 1. In this case, p_1, p_2, p_1, and p_3 are requested in this order in time steps T_2, T_3, T_4, and T_5. The five requests are shown in Figure 7.5b. Analogously to the first case, it can be shown that using s_2 causes cost 2, while moving s_1 causes cost 4. If BBKS has cost 2, BGUESS has cost 0, and if BBKS has cost 4, BGUESS has cost 1.

It is crucial to note that, since BBKS is lazy and non-swapping, the server s_1 is positioned on p_1, and the server s_2 is positioned on p_3 afterwards. As a result, we have the same situation as at the beginning of T_1', and BGUESS can continue in the above fashion. In every time step, BGUESS guesses the correct bit if and only if BBKS has cost 2 in the corresponding five time steps. If BGUESS guesses the incorrect bit, BBKS has cost 4.

Clearly, the optimal cost for I is $(2n)/5$. Now suppose BGUESS guesses $\gamma n' = (\gamma n)/5$ bits correctly. For the competitive ratio c of BBKS, it follows that

$$c \geq \frac{\text{cost}(\text{BBKS}(I))}{\text{cost}(\text{OPT}(I))} = \frac{2\gamma \cdot n/5 + 4(1 - \gamma) \cdot n/5}{(2n)/5},$$

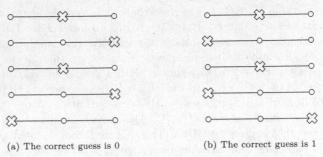

(a) The correct guess is 0   (b) The correct guess is 1

Figure 7.5. The two possible request sequences that are used by BGUESS.

and therefore $\gamma \geq 2 - c$. Recall that $\gamma \geq 1/2$ has to be satisfied in order to apply Theorem 7.8. This is ensured by requiring $2 - c \geq 1/2$, which yields $c \leq 3/2$. Then again, BBKS being c-competitive means that BGUESS guesses $\gamma n'$ bits correctly. From Theorem 7.8 we know that this requires that BGUESS uses at least $(1 + (1 - \gamma) \log_2(1 - \gamma) + \gamma \log_2 \gamma)n'$ advice bits, which increases in γ for $\gamma \geq 1/2$. Therefore, BGUESS has to read at least

$$(1 + (1 - \gamma) \log_2(1 - \gamma) + \gamma \log_2 \gamma)n'$$
$$= (1 + (c - 1) \log_2(c - 1) + (2 - c) \log_2(2 - c)) \cdot \frac{n}{5}$$

advice bits. Finally, note that the optimal cost of the instances constructed increases with n, which finishes the proof. $\qquad\square$

7.4.2 The Set Cover Problem

In this subsection, we introduce another online problem, which will serve as a second example of how to apply a reduction from bit guessing to bound the number of advice bits needed in order to achieve a small competitive ratio from below. In the *online set cover problem*, we are given a set X of k objects[8] together with a set family S consisting of sets of objects from X; both are given to an online algorithm with the first request. Some of the elements of X are then requested in consecutive time steps. An online algorithm must select sets from S such that all requests are contained in at least one of them. The goal is to do so while using as few sets as possible.

For ease of presentation, we will simply refer to the problem as "set cover." Let us define the problem formally and then give a simple example.

---

[8]Usually, these objects are simply natural numbers, that is, $X = \{1, 2, \ldots, k\}$; however, for our studies, it is easier to use the more abstract notion of "objects."

Definition 7.4 (Set Cover). The *online set cover problem* is an online minimization problem. The first request contains a *ground set* $X = \{s_1, s_2, \ldots, s_k\}$ and a set family $\mathcal{S} \subseteq \mathcal{P}(X)$ of size m; without loss of generality, $\emptyset \notin \mathcal{S}$. In every time step (including the first one), an object (that is, an element of X) is requested. Immediately after each request s, an online algorithm for set cover has to specify a set $S_i \in \mathcal{S}$ such that $s \in S_i$ unless s is contained in a set that was taken in an earlier time step. The set of requested objects is denoted by $X' \subseteq X$. A feasible solution for the problem is any set family $\{S_1, S_2, \ldots, S_t\} \subseteq \mathcal{S}$ such that

$$X' \subseteq \bigcup_{i=1}^{t} S_i .$$

The objective is to minimize t, that is, to use as few sets as possible.

Example 7.2. Let ALG be some online algorithm for set cover, and consider the ground set

$$X = \{s_1, s_2, s_3, s_4, s_5, s_6, s_7, s_8\}$$

and the set family

$$\mathcal{S} = \{\{s_1, s_3, s_6\}, \{s_2, s_3, s_5, s_8\}, \{s_4, s_7\}, \{s_6, s_7, s_8\}\} ,$$

which are given to ALG with the first request. The first object that is requested is s_4. Since there is only one set contained in $\mathcal{S}$ that contains s_4, any online algorithm answers by taking the set $\{s_4, s_7\}$. The next request is s_3, and ALG may decide to take the set $\{s_2, s_3, s_5, s_8\}$ since it contains more objects than the other set that contains s_3. However, if the next request is s_6, ALG has to take an additional set; suppose it chooses the set $\{s_6, s_7, s_8\}$. In the case that the last request is s_1, ALG has to take yet another set. All in all, we have

$$I = ((X, \mathcal{S}, s_4), s_3, s_6, s_1) \quad \text{and} \quad X' = \{s_4, s_3, s_6, s_1\} ,$$

and an optimal solution uses the two sets $\{s_4, s_7\}$ and $\{s_1, s_3, s_6\}$, while ALG chooses the four sets $\{s_4, s_7\}$, $\{s_2, s_3, s_5, s_8\}$, $\{s_6, s_7, s_8\}$, and $\{s_1, s_3, s_6\}$; thus ALG has cost 4, while the optimal cost is 2. $\diamondsuit$

Note that the input length n is bounded from above by the size k of the set X; we had a similar situation for JSS, which we studied in Chapter 5. However, there are now two parameters in the game, namely k and m. Thus, the first question is which of the two we choose to measure the achievable competitive ratio and the advice complexity; throughout this subsection, we will give bounds with respect to both k and m. An upper bound on the advice needed to compute an optimal solution can easily be obtained.

Theorem 7.11. *There are optimal online algorithms* SCLIN1 *and* SCLIN2 *with advice for set cover that use* $k - 1$ *or* m *advice bits, respectively.*

Proof. Recall that any online algorithm for set cover knows both X and $\mathcal{S}$ in advance. The online algorithm SCLIN1 reads one bit for every element of X, and that bit is 1 if and only if the corresponding object is contained in the input. After that, SCLIN1 can compute an optimal solution and only include sets that are part of it. For the first request, however, the algorithm does not need to use any advice. Thus, $k - 1$ advice bits are sufficient. SCLIN2 reads one advice bit for every set in $\mathcal{S}$. This way, it gets information about some fixed optimal solution of the instance. It only chooses sets according to this solution. Note that the two bounds are incomparable in the sense that the relationship between k and m can be (almost) arbitrary. $\square$

Note that SCLIN1 gets advice about the input, and has to compute the solution on its own. Conversely, SCLIN2 gets information about an optimal solution and only needs to choose the sets from $\mathcal{S}$ accordingly. Next, we complement these bounds with lower bounds. To this end, we construct a set of instances that already reminds us of guessing bits. Let us first give an example.

Example 7.3. Let ALG be some online algorithm for set cover, and consider the ground set

$$X = \{a_1, a_2, a_3, a_4\} \cup \{b_{1,1}, b_{2,1}, b_{3,1}, b_{4,1}\} \cup \{b_{1,2}, b_{2,2}, b_{3,2}, b_{4,2}\}$$

and the set family

$$\mathcal{S} = \{\{a_1, b_{1,1}\}, \{a_1, b_{1,2}\}, \{a_2, b_{2,1}\}, \{a_2, b_{2,2}\},$$
$$\{a_3, b_{3,1}\}, \{a_3, b_{3,2}\}, \{a_4, b_{4,1}\}, \{a_4, b_{4,2}\}\} ,$$

which are given to ALG with the first request. The first object that is requested is a_1. ALG has exactly two possible answers; the requested object is uncovered, and there are two sets in $\mathcal{S}$ in which it is contained. Both these sets cover an additional object, namely $b_{1,1}$ or $b_{1,2}$, respectively. In the next time step, exactly one of these two objects is requested. Depending on its previous choice, ALG might have to take another set. Inputs from this set continue in this fashion until every a_i with $1 \leq i \leq k/3$ is requested together with either $b_{i,1}$ or $b_{i,2}$ for every i. Clearly, an optimal solution for such an instance uses exactly $k/3$ sets. $\diamond$

Note that, for any instance from the set described above, there are exactly $n = (2/3)k$ requests and the size of $\mathcal{S}$ is $m = (2/3)k$. We use this set of instances in the remainder of this chapter. We start by showing that every optimal online algorithm with advice needs a number of advice bits that is linear in both k and m.

Theorem 7.12. *Every optimal online algorithm with advice for set cover has to use at least* $\max\{k/3, m/2\}$ *advice bits.*

Proof. Let k be any multiple of 3; consider the ground set

$$X = \{a_1, a_2, \ldots, a_{k/3}\} \cup \{b_{1,1}, b_{2,1}, \ldots, b_{k/3,1}\} \cup \{b_{1,2}, b_{2,2}, \ldots, b_{k/3,2}\}$$

and the set family

$$\mathcal{S} = \{\{a_1, b_{1,1}\}, \{a_1, b_{1,2}\}, \{a_2, b_{2,1}\}, \{a_2, b_{2,2}\}, \ldots, \{a_{k/3}, b_{k/3,1}\}, \{a_{k/3}, b_{k/3,2}\}\}.$$

We construct a set $\mathcal{I}$ of instances of set cover as suggested in Example 7.3. There are $(2/3)k$ time steps. In odd time steps, the objects a_i with $1 \leq i \leq k/3$ are requested in ascending order. In the jth even time step, either $b_{j,1}$ or $b_{j,2}$ is requested; $\mathcal{I}$ covers all possibilities. It is immediate that there is an optimal solution that uses exactly $k/3$ sets from $\mathcal{S}$ for any $I \in \mathcal{I}$.

Now we claim that any online algorithm with advice that is optimal for set cover needs to use at least $k/3$ advice bits. For a contradiction, assume there is an online algorithm ALG that uses fewer advice bits, but is still optimal. There are exactly $2^{k/3}$ instances in $\mathcal{I}$. Since ALG uses fewer than $k/3$ advice bits, by the pigeonhole principle, it uses the same advice string for two instances, say I_1 and I_2. Consider the time step T_i, in which I_1 and I_2 differ for the first time. Since all instances in $\mathcal{I}$ are identical for the odd time steps, without loss of generality, we assume that in I_1, the object $b_{i/2,1}$ is requested, while $b_{i/2,2}$ is requested in I_2. In order to be optimal, the set $\{a_{i/2}, b_{i/2,1}\}$ has to be chosen for I_1, and $\{a_{i/2}, b_{i/2,2}\}$ has to be chosen for I_2. However, when $a_{i/2}$ was requested in the preceding time step T_{i-1}, ALG was not able to distinguish between the two instances, because it so far only saw their common prefix. Since the advice was the same, ALG chooses the same set for both instances and consequently needs to take an additional set in T_i for one of the instances. Therefore, on one of the two instances, ALG's cost is at least $k/3 + 1$, which contradicts its optimality. Thus, every optimal online algorithm with advice needs to use at least $k/3$ bits of advice.

Since $m = (2/3)k$, the second claim of the theorem (that is, the second argument of the max-expression) follows immediately from the same set of instances. $\qquad\square$

Exercise 7.13. Improve the bound of Theorem 7.12 by increasing the sets within $\mathcal{S}$.

Now that we have (asymptotically) tight bounds on the number of advice bits that allow us to produce an optimal output for set cover, we ask how much information is needed to obtain an "almost optimal" solution. To this end, we again use a reduction from bit guessing with known history. The idea of the following proof is rather similar to the proof of Theorem 7.12. The basic difference is that, instead of simply arguing about optimality, we can use our knowledge about bit guessing.

Theorem 7.13. *For every c with $c \leq 3/2$, every c-competitive online algorithm with advice for set cover has to use at least*

$$(1 + (c-1)\log_2(c-1) + (2-c)\log_2(2-c)) \cdot \max\left\{\frac{k}{3}, \frac{m}{2}\right\}$$

advice bits.

Proof. We reduce bit guessing with known history to set cover. Let BBsc be some online algorithm with advice for set cover. We construct an online algorithm BGuess with advice for bit guessing with known history that uses BBsc as a black box. Whenever BBsc asks for advice, BGuess simply copies it from its own tape.

In T_1', BGuess is given the length n' of the string it should guess as the first request of I'. BGuess creates an input I for BBsc of length $n = 2n'$ by first constructing a set X of size $k = (3/2)n$ and a set family S of size $m = n$ as in the proof of Theorem 7.12. Then it gives the first request (X, S, a_1) to BBsc. BBsc has to answer this request by selecting either $\{a_1, b_{1,1}\}$ or $\{a_1, b_{1,2}\}$. In the former case, BGuess guesses 0 in T_1', otherwise it guesses 1. In T_2', the correct guess is revealed to BGuess. Depending on this feedback, BGuess requests $b_{1,1}$ if the correct bit was 0 and $b_{1,2}$ if it was 1. We again distinguish two cases.

Case 1. Suppose the correct guess is 0. Then BGuess requests $b_{1,1}$ in T_2.

> *Case 1.1.* If BBsc used the set $\{a_1, b_{1,1}\}$ in T_1, it does not have to use another set and therefore has cost 1 in the first two time steps.

> Since BGuess guesses 0 in this case, it has cost 0 in T_1'.

> *Case 1.2.* If BBsc used the set $\{a_1, b_{1,2}\}$ in T_1, it must use another set in T_2 (namely the set $\{a_1, b_{1,1}\}$) in order to cover the request $b_{1,1}$. Therefore, it has cost 2 in the first two time steps.

> Since BGuess guesses 1 in this case, it has cost 1 in T_1'.

Case 2. Suppose the correct guess is 1. Analogously to the first case, it can be shown that BGuess has cost 0 in T_1' if and only if BBsc has cost 1 in the first two time steps; otherwise, BGuess has cost 1 in T_1'.

None of the objects involved so far is requested in any of the remaining time steps; hence, we can analyze them independently. BGuess proceeds as above, and thus whenever BGuess guesses a bit correctly, BBsc has cost 1 in the corresponding two time steps.

Clearly, the optimal cost on I is $n' = n/2$. Now suppose BGuess guesses $\gamma n' = \gamma n/2$ bits correctly. For the competitive ratio c of BBsc, we have

$$c \geq \frac{\text{cost}(\text{BBsc}(I))}{\text{cost}(\text{Opt}(I))} = \frac{n' + (1 - \gamma)n'}{n'} ,$$

and therefore $\gamma \geq 2 - c$. Since $\gamma \geq 1/2$, this again requires that $c \leq 3/2$. We know that BGuess needs to read at least

$$(1 + (1 - \gamma)\log_2(1 - \gamma) + \gamma \log_2 \gamma)n'$$
$$= (1 + (c - 1)\log_2(c - 1) + (2 - c)\log_2(2 - c)) \cdot \frac{n}{2}$$

advice bits to guess a fraction γ of all bits correctly.

The claims of the theorem follow from $n = (2/3)k$ and $n = m$. Moreover, we again note that the optimal cost increases with n. $\qquad\square$

Note that if c tends to 1, the bound from Theorem 7.13 tends to the bound given in Theorem 7.12.

Exercise 7.14. Give a reduction from bit guessing with unknown history to obtain the same bound as in Theorem 7.13; use the same X and $\mathcal{S}$.

Exercise 7.15. In Exercise 7.13, we gave a better bound on the number of advice bits necessary to compute optimal solutions by increasing the sets in $\mathcal{S}$. By doing so, generalize Theorem 7.13 by giving a reduction from string guessing with known history and alphabet size $\sigma \geq 2$. To this end, use the result of Exercise 7.11.

7.4.3 The Disjoint Path Allocation Problem

The third problem that we study as an example of using reductions from bit guessing is called the *disjoint path allocation problem*. This problem is concerned with establishing connections in a network; we assume the network topology is a very simple one, namely a path. Unlike the previous examples, this problem is a maximization problem. Although bit guessing is a minimization problem, it is still possible to reduce from it. As always, we start with a formal definition of the problem.

Definition 7.5 (Disjoint Path Allocation). The *disjoint path allocation problem* (DPA for short) is an online maximization problem. The first request contains the length ℓ of the underlying path P; the vertices of the path are denoted by $v_0, v_1, \ldots, v_\ell$. In every time step (including the first one), a subpath of P is requested; we assume that such a subpath is represented by a pair (v_i, v_j) containing its end vertices v_i and v_j with $0 \leq i < j \leq \ell$. If such a path does not share any edge with a previously granted connection (accepted path), an online algorithm for DPA has to decide whether to grant this connection; this decision is final. If the subpath does share an edge with a previously accepted one, it cannot be granted (we call such a subpath "blocked"). The objective is to grant as many requests as possible.

Let us again start with an example to get a better feeling for the problem.

Example 7.4. Let ALG be some online algorithm for DPA and suppose we are given a path of length 20 with the first request. The complete instance is depicted in Figure 7.6. The first request contains the subpath (v_0, v_6). If ALG decides to grant this request, and also the next one (v_9, v_{14}), it cannot grant any of the subsequent requests (v_4, v_7), (v_{13}, v_{16}), (v_6, v_{12}), (v_{14}, v_{20}), (v_1, v_4), and (v_{12}, v_{14}). The gain of ALG is therefore 2. An optimal solution has twice the gain by granting, for instance, the requests (v_0, v_6), (v_6, v_{12}), (v_{14}, v_{20}), and (v_{12}, v_{14}). $\qquad\diamond$

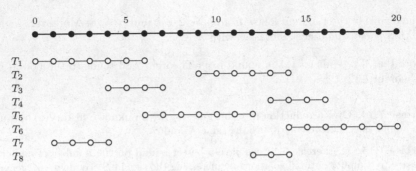

Figure 7.6. An instance on a path of length 20. The given path P contains black vertices, while the requests contain white vertices.

In principle, we could measure the advice complexity of DPA in either the number of requests n or the length ℓ of the path P. For our studies, we mostly consider ℓ.

Exercise 7.16. Show that there is no competitive online algorithm for DPA.

While it is easy to get an upper bound of n on the number of advice bits sufficient to compute an optimal solution for DPA, it is a little more tricky to get a bound of ℓ.

Theorem 7.14. *There are optimal online algorithms* DLIN1 *and* DLIN2 *with advice for DPA that use* n *or* ℓ *advice bits, respectively.*

Proof. As already mentioned, it is straightforward to give an upper bound of n; for every request, simply encode whether it is part of some fixed optimal solution or not. DLIN1 can simply read one bit per time step, and therefore no self-delimiting encoding is needed.

In order to prove that it is also sufficient to use ℓ advice bits, consider the following advice string. At position $i + 1$ (recall that the vertices of P start with v_0), a 1 is written if and only if, in some fixed optimal solution, vertex v_i is the left end vertex of a granted request. This way, $\ell + 1$ bits are used. Since DLIN2 knows ℓ, it knows how many bits to read. Now when a request (v_i, v_j) is given, DLIN2 accepts it only if position $i + 1$ on the advice tape is 1 and there is no 1 on the advice tape for any other vertex between v_i and v_j; whether position $j + 1$ contains a 0 or 1 does not matter. This way, DLIN2 never grants a request that blocks any other requests that are granted by the fixed optimal solution. Furthermore, it will always find a request to accept for every position on the tape that is 1.

Finally, we note that the last position $\ell + 1$ on the advice tape cannot be 1 since no request has its left end vertex at the last vertex v_ℓ. DLIN2 can therefore assume that this bit is 0. Hence, reading ℓ advice bits is sufficient. □

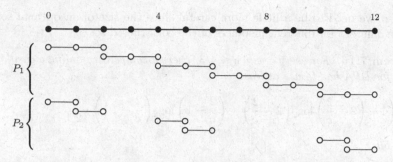

Figure 7.7. An instance from $\mathcal{I}$ on a path of length 12. In P_1, the second, fourth, and fifth requests should be granted, in order to grant as many requests as possible.

Next, we complement this upper bound with a lower bound. Similarly to the set cover problem, we use a set of instances that will come in handy later, when we apply a reduction from bit guessing.

Theorem 7.15. *Every optimal online algorithm with advice for DPA has to use at least $\ell/2$ advice bits.*

Proof. Let ℓ be even, and consider the following set $\mathcal{I}$ of instances on paths of length ℓ. Every instance from $\mathcal{I}$ is divided into two phases P_1 and P_2. Phase P_1 always contains the same requests

$$(v_0, v_2), (v_2, v_4), \ldots, (v_{\ell-2}, v_\ell) ,$$

which are offered in this order in the first $\ell/2$ time steps. Then, in P_2, for some of the above requests, two consecutive intersecting requests are given. An example of such an instance is shown in Figure 7.7.

We call a request from P_1 "open" if there are two requests intersecting with it in P_2; otherwise, it is called "closed." $\mathcal{I}$ contains every instance that corresponds to a possible way to open the requests of P_1. As a result, there are $2^{\ell/2}$ instances in $\mathcal{I}$. For any given instance $I \in \mathcal{I}$, there is a unique optimal solution $\text{OPT}(I)$ that grants exactly the closed requests in P_1, and is therefore able to grant all requests from P_2 as well.

For a contradiction, let ALG be some optimal online algorithm with advice for DPA that uses fewer than $\ell/2$ advice bits. Then there are two instances I_1 and I_2 in $\mathcal{I}$ that get the same advice. This implies that ALG grants the same requests in P_1. However, there is at least one request in P_1 that is open in one of the two instances, but closed in the other (otherwise I_1 and I_2 would not be different). Without loss of generality, assume the request is open in I_1. If ALG grants the request, it is not optimal for I_1; if it does not grant the request, it is not optimal for I_2. As a result, we get a contradiction, and ALG cannot be optimal. $\qquad\square$

Now we give a lower bound on the advice complexity to obtain a small competitive ratio. This time, we use bit guessing with unknown history in our reduction. In doing so, we need to be a little more careful since the size of an optimal solution may be different for different instances of the constructed set.

Theorem 7.16. *For every c with $c \leq 4/3$, every c-competitive online algorithm with advice for DPA has to use at least*

$$\left(1 + \left(2 - \frac{2}{c}\right) \log_2 \left(2 - \frac{2}{c}\right) + \left(\frac{2}{c} - 1\right) \log_2 \left(\frac{2}{c} - 1\right)\right) \cdot \frac{\ell}{2}$$

advice bits.

Proof. We reduce bit guessing with unknown history to DPA. Let BBDPA be some online algorithm with advice for DPA. As before, BGUESS uses BBDPA as a black box.

In T_1', as the first request of an instance I', BGUESS is given the length n' of the string it should guess and sets $\ell = 2n'$. The idea is to use the same set of instances as in the proof of Theorem 7.15. Thus, BGUESS first creates the input by setting the first request to $(\ell, (v_0, v_2))$. If BBDPA grants (v_0, v_2), BGUESS guesses 1 in T_1'; otherwise it guesses 0. It proceeds by requesting all remaining subpaths from P_1 in time steps $T_2, T_3, \ldots, T_{\ell/2}$ and guessing accordingly.

In the last time step $T_{n'+1}'$, BGUESS is told which guesses were correct. With this knowledge, it starts P_2 of the instance I for BBDPA. If the ith bit of I' is 0, BGUESS requests two consecutive subpaths of length 1 that intersect with the ith request of P_1. If the correct guess was 1, BGUESS does not request anything that intersects with this request. We distinguish two cases depending on the correct guess of the ith bit.

Case 1. Suppose the correct guess is 0. In this case, an optimal solution does not grant the ith request from P_1, but the two requests of length 1 that are given in P_2 and that both intersect with the ith request.

  Case 1.1. Suppose BBDPA does not grant the ith request from P_1. Then it can grant the two requests in P_2, which is optimal.

  Since BGUESS guesses 0 in this case, it has cost 0 in T_i'.

  Case 1.2. Suppose BBDPA grants the ith request from P_1. Then it has gain 1 in T_i, but it cannot grant either of the requests of length 1 in P_2.

  Since BGUESS guesses 1 in this case, it has cost 1 in T_i'.

Case 2. Suppose the correct guess is 1. In this case, an optimal solution grants the ith request from P_1. Analogously to the first case, it can easily be shown that if BBDPA has gain 1, BGUESS has cost 0, and if BBDPA has gain 0, BGUESS has cost 1.

It follows that, for every bit BGUESS guesses incorrectly, BBDPA is able to grant one fewer subpath compared to the optimal solution of I. Now suppose BGUESS guesses $\gamma n'$ bits correctly, and therefore makes $(1 - \gamma)n'$ incorrect guesses. By the above reasoning, we have

$$\text{gain}(\text{BBDPA}(I)) = \text{gain}(\text{OPT}(I)) - (1 - \gamma)n' . \tag{7.7}$$

Moreover, we can bound the optimal gain by

$$n' \leq \text{gain}(\text{OPT}(I)) \leq 2n' . \tag{7.8}$$

For the competitive ratio c of BBDPA we have

$$
\begin{aligned}
c &\geq \frac{\text{gain}(\text{OPT}(I))}{\text{gain}(\text{BBDPA}(I))} \\
&\geq \frac{\text{gain}(\text{OPT}(I))}{\text{gain}(\text{OPT}(I)) - (1 - \gamma)n'} \\
&\quad \textit{(as a consequence of (7.7))} \\
&= 1 + \frac{(1 - \gamma)n'}{\text{gain}(\text{OPT}(I)) - (1 - \gamma)n'} \\
&\geq 1 + \frac{1 - \gamma}{1 + \gamma} ,
\end{aligned}
$$

(due to the right-hand side of (7.8))

and with this we obtain

$$\gamma \geq \frac{2}{c} - 1 , \tag{7.9}$$

and thus, to satisfy $\gamma \geq 1/2$, it must hold that $c \leq 4/3$. We know from Theorem 7.7 that BGUESS needs to read at least $(1 + (1 - \gamma)\log_2(1 - \gamma) + \gamma \log_2 \gamma)n'$ advice bits to guess a fraction γ of all bits correctly. Due to (7.9), we conclude that any c-competitive online algorithm for DPA needs to read at least

$$
\begin{aligned}
&\left(1 + \left(2 - \frac{2}{c}\right) \log_2 \left(2 - \frac{2}{c}\right) + \left(\frac{2}{c} - 1\right) \log_2 \left(\frac{2}{c} - 1\right)\right)n' \\
&= \left(1 + \left(2 - \frac{2}{c}\right) \log_2 \left(2 - \frac{2}{c}\right) + \left(\frac{2}{c} - 1\right) \log_2 \left(\frac{2}{c} - 1\right)\right) \cdot \frac{\ell}{2}
\end{aligned}
$$

advice bits. Finally, note that the optimal gain grows with ℓ. $\qquad\square$

Exercise 7.17. Give a reduction from bit guessing with known history to obtain the same bound as in Theorem 7.16.

Exercise 7.18. As a means to give an online algorithm more power, we can reformulate DPA to allow for *preemption*, which means that an online algorithm is allowed to remove subpaths it granted before. It is, however, not allowed to grant a connection it discarded before. Also, we demand that the online algorithm has a feasible solution in every time step (that is, it never grants two overlapping requests at any time). Give a reduction from bit guessing with unknown history to this problem.

7.5 Historical and Bibliographical Notes

Emek et al. [58, 60] introduced a problem they called "general matching pennies," which they used within a reduction to prove lower bounds on the competitive ratio of online algorithms with advice for metrical task systems. The string guessing problem as we defined it in this chapter was introduced by Böckenhauer et al. [26, 27]. Although the concept of reductions already appeared in the aforementioned papers, a first attempt to formalize this concept was made by Sprock [134] and later refined by Hammann [73].

Example 7.1 is due to Gebauer [67]. Krug showed that it indeed helps to know the history for the bit guessing problem if one error is allowed [108]. Smula [132] studied the advice complexity of the bit guessing problem when the adversary is allowed to use randomization, that is, the oracle does not know the exact input, but a set of instances such that each instance from this set is chosen by the adversary with a certain probability. Moreover, she showed a reduction to the online set cover problem in this probabilistic setting [132].

The k-server problem was already introduced in Chapter 4. The reduction we presented is due to Smula [132]. The studied version of the online set cover problem was introduced by Alon et al. [8, 9] (in this paper, the authors studied a weighted version of the problem). Komm et al. [103] first studied the advice complexity of the set cover problem. A reduction from the string guessing problem to the online set cover problem was given by Böckenhauer et al. [27] together with a reduction to the online clique problem.

As already mentioned, DPA was one of the first problems that were studied within our model of advice complexity [30] (together with paging and JSS). In this paper, most bounds were given with respect to the input length. The proof of Theorem 7.15 can be found in the corresponding technical report [31]. An improved analysis with bounds with respect to the path length ℓ was made by Barhum et al. [16]. They showed that the bound of $\ell/2$ of Theorem 7.15 can be improved by a factor of roughly 2, and thus the bound of Theorem 7.14 is tight. Together with the results of Gebauer et al. [68], the investigations of Barhum et al. [16] show that the problem has a very interesting threshold behavior.

Dietiker [52] reduced the bit guessing problem to a variant of DPA where every request has the same length. The reduction presented in this chapter is due to Smula [132]. Selečéniová [129] studied DPA with preemption, and she showed the linear lower bound of Exercise 7.18.

In order to make the reductions from bit guessing more uniform, we slightly redefined set cover and DPA; for the former problem X and $\mathcal{S}$ are usually known from the start and thus problem parameters. To have a reduction that works for arbitrary sizes of X and $\mathcal{S}$, we made them part of the first request. Likewise, the length of the path ℓ for DPA is usually fixed. Moreover, DPA is often defined on general graphs instead of paths; however, since we mostly considered lower bounds, restricting ourselves to path networks makes our results only stronger.

The proofs of Lemma 7.1 and Exercise 7.9 are taken from the textbook of Guruswami et al. [70].

Problems on Graphs

8

In this chapter, we deal with a large class of computational problems, namely graph problems. We already described two prominent examples of graph problems at the beginning of this book. The difference is that, here, the graph is not known in advance; not even its size. In every time step, a vertex is revealed together with all edges to previously revealed vertices; an online algorithm has to base its answer for the current time step on the knowledge of the part of the graph that is known so far (and of course on its previous answers). In this chapter, we basically study two online graph problems.

The first problem we investigate is graph coloring in an online setting. We start by showing that this problem does not allow for a competitive deterministic online algorithm, even if the input graph is a tree. The given lower bound on the competitive ratio is roughly $\log_2 n$ for graphs with n vertices (that is, instances with n requests); this bound is tight. For bipartite graphs, there is an online algorithm that has a competitive ratio of at most $2\log_2 n$. Moreover, we study a "first fit" strategy. It turns out that this approach is bad for general bipartite graphs, but gives a best possible online coloring on trees. Next, we study online algorithms with advice on bipartite graphs; here, we show an almost matching linear upper and lower bound.

As the second problem, we look at the minimum spanning tree problem (MSTP), which was already briefly discussed in Chapter 1; more precisely, in Exercise 1.3, we have seen that a greedy approach (the algorithm KRUSKAL) is very successful for MSTP in the offline case. This result will be very valuable also for the online setting, in particular when we consider restricted classes of input graphs. We show that a greedy approach is rather successful also in the online setting if the input graph is complete and has a cost function that satisfies the triangle inequality. As a part of our investigation, we also revisit another graph problem that we had a brief look at in Chapter 1, namely the traveling salesman problem. If the graph does not have these properties, both deterministic and randomized online algorithms perform very poorly. We also study online algorithms with advice for the MSTP. First, we

© Springer International Publishing Switzerland 2016
D. Komm, *An Introduction to Online Computation*,
Texts in Theoretical Computer Science. An EATCS Series,
DOI 10.1007/978-3-319-42749-2_8

show that roughly $n \log_2 n$ advice bits are both necessary and sufficient to produce an optimal output. Then we establish a lower bound on small competitive ratios by a reduction from the bit guessing problem, which we studied in the preceding chapter. Finally, we again use the analysis of KRUSKAL to obtain some simple online algorithms with advice for certain graph classes. We also briefly touch a couple of other online problems, namely the online vertex cover problem, and the online independent set problem.

8.1 Introduction

Many computational problems are graph problems, that is, the input consists of a finite set of vertices and a finite set of edges, possibly with some associated edge weights. In Chapter 1, we already briefly discussed two offline graph problems, namely the traveling salesman problem and the minimum spanning tree problem. Moreover, some of the online problems we have dealt with so far were defined using graphs, such as the k-server problem and the disjoint path allocation problem. However, for these problems, the graphs were usually, at least in parts, known in advance. In the online setting used in this chapter, the graph is presented vertex by vertex; together with every vertex that is revealed, all edges to previously presented vertices are given. Essentially, *online graph problems* are just those online problems where the input has this particular form. Throughout this chapter, graphs are always undirected. Let us continue with a formal definition.

Definition 8.1 (Online Graph Problem). Let $G = (V, E)$ be an undirected graph with vertex set $V = \{v_1, v_2, \ldots, v_n\}$ and edge set $E = \{e_1, e_2, \ldots, e_m\}$; if G is weighted, then additionally there is a weight function weight: $E \to \mathbb{R}^+$. Let $\prec$ be a total ordering on V such that, without loss of generality, $v_1 \prec v_2 \prec \ldots \prec v_n$. An *online graph problem* is an online problem where the input corresponds to the vertices V, which are presented gradually such that, in time step T_i with $1 \leq i \leq n$, the vertex v_i (that is, the ith vertex according to $\prec$) is presented together with all edges $\{v_j, v_i\}$ for $v_j \prec v_i$ (that is, all edges that connect v_i to vertices that were presented earlier). In the deterministic setting, the answer y_i only depends on $v_1, v_2, \ldots, v_i$, the edges between these vertices (that is, the part of the graph that is known in T_i), and $y_1, y_2, \ldots, y_{i-1}$.

For most of the problems studied in this chapter, the input is given by an online graph as in Definition 8.1. The terms *online graph maximization problem* and *online graph minimization problem* are defined in the obvious way.

An example of how a graph can be presented is depicted in Figure 8.1. For ease of presentation, we will usually define $\prec$ implicitly by describing how the vertices are revealed. If the graph is weighted, then the cost function (gain function, respectively) depends on the associated weight function. Whenever we speak of "G" in this

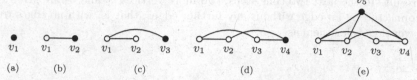

Figure 8.1. Online presentation of a graph. The most recently presented vertex is filled. The corresponding instance consists of five time steps.

chapter, this means the whole graph that represents the input. For convenience, we sometimes write, for instance, $\text{ALG}(G)$ instead of $\text{ALG}(I)$.

One thing that makes many online graph problems hard is that many of the vertices may appear as *isolated vertices*, that is, as vertices that do not have an edge at the point in time when they are revealed, but may have edges in G that are shown later (see, for instance, Example 8.1). Throughout this chapter, G is connected.

8.2 The Coloring Problem

We start with a famous graph problem where the goal is to color the vertices of a given graph. The crucial restriction is that any two vertices that are connected by an edge must not have the same color. Let us give a formal definition.

> **Definition 8.2 (Online Coloring).** The *online coloring problem* is an online graph minimization problem on unweighted graphs. An online algorithm for online coloring has to assign a natural number (a *color*) to each revealed vertex such that no two vertices that are connected by an edge have the same color. The goal is to minimize the total number of colors used.

We will simply speak of *coloring* in this context. For any graph G, $\chi(G)$ denotes the *chromatic number* of G, which is the smallest number of colors with which G can be colored. Let us start with an example that already suggests that the problem is hard in an online setting. In fact, the underlying idea of the following example will be used to obtain some of the subsequent results.

Example 8.1. Let ALG be an online algorithm for coloring; when the vertex v_1 is presented in the first time step, ALG starts by assigning color 1 to it, such that we get

①
v_1

as a result. In the next two time steps, two more vertices v_2 and v_3 are given that are connected by an edge without any further edges, that is, with no edges to v_1. ALG can thus color them as

and has used two colors so far. At this point, this is an optimal coloring, since any solution clearly needs to use two colors at least.

Next, however, the adversary requests a vertex v_4 that is connected to both v_1 and v_3, which forces ALG to use a third color, and thus to produce

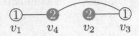

as a result. It is easy to see that

is an optimal solution that uses two colors instead of three.   ◇

8.2.1 Deterministic Algorithms

Coloring is hard for deterministic online algorithms; in particular, there is no competitive algorithm. This is already true for *bipartite graphs*, that is, graphs for which we can partition the vertices into two groups (so-called *shores*) such that there is no edge between any two vertices within one shore.

Observation 8.1. *Bipartite graphs are exactly the graphs that are 2-colorable (in other words, bipartite graphs have chromatic number 2).*

Indeed, if a graph is bipartite, we can simply assign color 1 to the first shore and color 2 to the second one. Conversely, if a graph is 2-colorable, we can define the shores with respect to a valid 2-coloring. The following theorem is proven by applying the idea from Example 8.1 and iterating it. The resulting instance is even more restricted than general bipartite graphs; it is a tree.

Theorem 8.1. *Every deterministic online algorithm for coloring uses at least* $\log_2 n + 1$ *colors.*

Proof. Let ALG be some deterministic online algorithm for coloring. In what follows, we show that, for any natural number k, there is a tree $\mathcal{T}_k$ and a total ordering $\prec_k$ on its vertices such that ALG has to use at least k colors to color it. To this end, we start as in Example 8.1, and then construct larger and larger trees. Essentially, every tree $\mathcal{T}_i$ is composed of smaller trees $\mathcal{T}_1, \mathcal{T}_2, \ldots, \mathcal{T}_{i-1}$. We construct the trees as follows.

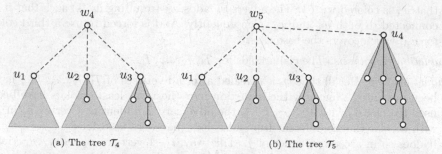

(a) The tree $\mathcal{T}_4$ (b) The tree $\mathcal{T}_5$

Figure 8.2. The construction of $\mathcal{T}_4$ and $\mathcal{T}_5$ by adding w_4 or w_5, respectively, to the already revealed trees.

- $\mathcal{T}_1$ consists of one single vertex w_1.
- $\mathcal{T}_2$ consists of two vertices v and w_2 that are connected by an edge.
- For $i \geq 3$, $\mathcal{T}_i$ consists of a vertex w_i that is connected to some specific vertices $u_1, u_2, \ldots, u_{i-1}$; every u_j with $1 \leq j \leq i-1$ is chosen from the tree $\mathcal{T}_j$ in a specific way that will be explained shortly.

The vertices are presented such that vertices from $\mathcal{T}_1$ are given first according to $\prec_1$, then the vertices from $\mathcal{T}_2$ according to $\prec_2$, and so on; finally, the vertex w_k is presented; this defines $\prec_k$.

An example of how the trees are constructed is depicted in Figure 8.2. First, we prove by induction that $\mathcal{T}_k$ has exactly 2^{k-1} vertices.

Base Case. Since $\mathcal{T}_1$ contains a single vertex and $\mathcal{T}_2$ contains two vertices, the base case is covered.

Induction Hypothesis. The claim holds for $\mathcal{T}_1, \mathcal{T}_2, \ldots, \mathcal{T}_{i-1}$.

Induction Step. Now consider $\mathcal{T}_i$. By the induction hypothesis, we have that $\mathcal{T}_j$ contains 2^{j-1} vertices, where $1 \leq j \leq i-1$. Since $\mathcal{T}_i$ also contains all these vertices and an additional vertex w_i, the total number of vertices of $\mathcal{T}_i$ is exactly

$$1 + \sum_{j=1}^{i-1} 2^{j-1} = 1 + \sum_{j=0}^{i-2} 2^j = 2^{i-1} ,$$

as claimed.

Now we show that ALG needs to use at least k colors for $\mathcal{T}_k$. This can be done by an easy induction as well.

Base Case. Without loss of generality, suppose ALG colored the vertices of $\mathcal{T}_2$, that is, v and w_2, such that v gets color 1 and w_2 gets color 2. If a third color was used to color w_1, then w_3 can be connected to $\mathcal{T}_1$ and $\mathcal{T}_2$ in any way such that the result is a tree, and we are done. Thus assume, again without loss of generality,

245

that w_1 is colored with 1. The adversary adds w_3 (resulting in $\mathcal{T}_3$) such that it is connected to both w_1 and w_2. Consequently, ALG is forced to use a third color for w_3, which covers the base case.

Induction Hypothesis. The claim holds for $\mathcal{T}_1, \mathcal{T}_2, \ldots, \mathcal{T}_{i-1}$.

Induction Step. Recall that w_i is revealed after all vertices of $\mathcal{T}_1, \mathcal{T}_2, \ldots, \mathcal{T}_{i-1}$ have been presented. Since, by the induction hypothesis, at least j colors have been used to color $\mathcal{T}_j$ with $1 \le j \le i - 1$, the adversary can identify a vertex u_j in $\mathcal{T}_j$ with a color that is different from all colors that were used for $u_1, u_2, \ldots, u_{j-1}$; it does so in ascending order of j. This way, $i - 1$ vertices $u_1, u_2, \ldots, u_{i-1}$ are identified that have pairwise distinct colors, and they can all be connected to w_i. Therefore, w_i has to get a different color, which results in a total of at least i colors.

It follows that ALG uses at least k colors to color $\mathcal{T}_k$; since we have already shown that the number n of vertices of $\mathcal{T}_k$ is 2^{k-1}, we get that ALG uses at least $k = \log_2 n + 1$ colors, which proves the claim. □

Theorem 8.1 and Observation 8.1 imply the following corollary.

Corollary 8.1. *No deterministic online algorithm for coloring is competitive.* □

Next, we show that the bound of Theorem 8.1 is tight up to a factor of 2, even for general bipartite graphs. Consider the online algorithm CBIP that does the following. Whenever a vertex v is revealed, it investigates the component (that is, the connected subgraph) that v belongs to, with respect to the part of the graph it already knows. The vertices of this component can be partitioned into two independent sets (each of which is a subset of one shore of the whole graph). Then, v is given the smallest color that is not present in the independent set v does not belong to.

Theorem 8.2. CBIP *is strictly* $2 \log_2 n$-*competitive for coloring on bipartite graphs.*

Proof. In the following, let $\mathrm{num}\colon \mathbb{N}^+ \to \mathbb{N}^+$ be a function that is defined such that $\mathrm{num}(i)$ gives the minimum number of vertices required so that CBIP uses color i. We now show by induction on i that, for $i \ge 2$, $\mathrm{num}(i) \ge \lceil 2^{i/2} \rceil$.

Base Case. In order to force CBIP to use two colors, clearly at least two vertices are needed; to make sure CBIP uses three colors, more than three vertices are necessary (a bipartite graph does not contain a triangle, thus three vertices are not sufficient). Since $\mathrm{num}(2) = 2 = \lceil 2^{2/2} \rceil$ and $\mathrm{num}(3) > 3 = \lceil 2.828 \rceil = \lceil 2^{3/2} \rceil$, the base case is covered.

Induction Hypothesis. The claim holds for $\mathrm{num}(i - 2)$.

Induction Step. Consider an arbitrary time step in which a vertex v is revealed. If v is not connected to any other already known vertex, it gets color 1, which does not increase the overall number of colors. Otherwise, let C_v denote the component

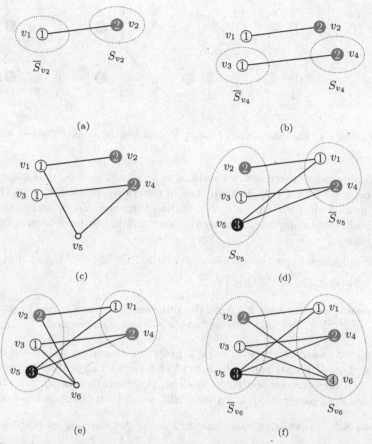

Figure 8.3. Six time steps and the intermediate solutions computed by CBIP.

that contains v with respect to the subgraph of the whole graph G that CBIP already knows in the current time step. Since G is bipartite, C_v is bipartite as well, and CBIP partitions the vertices into two independent sets; let S_v denote the independent set v belongs to, and let $\overline{S}_v$ be the other one.

CBIP then inspects $\overline{S}_v$ and colors v with the smallest color not used for the vertices of $\overline{S}_v$. If this is color i, it follows that $\overline{S}_v$ is colored using all colors from 1 to $i-1$. Let v' be a vertex in $\overline{S}_v$ that has color $i-1$. In the time step where v' was revealed, it was in some component $C_{v'}$ such that the vertices in the independent set not containing v' were assigned all colors from 1 to $i-2$. All these vertices are in C_v, and must belong to S_v; therefore, S_v is colored with all colors from 1 to $i-2$. An example is shown in Figure 8.3.

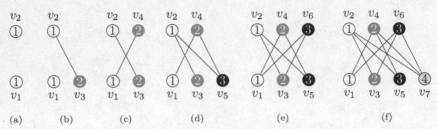

Figure 8.4. The construction of instances as used in the proof of Theorem 8.3.

As a consequence, there are two vertices $v_j \in \overline{S}_v$ and $v_l \in S_v$ that are given the same color $i - 2$ by CBIP. Without loss of generality, assume $v_j \prec v_l$, that is, v_l gets revealed after v_j. In the corresponding time step T_l, v_j and v_l must have been in different components; otherwise they would not have been assigned the same color.

By the induction hypothesis, we have $\operatorname{num}(i-2) \geq \lceil 2^{(i-2)/2} \rceil$, and thus

$$\operatorname{num}(i) \geq 2 \cdot \lceil 2^{(i-2)/2} \rceil \geq \lceil 2^{i/2} \rceil .$$

As a result, if CBIP uses k colors, the number of vertices n has to satisfy $n \geq \operatorname{num}(k) \geq \lceil 2^{k/2} \rceil \geq 2^{k/2}$, and thus we have $k \leq 2 \log_2 n$ as claimed. □

A straightforward strategy to color a graph in an online fashion would be to follow a somewhat greedy approach. FIRSTFIT is such an algorithm; for every vertex presented, it uses the smallest color possible. However, in general, this strategy is not successful; in particular, it is exponentially worse than CBIP on bipartite graphs.

Theorem 8.3. FIRSTFIT *uses at least $n/2$ colors for coloring on bipartite graphs.*

Proof. We construct a set $\mathcal{I}^{(n)}$ of instances of even length n as follows. For every even n, consider the following bipartite graph where all vertices with odd index are part of the first shore, and all vertices with even index are in the second shore. In the first two time steps, two vertices v_1 and v_2 are presented without any edge between them; in other words, these vertices are isolated. By definition, FIRSTFIT assigns to both of them the smallest color 1. Then, v_3 is presented in time step T_3 together with an edge to v_2, and afterwards v_4 is presented with an edge to v_1 in T_4; since color 1 is not available, again, by definition, FIRSTFIT gives both new vertices color 2. Next, in T_5, the vertex v_5 is presented with edges to both v_2 and v_4; FIRSTFIT is now forced to color v_5 with color 3. The adversary continues in this fashion; the idea of the construction is depicted in Figure 8.4. More precisely, in every odd time step, a vertex v_{2i-1} with $2 \leq i \leq n/2$ is given with edges to all vertices $v_2, v_4, \ldots, v_{2i-2}$, which means it is connected to all previously revealed vertices with an even index. Likewise, in every even time step, a vertex v_{2i} with $2 \leq i \leq n/2$ is presented together with edges to the vertices $v_1, v_3, \ldots, v_{2i-3}$, which means it is connected to all previously revealed vertices with an odd index, except for the one presented just beforehand. We now prove by induction on the number of vertices that FIRSTFIT needs to use $n/2$ colors. More specifically, we show that if a vertex v_{2i-1} is given, the assigned color is i; if a vertex v_{2i} is given, the algorithm also assigns color i to it.

Base Case. For the first odd vertex $v_1 = v_{2\cdot 1-1}$, color 1 is assigned and, for the first even vertex $v_2 = v_{2\cdot 1}$, color 1 is assigned as well. This covers the base case.

Induction Hypothesis. The claim holds for $v_1, v_2, \ldots, v_{j-1}$.

Induction Step. We now consider two cases depending on whether the index of the current vertex is odd or even.

Case 1. Suppose j is odd, that is, $j = 2i - 1$ for some i with $2 \le i \le n/2$. Let $v_2, v_4, \ldots, v_{2i-2}$ be the $i-1$ vertices with even index that were presented before v_j. By the construction of the instances in $\mathcal{I}^{(n)}$, v_j is connected to all of these vertices, and by induction (note that $v_{2i-2} = v_{j-1}$), they are colored with $1, 2, \ldots, i-1$. As a result, FIRSTFIT uses color i to color $v_j = v_{2i-1}$.

Case 2. Suppose j is even, that is, $j = 2i$ for some i with $2 \le i \le n/2$. Then v_j is connected to the $i-1$ vertices $v_1, v_3, \ldots, v_{2i-3}$, and the claim again follows from the induction hypothesis (this time, $v_{2i-3} = v_{j-3}$).

The claim of the theorem finally follows for $i = n$. $\qquad\qquad\square$

Exercise 8.1. Surprisingly, FIRSTFIT performs as good as possible if the input is a tree. Prove that it obtains a competitive ratio of $\log_2 n + 1$ in this case.

Hint. Use an approach similar to the proof of Theorem 8.2 by defining a function num.

8.2.2 Advice Complexity

Now let us investigate what can be done with advice. To color a graph optimally, it is obviously sufficient to tell an online algorithm with advice which color to use for every vertex; this amounts to $n\lceil \log_2(\chi(G)) \rceil$ advice bits for any graph G plus logarithmic advice to encode $\chi(G)$ and n as shown in Section 3.2. Since $\chi(G)$ is at most n (in the case of complete graphs), we get an upper bound of $\mathcal{O}(n \log n)$ advice bits.

Let us again focus on bipartite graphs. The considerations above immediately imply that n bits of advice are sufficient. Using a simple idea, we can save one advice bit (this is true for any graph).

Theorem 8.4. *There is an optimal online algorithm* CLIN1 *with advice for coloring on bipartite graphs that uses $n - 1$ advice bits.*

Proof. CLIN1 always assigns color 1 to the first vertex presented. For each other vertex, it reads one advice bit that indicates its color. $\qquad\qquad\square$

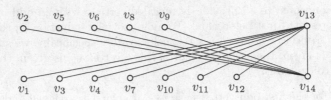

Figure 8.5. An instance I_s as used in the proof of Theorem 8.5 corresponding to the string $s = 010011011000$.

Exercise 8.2. Show the existence of an algorithm CLIN2 that improves the bound of Theorem 8.4 to $n-2$ advice bits.

Hint. Distinguish the instances depending on how many isolated vertices they contain.

Next, we prove that the bound of Exercise 8.2 is tight up to one bit.

Theorem 8.5. *Every optimal online algorithm with advice for coloring on bipartite graphs has to use at least $n-3$ advice bits.*

Proof. We construct a set $\mathcal{I}^{(n)}$ of instances of length n as follows. Every instance starts by requesting $n-2$ vertices that are all isolated. For every n, let $s = s_1 s_2 \ldots s_{n-2}$ denote a binary string. In the instance $I_s \in \mathcal{I}^{(n)}$, vertex v_i is part of the first shore if and only if $s_i = 0$, for all i with $1 \le i \le n-2$. This is revealed only in the last two time steps. More precisely, v_{n-1} is connected to all vertices from the first shore, and v_n is connected to all vertices from the second shore. Furthermore, v_{n-1} is connected to v_n (to ensure that the graph is connected); see Figure 8.5. Consequently, for every instance I_s, there is an optimal solution that assigns, say, color 1 to all vertices that correspond to a bit that is 0, and color 2 to all vertices that correspond to a bit that is 1. As usual, we can now apply the pigeonhole principle to argue that an online algorithm needs a different advice string for every I_s. However, we need to be careful due to the symmetry of the solutions. It is easy to see that, for every I_s, there are in fact two optimal solutions (one that assigns color 1 to the vertices of the first shore, and one that assigns color 2 to them); thus, the optimal solutions are not unique.

To take this into account, without loss of generality, we assume that the vertex presented first always gets color 1; in this case, there are 2^{n-3} strings $0 s_2 s_3 \ldots s_{n-2}$ to consider. If an online algorithm ALG with advice uses the same advice string for two instances I_s and $I_{s'}$, it will assign the first $n-2$ vertices to the same shores. Finally, the last two vertices are revealed and they are connected in I_s ($I_{s'}$, respectively) according to s (s', respectively). Since ALG computed the same solution for both instances until T_{n-2}, for one of them there is a vertex v among the last two vertices that needs to get a third color. Hence, this solution is not optimal, and it follows that every optimal online algorithm with advice needs to use at least $n-3$ advice bits. □

8.3 The Minimum Spanning Tree Problem

In Chapter 1, we already mentioned the minimum spanning tree problem. Here, we want to look at what can be done if the graph is not known in advance. With every vertex revealed, an online algorithm has to choose a number of edges that should be part of the resulting spanning tree. The formal definition is as follows.

> **Definition 8.3 (Online Minimum Spanning Tree).** The *online minimum spanning tree problem* is an online graph minimization problem on weighted graphs. In every time step, an online algorithm must decide, for each newly presented edge, whether it is part of the computed solution or not, unless taking this edge would close a cycle.

As in Section 1.1, we will use the abbreviation MSTP in what follows. For this problem, it can theoretically happen that an online algorithm does not output a feasible solution. In this case, we say that the solution has an arbitrarily large *penalty cost* λ. No algorithm that has cost λ is competitive. Also note that the input graph is not necessarily complete (in contrast to the offline version we defined in Section 1.1). In general, this makes it very hard for any deterministic online algorithm for the MSTP; as soon as the partial solution that is computed is not connected, the adversary can end the input. When given advice, however, this changes; therefore, our main interest is to study online algorithms with advice for the problem.

8.3.1 Deterministic and Randomized Algorithms

First, let us show that the strict competitive ratio of any deterministic online algorithm is arbitrarily large. To this end, we use an idea that is closely related to the hard instances of the simple knapsack problem used in the proof of Theorem 6.1. Let ALG be some deterministic online algorithm for the MSTP. Let $\varepsilon > 0$, and consider the following set of two instances. In the first two time steps, two vertices v_1 and v_2 are revealed that are connected by an edge of weight $1/\varepsilon$. We distinguish two cases.

Case 1. Suppose ALG decides not to take the edge $\{v_1, v_2\}$. Then the input ends, and ALG did not compute a feasible solution. Therefore, it has to pay the penalty λ and thus is not competitive by definition.

Case 2. Suppose ALG takes the edge. Then a third vertex v_3 is revealed that has edges to both v_1 and v_2; each edge has a weight of $1/2$. As a result, the optimal cost is 1, while ALG's cost is $1/\varepsilon$.

The corresponding two instances I_1 and I_2 are shown in Figures 8.6a and 8.6b. Next, we generalize this idea by constructing *widgets* that are similar to I_1 and I_2. However, we want to be a little less "unfair" and therefore assume in what follows

251

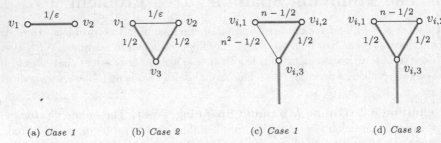

(a) *Case 1*   (b) *Case 2*   (c) *Case 1*   (d) *Case 2*

Figure 8.6. (a) and (b) show the instances used to prove that the strict competitive ratio of any deterministic online algorithm for the MSTP is arbitrarily large; (c) and (d) show the instances I_1 and I_2 used in the proof of Theorem 8.6. The thick gray lines mark optimal solutions.

that we are given a deterministic algorithm that always computes a feasible solution, and that thus never pays λ in any time step.

Theorem 8.6. *No deterministic online algorithm for the MSTP is competitive.*

Proof. Let $n = 3k + 1$ for some natural number k, and let ALG be a deterministic online algorithm for the MSTP that always produces some feasible solution. We construct an instance I of length n that consists of k *widgets*. A widget W_i with $1 \leq i \leq k$ has three vertices $v_{i,1}$, $v_{i,2}$, and $v_{i,3}$ as depicted in Figures 8.6c and 8.6d; which one is chosen depends on whether ALG takes the first edge $\{v_{i,1}, v_{i,2}\}$ of weight $n - 1/2$ of W_i or not. The last request is a vertex w that is connected to exactly the vertex $v_{i,3}$ of every widget W_i by edges of weight $1/k$ each. We distinguish two cases for any given widget.

Case 1. Suppose ALG does not take the edge of weight $n - 1/2$. Then it has to take the next two edges, which gives a total cost of n^2, while an optimal solution has cost n; see Figure 8.6c.

Case 2. Suppose ALG takes this edge. Then it has to take another edge of weight $1/2$, and its total cost for the current widget is thus n. Conversely, an optimal solution has cost 1; see Figure 8.6d.

In both cases, the cost of ALG is n times larger than the optimal cost. Finally, both ALG's solution and the optimal one have to take k edges of weight $1/k$ each to connect w to the widgets. Let δ denote the number of widgets where ALG took the first edge; we obtain

$$\text{cost}(\text{ALG}(I)) = \delta n + (k - \delta)n^2 + 1 = n(\delta + (k - \delta)n) + 1 \,,$$

and, since $\text{cost}(\text{OPT}(I)) = \delta + (k - \delta)n + 1$, it follows that

$$\text{cost}(\text{ALG}(I)) \geq n(\text{cost}(\text{OPT}(I)) - 1) \,.$$

This way, we construct instances for infinitely many n. As a result, the competitive ratio of ALG cannot be constant. $\qquad\square$

It does not look much brighter for randomized online algorithms. We leave the proof of this fact as an exercise for the reader.

Exercise 8.3. Show that randomized online algorithms for the MSTP are also not strictly competitive in expectation.

Exercise 8.4. Generalize Exercise 8.3 to general competitiveness.

8.3.2 Advice Complexity

Now we consider online algorithms with advice. As usual, a first question deals with how much additional information is necessary and sufficient to obtain an optimal solution. It turns out that the number of advice bits is superlinear in the number of requests. An upper bound can be given rather easily.

Theorem 8.7. *There is an optimal online algorithm* PARENT *with advice for the MSTP that uses* $n\lceil \log_2 n\rceil + 2\lceil \log_2(\lceil \log_2 n\rceil)\rceil$ *advice bits.*

Proof. Using a self-delimiting encoding (see Section 3.2), the first $2\lceil \log_2(\lceil \log_2 n\rceil)\rceil$ bits give the number $\lceil \log_2 n\rceil$; PARENT does not need to know n. Recall that we ignore the cases where n is smaller than 3. Then, for every vertex v revealed, PARENT reads the index of the parent vertex of v in a fixed optimal solution; this needs $\lceil \log_2 n\rceil$ advice bits in every time step (as the maximum degree of any graph is $n-1$). If the current vertex is the root, the advice is just the index of this vertex. Note that if the parent vertex is already revealed, the edge to the current vertex is still only revealed in the current time step. If the parent vertex is not yet revealed, PARENT stores the information to take the corresponding edge in a later time step. This way, PARENT can take exactly the edges that belong to the optimal solution. $\qquad\square$

The online algorithm PARENT follows a very simple strategy; still, it uses a number of advice bits that is asymptotically best possible.

Theorem 8.8. *Every optimal online algorithm with advice for the MSTP has to use* $\Omega(n \log n)$ *advice bits.*

Proof. Let $n = 2k+1$ for some natural number k; we construct a set $\mathcal{I}^{(n)}$ of instances of length n with vertices $v_1, v_2, \ldots, v_k, u_1, u_2, \ldots, u_k, w$. For every $I \in \mathcal{I}^{(n)}$, the first k vertices (the *v-vertices*) are presented according to a permutation of their indices; more precisely, for an instance $I \in \mathcal{I}^{(n)}$, there is a permutation π_I such that $v_{\pi_I(1)} \prec v_{\pi_I(2)} \prec \ldots \prec v_{\pi_I(k)}$. Of course, the "real" indices are hidden; for any online algorithm, the first k vertices are just identified by the time step in which they are revealed. Every vertex u_i with $1 \le i \le k$ is connected to exactly the $k-i+1$ vertices

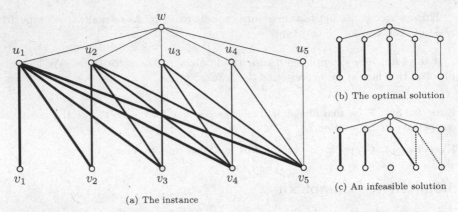

(a) The instance

(b) The optimal solution

(c) An infeasible solution

Figure 8.7. A sample instance as used in the proof of Theorem 8.8 for $k = 5$. The indices of the v-vertices are not known to an online algorithm, that is, they are presented in some arbitrary ordering (according to a permutation). Depending on their thickness, the edges connecting the u-vertices to the v-vertices have weights 5, 4, 3, 2, and 1. (b) An optimal solution takes the edges $\{w, u_i\}$ and $\{u_i, v_i\}$ for $1 \le i \le 5$. (c) The online algorithm picks the edge $\{u_3, v_4\}$, which leads to an infeasible solution.

$v_i, v_{i+1}, \ldots, v_k$ by edges each of weight $k - i + 1$; u_i is revealed in time step T_{k+i}. Finally, a vertex w is presented, which is connected to every vertex u_i by an edge of weight 1; an example for $k = 5$ is shown in Figure 8.7. Note that, for every instance from $\mathcal{I}^{(n)}$, there is a unique optimal solution that takes exactly the edges $\{v_i, u_i\}$ and $\{w, u_i\}$, for $1 \le i \le k$. This way, it takes one edge of every weight between 1 and k; together with the k edges $\{w, u_i\}$ of weight 1 each, we get

$$\text{cost}(\text{OPT}(I)) = k + \sum_{i=1}^{k} i = \frac{k(k+3)}{2} \, ,$$

for every $I \in \mathcal{I}^{(n)}$. Every other feasible solution for a given I is more expensive. Without loss of generality, we will always assume that no online algorithm takes two edges with the same weight (except the $k + 1$ edges each of weight 1); otherwise, it cannot compute an optimal solution.

We now use the usual approach employing the pigeonhole principle in order to show that every online algorithm with advice needs to use at least $\log_2(k!)$ advice bits to be optimal. For a contradiction, assume that ALG is an optimal online algorithm with advice that uses fewer than $\log_2(k!)$ advice bits. Then, there are two instances I_1 and I_2 contained in $\mathcal{I}^{(n)}$ that get the same advice string. Suppose that the corresponding permutations π_{I_1} and π_{I_2} differ for the first time for the index i, that is, the vertex v_i is at two different positions for the two instances. This means that the v-vertex revealed in time step T_i (that is, either $v_{\pi_{I_1}(i)}$ or $v_{\pi_{I_2}(i)}$, depending on the given instance) needs to be connected to the corresponding u-vertex (that is, either $u_{\pi_{I_1}(i)}$ or $u_{\pi_{I_2}(i)}$, depending on the given instance) in order to get an optimal solution; without loss of generality, let $\pi_{I_1}(i) < \pi_{I_2}(i)$. However, up to the ith u-vertex, both instances I_1 and I_2 look the same to ALG. Thus, the algorithm connects it to the same v-vertex, which cannot be optimal for both instances and thus contradicts the optimality of ALG.

Finally, using Stirling's approximation and the same calculations as in the proof of Theorem 4.9, we conclude that

$$\log_2(k!) \geq k(\log_2 k - \beta),$$

where $e = 2.718\ldots$ is Euler's number and $\beta = \log_2 e < 1.443$. The claim follows from $k = (n-1)/2$. $\qquad\square$

Next, we show that a linear number of advice bits is necessary to obtain a competitive ratio close to 1; to this end, we give a reduction from the bit guessing problem (see Chapter 7).

Theorem 8.9. *For every c with $c \leq 1.125$, every c-competitive online algorithm with advice for the MSTP has to use at least*

$$\left(1 + (3c-3)\log_2(3c-3) + (4-3c)\log_2(4-3c)\right) \cdot \frac{n-1}{3}$$

advice bits.

Proof. We reduce bit guessing with known history to the MSTP. Let BBMST be some online algorithm with advice for the MSTP. We again assume that BBMST always creates a feasible output, and design an online algorithm BGUESS with advice for bit guessing with known history that uses BBMST as a black box. As in the reductions given in Section 7.4, whenever BBMST asks for advice, BGUESS simply copies it from its own tape.

In the first time step T_1', BGUESS is given the length n' of the string it is supposed to guess. BGUESS creates an input I for BBMST of length $n = 3n' + 1$. More precisely, for every bit that is to be guessed, BBMST is given three vertices. The vertices associated with time step T_i' with $1 \leq i \leq n'$ are called $v_{i,1}$, $v_{i,2}$, and $v_{i,3}$, and they form a *widget* W_i similar to those in the proof of Theorem 8.6.

Initially, BGUESS generates two vertices $v_{i,1}$ and $v_{i,2}$ that are connected by an edge of weight 2 in two consecutive time steps. If BBMST chooses to take this edge, BGUESS guesses the corresponding bit to be 0; if BBMST does not take the edge, BGUESS outputs 1. Next, BGUESS is told whether its guess was correct. Depending on this feedback, BGUESS extends the input that is given to BBMST as shown in Figure 8.8a if the correct guess was 0, and as depicted in Figure 8.8b if it was 1. We can make a simple case distinction.

Case 1. Suppose the correct guess is 0. In this case, $v_{i,3}$ is connected by an edge of weight 1 and an edge of weight 3. The optimal solution therefore takes the first edge $\{v_{i,1}, v_{i,2}\}$ and additionally $\{v_{i,2}, v_{i,3}\}$, amounting to a cost of 3 for W_i; if BBMST did not take this edge, it pays an extra cost of 1.

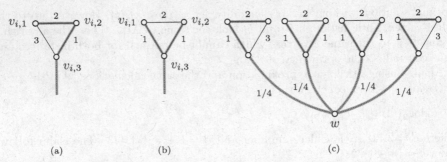

Figure 8.8. The widgets used in the reduction given in the proof of Theorem 8.9.

Case 2. Suppose the correct guess is 1. Then $v_{i,3}$ is connected by two edges each of weight 1. The optimal solution takes these two new edges and has cost 2 for W_i; if BBMST did take the edge $\{v_{i,1}, v_{i,2}\}$, its cost is again larger by 1.

To sum up, for every time step where BGUESS guesses incorrectly, the cost of BBMST increases by 1 compared to the optimal cost. Finally, again a vertex w is revealed in time step T_n that is connected to all widgets by edges each of weight $1/n'$.

Now suppose BGUESS guesses $\gamma n' = \gamma(n-1)/3$ bits correctly. Then it follows that

$$\text{cost}(\text{BBMST}(I)) = \text{cost}(\text{OPT}(I)) + (1-\gamma)n', \qquad (8.1)$$

and

$$2n' + 1 \leq \text{cost}(\text{OPT}(I)) \leq 3n' + 1. \qquad (8.2)$$

We can bound the competitive ratio c of BBMST from below by

$$c \geq \frac{\text{cost}(\text{BBMST}(I))}{\text{cost}(\text{OPT}(I))} \geq 1 + \frac{(1-\gamma)n'}{\text{cost}(\text{OPT}(I))}$$

as a consequence of (8.1), and thus

$$\gamma \geq 1 - \frac{(c-1) \cdot \text{cost}(\text{OPT}(I))}{n'}.$$

Together with (8.2), we obtain

$$\gamma \geq 1 - \frac{(c-1)(3n'+1)}{n'} \geq 1 - \frac{(c-1)4n'}{n'} \geq 5 - 4c,$$

and, since $\gamma \geq 1/2$ needs to be satisfied, we require that $c \leq 1.125$.

From Theorem 7.8, we know that BGUESS needs to read at least

$$(1 + (1-\gamma)\log_2(1-\gamma) + \gamma \log_2 \gamma)n'$$

advice bits in order to guess a fraction γ of all bits correctly. Since this function grows with γ for $\gamma \geq 1/2$, and since $\gamma \geq 4 - 3c$, we get that at least

$$(1 + (1 - (4 - 3c)) \log_2(1 - (4 - 3c)) + (4 - 3c) \log_2(4 - 3c))n'$$
$$= (1 + (3c - 3) \log_2(3c - 3) + (4 - 3c) \log_2(4 - 3c)) \cdot \frac{n-1}{3}$$

advice bits are needed. Finally, note that the optimal cost of the instances constructed increases with n, which finishes the proof. $\qquad\square$

Exercise 8.5. Still assuming we consider online algorithms that compute feasible solutions, how does the bound of Theorem 8.9 change if we only consider graphs of degree at most 3? What about if we allow degree 4?

Exercise 8.6. The *online minimum vertex cover problem* (MVCP) is an online minimization problem where the objective is to find a smallest set $C \subseteq V$ for a given graph $G = (V, E)$ such that, for each edge in E, at least one of its endpoints is in C. Using a bit guessing reduction, show that a linear number of advice bits is necessary for any online algorithm with advice to achieve a small competitive ratio.

Exercise 8.7.* The *online maximum independent set problem* (MISP) is an online graph maximization problem. In every time step, an online algorithm either accepts or discards the presented vertex. The goal is to compute a set of vertices such that there is no edge between any pair of them in the graph G. We want to study online algorithms for this problem that are allowed to use preemption; the idea is analogous to that from Exercise 7.18. More precisely, an online algorithm is allowed to remove vertices from its solution that it previously accepted, but it cannot accept vertices that were already discarded. We demand that the given algorithm has a feasible solution in every time step; thus, it cannot accept two vertices that are connected by an edge and later preempt one of them. Use a string guessing reduction (that is, we allow an arbitrary alphabet size $\sigma \geq 2$) to give a linear lower bound on the number of advice bits necessary to compute solutions with a small competitive ratio.

8.3.3 Special Graph Classes

In this subsection, we want to investigate graphs with particular properties. Moreover, our aim is to observe some interesting connections between algorithms for the offline version of the problem and online environments. First, recall that the definition of the MSTP diverges from that given in Exercise 1.3 in that, in the classical version, we consider complete graphs. Second, we want to restrict the weight function such that it satisfies the triangle inequality, that is, for any three vertices v_i, v_j, and v_k, we have

$$\text{weight}(\{v_i, v_j\}) \leq \text{weight}(\{v_i, v_k\}) + \text{weight}(\{v_k, v_j\})$$

(analogously to Definition 4.1). From now on, we consider *metric graphs*, which are complete undirected graphs with a weight function that satisfies the triangle inequality. We now leave the MSTP for a while and return to another classical problem that we already discussed in Section 1.1, namely the *traveling salesman problem*. We start by proving the following technical lemma, which we will need to analyze the MSTP.

Lemma 8.1. *Let $G = (V, E)$ be a metric graph with a weight function* weight$: E \to \mathbb{R}^+$*; let $H_{opt} := \text{OPT}(G)$ be a minimum Hamiltonian cycle in G. If there is a function* lab$: V \to \mathbb{R}^+$ *such that*

(i) $\min\{\text{lab}(v_i), \text{lab}(v_j)\} \leq \text{weight}(\{v_i, v_j\})$*, for all $v_i, v_j \in V$, and*

(ii) $\text{lab}(v) \leq \text{cost}(H_{opt})/2$*, for all $v \in V$,*

then

$$\sum_{v \in V} 2 \cdot \text{lab}(v) \leq (\lceil \log_2 n \rceil + 1) \cdot \text{cost}(H_{opt}) .$$

Proof. Let $V = \{v_1, v_2, \ldots, v_n\}$ and, without loss of generality, suppose $\text{lab}(v_1) \geq \text{lab}(v_2) \geq \ldots \geq \text{lab}(v_n)$.[9] For any k with $1 \leq k \leq n$, we consider the induced subgraph G_k of G with vertices $\{v_i \mid 1 \leq i \leq \min\{2k, n\}\}$. Let H_k denote a Hamiltonian cycle in G_k that visits all vertices of G_k in the same order as they are visited in H_{opt}. For every edge $\{v_i, v_j\}$ in H_k, H_{opt} connects v_i and v_j by a path in G that is at least as expensive as the direct edge due to the triangle inequality. Thus, we have

$$\text{cost}(H_{opt}) \geq \text{cost}(H_k) . \tag{8.3}$$

Due to (i), we obtain

$$\text{cost}(H_k) = \sum_{\{v_i, v_j\} \in H_k} \text{weight}(\{v_i, v_j\}) \geq \sum_{\{v_i, v_j\} \in H_k} \min\{\text{lab}(v_i), \text{lab}(v_j)\} . \tag{8.4}$$

Now let us have a look at the right-hand side of (8.4). Every $v \in V$ appears at most twice as a summand; moreover, the number of summands is equal to the number of edges in H_k, that is, $\min\{2k, n\}$. Since the labels are decreasing with increasing indices, we get

$$\sum_{\{v_i, v_j\} \in H_k} \min\{\text{lab}(v_i), \text{lab}(v_j)\} \geq \sum_{i=k+1}^{\min\{2k,n\}} 2 \cdot \text{lab}(v_i) . \tag{8.5}$$

All in all, (8.3) to (8.5) imply

$$\text{cost}(H_{opt}) \geq \sum_{i=k+1}^{\min\{2k,n\}} 2 \cdot \text{lab}(v_i) . \tag{8.6}$$

---

[9]Keep in mind that we are dealing with an offline problem now, and that the labeling of the vertices has nothing to do with any presentation order.

Next, we sum (8.6) for all values of k that are a power of two and smaller than n, that is, $1, 2, 4, \ldots, 2^{\lceil \log_2 n \rceil - 1}$, yielding

$$\sum_{j=0}^{\lceil \log_2 n \rceil - 1} \text{cost}(H_{\text{opt}}) \geq \sum_{j=0}^{\lceil \log_2 n \rceil - 1} \sum_{i=2^j+1}^{\min\{2^{j+1}, n\}} 2 \cdot \text{lab}(v_i) \, .$$

Simplifying this inequality, we finally get

$$\lceil \log_2 n \rceil \cdot \text{cost}(H_{\text{opt}}) \geq \sum_{i=2}^{n} 2 \cdot \text{lab}(v_i)$$

$$\Longleftrightarrow \quad \lceil \log_2 n \rceil \cdot \text{cost}(H_{\text{opt}}) + 2 \cdot \text{lab}(v_1) \geq \sum_{v \in V} 2 \cdot \text{lab}(v)$$

(by adding $2 \cdot \text{lab}(v_1)$ on both sides)

$$\Longleftrightarrow \quad \lceil \log_2 n \rceil \cdot \text{cost}(H_{\text{opt}}) + 2 \cdot \max_{1 \leq i \leq n}(\text{lab}(v_i)) \geq \sum_{v \in V} 2 \cdot \text{lab}(v) \, . \tag{8.7}$$

(due to the definition of lab*)*

Note that, until this point, we did not use (ii). Together with (8.7), this assumption now finally implies that

$$(\lceil \log_2 n \rceil + 1) \cdot \text{cost}(H_{\text{opt}}) \geq \sum_{v \in V} 2 \cdot \text{lab}(v)$$

as claimed. $\qquad \square$

We now use this result to prove an upper bound for the MSTP on metric graphs. To this end, we need to establish a connection between spanning trees and Hamiltonian cycles. We leave the proof of the following lemma as an exercise for the reader.

Lemma 8.2. *Let G be some metric graph, and let S be a spanning tree of G. Then, there is a Hamiltonian cycle in G such that $\text{cost}(H) \leq 2 \cdot \text{cost}(S)$.*

Exercise 8.8. Prove Lemma 8.2.

Exercise 8.9. Show that Exercise 8.8 implies a 2-approximation algorithm DOUBLE for the TSP on metric graphs.

Consider the online algorithm MSTGREEDY that chooses, in every time step, the cheapest edge that connects the vertex that was just revealed to the tree that was computed so far.

Theorem 8.10. MSTGREEDY *is strictly $\lceil \log_2 n \rceil$-competitive for the MSTP on metric graphs.*

Proof. Let I be an instance of the MSTP on a metric graph $G = (V, E)$ with $V = \{v_1, v_2, \ldots, v_n\}$ and a weight function weight: $E \to \mathbb{R}^+$; let $v_1 \prec v_2 \prec \ldots \prec v_n$, that is, vertex v_i is presented in time step T_i together with an edge to each v_j with $1 \leq j < i$. In every time step T_i, MSTGREEDY constructs a tree on the vertices of the graph revealed so far by connecting v_i to the tree constructed in T_{i-1} using the cheapest edge that is already known. Note that MSTGREEDY's solution is therefore valid in every time step. For the sake of an easier notation, let G_i denote the graph that is revealed up to T_i with $1 \leq i \leq n$, and let $S_i := \text{MSTGREEDY}(G_i)$ ($S_{\text{opt},i} := \text{OPT}(G_i)$, respectively) be the solutions computed until T_i. We now show that S_i is at most $\lceil \log_2 n \rceil$ times more expensive than $S_{\text{opt},i}$ for every G_i. In the following, let $H_{\text{opt},i}$ be a minimum Hamiltonian cycle in G_i.

For every vertex v_i with $2 \leq i \leq n$, we define

$$\text{lab}(v_i) := \min_{1 \leq j < i} (\text{weight}(\{v_j, v_i\})) ,$$

that is, the weight of a cheapest edge connecting v_i to some vertex v_j that is presented before v_i. As a consequence, the edge used by MSTGREEDY in T_i has a weight of exactly $\text{lab}(v_i)$. Furthermore, we set

$$\text{lab}(v_1) := \max_{1 \leq j \leq n} (\text{weight}(\{v_1, v_j\})) ,$$

which implies

$$\text{lab}(v_1) \geq \max_{1 \leq j \leq n} (\text{lab}(v_j)) \geq \max_{1 \leq j \leq i} (\text{lab}(v_j)) , \tag{8.8}$$

for every i with $1 \leq i \leq n$. It follows that

$$\text{cost}(S_i) \leq \sum_{j=2}^{i} \text{lab}(v_j)$$

$$= \left(\sum_{j=1}^{i} \text{lab}(v_j) \right) - \text{lab}(v_1)$$

$$\leq \left(\sum_{j=1}^{i} \text{lab}(v_j) \right) - \max_{1 \leq j \leq i} (\text{lab}(v_j)) \tag{8.9}$$

$$\text{\textit{(due to (8.8))}}$$

Now consider any two vertices v_j and $v_{j'}$ in S_i with $j < j'$. By the definition of lab, we have $\text{lab}(v_{j'}) \leq \text{weight}(\{v_j, v_{j'}\})$, which satisfies (i) of Lemma 8.1 for G_i. Thus, we can apply an intermediate result from the proof of Lemma 8.1. We get

$$\text{cost}(S_i) \leq \left(\sum_{j=1}^{i} \text{lab}(v_j) \right) - \max_{1 \leq j \leq i} (\text{lab}(v_j))$$

$$\text{\textit{(shown in (8.9))}}$$

$$\leq \lceil \log_2 i \rceil \cdot \mathrm{cost}(H_{\mathrm{opt},i})/2$$

(due to (8.7) in the proof of Lemma 8.1)

$$\leq \lceil \log_2 i \rceil \cdot \mathrm{cost}(S_{\mathrm{opt},i}) \,,$$

(which follows from Lemma 8.2)

which proves the claim for $i = n$ and $S_{\mathrm{opt},i} = \mathrm{OPT}(G)$. $\qquad\square$

Recall that TSPGREEDY performs very poorly for the TSP on general graphs. The algorithm is a lot better on metric graphs, although still worse than the algorithm DOUBLE from Exercise 8.9.

Exercise 8.10. In Exercise 1.2, we have shown that TSPGREEDY, that is, the greedy algorithm for the TSP that starts at some vertex and always chooses the cheapest edge, has an approximation ratio that is arbitrarily bad. Use Lemma 8.1 to show that TSPGREEDY is a $(\lceil \log_2 n \rceil + 1)$-approximation algorithm for the TSP on metric graphs.

After reviewing the offline version of the TSP, let us now look at the offline version of the MSTP for a second. We already know (see Exercise 1.3) that the decision version of the classical MSTP is in $\mathcal{P}$ due to the algorithm KRUSKAL (among others). This enables us to deduce some interesting results for the online version. However, we first need another online model in order to analyze the algorithm. In the following model, the underlying graph G is known to the online algorithm and the edge weights appear online, one per time step; we call this the *edge-by-edge* model.

Consider a deterministic online algorithm ONKRUSKAL for this setting where the edge weights are restricted to two values a and b with $a < b$. This algorithm computes a greedy solution by taking all edges of weight a if this does not close a cycle. Edges of weight b are only taken if otherwise the algorithm could not compute a feasible solution; see Algorithm 8.1.

Theorem 8.11. ONKRUSKAL *is optimal for the MSTP on graphs with edge weights a and b in the edge-by-edge model.*

Proof. Consider any graph G with edge weights a and b only, and a minimum spanning tree $S_{\mathrm{opt}} := \mathrm{OPT}(G)$. Recall that every spanning tree contains exactly $n - 1$ edges. Suppose S_{opt} contains δ edges of weight a and $(n - 1) - \delta$ edges of weight b. What we need to prove is thus that $S := \mathrm{ONKRUSKAL}(G)$ also contains δ edges of weight a, and we are done.

To this end, we show that S can be transformed into S_{opt} without increasing its cost. Consider any ordering of the edges in S_{opt}, and let e be the first edge in S_{opt} of weight a that is not contained in S. If there is no such edge, the claim follows immediately. If ONKRUSKAL did not take e when it was offered, the only possible reason could have been that this would close a cycle C in S. If C does not contain an edge of weight b, we can remove an arbitrary edge that is not contained

```
for every request x do
    if taking x closes a cycle
        discard x;
    elsif weight(x) = a
        use x;
    else
        S₁ := First subtree that contains a vertex of x;
        S₂ := Second subtree that contains a vertex of x;
        if there is no yet unrevealed path that connects S₁ and S₂
            use x;
        else
            discard x;
end
```

Algorithm 8.1. The online version of KRUSKAL.

in S_{opt} (clearly, such an edge must exist) from C and insert e instead. This does not change the cost of the computed solution; also, it does not influence which edges the algorithm takes in subsequent time steps, because the subtrees of the intermediate solution of ONKRUSKAL contain the same vertices. If C contains at least one edge of weight b, let e' denote the last such edge that was revealed. Removing e' from S results in two subtrees. When e' was presented, the edge e was not yet presented (otherwise, ONKRUSKAL would have chosen it since it takes all edges of weight a that do not close a cycle); thus, there was a so far unrevealed path that connected the two subtrees, and ONKRUSKAL would not have chosen e', which is a contradiction. We can continue this way to transform S without increasing its cost. □

Now we return to online graph problems as defined in Definition 8.1, that is, the vertices are revealed online together with edges to known vertices. Theorem 8.11 has some interesting consequences for online algorithms with advice for particular graph classes if the given algorithm knows that it is dealing with a graph from this class.

Theorem 8.12. *There is an optimal online algorithm* EMB *with advice for the MSTP on complete graphs with edge weights* a *and* b *that uses* $\mathcal{O}(\log n)$ *advice bits.*

Proof. Let G be a complete graph with n vertices and edge weights a and b only. First, EMB reads $\lceil \log_2 n \rceil + 2\lceil \log_2(\lceil \log_2 n \rceil) \rceil$ advice bits to obtain n. After that, the algorithm knows the structure of the underlying graph. Let G' be an unweighted complete graph with n vertices; EMB successively "embeds" G into G'. Since all vertices have edges to all other vertices, EMB can assign any given vertex v of G to any unused vertex v'. Together with v, some edges are revealed. EMB simulates the behavior of ONKRUSKAL when these edges are given one after the other (that is, in the edge-by-edge model). It follows that EMB computes an optimal solution. □

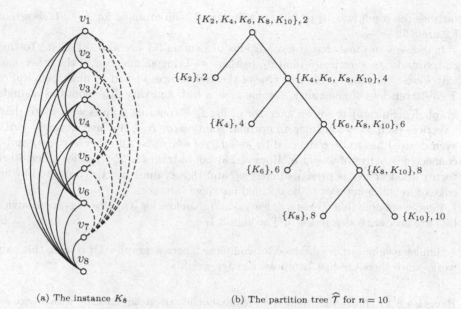

(a) The instance K_8 (b) The partition tree $\widehat{\mathcal{T}}$ for $n = 10$

Figure 8.9. (a) shows a sample instance K_8; edges of weight a are dashed, while edges of weight b are solid; (b) shows the partition tree $\widehat{\mathcal{T}}$ for $n = 10$.

For complete graphs with two edge weights, we can give a complementing lower bound. The idea behind the following theorem is that an online algorithm needs to know the input length in order to be optimal.

Theorem 8.13. *Every optimal online algorithm with advice for the MSTP on complete graphs with edge weights a and b has to use at least $\log_2 n - 1$ advice bits.*

Proof. We prove the claim using partition trees, which we introduced in Section 3.3 (see Definition 3.3). For any even n, consider the following set of instances $\mathcal{I}^{(\leq n)}$ that consists of the graphs $K_2, K_4, \ldots, K_n$; K_i with $2 \leq i \leq n$ is a complete graph with an even number i of vertices $v_1, v_2, \ldots, v_i$, and we set $v_1 \prec v_2 \prec \ldots \prec v_i$. For every j with $1 < j \leq i$, the vertex v_j is connected to all vertices $v_{j'}$ with $1 \leq j' < j$ by edges of weight a if j is odd, and by edges of weight b if j is even. K_8 is shown in Figure 8.9a.

Next, we construct a partition tree $\widehat{\mathcal{T}}$ for $\mathcal{I}^{(\leq n)}$. Every instance starts with the two vertices v_1 and v_2, which are connected by an edge of weight b. Therefore, we label the root $\hat{r}$ with $\mathcal{I}^{(\leq n)}$ and 2. For every vertex $\hat{v}$ of $\widehat{\mathcal{T}}$ that is labeled by a set of instances $\mathcal{I}_{\hat{v}}^{(\leq n)}$ with more than one element and a natural number $\rho_{\hat{v}}$, we label its two children such that the left one contains the smallest graph from $\mathcal{I}_{\hat{v}}^{(\leq n)}$ and $\rho_{\hat{v}}$, and the right one contains the other graphs from $\mathcal{I}_{\hat{v}}^{(\leq n)}$ and $\rho_{\hat{v}} + 2$. This clearly satisfies the conditions (i) to (iii) of Definition 3.3; an example for $\mathcal{I}^{(\leq 10)}$ is shown in Figure 8.9b.

It remains to show that the conditions of Lemma 3.1 are also satisfied. To this end, consider two vertices $\hat{v}_1$ and $\hat{v}_2$, neither one being an ancestor of the other, and with lowest common ancestor $\hat{v}$. One of the two vertices $\hat{v}_1$ and $\hat{v}_2$ must be a leaf of $\widehat{\mathcal{T}}$. Without loss of generality, assume $\hat{v}_1$ is a leaf, and thus $\mathcal{I}_{\hat{v}_1}^{(\leq n)}$ contains a single graph K_i. Since $\hat{v}_2$ is not an ancestor of $\hat{v}_1$, $\mathcal{I}_{\hat{v}_2}^{(\leq n)}$ contains graphs with more than i vertices each. Now consider an optimal solution for K_i. The last vertex v_i (with even degree) has to be connected by an edge of weight b. All other vertices can be connected by edges of weight a. However, for all instances in $\mathcal{I}_{\hat{v}_2}^{(\leq n)}$, at least one other vertex of odd index is presented after v_i, and thus v_i must not be connected by an edge of weight b in order to be optimal for these instances.

Finally, we note that $\widehat{\mathcal{T}}$ has $n/2$ leaves, and therefore $\log_2(n/2) = \log_2 n - 1$ advice bits are necessary as a result of Theorem 3.1. $\qquad\square$

Similar results can be obtained for complete bipartite graphs. Of course, this only works since there are just two possible edge weights.

Exercise 8.11. Prove that there is an optimal online algorithm EMBBIP with advice for the MSTP on complete bipartite graphs with edge weights a and b that uses $\mathcal{O}(\log n)$ advice bits.

Exercise 8.12. Prove that $\log_2(n-1) - 1$ advice bits are necessary to be optimal for the MSTP on complete bipartite graphs with edge weights a and b.

Finally, let us consider the case that there are three possible weights. To keep the calculations simple, let these weights be 1, 2, and 3. We prove in the following that we can at least obtain a small competitive ratio with logarithmic advice. The following algorithm is called MSTONE since it uses one advice bit to distinguish between two deterministic strategies; the additional logarithmic number of bits is only used to communicate the size of the input graph.

The idea of the following proof once again relies on the optimality of KRUSKAL. In the offline setting with weights 1, 2, and 3, all edges of weight 1 can be taken (as long as they do not close a cycle). After that, we can take edges of weight 2 and finally those of weight 3. Surely, taking edges of weight 1 should also be done in the online setting. However, it is not clear whether taking an edge of weight 2 is a good idea (maybe otherwise we would have to take an edge of weight 3 later) or a bad idea (maybe this prevents us from taking an edge of weight 1). Essentially, the single advice bit tells MSTONE whether it should take edges of weight 2 or not (except for the last time step).

Theorem 8.14. *There is a strictly 1.4-competitive online algorithm* MSTONE *with advice for the MSTP on complete graphs with edge weights 1, 2, and 3 that uses* $\mathcal{O}(\log n)$ *advice bits.*

Proof. With $\lceil \log_2 n \rceil + 2\lceil \log_2(\lceil \log_2 n \rceil) \rceil$ advice bits, the input length n is encoded in a self-delimiting way. Then, one additional bit is read to choose one of the following two strategies.

Case 1. If the bit is 0, MSTONE takes all edges of weight 1 greedily in the first $n-1$ time steps unless a cycle is closed. In the last time step, the remaining edges are taken in order to compute a feasible solution, that is, to connect all components it computed so far; this is always possible since the input graph is complete.

Case 2. If the bit is 1, MSTONE follows a similar strategy, but takes edges of weights either 1 or 2 in the first $n-1$ time steps.

Let us analyze how the oracle should choose the value of the bit. For the second strategy, we define so-called *suboptimal* edges. Suppose that, in some time step, an edge of weight 1 is presented, but MSTONE cannot take it since it closes a cycle and this cycle contains an edge of weight 2 that was taken earlier. For each such cycle, we pick one arbitrary but fixed edge of weight 2 and call it suboptimal. Since no edge of weight 1 can close two cycles (otherwise, there would have been a larger cycle already), it follows that there are at least as many edges of weight 1 as there are suboptimal edges. In what follows, let δ be such that the oracle tells MSTONE to use the second strategy if the number of suboptimal edges that it would choose is less than $\delta(n-1)$.

We know from Exercise 1.3 that the offline algorithm KRUSKAL is optimal for the MSTP. For the given instance I, we will therefore compare MSTONE's solution to KRUSKAL(I).

Now suppose MSTONE uses the first strategy on I. By construction, there must be more than $\delta(n-1)$ suboptimal edges and therefore at least that many edges of weight 1. Clearly, MSTONE chooses all these edges of weight 1, and, in the worst case, all remaining edges that are taken in the last time step have weight 3, while KRUSKAL(I) takes edges of weight 2 instead. Thus, the performance of MSTONE on I in this case can be bounded from above by

$$\frac{\delta(n-1) + (1-\delta)(n-1) \cdot 3}{\delta(n-1) + (1-\delta)(n-1) \cdot 2} = \frac{3-2\delta}{2-\delta}. \tag{8.10}$$

Conversely, if MSTONE uses the second strategy, there are fewer than $\delta(n-1)$ suboptimal edges in I. Since MSTONE never takes an edge of weight 3 to connect two components unless there is no other choice (that is, in the last time step), the only edges that contribute to MSTONE's solution being larger than cost(KRUSKAL(I)) are the suboptimal edges. With this, we get an upper bound on the performance on I of

$$\frac{\delta(n-1) \cdot 2 + \Delta}{\delta(n-1) + \Delta}, \tag{8.11}$$

where Δ is the cost of the other edges (which is the same for both solutions). Note that (8.11) is maximized if Δ is minimized, and thus we get an upper bound of

$$\frac{\delta(n-1)\cdot 2 + (1-\delta)(n-1)}{\delta(n-1) + (1-\delta)(n-1)} = 1 + \delta. \tag{8.12}$$

It remains to choose δ. To this end, note that (8.10) decreases with δ, while (8.12) increases with δ (we had a similar situation for the simple knapsack problem; see Figure 6.5). Thus, a best strategy is to choose δ such that the two performances are equal, which results in

$$\frac{3 - 2\delta}{2 - \delta} = 1 + \delta \iff \delta = \frac{1}{2}\left(3 - \sqrt{5}\right).$$

Plugging this value into one of the two functions finally yields an upper bound of $(5 - \sqrt{5})/2 \leq 1.4$ on the strict competitive ratio. $\qquad\square$

The results of this subsection show an interesting interplay between the online and offline formulations of the problem, and how advice can help to build a bridge between them.

8.4 Historical and Bibliographical Notes

An introduction to graph theory is, for instance, given in the books by Diestel [51] and West [144]. Graph coloring is certainly one of the oldest and best-studied problems on graphs; the decision problem of the offline version is also among "Karp's 21 $\mathcal{NP}$-complete problems" [93].

The online algorithm CBIP is due to Lovász et al. [113]; the proof presented here that this algorithm is strictly $\log_2 n$-competitive (see Theorem 8.2) follows that given by Kierstead and Trotter [95]. The lower bound for trees (see Theorem 8.1) is due to Bean [17]; it was independently discovered by Gyárfás and Lehel [72]. For bipartite graphs, Bianchi et al. [22] improved this bound from $\log_2 n + 1$ to roughly $1.137 \log_2 n - 0.499$, which was then improved to $2 \log_2 n - 10$ by Gutowski et al. [71]; note that this most recent bound matches the upper bound (see Theorem 8.2) up to the small additive constant of 10.

The lower bound for FirstFit on bipartite graphs can be found in the overview by Kierstead and Trotter [95]. To the best of our knowledge, Steffen [135] was the first to prove the statement from Exercise 8.1.

Bianchi et al. [22] studied the advice complexity of coloring on bipartite graphs. Forišek et al. [64] studied coloring with advice on paths. Seibert et al. [128] considered coloring 3-colorable graphs with advice, and in particular how much information is needed to color them with at most four colors. Burjons et al. [43] considered coloring with advice against a randomized adversary.

The polynomial-time ($\lceil \log_2 n \rceil + 1$)-approximation algorithm TSPGreedy (and thus Lemma 8.1 and Exercise 8.10) is due to Rosenkrantz et al. [127]. The

2-approximation algorithm DOUBLE (see Exercise 8.9) was also mentioned by Rosenkrantz et al. [127], but it was known beforehand. Also recall that the Christofides algorithm, which has an approximation ratio of $3/2$, was introduced in 1976 [44]. The strictly $\lceil \log_2 n \rceil$-competitive online algorithm MSTGREEDY is due to Imase and Waxman [85]; their bound originally works in a slightly different setting, which they called the dynamic Steiner tree problem. Here, the underlying graph is known and only the terminals are revealed online; however, the greedy approach also works for our setting since it only considers vertices that were presented earlier.

Online algorithms with advice for the MSTP were studied by Bianchi et al. [21]; the results given in this chapter are mainly based on this publication (see also Brülisauer [41], on which especially the usage of Kruskal's algorithm in Subsection 8.3.3 is based). Barhum [15] studied the Steiner tree problem in an online model where the graph is known in advance and the terminal vertices are revealed online; an online algorithm for the problem must have a feasible Steiner tree in every time step. For n vertices and t terminals, he showed that using $q \log_2 n$ advice bits with $0 \le q \le n-1$ allows for an $\mathcal{O}(\log(t/q))$-competitive online algorithm with advice and that this bound is tight.

Boyar et al. [36] introduced the *asymmetric string guessing problem*, which allowed them to do reductions to a large number of online problems. For many problems on graphs, this variant of string guessing is better suited for proving hardness results than the variant we introduced in Chapter 7. Moreover, they identified a class of "hard" online problems they called *AOC-complete*; these problems, which include DPA and the MISP, have the same advice complexity as asymmetric string guessing. Komm et al. [99] studied a large class of graph problems that are characterized by *hereditary graph properties*. They used reductions from both classical and asymmetric string guessing to establish different results with and without preemption; one of their results is a generalization of Exercise 8.7.

Solutions to Exercises

Exercise 1.1. It does not help in general to modify KNGREEDY as proposed in the exercise statement. The algorithm still has an approximation ratio that converges to 2 on the worst-case instance constructed in (1.1) as, after packing the object of weight $B/2 + 1$, there is no more room for any of the other objects. The only change necessary in the analysis is to give this statement.

Exercise 1.2. Let γ be a given positive integer. For any even $n \geq 4$, we construct a graph with n vertices such that the cost of TSPGREEDY's solution is γ times larger than the optimal cost; the idea is shown in Figure 9.1. All edges of the zigzag path starting at the vertex v at the lower left-hand corner and ending at w have weight 1; the edge back from w to v has weight $(2\gamma - 1)n + 1$. The horizontal edges have weight 2. Of course, this is not yet an instance of the TSP as the graph has to be complete. We simply define all remaining edges to have a weight of $2\gamma n$. For convenience, they are not shown in the figure.

First, assume TSPGREEDY starts at v. Then, it is lured into following the zigzag path until it ends up at w. Now it must close the cycle by taking the edge of weight $(2\gamma - 1)n + 1$ from w back to v; see Figure 9.1a. On the other hand, there is an optimal solution that starts at v, takes the horizontal path, followed by a vertical edge to arrive at w. After that, it returns to v again following the upper horizontal path and finally the vertical edge on the left; see Figure 9.1b. The total cost is $2(n-1) + 2 = 2n$, and thus we obtain a lower bound of

$$\frac{(2\gamma - 1)n + 1 + n - 1}{2n} = \gamma$$

on the approximation ratio as claimed. It is easy to see that a similar argumentation is possible if TSPGREEDY starts at any other vertex, which may even result in a more expensive solution.

Finally, note that we could also choose γ to be some function of n.

© Springer International Publishing Switzerland 2016
D. Komm, *An Introduction to Online Computation*,
Texts in Theoretical Computer Science. An EATCS Series,
DOI 10.1007/978-3-319-42749-2

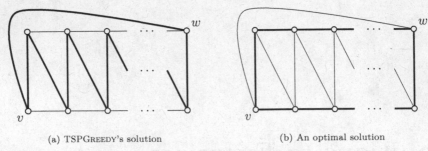

(a) TSPGREEDY's solution   (b) An optimal solution

Figure 9.1. A hard instance for TSPGREEDY as used in the solution of Exercise 1.2.

Exercise 1.3. First, we argue that KRUSKAL is consistent for MSTP. To this end, we use the fact that any spanning tree contains exactly $n - 1$ edges. For a given instance G, let $S :=$ KRUSKAL(G) denote the solution that is computed by KRUSKAL. S contains $n - 1$ edges as well, as there are $n - 1$ rounds and exactly one edge is added to S in any of them. Clearly, S does not contain a cycle since KRUSKAL never picks an edge that closes one. For a contradiction, suppose that S is not connected; then S is a forest, and consequently contains fewer than $n - 1$ edges, which is a direct contradiction. On the other hand, S must contain every vertex of G by the same reasoning.

Now we prove that S is optimal. We do this by showing that there is an optimal solution for G that contains all the edges that are chosen in the $n - 1$ rounds $R_1, R_2, \ldots, R_{n-1}$ by induction on the round number i.

Base Case. In round R_1, an edge e_1 that has the smallest weight in G is chosen to be part of S. Now consider any optimal solution $S_{\mathrm{opt}} :=$ OPT(G) for G. If S_{opt} contains e_1, the claim follows immediately. If S_{opt} does not contain e_1, then adding e_1 to S_{opt} creates a graph that contains a cycle. All other edges in this cycle have at least the same weight as e_1. Thus, removing one of them leads to a spanning tree that contains e_1, and that has a weight which is not larger than the weight of S_{opt}.

Induction Hypothesis. The claim holds for $i - 1$.

Induction Step. Let S_{i-1} denote the subtree of S that contains the $i - 1$ edges that have been added to S in the previous rounds $R_1, R_2, \ldots, R_{i-1}$, and let e_i denote the edge that is chosen in round R_i resulting in a tree S_i. Now consider an optimal solution S_{opt} that has S_{i-1} as a subgraph. By the induction hypothesis, such a solution exists. If S_{opt} contains e_i, we are again done; otherwise, adding e_i to S_{opt} closes a cycle. At least one of the edges in this cycle is not contained in S_i. As a consequence, this edge cannot have a weight smaller than that of e_i, and removing it results in a spanning tree that has a weight which is not larger than that of S_{opt}.

The claim follows.

Exercise 1.4. Suppose there is a c-competitive online algorithm ALG for paging that starts with the same cache content as OPT as in Definition 1.7. We then easily design an online algorithm ALG′ that may start with any cache content, and imitates the original algorithm. In the worst case, the pages that are originally in the caches of ALG and OPT get requested before ALG removes them. This causes a page fault for ALG′ but not for ALG or OPT. However, this can happen at most k times; thus we have $\mathrm{cost}(\mathrm{ALG}'(I)) \leq \mathrm{cost}(\mathrm{ALG}(I)) + k$ for every instance I. Now, if ALG is c-competitive, there is some constant α such that $\mathrm{cost}(\mathrm{ALG}(I)) \leq c \cdot \mathrm{cost}(\mathrm{OPT}(I)) + \alpha$ for all I, and therefore $\mathrm{cost}(\mathrm{ALG}'(I)) \leq c \cdot \mathrm{cost}(\mathrm{OPT}(I)) + \alpha + k$ for all I. Since $\alpha + k$ is also constant with respect to $|I|$, the claim follows.

Of course, if we speak about the strict competitive ratio, things change. Suppose a page that is initially in the cache of ALG but not in that of ALG′ is requested n times; call this instance I'. Then ALG is optimal since $\mathrm{cost}(\mathrm{ALG}(I')) = \mathrm{cost}(\mathrm{OPT}(I')) = 0$, but the strict competitive ratio of ALG′ is unbounded (it is not even defined, to be precise).

Exercise 1.5. Let ALG be any online algorithm for paging that replaces an arbitrary number of pages in every time step. We design another online algorithm ALG′ for paging that imitates ALG, but only replaces pages if a page fault occurs. Suppose a page p is requested that is not in the cache of ALG′ in the corresponding time step; we distinguish two cases depending on whether p also causes a page fault for ALG.

Case 1. Suppose p is also missing in the cache of ALG in this time step, and ALG removes some page p'. If p' is also in the cache of ALG′, it also replaces p'. If p' is not in the cache of ALG′, then ALG′ replaces a page p'' that is not in ALG's cache (such a page must always exist). Thus, the overall cost increases by 1 for both algorithms.

Case 2. Conversely, if p is in ALG's cache, it must have been loaded into it in some preceding time step, because both algorithms started with the same cache content. In the time step where ALG loaded p into the cache for the last time, this was not to replace a page due to a page fault, because otherwise p would also be in the cache of ALG′ (due to case 1). As a consequence, ALG already caused an additional cost of 1 compared to ALG′.

It follows that ALG′ never pays more than ALG.

Exercise 1.6. Let ALG be any online algorithm for paging that removes an arbitrary number of pages in every time step. We design an algorithm ALG′ that imitates ALG, but whenever ALG removes a page just marks this page as removed instead. If, on a page fault, ALG loads some page p into an empty cache cell and p is also not in the cache of ALG′, ALG′ replaces a page that is marked as removed with p. Such a page must always exist. This way, the set of pages in the cache of ALG′ is a superset of the pages that ALG has in its cache, and ALG′ does not cause more page faults than ALG.

Exercise 1.7. We can prove that LRU is k-competitive analogously to the proof of Theorem 1.4; consider a fixed input together with its k-phase partition. We already know that OPT has to make at least N page faults in total, so it only remains to show that LRU makes at most k page faults per phase P_i.

Since at most k different pages are requested during P_i, we are again done if we can show that no single page causes two page faults in this phase. Let p be the first page that causes a page fault during P_i. After that, p is the most recently used page in the cache, and it does not get removed for the next $k - 1$ distinct requests. Since there are at most k distinct pages requested during P_i, p does not cause a second page fault in this phase.

Exercise 1.8. Again we consider an input and its k-phase partition according to Definition 1.8. Recall that the first phase starts with the first page fault. In general, a phase P_i always starts with FWF emptying its cache, and then filling it up with every page fault that is encountered. Since the cache is full after exactly k different pages were requested, no single page can cause more than one page fault, because a page that is loaded into the cache during P_i is not removed as there is always enough free space. Together with the same reasoning as in the proof of Theorem 1.4 about OPT, the claim follows.

Exercise 1.9. Let I be any instance of paging, and consider the phase partition as defined in the exercise statement; suppose there are N phases in total. Let $P_{\mathrm{FIFO},i}$ be an arbitrary phase with $1 \le i \le N - 1$; our goal is to show that OPT also has to make at least one page fault in it. For $P_{\mathrm{FIFO},1}$, we immediately see that both FIFO and OPT make exactly one page fault.

For every i with $2 \le i \le N - 1$, let p denote the page that caused the last page fault for FIFO in phase $P_{\mathrm{FIFO},i-1}$. All pages that cause a page fault for FIFO during $P_{\mathrm{FIFO},i}$ are not removed before the end of phase $P_{\mathrm{FIFO},i}$. It follows that the cost of FIFO during $P_{\mathrm{FIFO},i}$ is not increased by requesting the same page multiple times. In other words, no page causes more than one page fault during $P_{\mathrm{FIFO},i}$. The page p is evicted by FIFO with the kth page fault in $P_{\mathrm{FIFO},i}$; requesting it during $P_{\mathrm{FIFO},i}$ therefore does not cause any additional cost. Since p caused the last page fault in $P_{\mathrm{FIFO},i-1}$ for FIFO and this phase was ended right afterwards, p must also be in the cache of OPT at the beginning of $P_{\mathrm{FIFO},i}$. Accordingly, there are $k - 1$ pages (namely at most all other ones in the cache of OPT at the beginning of phase $P_{\mathrm{FIFO},i}$) that can be requested and cause a page fault for FIFO, but no page fault for OPT. Thus, OPT has to make at least one page fault during phase $P_{\mathrm{FIFO},i}$; in general, OPT causes at least one page fault for every k page faults of FIFO.

The only exception is the last phase $P_{\mathrm{FIFO},N}$ since it may not be complete. Then again, if this is the case, FIFO causes fewer than k page faults in $P_{\mathrm{FIFO},N}$; it follows that the number of page faults caused by FIFO in $P_{\mathrm{FIFO},1}$ and $P_{\mathrm{FIFO},N}$ is at most k. Recall that OPT also causes one page fault in $P_{\mathrm{FIFO},1}$. Conversely, if $P_{\mathrm{FIFO},N}$ is complete, OPT causes one page fault per phase. Thus, it even follows that FIFO is strictly k-competitive.

Exercise 1.10. We consider FIFO for two cache sizes 3 and 4. As always, the cache is initialized as (p_1, p_2, p_3) or (p_1, p_2, p_3, p_4), respectively. Suppose we are given the instance

$$(p_5, p_6, p_7, p_8, p_5, p_6, p_9, p_5, p_6, p_7, p_8, p_9) \ .$$

First, consider FIFO with cache size 3. Independently of how the three pages that are initially in the cache are removed, FIFO's cache has the form

p_5	p_6	p_7

after the first three requests; so far, FIFO made three page faults. On the next four requests p_8, p_5, p_6, p_9, the cache contents are

p_8	p_6	p_7

,

p_8	p_5	p_7

,

p_8	p_5	p_6

,

p_9	p_5	p_6

causing a page fault in every time step. The next two requests p_5 and p_6 do not cause page faults. Finally, when p_7 and p_8 are requested, FIFO's cache content changes to

p_9	p_7	p_6

and

p_9	p_7	p_8

and the last request p_9 does not cause any page fault. This sums up to nine page faults in total.

Now consider FIFO with cache size 4 on the same instance. After the first four requests, the cache content is

p_5	p_6	p_7	p_8

,

and there were four page faults so far. The next two requests p_5 and p_6 do not cause page faults. However, the subsequent requests p_9, p_5, p_6, p_7, p_8, p_9 cause one page fault each, and the cache contents are

p_9	p_6	p_7	p_8

,

p_9	p_5	p_7	p_8

,

p_9	p_5	p_6	p_8

,

p_9	p_5	p_6	p_7

,

p_8	p_5	p_6	p_7

,

p_8	p_9	p_6	p_7

.

Thus, in total there are 10 page faults, although the cache size is larger.

Exercise 1.11. In this case, we can indeed prove a stronger lower bound that is closer to the one for LIFO. For any n that is larger than $2k$ and a multiple of 2, the adversary creates the instance

$$I = (p_1, p_1, p_2, p_2, \ldots, p_{k-1}, p_{k-1}, \underbrace{p_{k+1}, p_k, p_{k+1}, p_k, \ldots, p_{k+1}, p_k}_{n-2(k-1) \text{ requests}})$$

on which $\mathrm{OPT}(I)$ causes one page fault by replacing any page different from p_k in time step $2(k-1) + 1$. LFU as defined in the exercise statement, however, causes a page fault in every of the last $n - 2(k-1)$ time steps. Therefore, its competitive ratio is at least $n - 2(k-1)$.

Exercise 1.12. The online algorithm MAX is not competitive and the argument is very similar to the one for LIFO. If the request sequence is given by $I = (p_{k+1}, p_k, p_{k+1}, p_k, \ldots)$, the cost of MAX grows linearly in the input length n, because it evicts the pages $p_k, p_{k+1}, p_k, p_{k+1}, \ldots$ while OPT(I) simply removes an arbitrary page different from p_k in time step T_1. Obviously, we can construct an analogous hard instance $(p_{k+1}, p_1, p_2, p_1, p_2, \ldots)$ for MIN.

Exercise 1.13. The algorithm WALK implements a FIFO strategy where we have a special strategy to evict the first k pages in the cache, namely in the order $p_1, p_2, \ldots, p_k$. After that, the cache is just treated like a queue and WALK's competitive ratio is k according to Theorem 1.4.

Exercise 1.14. From the theoretical point of view that we take, this approach does not help at all. LOCAL is clearly not competitive and we can easily show this analogously as for LIFO. The adversary simply constructs the input $I = (p_{k+1}, p_1, p_{k+1}, p_1, \ldots)$; again, OPT($I$) makes one page fault by, for instance, removing page p_2 at the beginning, while LOCAL makes n page faults in total.

Exercise 1.15. At the beginning of each phase P_i, FWF empties the cache and loads the requested page. All pages that are requested during P_i with $1 \leq i \leq N$ are not removed during this phase until there are k requests to different pages in total and the cache is full. If a $(k+1)$th distinct page is requested, a marking algorithm starts a new phase P_{i+1}, and only then FWF empties its cache again. It follows that the pages in the cache of FWF at any given time step are exactly those that would be marked, and since none of them are removed in the same phase, FWF is a marking algorithm.

Exercise 1.16. According to Theorem 1.8, every marking algorithm is (strictly) k-competitive and according to Theorem 1.6, LIFO is not competitive. Thus, LIFO cannot be a marking algorithm.

Neither is FIFO, as we can show using the input

$$(p_{k+1}, p_{k+2}, \ldots, p_{2k}, p_{2k+1}, p_{k+2}, p_{2k+2}) \,.$$

The first phase P_1 starts with the first request; P_1 ends after the request p_{2k} and all requested pages are now in the cache. At the beginning of the second phase P_2, FIFO removes p_{k+1}, which has now been in the cache for the longest time. When p_{2k+2} is requested, FIFO removes p_{k+2}. A marking algorithm, on the other hand, does not remove p_{k+2} as it was requested in P_2 and thus marked.

Exercise 1.17. If we consider (h, k)-paging for $k < h$, the situation becomes hopeless for any online algorithm ALG. Suppose that $m = h = k + 1$. For any instance I, OPT(I) has all pages available in its memory from the start, so it never causes any page fault, whereas ALG can again be forced to make a page fault in every time step.

Exercise 1.18. We use the same idea as in the proof of Theorem 1.5. Let $n = N \cdot k$, for some $N \in \mathbb{N}^+$. Recall that k is the size of ALG's cache and h is the size of OPT's cache; the caches are initialized as $(p_1, p_2, \ldots, p_k)$ and $(p_1, p_2, \ldots, p_h)$, respectively. This time, let $m = 2k + 1$, which means that, at any given time step, there are always $k - h + 1$ pages that are neither in ALG's cache nor in OPT's cache, even in cases where their contents are disjoint.

The input I is again subdivided into N phases of k-requests each, and the adversary makes sure that ALG causes a page fault in every time step. Consider phase P_1; I starts with the $k - h + 1$ pages $p_{k+1}, p_{k+2}, \ldots, p_{2k-h+1}$, which causes $k - h + 1$ page faults for both ALG and OPT. Now let S denote the set of $k + 1$ different pages that were in OPT's cache at the beginning of the phase or that were requested during the first $k - h + 1$ time steps. At this point, OPT can have any arbitrary subset of size $h - 1$ of S in its cache; on the other hand, there is at least one page in S that is not in ALG's cache. Thus, the adversary can ensure that ALG causes a page fault in each of the $h - 1$ subsequent time steps. Doing so, it requests at most $h - 1$ different pages, and these are all in OPT's cache. Therefore, ALG causes k page faults, and OPT causes $k - h + 1$.

This procedure is iterated N times, where every phase starts with the adversary requesting $k - h + 1$ pages that are in neither of the two caches. Of course, at the beginning of any phase P_i with $2 \leq i \leq N$, the cache content of OPT is not necessarily a subset of ALG's cache content.

Exercise 2.1. Let σ be the size of the alphabet of the random tape of some randomized algorithm ALG_σ. Moreover, let p be the smallest prime number which is larger than σ. We now define a problem Π_p where the only task is to output a number between 1 and p with equal probability, that is, with probability $1/p$.

We can now argue in exactly the same way as for the algorithm THREE$'$. If there were a number $n' \in \mathbb{N}$ such that ALG_σ were able to output the numbers with the same probability, we would have to evenly distribute the $\sigma^{n'}$ different behaviors of RAND_σ among the p different outputs; but since p is not a prime factor of σ, nor is p a prime factor of any power of σ, and thus does not divide $\sigma^{n'}$.

Exercise 2.2. If we count as the exercise suggests, we distinguish the cases in which one random string is a proper prefix of another one. Suppose we are given a randomized online algorithm RAND for which the following holds. There is some random string s and a proper prefix s' of s such that the two corresponding deterministic online algorithms A_s and $A_{s'}$ are different. This means that there is at least one instance I such that A_s works differently than $A_{s'}$. However, this leads to a contradiction. If RAND has read s', its behavior is fully determined by I and s'. Thus, it will either always continue reading random bits and act like A_s or read no further random bits and act like $A_{s'}$.

Exercise 2.3. We start by proving the first part of the inequality, which can be done analogously to the proof of Lemma 2.1. In particular, for every deterministic online algorithm A_j, we have

$$\mathbb{E}_{\text{ADV}}[\text{gain}(A_j(\mathcal{I}))] = \sum_{i=1}^{\mu} \text{Pr}_{\text{ADV}}[I_i] \cdot \text{gain}(A_j(I_i))$$

and

$$\mathbb{E}_{\text{ADV}}[\mathbb{E}_{\text{RAND}}[\text{gain}(\text{RAND}(\mathcal{I}))]] = \sum_{i=1}^{\mu} \text{Pr}_{\text{ADV}}[I_i] \cdot \mathbb{E}_{\text{RAND}}[\text{gain}(\text{RAND}(I_i))]$$

$$= \sum_{j=1}^{\ell} \text{Pr}_{\text{RAND}}[A_j] \cdot \mathbb{E}_{\text{ADV}}[\text{gain}(A_j(\mathcal{I}))] .$$

Now suppose that the expected optimal gain is at least c times larger than the expected gain of every deterministic online algorithm. Then,

$$\mathbb{E}_{\text{ADV}}[\mathbb{E}_{\text{RAND}}[\text{gain}(\text{RAND}(\mathcal{I}))]] = \sum_{j=1}^{\ell} \text{Pr}_{\text{RAND}}[A_j] \cdot \mathbb{E}_{\text{ADV}}[\text{gain}(A_j(\mathcal{I}))]$$

$$\leq \sum_{j=1}^{\ell} \text{Pr}_{\text{RAND}}[A_j] \cdot \frac{1}{c} \cdot \mathbb{E}_{\text{ADV}}[\text{gain}(\text{OPT}(\mathcal{I}))]$$

$$= \frac{1}{c} \cdot \mathbb{E}_{\text{ADV}}[\text{gain}(\text{OPT}(\mathcal{I}))] .$$

By the same arguments as in the proof of Lemma 2.1, we can again "derandomize" the adversary, and get the result that there is some $I \in \mathcal{I}$ such that

$$c \leq \frac{\text{gain}(\text{OPT}(I))}{\mathbb{E}_{\text{RAND}}[\text{gain}(\text{RAND}(I))]} ,$$

which proves the statement if the maximum is given by the first argument of the max-expression.

Now we look at the second part. To this end, following the hint from the exercise statement, we consider the reciprocal strict competitive ratio, that is,

$$\frac{\text{gain}(A_j(I))}{\text{gain}(\text{OPT}(I))} ,$$

for any online algorithm A_j and instance I. Note that this expression always has a value between 0 and 1, and A_j is better the larger it gets. We can now compute a bound on the reciprocal strict competitive ratio of RAND with respect to Pr_{ADV}; the important thing is that, in this case, we can again change the order of summation.

$$\mathbb{E}_{\text{ADV}}\left[\frac{\mathbb{E}_{\text{RAND}}[\text{gain}(\text{RAND}(\mathcal{I}))]}{\text{gain}(\text{OPT}(\mathcal{I}))}\right]$$

$$= \mathbb{E}_{\mathrm{ADV}} \left[\frac{\sum_{j=1}^{\ell} \mathrm{Pr}_{\mathrm{RAND}}[A_j] \cdot \mathrm{gain}(A_j(\mathcal{I}))}{\mathrm{gain}(\mathrm{OPT}(\mathcal{I}))} \right]$$

$$= \sum_{j=1}^{\ell} \left(\mathrm{Pr}_{\mathrm{RAND}}[A_j] \sum_{i=1}^{\mu} \mathrm{Pr}_{\mathrm{ADV}}[I_i] \cdot \frac{\mathrm{gain}(A_j(I_i))}{\mathrm{gain}(\mathrm{OPT}(I_i))} \right)$$

$$= \sum_{j=1}^{\ell} \mathrm{Pr}_{\mathrm{RAND}}[A_j] \cdot \mathbb{E}_{\mathrm{ADV}} \left[\frac{\mathrm{gain}(A_j(\mathcal{I}))}{\mathrm{gain}(\mathrm{OPT}(\mathcal{I}))} \right].$$

Now suppose that

$$\left(\mathbb{E}_{\mathrm{ADV}} \left[\frac{\mathrm{gain}(A_j(\mathcal{I}))}{\mathrm{gain}(\mathrm{OPT}(\mathcal{I}))} \right] \right)^{-1} \geq c \,,$$

and therefore

$$\mathbb{E}_{\mathrm{ADV}} \left[\frac{\mathrm{gain}(A_j(\mathcal{I}))}{\mathrm{gain}(\mathrm{OPT}(\mathcal{I}))} \right] \leq \frac{1}{c} \,,$$

for any deterministic online algorithm A_j. As a consequence, it follows that

$$\mathbb{E}_{\mathrm{ADV}} \left[\frac{\mathbb{E}_{\mathrm{RAND}}[\mathrm{gain}(\mathrm{RAND}(\mathcal{I}))]}{\mathrm{gain}(\mathrm{OPT}(\mathcal{I}))} \right] = \sum_{j=1}^{\ell} \mathrm{Pr}_{\mathrm{RAND}}[A_j] \cdot \mathbb{E}_{\mathrm{ADV}} \left[\frac{\mathrm{gain}(A_j(\mathcal{I}))}{\mathrm{gain}(\mathrm{OPT}(\mathcal{I}))} \right]$$

$$\leq \sum_{j=1}^{\ell} \mathrm{Pr}_{\mathrm{RAND}}[A_j] \cdot \frac{1}{c}$$

$$= \frac{1}{c} \,.$$

Hence, there is an instance $I \in \mathcal{I}$ such that

$$\frac{\mathbb{E}_{\mathrm{RAND}}[\mathrm{gain}(\mathrm{RAND}(I))]}{\mathrm{gain}(\mathrm{OPT}(I))} \leq \frac{1}{c} \,,$$

and thus

$$c \cdot \mathbb{E}_{\mathrm{RAND}}[\mathrm{gain}(\mathrm{RAND}(I))] \leq \mathrm{gain}(\mathrm{OPT}(I)) \,.$$

This concludes the second part of the claim, and thus proves Yao's principle for finite maximization problems.

Exercise 2.4. Suppose we can construct $\mathcal{I}_1, \mathcal{I}_2, \ldots$ as before, and are able to show

$$\max \left\{ \frac{\mathbb{E}_{\mathrm{ADV},i}[\mathrm{gain}(\mathrm{OPT}(\mathcal{I}_i))]}{\max_j (\mathbb{E}_{\mathrm{ADV},i}[\mathrm{gain}(A_j(\mathcal{I}_i))])}, \min_j \left(\left(\mathbb{E}_{\mathrm{ADV},i} \left[\frac{\mathrm{gain}(A_j(\mathcal{I}_i))}{\mathrm{gain}(\mathrm{OPT}(\mathcal{I}_i))} \right] \right)^{-1} \right) \right\} \geq c \,,$$

for every $i \in \mathbb{N}^+$. Then it follows that there are instances $I_i \in \mathcal{I}_i$ with

$$\frac{\text{gain}(\text{OPT}(I_i))}{\mathbb{E}_{\text{RAND}}[\text{gain}(\text{RAND}(I_i))]} \geq c \, .$$

The remainder of the discussion is analogous to the proof of Theorem 1.3.

Exercise 2.5. Again, for a contradiction, suppose that both conditions (i) and (ii) are true, but there still is a randomized online algorithm RAND that is $(c - \varepsilon)$-competitive in expectation for Π, where $\varepsilon > 0$. By the same reasoning as in the proof of Theorem 2.5, we get the counterpart of (2.7) as

$$\mathbb{E}_{\text{ADV},i}[\text{gain}(\text{OPT}(\mathcal{I}_i))] \leq (c - \varepsilon) \cdot \mathbb{E}_{\text{RAND}}[\mathbb{E}_{\text{ADV},i}[\text{gain}(\text{RAND}(\mathcal{I}_i))]] + \alpha \, . \quad (9.1)$$

Moreover, we easily obtain

$$\max_j(\mathbb{E}_{\text{ADV},i}[\text{gain}(A_j(\mathcal{I}_i))]) \geq \mathbb{E}_{\text{RAND}}[\mathbb{E}_{\text{ADV},i}[\text{gain}(\text{RAND}(\mathcal{I}_i))]] \, . \quad (9.2)$$

With (9.1) and (9.2), we get

$$\mathbb{E}_{\text{ADV},i}[\text{gain}(\text{OPT}(\mathcal{I}_i))] \leq (c - \varepsilon) \cdot \max_j(\mathbb{E}_{\text{ADV},i}[\text{gain}(A_j(\mathcal{I}_i))]) + \alpha \, ,$$

which is equivalent to (assuming that the maximum of the expected gain achievable by any deterministic online algorithm is not zero)

$$\frac{\mathbb{E}_{\text{ADV},i}[\text{gain}(\text{OPT}(\mathcal{I}_i))]}{\max_j(\mathbb{E}_{\text{ADV},i}[\text{gain}(A_j(\mathcal{I}_i))])} - \frac{\alpha}{\max_j(\mathbb{E}_{\text{ADV},i}[\text{gain}(A_j(\mathcal{I}_i))])} \leq c - \varepsilon \, . \quad (9.3)$$

In the last step, the argument is a little different from that in the proof of Theorem 2.5. Due to (i), the first term of (9.3) is again at least c. From (ii), it follows that the expected optimal gain increases unboundedly as n increases; but this means that also the expected gain of RAND has to increase unboundedly in n, since otherwise RAND would not be $(c - \varepsilon)$-competitive (recall that c is a constant). Consequently, also $\max_j(\mathbb{E}_{\text{ADV},i}[\text{gain}(A_j(\mathcal{I}_i))])$ increases unboundedly. Hence, there are infinitely many sets of instances such that the second term of (9.3) is smaller than ε, which is a contradiction.

Exercise 2.6. Again, for a contradiction, suppose that both conditions (i) and (ii) are true for all randomized online algorithms for Π, and there still is a randomized online algorithm RAND that is $(c - \varepsilon)$-competitive for Π, where $\varepsilon > 0$. By the same reasoning as in the proof of Theorem 2.8, we get the counterpart of (2.11) as

$$\mathbb{E}_{\text{ADV},i}[\text{gain}(\text{OPT}(\mathcal{I}_i))] \leq (c - \varepsilon) \cdot \mathbb{E}_{\text{RAND}}[\mathbb{E}_{\text{ADV},i}[\text{gain}(\text{RAND}(\mathcal{I}_i))]] + \alpha \, . \quad (9.4)$$

Furthermore, we have

$$\sup_j(\mathbb{E}_{\text{ADV},i}[\text{gain}(A_j(\mathcal{I}_i))]) \geq \mathbb{E}_{\text{RAND}}[\mathbb{E}_{\text{ADV},i}[\text{gain}(\text{RAND}(\mathcal{I}_i))]] \, . \quad (9.5)$$

With (9.4) and (9.5), we get

$$\mathbb{E}_{\mathrm{ADV},i}[\mathrm{gain}(\mathrm{OPT}(\mathcal{I}_i))] \leq (c-\varepsilon) \cdot \sup_j(\mathbb{E}_{\mathrm{ADV},i}[\mathrm{gain}(A_j(\mathcal{I}_i))]) + \alpha \,,$$

which is equivalent to (assuming that the supremum of the expected gain achievable by any deterministic online algorithm is not zero)

$$\frac{\mathbb{E}_{\mathrm{ADV},i}[\mathrm{gain}(\mathrm{OPT}(\mathcal{I}_i))]}{\sup_j(\mathbb{E}_{\mathrm{ADV},i}[\mathrm{gain}(A_j(\mathcal{I}_i))])} - \frac{\alpha}{\sup_j(\mathbb{E}_{\mathrm{ADV},i}[\mathrm{gain}(A_j(\mathcal{I}_i))])} \leq c - \varepsilon \,. \tag{9.6}$$

Now we can argue similarly to the proof of Theorem 2.8. From (ii), it follows that there is an infinite increasing sequence $i_1, i_2, \ldots$ for which the expected optimal gain increases unboundedly; but this means that also the expected gain of RAND must increase unboundedly for this sequence, since otherwise RAND would not be $(c-\varepsilon)$-competitive. Then again, in this case $\sup_j(\mathbb{E}_{\mathrm{ADV},i}[\mathrm{gain}(A_j(\mathcal{I}_i))])$ must increase unboundedly as well, and thus the second term of (9.6) is smaller than ε for infinitely many i. Hence, for infinitely many i, we get a contradiction to (i).

Exercise 2.7. Such an instance is given by $(p_8, p_2, p_3, p_4, p_5)$. After p_8 is requested, the cache contents look as follows.

$Mark_1$: | p_8 | p_2 | p_3 | p_4 | p_5 | p_6 | p_7 |

$Mark_2$: | p_1 | p_8 | p_3 | p_4 | p_5 | p_6 | p_7 |

$Mark_3$: | p_1 | p_2 | p_8 | p_4 | p_5 | p_6 | p_7 |

$Mark_4$: | p_1 | p_2 | p_3 | p_8 | p_5 | p_6 | p_7 |

The next requests are all unmarked old pages. First, p_2 is requested and $Mark_2$ evicts p_7 to make sure its cache content is different from all other algorithms in strat(RMARKBARELY).

$Mark_1$: | p_8 | p_2 | p_3 | p_4 | p_5 | p_6 | p_7 |

$Mark_2$: | p_1 | p_8 | p_3 | p_4 | p_5 | p_6 | p_2 |

$Mark_3$: | p_1 | p_2 | p_8 | p_4 | p_5 | p_6 | p_7 |

$Mark_4$: | p_1 | p_2 | p_3 | p_8 | p_5 | p_6 | p_7 |

Then, p_3 and p_4 are requested, and $Mark_3$ and $Mark_4$ remove p_6 and p_5 respectively to load them.

$Mark_1$: | p_8 | p_2 | p_3 | p_4 | p_5 | p_6 | p_7 |

$Mark_2$: | p_1 | p_8 | p_3 | p_4 | p_5 | p_6 | p_2 |

$Mark_3$: | p_1 | p_2 | p_8 | p_4 | p_5 | p_3 | p_7 |

$Mark_4$: | p_1 | p_2 | p_3 | p_8 | p_4 | p_6 | p_7 |

Last, p_5 is requested, and there is no possibility left for $Mark_4$ to replace a page such that its cache content stays different from all other ones.

Exercise 2.8. Let $\varepsilon > 0$, and consider a constant $c < (1 - \varepsilon)k$. We use the same argumentation as in the proof of Theorem 2.13, but we need to pay a bit more attention at some places. Let n_0 and f be defined as above, and suppose there is a randomized online algorithm RAND that has a performance of c on instances of length $n \geq n_0$ with a probability of $1 - 1/f(n)$. In other words, there is a constant α such that, for every instance I of paging with $|I| = n \geq n_0$, the cost of RAND on I is at most $c \cdot \text{cost}(\text{OPT}(I)) + \alpha$ with a probability of $1 - 1/f(n)$.

Now let β be the smallest constant with $\beta \geq \alpha$ such that β/ε is a multiple of k; furthermore, let $n' \geq n_0$ be a natural number that is a large multiple of β/ε such that

$$\frac{1}{k^{\beta/\varepsilon - 1}} > \frac{1}{f(n')} \ .$$

Similarly to the proof of Theorem 2.13, we design a randomized online algorithm RAND'. For every instance of length β/ε, RAND' simulates RAND on an instance of length n' by repeating each request $n'/(\beta/\varepsilon)$ times. It follows that RAND' has a performance of c on inputs of length β/ε with probability $1 - 1/f(n')$.

Now consider an instance I' of length β/ε that is constructed the same way as the instance of length k in the proof of Theorem 2.13. RAND' has cost β/ε on I' with a constant probability of at least $1/k^{\beta/\varepsilon - 1}$. We also know that

$$\text{cost}(\text{OPT}(I')) \leq \frac{\beta}{k\varepsilon} \ ,$$

because β/ε is a multiple of k and $\text{OPT}(I')$ makes at most one page fault every k requests (by the same arguments as in the proof of Theorem 1.5).

This is a contradiction as the performance of RAND' on I' can be bounded from below by

$$\frac{\beta/\varepsilon - \alpha}{\beta/(k\varepsilon)} \geq \frac{\beta/\varepsilon - \beta}{\beta/(k\varepsilon)} = (1 - \varepsilon)k > c$$

with a probability of at least $1/k^{\beta/\varepsilon - 1}$.

Exercise 2.9. This does not change the asymptotic statement of Theorem 2.14. In this case, the only difference is that, when bounding the probability that RMARK has a cost that is larger than its expected cost, we use

$$\mathbb{E}[\text{cost}(\text{RMARK}(I))] \leq 2H_k \cdot \text{cost}(\text{OPT}(I)) + \alpha$$

instead of (2.28). This gives

$$\Pr[\text{cost}(\text{RMARK}(I)) \geq (2H_k + \varepsilon) \cdot \text{cost}(\text{OPT}(I))]$$

$$\leq \Pr\left[\text{cost}(\text{RMARK}(I)) \geq \frac{(2H_k + \varepsilon) \cdot (\mathbb{E}[\text{cost}(\text{RMARK}(I))] - \alpha)}{2H_k}\right]$$

$$= \Pr\left[\sum_{i=1}^{N}(C_i - \mathbb{E}[C_i]) \geq \frac{\varepsilon \cdot (\mathbb{E}[\text{cost}(\text{RMARK}(I))] - \alpha)}{2H_k} - \alpha\right].$$

Now we can again use Hoeffding's inequality together with the bounds of a_i and b_i from (2.27) and the lower bound of N for RMARK's expected cost. This yields

$$\Pr\left[\sum_{i=1}^{N}(C_i - \mathbb{E}[C_i]) \geq \frac{\varepsilon \cdot (\mathbb{E}[\text{cost}(\text{RMARK}(I))] - \alpha) - 2H_k\alpha}{2H_k}\right]$$

$$\leq \exp\left(-\frac{(\varepsilon \cdot (\mathbb{E}[\text{cost}(\text{RMARK}(I))] - \alpha) - 2H_k\alpha)^2}{4H_k^2 \sum_{i=1}^{N}(b_i - a_i)^2}\right)$$

$$\leq \exp\left(-\frac{(\varepsilon N - \alpha(\varepsilon + 2H_k))^2}{4H_k^2 N k^2}\right),$$

which again can be bounded by

$$\frac{1}{e^{\Omega(N)}}$$

since ε, α, and k are constant.

Exercise 2.10. In this case, we cannot follow similar reasoning to the case when the parameter k was fixed. We show that BREAKEVEN cannot be better than $(2 - 1/k)$-competitive. For a contradiction, suppose there are constants $\varepsilon > 0$ and $\alpha > 0$ such that, for every instance I of the ski rental problem, we have

$$\text{cost}(\text{BREAKEVEN}(I)) \leq (1 - \varepsilon)\left(2 - \frac{1}{k}\right) \cdot \text{cost}(\text{OPT}(I)) + \alpha. \tag{9.7}$$

Consider the following instance I of length $k + 1$. The first request is

$$k := \left\lfloor \frac{\alpha + \varepsilon}{2\varepsilon} \right\rfloor + 1 \tag{9.8}$$

and corresponds to the cost of buying the skis; the subsequent requests are "good." From Theorem 2.15, we know that

$$\text{cost}(\text{BREAKEVEN}(I)) = 2k - 1 \quad \text{and} \quad \text{cost}(\text{OPT}(I)) = k. \tag{9.9}$$

Together, (9.7) and (9.9) imply

$$2k - 1 \leq (1 - \varepsilon)\left(2 - \frac{1}{k}\right)k + \alpha \iff k \leq \frac{\alpha + \varepsilon}{2\varepsilon},$$

which is a contradiction to (9.8).

Exercise 3.1. We give two ideas. One possible alternative is to first encode the length of m in unary with, for instance, a sequence of this many 1s followed by one 0. To save a bit, the 0 can be written at position m. This is basically the same approach as the one we followed before; the only difference is that we now write in front the bits that were previously written at even positions, followed by the bits that were written at odd positions.

The second idea is to map all strings of length n over an alphabet $\{0, 1, \#\}$ to binary strings of length $2n$ by a mapping h. One possible way is to define

$$h(0) = 00, \quad h(1) = 11, \quad \text{and} \quad h(\#) = 01 ,$$

which can be decoded in straightforward fashion, and to use this mapping for encoding the length of m; here, $\#$ serves as a delimiter.

Exercise 3.2. For ease of presentation, for any $x \in \mathbb{N}^+$, let

$$f(x) := \lceil \log_2 x \rceil \quad \text{and} \quad f_i(x) := \underbrace{f(f(\ldots f(x)\ldots))}_{i} .$$

To encode a natural number m, we can simply iterate the procedure we have used before as suggested by the exercise statement. This leads to an upper bound of

$$f(m) + f_2(m) + \ldots + 2f_k(m)$$

for k iterations.

Of course, the algorithm must know the value of k in advance. Moreover, the leading term stays $\lceil \log_2 m \rceil$. We see that the number of "reasonable" iterations depends on the size of m; for instance, to encode the number 43 as in Example 3.2, we obtain

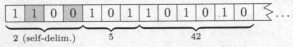

for $k = 3$. The algorithm now first reads the self-delimiting encoding of 2 without having further information. Then it reads the next three bits and decodes them, which gives 5. Finally, it reads the next six bits yielding 42. We observe that this requires more bits than the original approach from Example 3.2.

Exercise 3.3. With three bits, we can encode $2^3 = 8$ different numbers. However, since one combination is reserved as the delimiter, there only remain seven different possibilities. Consider an arbitrary string of length n that is a multiple of 3. The first $n - 3$ bits encode information and thus there are $7^{(n-3)/3} < 1.92^n$ different possibilities. Now consider our approach. We need at most $2\lceil \log_2 n \rceil$ bits to encode the length of the part of the string that carries the actual information in a self-delimiting way. Thus, there remain at least $n - 2\lceil \log_2 n \rceil$ bits to encode the actual information. Therefore, we have $2^{n-2\lceil \log_2 n \rceil}$ possibilities in this case. It remains to verify that

$$2^{n-2\lceil \log_2 n \rceil} > 1.92^n .$$

holds for n tending to infinity. To this end, observe that $n - 2\lceil \log_2 n \rceil$ is larger than $n - \varepsilon n$ as n tends to infinity, for any $\varepsilon > 0$, and

$$2^{(1-\varepsilon)n} > 1.92^n \,,$$

which finishes the proof.

Exercise 3.4. The algorithm PLIN3 already fulfills this condition if the initialization is skipped at the beginning. This can cause at most k additional page faults, which can be hidden in the additive constant α from Definition 3.2. Since one advice bit is read for each of the n requests, we are done.

Exercise 3.5. In the case that the cache is empty at the beginning, we do not need to initialize the cache and consequently get an upper bound of n on the advice complexity to compute an optimal solution.

   If the caches are initialized differently, however, there is no optimal online algorithm, not even with advice, since the adversary can always request a page at the beginning that is only in the cache of OPT but not in that of the algorithm. This causes at least one page fault the algorithm cannot make up for.

Exercise 3.6. If there are only $k + 1$ pages in total, then there is an optimal solution that only makes a page fault in at most every kth time step; the corresponding algorithm is the aforementioned offline algorithm LFD. Let PLIN4 be an online algorithm that reads $\lceil \log_2 k \rceil$ advice bits whenever it causes a page fault. These advice bits encode the index of the page LFD replaces in the cache. For the next $k - 1$ time steps, LFD does not cause any other page fault. Since the input length n is not necessarily a multiple of k, $\lceil \log_2 k \rceil$ advice bits must be read at most $\lceil n/k \rceil$ times.

Exercise 3.7. We use the same set $\mathcal{I}^{(n)}$ of instances as in the proof of Theorem 3.3, and construct a partition tree $\widehat{\mathcal{T}}$ of $\mathcal{I}^{(n)}$ such that its levels roughly correspond to the phases; an example is shown in Figure 9.2. The root $\hat{r}$ of $\widehat{\mathcal{T}}$ is labeled by $\mathcal{I}^{(n)}$ and 1 (since the same page $\bar{p}_1$ is requested initially and is therefore the common prefix of all instances), according to condition (iii) of Definition 3.3. $\widehat{\mathcal{T}}$ is k-ary; the k children of $\hat{r}$ correspond to the k different possibilities to choose the page p_1' that is not requested during P_1. We denote the corresponding children of $\hat{r}$ by $\hat{v}_{1,1}, \hat{v}_{1,2}, \ldots, \hat{v}_{1,k}$, and the corresponding sets are therefore $\mathcal{I}_{1,1}^{(n)}, \mathcal{I}_{1,2}^{(n)}, \ldots, \mathcal{I}_{1,k}^{(n)}$. The sets clearly partition $\mathcal{I}^{(n)}$, and all instances in one set have the same prefix of length $k + 1$ ($\bar{p}_1$ followed by the same $k - 1$ pages that were initially in the cache and the second new page $\bar{p}_2$). Thus, we can define $\rho_{\hat{v}_{1,1}} = \rho_{\hat{v}_{1,2}} = \ldots = \rho_{\hat{v}_{1,k}} := k + 1$. We can continue in this fashion to describe the vertices $\hat{v}_{2,1}, \hat{v}_{2,2}, \ldots, \hat{v}_{2,k^2}$ on the next level. The instances that correspond to these vertices all start with the first $k + 1$ requests of their parent; then, all instances belonging to the same vertex request the same $k - 1$ pages that are in the optimal cache at the beginning of this phase and the third new page $\bar{p}_3$. Therefore, we have $\rho_{\hat{v}_{2,1}} = \rho_{\hat{v}_{2,2}} = \ldots = \rho_{\hat{v}_{2,k^2}} := 2k + 1$, and

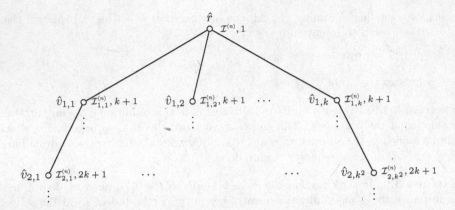

Figure 9.2. The partition tree constructed in the solution of Exercise 3.7.

so on. It follows that (i) and (ii) of Definition 3.3 are also satisfied. The leaves of $\widehat{\mathcal{T}}$ are labeled by (sets of) single instances and n.

Now consider any two vertices $\hat{v}_1$ and $\hat{v}_2$, neither one being an ancestor of the other and with lowest common ancestor $\hat{v}$. This means that both instances have the same common prefix of length $\rho_{\hat{v}}$. The last request of this prefix was a request for a page that was never requested before. Since $\hat{v}_1$ and $\hat{v}_2$ are in two different subtrees of $\hat{v}$, there were two different pages that needed to be replaced by this page in order to compute an optimal solution. Therefore, $[O_1]_{\rho_0}$ and $[O_2]_{\rho_0}$ must be different, which shows that the condition of Lemma 3.1 is satisfied.

Since there are n/k phases, $\widehat{\mathcal{T}}$ has a height of n/k. With this and the fact that $\widehat{\mathcal{T}}$ is k-ary, we get $w = k^{n/k}$ for the number w of leaves of $\widehat{\mathcal{T}}$. As a result, Theorem 3.1 implies the claimed lower bound.

Exercise 3.8. In this case, the single deterministic strategies are not necessarily all chosen with the same probability. In the proof of Theorem 3.7, we were able to bound

$$\frac{1}{2^{b(n)}} \sum_{i=1}^{2^{b(n)}} c_{i,j} = \frac{\mathbb{E}[\mathrm{cost}(\mathrm{RAND}(I_i))] - \alpha}{\mathrm{cost}(\mathrm{OPT}(I_i))}$$

by summing over all columns of a fixed row.

An analogous computation is not possible in this case, because the different columns of the new $(\mu(n) \times \ell(n))$-matrix $\mathcal{M}'$ are not all equally likely. Consequently,

$$\frac{1}{\ell(n)} \sum_{i=1}^{\ell(n)} c_{i,j} = \frac{\sum_{j=1}^{\ell(n)} \left(\frac{1}{\ell(n)} \cdot \mathrm{cost}(A_j(I_i)) - \alpha \right)}{\mathrm{cost}(\mathrm{OPT}(I_i))}$$

$$\neq \frac{\sum_{j=1}^{\ell(n)} (\Pr[A_j] \cdot \mathrm{cost}(A_j(I_i)) - \alpha)}{\mathrm{cost}(\mathrm{OPT}(I_i))}$$

$$= \frac{\mathbb{E}[\text{cost}(\text{RAND}(I_i))] - \alpha}{\text{cost}(\text{OPT}(I_i))}$$

in general.

Exercise 4.1. Let G be an arbitrary graph with edge weights of 1 and 2 only. If G has only one or two vertices, the claim follows trivially. So let there be at least three vertices. For any two vertices p_1 and p_2 we have $\text{dist}(p_1, p_2) \leq 2$ by the definition of G. No path via any vertex p_3 can be cheaper since, also by definition, both $\text{dist}(p_1, p_3) \geq 1$ and $\text{dist}(p_3, p_2) \geq 1$. As a result, the triangle inequality holds for every such graph.

Exercise 4.2. Let ALG be some non-lazy online algorithm for k-server. We construct a lazy online ALG$'$ as follows. For an input of length n, a solution of ALG can be represented by a sequence $(S_1, S_2, \ldots, S_n)$, where S_i with $1 \leq i \leq n$ is a set of pairs $(j, p_{i,j})$ with $1 \leq j \leq k$. Each such pair corresponds to the index of a server and a point to which this server is moved in the ith time step. If a server is already positioned on the requested point in time step T_i, the corresponding pair is contained in S_i as well.

The output of ALG$'$ is a sequence of n server indices; if a server is already positioned on the requested point, the corresponding index is also part of this sequence. ALG$'$ now simulates ALG as follows. For every request x_i, ALG$'$ outputs an index from a pair from S_i such that the corresponding server is moved to x_i and the cost is minimized. Obviously, such a pair must always exist. Therefore, ALG$'$ is consistent for k-server as a direct consequence of the consistency of ALG.

Now we argue why the cost of ALG$'$ cannot be larger than that of ALG. The two algorithms start with their servers at the same positions. If we consider a fixed server s_j with $1 \leq j \leq k$, we see that the sum of the distances that this server travels in the solution of ALG$'$ cannot be larger than in that of ALG. This follows from the fact that s_j is positioned successively at points at which it is also positioned by ALG in the same order. However, ALG may also move s_j to other points in between; due to the triangle inequality, this cannot lead to a smaller cost.

Exercise 4.3. In principle, a similar argumentation as in the solution of Exercise 4.2 would be possible. However, there is a difference when it comes to the complexity of the algorithm since the triangle inequality does not hold anymore. More specifically, suppose that ALG uses a server s_j with $1 \leq j \leq k$ in some time step to answer a request, and ALG$'$ also wants to use s_j, but it is located at some other point. In this case, ALG$'$ must either make sure that s_j moves exactly the same way as this server moved in ALG's solution so far, or it must compute the shortest way to the new position. As a consequence, ALG$'$ may use a lot more memory than in Exercise 4.2, or its time complexity is a lot worse.

Exercise 4.4. A first attempt to improve the bound is to set $\text{dist}(p_1, p_2)$ to $1 + \varepsilon$ instead of 2 for a given $\varepsilon > 0$. Using the same construction of an instance as in the proof of Theorem 4.2, this gives a bound of $n/(1 + \varepsilon)$.

A further improvement, however, is not possible. Of course, we could simply set $\text{dist}(p_1, p_2) = 1$; after the first request, KSGREEDY again has to choose some server to move to p_2. Since the adversary knows which server KSGREEDY uses in such a case, it can now request that server's previous position to force KSGREEDY to move another server. Without loss of generality, assume KSGREEDY first uses s_2, which is then positioned on p_3 after the second time step T_2. Next, the adversary requests p_2 again, but this time KSGREEDY might use s_1, which also corresponds to a greedy move. Now the adversary must request p_1 in order to make KSGREEDY move another server. This again leads to s_1 and s_2 being positioned on p_1 and p_3 as at the beginning. In total, the algorithm paid 4 so far, but OPT also had to pay 2. In general, all three vertices are requested every four requests if KSGREEDY always uses the two servers alternatingly to serve requests in which it may choose between them. Since there are only two servers, OPT also has to move at least one server every four requests. Thus, in this case, the competitive ratio of KSGREEDY is constant (it is at most 4).

Exercise 4.5. Let $\mathcal{M}$ be any metric space with at least $k+1$ points $p_1, p_2, \ldots, p_{k+1}$, and let the initial positions of the servers be $p_1, p_2, \ldots, p_k$. Moreover, the servers of an optimal algorithm are positioned on the points $p_1, p_2, \ldots, p_h$. Let ALG be any deterministic online algorithm for (h, k)-server. Following the hint from the exercise statement, we consider inputs $I = (x_1, x_2, \ldots, x_n)$ where the adversary always requests exactly the one point not covered by ALG in every time step.

Now we again consider a set of different algorithms with h servers each that work as follows. Every algorithm begins with a couple of non-greedy moves before the first request is processed. This time, every such algorithm moves one server to p_{k+1}; additionally, every algorithm covers a unique set of $h-1$ points from the remaining k points. Thus, there are

$$\binom{k}{h-1}$$

such algorithms in total. If some algorithm ALG_j with $1 \le j \le \binom{k}{h-1}$ does not cover some requested point x_i, ALG_j moves the server located at x_{i-1} to serve x_i. Similarly to the proof of Theorem 4.4, we are now going to show that, after the first moves in T_1, there are never two algorithms with the same $k+1-h$ uncovered points. The proof is again done by induction.

Base Case. The claim holds by construction after the first time step.

Induction Hypothesis. The claim holds for T_{i-1}.

Induction Step. Let us consider any two algorithms $\text{ALG}_{j'}$ and $\text{ALG}_{j''}$ in some time step T_i with $i \ge 2$. We can do a case distinction as in the proof of Theorem 4.4. The two cases that x_i is covered by both algorithms or only by one can be handled completely analogously. However, we need to take care of one additional case if $h < k$.

Case 3. If both algorithms do not have a server placed on x_i, they both move the server placed at x_{i-1}. As a consequence of the induction hypothesis, the algorithms covered different sets of points before; thus this identical movement leads to two different sets of covered points.

We conclude that all algorithms cover different sets of points. Now we need to compute how many of the above algorithms have the point x_i uncovered in time step T_i for $i \geq 2$. In time step T_{i-1}, the point x_{i-1} was requested; thus, every algorithm has a server placed on x_{i-1} at the beginning of T_i. Therefore, the number of algorithms that have no server placed on x_i at the beginning of T_i is equal to the number of possibilities to place $h - 1$ servers on the $k - 1$ points that are neither x_i nor x_{i-1}, which means that there are at most

$$\binom{k-1}{h-1}$$

algorithms that move a server from x_{i-1} to x_i. For ease of presentation, let us denote the sum of the distances that all algorithms move the serves at the beginning of T_1 by β; clearly, β is constant with respect to n. With a calculation similar to the one in the proof of Theorem 4.4, we get

$$\sum_{j=1}^{\binom{k}{h-1}} \mathrm{cost}(\mathrm{ALG}_j(I)) = \beta + \binom{k-1}{h-1} \cdot \sum_{i=2}^{n} \mathrm{dist}(x_{i-1}, x_i)$$

$$\leq \beta + \binom{k-1}{h-1} \cdot \mathrm{cost}(\mathrm{ALG}(I)) \, .$$

The average cost of an algorithm is thus at most

$$\left(\beta + \binom{k-1}{h-1} \cdot \mathrm{cost}(\mathrm{ALG}(I)) \right) \Big/ \binom{k}{h-1}$$

$$= \frac{(k-1)!}{(h-1)!(k-h)!} \cdot \frac{(h-1)!(k-h+1)!}{k!} \cdot \mathrm{cost}(\mathrm{ALG}(I)) + \beta \Big/ \binom{k}{h-1}$$

$$= \frac{k-h+1}{k} \cdot \mathrm{cost}(\mathrm{ALG}(I)) + \beta \Big/ \binom{k}{h-1} \, .$$

The remainder of the proof can be done analogously to the proof of Theorem 4.4.

Exercise 4.6. No, it does not, as it does not help for paging. In fact, we can follow the same strategy as described in Subsection 1.6.1 for paging in the obvious way. Instead of once, every point is requested $\ell + 1$ times. The request sequence is thus given by

$$(p_{k+1}, \underbrace{p_{k+1}, \ldots, p_{k+1}}_{\ell \text{ requests}}, p_i, \underbrace{p_i, \ldots, p_i}_{\ell \text{ requests}}, \ldots)$$

This way, no online algorithm can be better than k-competitive.

Exercise 4.7. There are m pages in total, and the cache has a size of k. As we have defined paging, the cache cannot be empty. By an easy counting argument, we get that there are

$$m \cdot (m-1) \cdot \ldots \cdot (m-k+1)$$

possible configurations. For k-server, we basically get the same number, where k and m are the number of servers and points of the metric space, respectively; but here, we also need to mention the case $m = \infty$, in which there is an infinite number of configurations.

Exercise 4.8. It is easy to change the definition and verify that a slight adaptation of the proof of Theorem 4.5 works; recall that $\Phi(x_0) = \beta$, for some $\beta \in \mathbb{R}$. So suppose we are dealing with an online minimization problem Π, but instead of (i) from Theorem 4.5, we have

(i) there is a constant $\gamma \in \mathbb{R}^+$ such that $\Phi(x_i) \geq -\gamma$, for all i with $1 \leq i \leq n$.

For a given online algorithm ALG, the same calculation as above gives

$$
\begin{aligned}
\text{cost}(\text{ALG}(I)) &= \sum_{i=1}^{n} \text{cost}(\text{ALG}(x_i)) \\
&= \Phi(x_0) - \Phi(x_n) + c \cdot \text{cost}(\text{OPT}(I)) \\
&\leq c \cdot \text{cost}(\text{OPT}(I)) + \beta + \gamma \,,
\end{aligned}
$$

and therefore ALG is c-competitive, where we set $\alpha := \beta + \gamma$ for the additive constant α of Definition 1.6.

Exercise 4.9. Again, we only need to make some slight modifications. Both the real cost and the amortized cost are random variables with respect to the random decisions made by the given randomized online algorithm RAND. Then, we define the potential function Φ analogously to the deterministic case. Recall that, for a randomized online algorithm for an online minimization problem, we compute (bounds on) the expected cost on a given instance. We also study both the expected real cost and the expected amortized cost on single requests. We replace the two conditions of Theorem 4.5 with

(i) $\mathbb{E}[\Phi(x_i)] \geq 0$, for all i with $1 \leq i \leq n$, and

(ii) $\mathbb{E}[\text{amcost}(\text{RAND}(x_i))] \leq c \cdot \text{cost}(\text{OPT}(x_i))$, for all i with $1 \leq i \leq n$.

Note that again $\Phi(x_0) = \beta$ for some $\beta \in \mathbb{R}$; since the initial configurations do not depend on any random decision of ALG, we have $\mathbb{E}[\Phi(x_0)] = \Phi(x_0)$. We obtain

$$\mathbb{E}[\text{cost}(\text{RAND}(I))] = \mathbb{E}\left[\sum_{i=1}^{n} \text{cost}(\text{RAND}(x_i))\right]$$

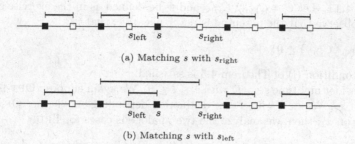

(a) Matching s with s_{right}

(b) Matching s with s_{left}

Figure 9.3. Two different matchings for the same configurations as described in the solution of Exercise 4.10; again, the servers of OPT are filled squares, those of DCov are not filled.

$$= \sum_{i=1}^{n} (\mathbb{E}[\text{amcost}(\text{RAND}(x_i))] + \mathbb{E}[\Phi(x_{i-1})] - \mathbb{E}[\Phi(x_i)])$$

(due to linearity of expectation)

$$= \mathbb{E}[\Phi(x_0)] - \mathbb{E}[\Phi(x_n)] + \sum_{i=1}^{n} \mathbb{E}[\text{amcost}(\text{RAND}(x_i))]$$

$$\leq \Phi(x_0) + c \cdot \text{cost}(\text{OPT}(I))$$

(due to the new conditions (i) and (ii))

$$\leq c \cdot \text{cost}(\text{OPT}(I)) + \beta ,$$

which proves that RAND is c-competitive in expectation.

Note that we can easily modify Φ to prove that RAND is strictly c-competitive similarly to Corollary 4.1; also, we can extend the notion of potential functions for randomized online algorithms to work for negative values of the potential similarly to Exercise 4.8.

Exercise 4.10. Consider two configurations as shown in Figure 9.3 after OPT made its move. There are two servers s_{left} and s_{right} next to s. Note that s_{left} is actually closer to s than s_{right}. All other distances between two consecutive servers are equal. A minimum-weight matching matches s and s_{right} as shown in Figure 9.3a. If it is required that we match s with s_{left}, this must lead to a more expensive matching. The reason is that there are more servers of OPT left of s_{left} than there are servers of DCov. Conversely, there are more servers of DCov right of s than there are servers of OPT. Consequently, one of the servers of OPT left of s_{left} must be matched to one of the servers of DCov right of s. It is easy to see that a minimum-weight matching under the above condition is the one shown in Figure 9.3b, which is more expensive than that in Figure 9.3a.

Exercise 4.11. Let $C = C_{\text{LRU}} \setminus C_{\text{OPT}}$ and Φ be defined as in the exercise statement. First, we observe that the potential is never negative, that is,

$$\Phi(C_{\text{LRU}}, C_{\text{OPT}}) \geq 0 \,,$$

and thus condition (i) of Theorem 4.5 is satisfied.

Now consider any time step T_i with $1 \leq i \leq n$. We again suppose OPT first serves the request x_i. We start with a case distinction depending on whether OPT causes a page fault on x_i; then, we analyze the two analogous cases for LRU.

Case 1. If OPT does not cause a page fault in T_i, C_{OPT} and thus C do not change. The potential therefore also stays the same.

Case 2. Suppose OPT causes a page fault. If it replaces a page that is not in C_{LRU}, the potential again does not change. Conversely, if the replaced page is also in C_{LRU}, the potential can increase by at most $k \cdot \text{cost}(\text{OPT}(x_i))$ since k is the largest value assigned by w and $\text{cost}(\text{OPT}(x_i)) = 1$.

Now we make another case distinction in order to bound the change in potential in T_i that is a consequence of LRU's actions.

Case 1. If LRU does not cause a page fault, then C_{LRU} and C do not change, and neither does the potential.

Case 2. The interesting case is when LRU causes a page fault. Since OPT already served the request x_i, the requested page $p = x_i$ is already in OPT's cache, but not in that of LRU. Note that there must be a page p' that is in LRU's cache, but not in that of OPT, that is, $p' \in C$. If LRU replaces p' with p, then, after serving x_i, the size of C is decreased by 1, and thus Φ is decreased by $w(p') \geq 1$. Conversely, if LRU replaces a page that is different from p', then $w(p')$ decreases by 1 since the page p is loaded into the cache. Thus, the potential decreases by at least $\text{cost}(\text{LRU}(x_i))$ due to LRU.

It follows that

$$\Phi(x_i) - \Phi(x_{i-1}) \leq k \cdot \text{cost}(\text{OPT}(x_i)) - \text{cost}(\text{LRU}(x_i)) \,,$$

and hence (ii) of Theorem 4.5 is also satisfied; as a consequence, LRU is k-competitive.

Note that, since both algorithms start with the same cache content, we have $\Phi(x_0) = 0$. Together with Corollary 4.1, it therefore immediately follows that LRU is even strictly k-competitive.

Exercise 4.12. Suppose we are given any weighted tree, where the weights are positive integers. An online algorithm DCOvT$'$ for such metric spaces works as follows. For any edge $\{p_1, p_2\}$ with a weight $\text{dist}(p_1, p_2)$ larger than 1, DCOvT$'$ inserts $\text{dist}(p_1, p_2) - 1$ vertices between p_1 and p_2 such that these two vertices are now connected by a path of length $\text{dist}(p_1, p_2)$. After that, all weights are removed from the tree and DCOvT$'$ simulates DCOvT on the constructed tree. DCOvT$'$

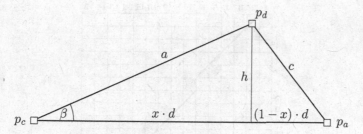

Figure 9.4. The triangle defined by p_a, p_c, and p_d used in the solution of Exercise 4.13.

keeps track of all the server positions of DCovT. If DCovT positions a server s at a vertex that does not exist in the weighted tree, DCovT' keeps s at its original position. If, on the other hand, s is moved to a vertex in the unweighted tree that corresponds to a vertex in the weighted tree, DCovT' moves s to this vertex. Clearly, DCovT' is also k-competitive.

Exercise 4.13. Consider the triangle defined by p_a, p_c, and p_d as depicted in Figure 9.4. Let h denote the altitude of the triangle that divides d into two parts of length xd and $(1-x)d$, for some x with $0 \leq x \leq 1$, which results in two new right triangles. Easily, $xd = a \cos \beta$ and, from $c^2 = h^2 + (1-x)^2 d^2$ and $a^2 = h^2 + x^2 d^2$, we get $c^2 - a^2 = d^2(1 - 2x)$, which implies

$$\frac{c^2 - a^2}{d^2} = 1 - 2\left(\frac{a \cos \beta}{d}\right),$$

and thus

$$c^2 = a^2 + d^2 - 2ad \cos \beta,$$

which proves the law.

Exercise 4.14. From the Pythagorean trigonometric identity, we know that

$$(\sin \psi)^2 + (\cos \psi)^2 = 1. \tag{9.10}$$

Together with the addition theorem from the hint of the exercise statement, we therefore obtain

$$\cos(2\psi) = (\cos \psi)^2 - (\sin \psi)^2 = 1 - 2(\sin \psi)^2$$

as claimed.

Exercise 5.1. Let ALG be any online algorithm for JSS and suppose ALG makes h_{ALG} horizontal, v_{ALG} vertical, and d_{ALG} diagonal moves on some given instance I. Thus, by Observation 5.1(iv), the delay of this schedule is $h_{\text{ALG}} = v_{\text{ALG}}$. The sum of d_{ALG} and h_{ALG} must be exactly m, because otherwise this solution would "leave the grid" on the right-hand side. As a result, $\text{cost}(\text{ALG}(I)) = d_{\text{ALG}} + h_{\text{ALG}} + v_{\text{ALG}} = m + v_{\text{ALG}}$.

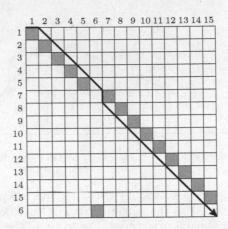

Figure 9.5. The instance from Exercise 5.3 together with an optimal solution.

Exercise 5.2. We relabel π_A to be the identity and obtain

$$\pi_A = (\,1\,,2,\,3\,,\,4\,,\,5\,,\,6\,,7,\,8\,,9,10,11,12,13,14,15,16,17,18,19,20)\,,$$
$$\pi_B = (13,3,10,18,14,17,6,11,2,12,\,8\,,\,7\,,15,\,5\,,19,\,9\,,20,\,4\,,\,1\,,16)$$

as a result.

Exercise 5.3. At first sight, it may seem that an optimal solution for the given instance has to make many delays since there are many positions where the two permutations are equal. However, if we take a closer look, we see that one delay is sufficient to schedule each task of each job, that is, we get an optimal solution

$$\text{Schedule}_{\text{OPT}}(\pi_A) = (1,2,3,4,5,6,-,7,8,\ 9\ ,10,11,12,13,14,15)\,,$$
$$\text{Schedule}_{\text{OPT}}(\pi_B) = (-,1,2,3,4,5,7,8,9,10,11,12,13,14,15,\ 6\ )\,.$$

Indeed, the optimality of this schedule is immediate since there is a collision in the first time step, which means that no solution can have a cost smaller than $m+1$. Both the instance and the described optimal solution are depicted in Figure 9.5.

Exercise 5.4. Let I be an instance of JSS such that there is an online algorithm ALG with delay d that makes at least one non-diagonal move without directly facing an obstacle in the current time step or having arrived at the border of the grid; we call such a move an "unambitious move."

We show how we can iteratively modify ALG to an ambitious online algorithm without increasing the delay. Consider the last unambitious move of ALG. Without loss of generality, let this move be horizontal. We change this move to a diagonal one; all following moves are also diagonal until an obstacle or the border is hit. In the former case, the obstacle is evaded by a horizontal move. After that, the new online algorithm continues as ALG does. We call this algorithm ALG$'$. We distinguish four cases on the subsequent moves of ALG$'$.

Case 1. If ALG′ arrives at the lower right-hand corner without hitting any obstacle or border, its cost on I is smaller than that of ALG, because instead of making an unnecessary horizontal move, it followed the main diagonal without encountering any obstacle.

Case 2. If ALG′ hits the right border without encountering another obstacle beforehand, the cost of ALG′ on I is again smaller than that of ALG.

Case 3. If ALG′ hits the bottom border, then the cost of ALG′ does not increase compared to that of ALG (note that, in this case, we cannot assume that the cost decreases; for instance, if the last two moves of ALG before hitting the border were horizontal and diagonal, the corresponding moves of ALG′ are now diagonal and horizontal, which does not change the cost).

Case 4. If ALG′ hits an obstacle, the cost does not increase. After the horizontal move of ALG′, both algorithms act identically.

As a result, we modified ALG such that it makes one fewer unambitious move without increasing its cost. If the modified algorithm ALG′ still makes some unambitious moves, we can obviously change it to an online algorithm ALG″ using the same approach. Again, the cost does not increase. This procedure is iterated until we finally get an ambitious online algorithm that has a delay of at most d.

Exercise 5.5. Let ALG be a deterministic online algorithm (that is, a strategy) from $\mathcal{D}_{2\lceil\sqrt{m}\rceil+1}$, that is, ALG follows a fixed diagonal diag_i, for some i with $-\lceil\sqrt{m}\rceil \leq i \leq \lceil\sqrt{m}\rceil$. The adversary simply blocks the whole diagonal diag_i. Thus, ALG does not make any diagonal move at all. At first, it makes a (possibly empty) number of non-diagonal moves to its starting position, then it encounters an obstacle in every time step and bypasses it with two non-diagonal moves, and finally it makes non-diagonal moves to get to the lower right-hand corner of the grid. This way, the cost of ALG is always $2m$. To bound the cost of an optimal solution, we distinguish two cases depending on the diagonal ALG chooses.

Case 1. If ALG uses the main diagonal diag_0, there is an optimal solution that has cost $m + 1$ by making a horizontal move at the beginning, a vertical move at the end, and only diagonal moves in between.

Case 2. If ALG chooses any other diagonal, the adversary places all obstacles that are not used to block diag_i on diag_{-i}. In this case, diag_0 does not contain any obstacle, and an optimal solution even has cost m.

Consequently, the competitive ratio of ALG is at least $2m/(m + 1)$, which is in essence as bad as it gets.

Exercise 5.6. In this case, the adversary needs to block two diagonals instead of one. With the same ideas as in the proof of Theorem 5.4, this results in a situation where the adversary can make sure that every second move of ALG is non-diagonal.

However, if ALG chooses the diagonal $diag_i$ for any $i \neq 0$, it even makes a non-diagonal move in each of the first and last i time steps. Thus, a best strategy ALG can choose in this case is to follow $diag_0$, which results in the online algorithm MDIAG. We know from Theorems 5.5 and 5.6 that this algorithm achieves a competitive ratio that is best possible.

Exercise 5.7. Let m_A denote the number of machines the first job uses, and let m_B be the number of machines used by B; without loss of generality, assume $m_A = 2m_B$. The total number of machines is $m = m_A$ and B uses half of them; it is not necessary to know in advance which ones. If we think about the graphical representation of instances of this modified version of JSS, we see that they contain twice as many columns as they contain rows.

Now consider an online algorithm ALG that simply evades every obstacle it hits with a horizontal move. As in the proof of Theorem 5.6, we note that at least every second move of ALG is diagonal. As a consequence, ALG hits the right border after m_A moves, that is, after m_A time steps. Note that m_A is even, thus the number of diagonal moves so far is at least as large as the number of horizontal moves, and thus it immediately follows that the algorithm arrives at the lower right-hand corner of the grid.

The overall cost of ALG is therefore m_A. Since every solution needs to make at least m_A moves in total, it follows that ALG is optimal.

Exercise 5.8. There are $2^{2\lceil \sqrt{m} \rceil}$ possible binary strings of length $2\lceil \sqrt{m} \rceil$ out of which the oracle provides one to the online algorithm, thus using at most $2\lceil \sqrt{m} \rceil$ bits in the proof of Theorem 5.11. The crucial part is that all of these strings have a very nice structural property, as noted in the hint of the exercise statement; due to Observation 5.1(iv), they contain as many ones as they contain zeros. If the solution can be represented by a shorter string, we just append zeros and ones alternatingly to obtain a string of length $2\lceil \sqrt{m} \rceil$ that still has this property. Recall that the algorithm knows m and therefore $\lceil \sqrt{m} \rceil$. It immediately follows that, for a fixed m, there exist

$$\binom{2\lceil \sqrt{m} \rceil}{\lceil \sqrt{m} \rceil} < \frac{4^{\lceil \sqrt{m} \rceil}}{\sqrt{\pi \lceil \sqrt{m} \rceil}}$$

such strings. Enumerating all possible strings in canonical order and then merely communicating the index of the string representing the instance at hand gives that it suffices to use

$$\log_2 \left(\frac{4^{\lceil \sqrt{m} \rceil}}{\sqrt{\pi \lceil \sqrt{m} \rceil}} \right) = \lceil \sqrt{m} \rceil \cdot \log_2 4 - \log_2 \left(\sqrt{\pi \lceil \sqrt{m} \rceil} \right)$$

$$\leq 2\lceil \sqrt{m} \rceil - \frac{1}{4} \log_2 m$$

bits of advice.

Exercise 5.9. Let d be an odd constant, and let $\gamma := d^2/4 - d$; note that $\gamma > -1$. As we have seen in Observation 5.1(iii), there are exactly m obstacles in the whole grid that represents the instance at hand. For a contradiction, suppose that each of the considered strategies has a cost of at least $m + \lceil(\gamma+m)/d\rceil + 1$. This means that at least $\lceil(\gamma+m)/d\rceil + 1$ obstacles are on the main diagonal, at least $\lceil(\gamma+m)/d\rceil$ obstacles are on diag_{-1} and diag_1, in general, at least

$$\left\lceil\frac{\gamma+m}{d}\right\rceil + 1 - i$$

obstacles have to be on diag_{-i} and diag_i, and finally

$$\left\lceil\frac{\gamma+m}{d}\right\rceil - \frac{d-3}{2}$$

obstacles are on $\text{diag}_{-(d-1)/2}$ and $\text{diag}_{(d-1)/2}$. Hence, we get a total of

$$\left\lceil\frac{\gamma+m}{d}\right\rceil + 1 + 2\sum_{i=1}^{(d-1)/2}\left(\left\lceil\frac{\gamma+m}{d}\right\rceil + 1 - i\right)$$

$$\geq \frac{\gamma+m}{d} + 1 + \left(\frac{\gamma+m}{d} + 1\right)(d-1) - 2\sum_{i=1}^{(d-1)/2} i$$

$$= \left(\frac{\gamma+m}{d} + 1\right)d - \frac{d^2-1}{4}$$

$$= m + d + \frac{d^2}{4} - d - \frac{d^2-1}{4}$$

$$= m + \frac{1}{4}$$

obstacles, which is strictly more than m and thus contradicts our assumption.

Exercise 5.10. Let ADIAG_d know d and read $\lceil\log_2 d\rceil$ bits in total that tell the algorithm which of the diagonal strategies from $\mathcal{D}_d$ to follow. As we have shown in Exercise 5.9, one of these strategies has a delay of at most $\lceil(\gamma+m)/d\rceil$, for $\gamma = d^2/4 - d$. Note that if the optimal solution has cost m, this solution must take the main diagonal. But in this case, ADIAG_d is always optimal, because there are no obstacles on diag_0 and the corresponding delay is therefore 0. Hence, without loss of generality, we may assume a lower bound of $m + 1$ on the cost of the optimal solution. To conclude from the above, we get a competitive ratio of ADIAG_d of at most

$$\frac{m + \left\lceil\frac{d^2/4-d+m}{d}\right\rceil}{m+1} \leq \frac{m + \frac{d^2/4-d+m}{d} + 1}{m+1}$$

$$= \frac{m + \frac{m}{d} + \frac{d}{4}}{m+1}$$

$$= 1 + \frac{1}{d} + \frac{d}{4(m+1)} - \frac{d+1}{d(m+1)}$$

as we claimed.

Exercise 5.11. Let m and l be even. We now describe how to sufficiently delay every possible diagonal strategy. Suppose we want to make sure that every strategy has a delay of at least l. At first, we place l obstacles in the center of the main diagonal, that is, in the cells $(m/2 - l/2 + 1, m/2 - l/2 + 1)$ to $(m/2 + l/2, m/2 + l/2)$. For now, let us focus on the cells that are in the lower right-hand quadrant of the $(m \times m)$-grid. For each i with $1 \le i \le (d-1)/2$, we create one *block* of obstacles. Block i consists of $l - i$ obstacles. All of these obstacles are put on the ith diagonal above the main one (that is, diag_i), in consecutive rows, just below the rows used by block $i - 1$. In particular, the obstacles of block 1 are located in the cells

$$\left(\frac{m+l}{2} + 2, \frac{m+l}{2} + 1 \right), \dots, \left(\frac{m+l}{2} + l, \frac{m+l}{2} + l - 1 \right),$$

the obstacles of block 2 are located in the cells

$$\left(\frac{m+l}{2} + l + 2, \frac{m+l}{2} + l \right), \dots, \left(\frac{m+l}{2} + 2l - 1, \frac{m+l}{2} + 2l - 3 \right),$$

etc. Hence, we need to use $l - i$ rows and $l - i + 1$ columns to build block i (the first column of the block is empty since block i is on a different diagonal than block $i - 1$).

To be able to successfully build all of the blocks, we need at least

$$\frac{l}{2} + 1 + (l - 1) + 1 + (l - 2) + \dots + 1 + \left(l - \frac{d-1}{2} \right)$$

columns. Clearly, if there are enough columns available, there are enough rows available as well. Since we have exactly $m/2$ columns, we have to make sure that

$$\frac{m}{2} \ge \frac{l}{2} + \sum_{i=1}^{(d-1)/2} (1 + l - i)$$

$$\iff \frac{m}{2} \ge \frac{l}{2} + \frac{d-1}{2}(1 + l) - \frac{d^2 - 1}{8}$$

$$\iff l \le \frac{m + \frac{d^2 + 3}{4} - d}{d}.$$

We can ensure this by taking l to be the smallest even integer such that

$$l \ge \frac{m + \frac{d^2+3}{4} - d}{d} - 2.$$

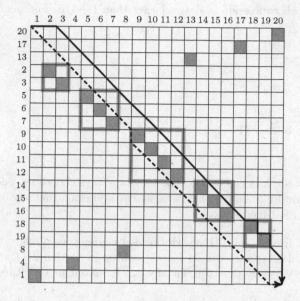

Figure 9.6. A hard instance for $\mathcal{D}_5$ from the solution of Exercise 5.11.

The same construction can be performed in the upper left-hand quadrant in a symmetric way. In every block, there is one free column. It remains to use the rows not used by any block (nor by the obstacles on the main diagonal) to put a single obstacle in every such free column. To do so, we use the upper right-hand and lower left-hand quadrant. It is straightforward to observe that this is always possible, even without using any diagonal neighboring the main one.

An example of this construction for $m = 20$, $l = 4$, and $\mathcal{D}_5$ is shown in Figure 9.6. It is clear that any optimal solution has a cost of exactly $m + 1$; an optimal solution follows the main diagonal until the first obstacle is hit. Afterwards, it makes one vertical move and follows the first diagonal below the main one (that is, diag_{-1}).

ADIAG_d computes a solution with a delay of at least l, that is, with a cost of at least

$$m + l \geq m + \frac{m + \frac{d^2 + 3}{4} - d}{d} - 2 = (m+1)\left(1 + \frac{1}{d}\right) - 4 - \frac{1}{d} + \frac{d^2 + 3}{4d}.$$

Therefore, the competitive ratio of ADIAG_d can be bounded from below by

$$\frac{(m+1)\left(1 + \frac{1}{d}\right) - 4 - \frac{1}{d} + \frac{d^2 + 3}{4d}}{m + 1} = 1 + \frac{1}{d} + \frac{d^2 - 16d - 1}{4d(m+1)}.$$

For $d \geq 17$, this expression is always larger than $1 + 1/d$. For smaller values of d, we can choose

$$m > -\frac{d^2 - 16d - 1}{4d\varepsilon} - 1$$

so that, for any given $\varepsilon > 0$,

$$1 + \frac{1}{d} + \frac{d^2 - 16d - 1}{4d(m+1)} > 1 + \frac{1}{d} - \varepsilon$$

is ensured.

Exercise 6.1. No, it does not, because we can always choose the additive constant α from Definition 1.6 to be B. Therefore, we can still claim that any online algorithm for the problem is 1-competitive.

Exercise 6.2. In this case, things do indeed change; we already faced a similar situation when dealing with the ski rental problem in Section 2.8 (more precisely, in Exercise 2.10). We show that still, for any $\varepsilon > 0$, no online algorithm is better than $1/\varepsilon$-competitive.

For a contradiction, suppose that there is a constant $\alpha > 0$ such that there is an online algorithm ALG for the simple knapsack problem that is better than $1/\varepsilon$-competitive with additive constant α, that is, for every instance I, we have

$$\text{gain}(\text{OPT}(I)) < \frac{1}{\varepsilon} \cdot \text{gain}(\text{ALG}(I)) + \alpha . \tag{9.11}$$

Now consider an instance I where the first request is a capacity

$$B := \frac{\alpha + 1}{\varepsilon} + \alpha ,$$

after which an object x of weight $\alpha + 1$ is offered. We again make a case distinction depending on whether ALG packs this object or not.

Case 1. If ALG does not pack x, no second object is offered. It follows that

$$\text{gain}(\text{ALG}(I)) = 0 \quad \text{and} \quad \text{gain}(\text{OPT}(I)) = \alpha + 1 ,$$

which immediately contradicts (9.11).

Case 2. If ALG packs x, a second object of weight B is offered, which implies that

$$\text{gain}(\text{ALG}(I)) = \alpha + 1 \quad \text{and} \quad \text{gain}(\text{OPT}(I)) = \frac{\alpha + 1}{\varepsilon} + \alpha$$

yielding

$$\text{gain}(\text{OPT}(I)) \geq \frac{1}{\varepsilon} \cdot \text{gain}(\text{ALG}(I)) + \alpha$$

again contradicting (9.11).

As a result, ALG is not better than $1/\varepsilon$-competitive.

Exercise 6.3. Let $\varepsilon > 0$, and let ALG be some c-competitive online algorithm for the simple knapsack problem defined as in the exercise statement; thus, for every instance I, we have

$$\text{gain}(\text{OPT}(I)) \leq c \cdot \text{gain}(\text{ALG}(I)) + \alpha . \tag{9.12}$$

Now let I' be some fixed instance, and consider the online algorithm ALG' that constructs an instance I from I' by multiplying every request (thus, the capacity and all weights) by a constant $\beta := \alpha/\varepsilon$. ALG' simulates ALG on I and packs the *unscaled* objects for I' corresponding to those that ALG packs for I. This way, if the solution of ALG is feasible for I, then the solution of ALG' is feasible for I', and we have

$$\beta \cdot \text{gain}\big(\text{ALG}'(I')\big) = \text{gain}(\text{ALG}(I)) \tag{9.13}$$

and also

$$\beta \cdot \text{gain}(\text{OPT}(I')) = \text{gain}(\text{OPT}(I)) . \tag{9.14}$$

From (9.12) to (9.14), we conclude

$$
\begin{aligned}
\text{gain}(\text{OPT}(I')) &= \frac{\text{gain}(\text{OPT}(I))}{\beta} \\
&\leq c \cdot \frac{\text{gain}(\text{ALG}(I)) + \alpha}{\beta} \\
&= c \cdot \text{gain}\big(\text{ALG}'(I')\big) + \frac{\alpha}{\beta} .
\end{aligned}
$$

Consequently, ALG' is c-competitive with an arbitrarily small constant ε.

Of course, with our considerations from Exercise 6.2, one may ask how meaningful this statement is. However, we could make the simple knapsack problem "fairer" by, for instance, disallowing arbitrarily small objects in the input. This way, there are c-competitive online algorithms for the problem whose competitive ratio depends on the weight of the smallest object in the input.

Exercise 6.4. The condition from the exercise statement does not really change much. Let n be some natural number. The adversary starts by offering a sequence of objects of weight ε, for some arbitrary $\varepsilon > 0$. For every deterministic online algorithm ALG, the adversary knows the time step (if it exists) in which ALG will pack the corresponding object into the knapsack. If there is such a time step T_i, it requests $n - i$ more objects of weight 1. If not, all n requests will offer objects of weight ε only. Then, by similar reasoning to the proof of Theorem 6.1, it follows that ALG cannot be better than $1/\varepsilon$-competitive. In the case that ALG does not pack any object into the knapsack, the optimal gain can in general even be larger than ε.

Exercise 6.5. Let $\varepsilon > 0$, and consider an instance that starts by offering two objects of weight $1/3 + \varepsilon$ and $2/3$. Since the objects do not both fit into the knapsack, any online algorithm ALG for the simple removable knapsack problem has at most one of the two packed in its knapsack at the beginning of time step T_3. We distinguish two cases depending on which it is.

Case 1. Suppose ALG packs the first object. Then, no other object is offered and the strict performance of ALG is

$$\frac{\frac{2}{3}}{\frac{1}{3} + \varepsilon} = \frac{2}{1 + 3\varepsilon},$$

which is larger than $3/2$, for any $\varepsilon < 1/9$.

Case 2. Suppose ALG packs the second object (possible after removing the first one). Then, another object of weight $2/3 - \varepsilon$ is offered. ALG may either keep the second object or (implying a smaller gain) remove it and pack the third one. In any case, its strict performance is at least $3/2$.

The claim follows.

Exercise 6.6. We use the same set $\mathcal{I}$ of instances as in the proof of Theorem 6.5, and construct a partition tree $\widehat{\mathcal{T}}$ of $\mathcal{I}^{(n)}$ with two levels. The root $\hat{r}$ is labeled by $\mathcal{I}^{(n)}$ and $n - 1$ since all instances have the same prefix of length $n - 1$ according to condition (iii) of Definition 3.3; $\hat{r}$ has 2^{n-1} children that correspond to the different binary strings, as in the proof of Theorem 6.5. The children, which are all leaves, are labeled accordingly, and they clearly partition $\mathcal{I}^{(n)}$. Now consider any two vertices $\hat{v}_1$ and $\hat{v}_2$, neither one being an ancestor of the other. By the construction of $\widehat{\mathcal{T}}$, the two vertices must be leaves with lowest common ancestor $\hat{r}$. Therefore, $[O_1]_{\rho_{\hat{r}}}$ and $[O_2]_{\rho_{\hat{r}}}$ must be different, which shows that the condition of Lemma 3.1 is satisfied. Since the number w of leaves of $\widehat{\mathcal{T}}$ is 2^{n-1}, Theorem 3.1 implies the claimed lower bound.

Exercise 6.7. Let $\varepsilon > 0$, let

$$\delta := \frac{\varepsilon}{2 - \varepsilon},$$

and let $\mathcal{I}$ be the same set of instances as in the proof of Theorem 6.12, but substitute ε by δ. Consider a probability distribution Pr_{ADV} over $\mathcal{I}$ such that each instance is drawn with probability $1/2$. In other words, the first object of weight δ is always offered, and the second one of weight 1 is offered in half of the cases. Obviously, $\mathcal{I}$ is finite. Moreover, there is also only a finite number of *generic algorithms* for $\mathcal{I}$; one that packs nothing, one that packs the first object and nothing else, one that packs the first object and possibly the second, and one that packs only the second if it is offered. Clearly, it suffices to consider the last two algorithms. We can thus apply Yao's principle for finite maximization problems, that is, Theorem 2.4. More specifically, we want to show that

$$\left(\mathbb{E}_{\text{ADV}} \left[\frac{\text{gain}(\text{ALG}(\mathcal{I}))}{\text{gain}(\text{OPT}(\mathcal{I}))} \right] \right)^{-1} \geq 2 - \varepsilon \tag{9.15}$$

for any deterministic online algorithm ALG for the simple knapsack problem.

So let ALG denote one of the above two deterministic online algorithms. This time, we make a case distinction depending on ALG's actions.

Case 1. Suppose that ALG packs the first object. Then, it cannot pack the second one if it is offered, which in turn happens with a probability of $1/2$; the gain of an optimal solution is δ or 1, respectively. Therefore, the strict expected competitive ratio of ALG is at least

$$\left(\frac{1}{2} \cdot \frac{\delta}{\delta} + \frac{1}{2} \cdot \frac{\delta}{1} \right)^{-1} = \left(\frac{1 + \delta}{2} \right)^{-1} = 2 - \frac{2\delta}{1 + \delta} = 2 - \varepsilon \,.$$

Case 2. Suppose that ALG does not pack the first object. Then, we have that ALG's gain is 0 if the second object is not offered. If the second object is offered, ALG's gain is 1. Thus, we get

$$\left(\frac{1}{2} \cdot \frac{0}{\delta} + \frac{1}{2} \cdot \frac{1}{1} \right)^{-1} = 2 \geq 2 - \varepsilon \,.$$

Consequently, (9.15) follows, and we can use Yao's principle to conclude that every randomized online algorithm has a strict expected competitive ratio of at least $2 - \varepsilon$.

Exercise 6.8. The proof can be done analogously to that of Theorem 6.1. Let $\varepsilon > 0$, and let ALG be any deterministic online algorithm for the simple γ-knapsack problem. At first, an object of weight $\gamma + \varepsilon$ is offered. If it is not packed, no further object is offered. If it is packed, a second object of weight 1 is offered and ALG has a performance of $1/(\gamma + \varepsilon)$ on this instance.

Exercise 6.9. This time, the proof can be done analogously to that of Theorem 6.12 or the solution of Exercise 6.7. Here, let us do the former. An object of weight $\varepsilon' := \varepsilon + \gamma$ is offered first, and then possibly another one of weight 1. Let RAND be any randomized online algorithm for the simple γ-knapsack problem, and let q denote the probability that RAND accepts the first object. By exactly the same arguments as in the proof of Theorem 6.12, it follows that it is a best strategy for RAND to set $q = 1/(2 - \varepsilon')$, and that its strict expected competitive ratio is, as a consequence, at least $2 - \varepsilon' = 2 - \gamma - \varepsilon$.

As mentioned above, we can again alternatively use Yao's principle as in the solution of Exercise 6.7 to get the same lower bound.

Exercise 6.10. Let ALG be any deterministic online algorithm for the general removable knapsack problem. For every n, consider the objects

$$(1, \sqrt[4]{n-1}), \underbrace{\left(\frac{1}{n-1}, \frac{1}{\sqrt{n-1}}\right), \left(\frac{1}{n-1}, \frac{1}{\sqrt{n-1}}\right), \dots, \left(\frac{1}{n-1}, \frac{1}{\sqrt{n-1}}\right)}_{n-1 \text{ times}} .$$

We can make an easy case distinction depending on how ALG chooses to pack them.

Case 1. Suppose ALG does not accept the first object. Then, $n-1$ objects are offered that each have a weight and a value of 1.

Case 2. Suppose ALG accepts the first object, and eventually it accepts another one from the sequence above. In order to do this, it must remove the first object. If this happens, again only objects of weight and value 1 are offered. Thus, the gain of ALG is again at most 1 and the optimal gain is $\sqrt[4]{n-1}$.

Case 3. Last, suppose ALG accepts the first object and no other one from the sequence above. Then, all n objects are offered, which leads to an optimal solution that accepts all objects except the first one and has a gain of $\sqrt{n-1}$.

In any case, the competitive ratio is at least $\sqrt[4]{n-1}$.

Exercise 7.1. The same argument as in the proof of Theorem 7.2 can be applied to any randomized online algorithm that chooses two complementary strings with probability 1/2 each.

Exercise 7.2. No randomized online algorithm that uses one random bit can do better than making an incorrect guess in every time step. Such an algorithm can only choose between two deterministic strategies. This implies that, in every time step, there always is a character that this algorithm does not output, and which is known to the adversary.

Note that this argument can easily be generalized. As long as $\sigma > 2^b$, where σ denotes the alphabet size and b is the number of random bits, any online algorithm reading at most b random bits has cost n.

Exercise 7.3. Due to the cost function, this does not work. The proof follows directly from the fact that fewer than $n-1$ advice bits are not sufficient to achieve this strict competitive ratio.

Exercise 7.4. Let RAND be any randomized online algorithm for the bit guessing problem either with or without history. In every time step, RAND guesses either 0 or 1 with some probability. Recall that the adversary knows these probabilities. When considering the known-history scenario, each of the concrete probabilities may depend on the previous guesses, the time step, and also on whether the preceding guesses were right or wrong. Still, the adversary can easily construct an instance such that the correct guess has a probability of at most 1/2.

As an example, suppose that RAND guesses 1 in time step T_1 with probability $2/3$. The adversary therefore chooses the answer 0, and RAND will guess right with probability $1/3$. In time step T_2, RAND might make a guess depending on the outcome in T_1; for instance, if the guess turned out to be correct, it guesses 0 or 1 with probability $1/2$ each, and if the guess was wrong, it guesses 0 with probability $1/4$ and 1 with probability $3/4$. The probability to guess 0 is therefore

$$\frac{1}{3} \cdot \frac{1}{2} + \frac{2}{3} \cdot \frac{1}{4} = \frac{1}{3}$$

and the probability to guess 1 is

$$\frac{1}{3} \cdot \frac{1}{2} + \frac{2}{3} \cdot \frac{3}{4} = \frac{2}{3} \,.$$

Consequently, the adversary chooses the answer 0 in T_2.

This way, RAND never guesses right with a probability larger than $1/2$, and therefore has an expected number of at most $n/2$ correct guesses in total. Note that this implies that it is a best strategy for RAND to guess 0 or 1 in every time step with probability $1/2$, which results in the online algorithm BGRONE.

Exercise 7.5. The construction of a partition tree $\widehat{\mathcal{T}}$ for the set $\mathcal{I}^{(n)}$ of all instances of length $n+1$ (that is, binary strings of length n) is straightforward. $\widehat{\mathcal{T}}$ is a binary tree, and its root $\hat{r}$ gets labeled with $\mathcal{I}^{(n)}$ and 1 (since all instances from $\mathcal{I}^{(n)}$ start with the length n of the string to be guessed). $\widehat{\mathcal{T}}$ has $n+1$ levels; $\hat{r}$ is on level 0 and the leaves are on level n. For every inner vertex $\hat{v}$ on level i with $0 \leq i \leq n$, its two children correspond to a correct guess 0 or 1 in time step T_i, respectively. Thus, all properties of a partition tree according to Definition 3.3 are satisfied. This way, the 2^n leaves of $\widehat{\mathcal{T}}$ correspond to all possible binary strings of length n. Consider two vertices $\hat{v}_1$ and $\hat{v}_2$ with lowest common ancestor $\hat{v}$, neither one being an ancestor of the other. In the first $\rho_{\hat{v}}$ time steps, all instances of both $\mathcal{I}_{v_1}^{(n)}$ and $\mathcal{I}_{v_2}^{(n)}$ are identical, but the next guess must be different in order to be optimal since $\hat{v}$ is the lowest common ancestor. Therefore, the conditions for Lemma 3.1 are satisfied. Hence, following Theorem 3.1, $\log_2(2^n) = n$ advice bits are necessary to be optimal.

Exercise 7.6. With $\lceil \log_2 \sigma \rceil$ advice bits, the character that appears most frequently in the input can be encoded. If an online algorithm with advice always guesses this character, it guesses at least n/σ characters correctly.

Exercise 7.7. Consider the following online algorithm that reads one advice bit that is equal to the bit that appears most frequently (that is, the majority bit) in the first three positions of the string. Thus, this algorithm makes at most one error while reading one bit. After that, it reads $n-3$ advice bits to guess the rest of the string without making another error; in total it uses $n-2$ advice bits.

Exercise 7.8. Suppose we want to make at most $r \in \mathbb{N}^+$ errors. Following the same idea as in the solution of Exercise 7.7, the online algorithm with advice reads one advice bit for the first $2r + 1$ bits of the string s it should guess. It will always guess the majority bit, and therefore, it will make at most r errors on this prefix. For the remaining bits of s, it reads one bit each, which means no more errors are made and $n - (2r + 1) + 1 = n - 2r$ advice bits are used in total.

Exercise 7.9. The proof can be done identically to that of Lemma 7.1. Analogously to (7.1), in the following, we show that

$$
\sigma^{-\mathcal{H}_\sigma(k)n} \sum_{i=0}^{kn} \binom{n}{i} (\sigma - 1)^i \leq 1 . \tag{9.16}
$$

We again start with the first factor of the left-hand side and obtain

$$
\begin{aligned}
\sigma^{-\mathcal{H}_\sigma(k)n} &= \sigma^{(-k \log_\sigma(\sigma-1) + k \log_\sigma k + (1-k) \log_\sigma(1-k))n} \\
&= \sigma^{\log_\sigma(\sigma-1)^{-kn}} \cdot \sigma^{\log_\sigma(k^{kn})} \cdot \sigma^{\log_\sigma((1-k)^{(1-k)n})} \\
&= \left(\frac{k}{\sigma - 1} \right)^{kn} (1 - k)^{(1-k)n} \\
&= \left(\frac{k}{(\sigma - 1)(1 - k)} \right)^{kn} (1 - k)^n .
\end{aligned} \tag{9.17}
$$

(again by multiplying by $(1-k)^{kn}/(1-k)^{kn}$)

Recall that, due to our assumptions, we have $k \leq 1 - 1/\sigma$. Now note that

$$
\begin{aligned}
& k \leq 1 - \frac{1}{\sigma} \\
\Longleftrightarrow\ & 1 - k \geq \frac{1}{\sigma} \\
\Longleftrightarrow\ & \sigma \geq \frac{1}{1 - k} \\
\Longleftrightarrow\ & \sigma \geq 1 + \frac{k}{1 - k} \\
& \qquad \textit{(by adding and subtracting k in the numerator)} \\
\Longleftrightarrow\ & 1 \geq \frac{k}{(1 - k)(\sigma - 1)} .
\end{aligned} \tag{9.18}
$$

Using (9.17), the left-hand side of (9.16) is equal to

$$
\sum_{i=0}^{kn} \binom{n}{i} (\sigma - 1)^i \left(\frac{k}{(\sigma - 1)(1 - k)} \right)^{kn} (1 - k)^n
$$

$$\leq \sum_{i=0}^{kn} \binom{n}{i} (\sigma-1)^i \left(\frac{k}{(\sigma-1)(1-k)} \right)^i (1-k)^n$$

(as a consequence of (9.18))

$$= \sum_{i=0}^{kn} \binom{n}{i} \left(\frac{k}{1-k} \right)^i (1-k)^n$$

$$= \sum_{i=0}^{kn} \binom{n}{i} k^i (1-k)^{n-i}$$

$$\leq 1 \,,$$

(due to the same arguments as in the proof of Lemma 7.1)

which finishes the proof.

Exercise 7.10. This proof can be done identically to that of Theorem 7.7; in essence, we again have to bound $|\mathcal{I}_\phi|$ from above. This time, consider a σ-ary fixed binary string s of length n. There are exactly

$$\binom{n}{i} (\sigma-1)^i$$

σ-ary strings that are different from s at exactly i positions (the first factor gives the number of possibilities to pick i positions; for each such possibility, each of these i positions has one of the $\sigma-1$ characters that are different from that of s at this position). Since there are σ^n different strings of length n that are feasible instances, we get

$$\frac{\sigma^n}{2^{b(n)}} \leq \sum_{i=0}^{(1-\gamma)n} \binom{n}{i} (\sigma-1)^i \leq \sigma^{\mathcal{H}_\sigma(1-\gamma)n} \,,$$

where we used the generalization of Lemma 7.1 from Exercise 7.9 (note that $1-\gamma \leq 1 - 1/\sigma$ since $\gamma \geq 1/\sigma$). Solving for $b(n)$, we obtain

$$\frac{\sigma^n}{2^{b(n)}} \leq \sigma^{(1-\gamma)n \log_\sigma(\sigma-1) - \gamma n \log_\sigma \gamma - (1-\gamma)n \log_\sigma(1-\gamma)}$$

$$\iff \quad \sigma^n \leq 2^{b(n)} \cdot \sigma^{\log_\sigma((\sigma-1)^{(1-\gamma)n})} \cdot \sigma^{\log_\sigma(\gamma^{-\gamma n})} \cdot \sigma^{\log_\sigma((1-\gamma)^{-(1-\gamma)n})}$$

$$\iff \quad \sigma^n \leq 2^{b(n)} \cdot (\sigma-1)^{(1-\gamma)n} \cdot \left(\frac{1}{\gamma} \right)^{\gamma n} \cdot \left(\frac{1}{1-\gamma} \right)^{(1-\gamma)n}$$

$$\iff \quad 2^{b(n)} \geq \sigma^n \cdot \left(\frac{1-\gamma}{\sigma-1} \right)^{(1-\gamma)n} \cdot \gamma^{\gamma n}$$

$$\iff \quad b(n) \geq \left(1 + (1-\gamma) \log_\sigma \left(\frac{1-\gamma}{\sigma-1} \right) + \gamma \log_\sigma \gamma \right) n \log_2 \sigma \,,$$

which proves the claim.

Exercise 7.11. We take the same steps that we made when dealing with the special case of $\sigma = 2$. In general, we can represent all σ^n instances of length n by a σ-ary tree $\mathcal{T} = (V, E)$ of height n; moreover, $\mathcal{I}_\phi$ now contains $\sigma^n / 2^{b(n)}$ instances. In essence, ALG traverses $\mathcal{T}$ the same way; it starts at the root $v_{n,1}$, and when guessing a character between 1 and σ, it chooses one of the σ subtrees of the current vertex. Then we can define the function size: $\mathbb{N} \times \mathbb{N} \to \mathbb{N}$ as above.

Next, we prove a more general version of Lemma 7.2. Let error: $V \to \mathbb{N}$ be defined as above, and again let v be an inner vertex of $\mathcal{T}$. If

$$m := \max\{\text{error}(u) \mid u \text{ is a child of } v\},$$

then, by the same arguments as in the proof of Lemma 7.2, it follows that

$$\text{error}(v) \geq \begin{cases} m+1 & \text{if, for at least two children } v' \text{ and } v'' \text{ of } v, \text{ it} \\ & \text{holds that error}(v') = \text{error}(v'') = m, \\ m & \text{else}. \end{cases}$$

Using this result, we can prove a generalization of Lemma 7.3; more precisely, we can show that, for r and h with $r \leq h \leq n$, we have

$$\text{size}(1, 0) = 1, \tag{9.19}$$
$$\text{size}(1, 1) = \sigma, \tag{9.20}$$
$$\text{size}(h, r) = \text{size}(h-1, r) + (\sigma - 1) \cdot \text{size}(h-1, r-1), \quad \text{for } r \geq 2. \tag{9.21}$$

As before, note that (9.19) and (9.20) speak about the vertices of $\mathcal{T}$ on level 1, and thus follow from the same considerations as in the proof of Lemma 7.3 (this time, there are σ leaves out of which ALG chooses one). Furthermore, (9.21) follows since the value gets maximized if there are r errors in one subtree and $r - 1$ errors in the other $\sigma - 1$ subtrees; an increase would result in a contradiction to the number of errors r due to the above generalization of Lemma 7.2.

Finally, for r and h with $r \leq h \leq n$, we show the closed form

$$\text{size}(h, r) = \sum_{i=0}^{r} \binom{h}{i} (\sigma - 1)^i$$

analogously to Lemma 7.4 by induction on h.

Base Case. Let $h = 1$. Again, it follows that either $r = 0$ or $r = 1$. Due to (9.19) and (9.20), we have

$$\text{size}(1, 0) = 1 = \sum_{i=0}^{0} \binom{1}{i} (\sigma - 1)^i \quad \text{and} \quad \text{size}(1, 1) = \sigma = \sum_{i=0}^{1} \binom{1}{i} (\sigma - 1)^i,$$

which covers the base case.

Induction Hypothesis. The claim holds for every $h' \leq h$, that is,

$$\text{size}(h', r) = \sum_{i=0}^{r} \binom{h'}{i} (\sigma - 1)^i.$$

Induction Step. We obtain

$$\text{size}(h+1, r) = \text{size}(h, r) + (\sigma - 1) \cdot \text{size}(h, r-1)$$

(as a consequence of the generalization of Lemma 7.3)

$$= \sum_{i=0}^{r} \binom{h}{i}(\sigma-1)^i + (\sigma - 1)\sum_{i=0}^{r-1}\binom{h}{i}(\sigma-1)^i$$

(using the induction hypothesis)

$$= \binom{h}{0}(\sigma-1)^0 + \sum_{i=1}^{r}\binom{h}{i}(\sigma-1)^i + \sum_{i=1}^{r}\binom{h}{i-1}(\sigma-1)^i$$

$$= \binom{h}{0}(\sigma-1)^0 + \sum_{i=1}^{r}\left(\binom{h}{i} + \binom{h}{i-1}\right)(\sigma-1)^i$$

$$= \binom{h+1}{0}(\sigma-1)^0 + \sum_{i=1}^{r}\binom{h+1}{i}(\sigma-1)^i$$

$$= \sum_{i=0}^{r}\binom{h+1}{i}(\sigma-1)^i .$$

As a result, we obtain

$$\frac{2^n}{2^{b(n)}} \leq \text{size}(n, (1-\gamma)n) = \sum_{i=0}^{r}\binom{n}{i}(\sigma-1)^i ,$$

and by the same calculations as in the solution of Exercise 7.10, which make use of the statement proven in Exercise 7.9,

$$b(n) \geq \left(1 + (1-\gamma)\log_\sigma\left(\frac{1-\gamma}{\sigma-1}\right) + \gamma\log_\sigma\gamma\right)n\log_2\sigma$$

follows.

Exercise 7.12. Let ALG be some swapping algorithm for 2-server on a path of length 2. Without loss of generality, assume that ALG is lazy; this implies that ALG never positions the two servers on the same point. We construct a non-swapping algorithm ALG' as follows. At the beginning, s_1 is positioned to the left of s_2. Now let T_i with $1 \leq i \leq n$ be the first time step in which ALG swaps the order of s_1 and s_2; we call such a move a "swapping move." Note that it is impossible that, at the beginning of T_i, s_1 is positioned on p_1 and s_2 is positioned on p_3. This is due to the fact that, since ALG is lazy, the only situation when it then moves a server is when p_2 is requested. No matter which server ALG moves (it only moves one, again due to being lazy), s_1 is still positioned to the left of s_2 afterwards. We can make a simple case distinction depending on the positions of the servers before the move (that is, at the beginning of T_i).

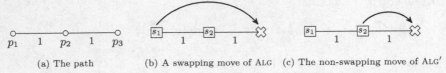

(a) The path   (b) A swapping move of ALG   (c) The non-swapping move of ALG$'$

Figure 9.7. Converting a swapping move to two non-swapping moves as in the solution of Exercise 7.12.

Case 1. Suppose s_1 is positioned on p_1, s_2 is positioned on p_2, and p_3 is requested. The only swapping move is to move s_1 to p_3, which induces a cost of 2. Instead, ALG$'$ moves s_2 to p_3, which leads to cost 1 for this time step; see Figure 9.7. After that, there is a (possibly empty) sequence of requests for either p_1 or p_3. These requests do not induce any cost for ALG$'$. Let T_j with $j > i$ be the first time step in which p_2 is requested. If T_j does not exist, we are done; otherwise, after serving the request in T_j, ALG has its two servers positioned on either p_1 and p_2 or p_2 and p_3. Moving either s_1 or s_2 to p_2, ALG$'$ has its two servers positioned on the same points as ALG after serving the request. Moreover, after T_j, the servers of ALG$'$ are still not swapped, and its cost up to now is at most as large as the cost of ALG. Clearly, ALG$'$ can now continue to answer requests in a way that induces a cost which is not larger than that of ALG.

Case 2. Suppose s_1 is positioned on p_2, s_2 is positioned on p_3, and p_1 is requested. This case can be handled completely analogously to case 1.

This construction can be applied iteratively to all remaining swapping moves.

Note that ALG$'$ is lazy as result of the laziness of ALG and the above construction.

Exercise 7.13. The general idea is to make the given online algorithm with advice choose between more than two sets in every time step. For instance, this time, let k be any multiple of 4; consider the ground set

$$X = \{a_1, a_2, \ldots, a_{k/4}\}$$
$$\cup \{b_{1,1}, b_{2,1}, \ldots, b_{k/4,1}\} \cup \{b_{1,2}, b_{2,2}, \ldots, b_{k/4,2}\} \cup \{b_{1,3}, b_{2,3}, \ldots, b_{k/4,3}\}$$

and the set family

$$\mathcal{S} = \{\{a_1, b_{1,1}\}, \{a_1, b_{1,2}\}, \{a_1, b_{1,3}\},$$
$$\{a_2, b_{2,1}\}, \{a_2, b_{2,2}\}, \{a_2, b_{2,3}\},$$
$$\ldots,$$
$$\{a_{k/4}, b_{k/4,1}\}, \{a_{k/4}, b_{k/4,2}\}, \{a_{k/4}, b_{k/4,3}\}\} \, .$$

In odd time steps, the objects a_i with $1 \le i \le k/4$ are requested. In the jth even time step, either $b_{j,1}$, $b_{j,2}$, or $b_{j,3}$ is requested; $\mathcal{I}$ covers all instances constructed in this way, and therefore has size $3^{k/4}$. By the same arguments as in the proof of Theorem 7.12, any optimal online algorithm with advice needs to use $\log_2(3^{k/4}) = (k \log_2 3)/4$ advice bits.

Generally, for some $l \geq 2$, for every a_i, we can put objects $b_{i,1}, b_{i,2}, \ldots, b_{i,l}$ into $\mathcal{S}$. We then obtain the general bound

$$\frac{\log_2 l}{l+1} \cdot k$$

on the number of advice bits, which is maximized for $l = 5$, yielding a lower bound of $0.4k$ advice bits.

For the instances constructed above, we have $m = (k/(l+1)) \cdot l$, and thus obtain a lower bound of

$$\frac{\log_2 l}{l} \cdot m ,$$

which is maximized for $l = 3$, giving a lower bound of roughly $0.528m$.

Exercise 7.14. The reduction given in the proof of Theorem 7.13 can easily be adapted to work for bit guessing with unknown history. To this end, we define X and $\mathcal{S}$ in the same way. However, in the first $k/3$ time steps, the objects $a_1, a_2, \ldots, a_{k/3}$ are requested. BGUESS makes its guesses according to the sets BBSC chooses, just as in the original proof. After it has guessed the n' bits, the correct string is revealed to BGUESS. Depending on this string, BGUESS requests the object $b_{i,1}$, for all i with $1 \leq i \leq k/3$, if and only if the correct guess for the ith bit was 0; otherwise, it requests $b_{i,2}$. This way, BBSC has to pick an additional set from $\mathcal{S}$ in the last $k/3$ time steps for every incorrect guess of BGUESS. The proof can then be finished analogously to that of Theorem 7.13.

Exercise 7.15. We again consider the instances from the solution of Exercise 7.13, but this time, there are σ different choices in every odd time step, where $\sigma \geq 2$ is the alphabet size of the given string guessing instance. More precisely, we construct an online algorithm SGUESS with advice, which, given an instance I' asking to guess a σ-ary string of length n', creates an instance I of length $n = 2n'$ with

$$
\begin{aligned}
X = \; & \{a_1, a_2, \ldots, a_{n'}\} \\
& \cup \{b_{1,1}, b_{2,1}, \ldots, b_{n',1}\} \\
& \cup \{b_{1,2}, b_{2,2}, \ldots, b_{n',2}\} \\
& \cup \ldots \\
& \cup \{b_{1,\sigma}, b_{2,\sigma}, \ldots, b_{n',\sigma}\}
\end{aligned}
$$

and the set family

$$
\begin{aligned}
\mathcal{S} = \; & \{\{a_1, b_{1,1}\}, \{a_1, b_{1,2}\}, \ldots, \{a_1, b_{1,\sigma}\}, \\
& \{a_2, b_{2,1}\}, \{a_2, b_{2,2}\}, \ldots, \{a_2, b_{2,\sigma}\}, \\
& \ldots, \\
& \{a_{n'}, b_{n',1}\}, \{a_{n'}, b_{n',2}\}, \ldots, \{a_{n'}, b_{n',\sigma}\}\} .
\end{aligned}
$$

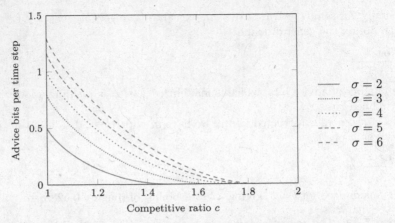

Figure 9.8. Lower bound on the average number of advice bits necessary per time step to be c-competitive for set cover with respect to n as shown in the solution of Exercise 7.15.

The reduction from string guessing with alphabet size σ works analogously to the proof of Theorem 7.13; note that $k = (\sigma + 1)n'$ and $m = \sigma n'$.

SGUESS requests the objects $a_1, a_2, \ldots, a_{n'}$ in odd time steps and one of the objects $b_{i,1}, b_{i,2}, \ldots, b_{i,\sigma}$ in the ith even time step. It guesses according to the concrete choice of the black box BBSC for set cover, and requests the objects according to the correct guesses. The optimal cost is obviously n'. If SGUESS guesses a fraction γ of all characters correctly, it follows for the competitive ratio c of BBSC that

$$c \geq \frac{\text{cost}(\text{BBSC}(I))}{\text{cost}(\text{OPT}(I))} = \frac{n' + (1 - \gamma)n'}{n'} \,,$$

and therefore $\gamma \geq 2 - c$. This time, since $\gamma \geq 1/\sigma$ has to be satisfied, it must hold that $c \leq 2 - 1/\sigma$. We know from Exercise 7.11 that SGUESS needs to read at least

$$\left(1 + (1 - \gamma) \log_\sigma \left(\frac{1 - \gamma}{\sigma - 1}\right) + \gamma \log_\sigma \gamma\right) n' \log_2 \sigma$$
$$\geq \left(1 + (c - 1) \log_\sigma \left(\frac{c - 1}{\sigma - 1}\right) + (2 - c) \log_\sigma (2 - c)\right) \cdot \frac{n}{2} \log_2 \sigma$$

advice bits to guess $\gamma n'$ characters correctly; this expression can easily be rewritten as a function of k or m, respectively. Lower bounds for different values of σ are shown in Figure 9.8.

Exercise 7.16. Let ALG be some online algorithm for DPA. Let ℓ be a square number, and consider the following set $\mathcal{I}$ of instances. The first request contains the length ℓ of P and a request $(v_0, v_{\sqrt{\ell}})$. If ALG grants this request, $\sqrt{\ell}$ consecutive requests of length 1 each are given. After that, the input ends. If ALG does not grant

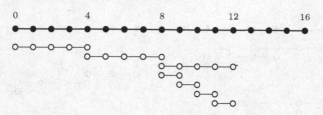

Figure 9.9. An instance from $\mathcal{I}$ on a path of length 16 as used in the solution of Exercise 7.16. In this example, ALG decides to grant the third request of length 4, which is followed by the adversary giving four requests each of length 1 that all intersect with the previously granted one.

the first request, another request $(v_{\sqrt{\ell}}, v_{2\sqrt{\ell}})$ of length $\sqrt{\ell}$ is sent, and the adversary continues in this manner until either $\sqrt{\ell}$ requests of length $\sqrt{\ell}$ have been offered or ALG accepts one of them. In the latter case, $\sqrt{\ell}$ requests each of length 1 are offered subsequently, which all intersect the subpath just granted; an example is shown in Figure 9.9. We make a case distinction depending on whether ALG grants a request of length $\sqrt{\ell}$.

Case 1. If ALG does not grant any of the $\sqrt{\ell}$ requests of length $\sqrt{\ell}$ each, its gain is 0, while the optimal gain is $\sqrt{\ell}$.

Case 2. Conversely, if ALG grants one of the requests of length $\sqrt{\ell}$, it cannot grant any of the $\sqrt{\ell}$ requests of length 1. Thus, its gain is 1, while the optimal gain is at least $\sqrt{\ell}$.

Since the gain of $\mathrm{OPT}(I)$ increases with ℓ, but the gain of ALG is at most 1, it follows that ALG is not competitive.

Exercise 7.17. The idea is to interleave the phases in the following way. After every request from P_1, BGUESS guesses the corresponding bit just as in the proof of Theorem 7.16. In the next time step, BGUESS gets feedback as to the correctness of this guess. If the correct guess was 0, BGUESS requests the two requests from P_2 that intersect with the previous request. If the correct guess was 1, it continues with the next request from P_1 (if there is any). Clearly, we have the same relationship between c and γ as in the proof of Theorem 7.16 and are able to conclude the same bound by the same reasoning.

Another possibility is to leave the phases as in the proof of Theorem 7.16, but have BGUESS store the feedback during P_1 and construct P_2 after all guesses have been made.

Exercise 7.18. We use the following set $\mathcal{I}$ of instances, which is different from the one used in the proofs of Theorems 7.15 and 7.16. There are again two phases P_1 and P_2. This time, the requests in P_1 are of length 3, and the consecutive requests of even time steps overlap the requests of odd time steps. In P_2, two requests of

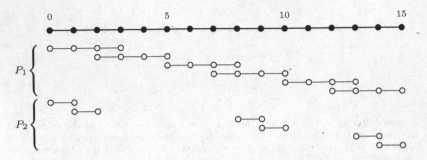

Figure 9.10. An instance from $\mathcal{I}$ on a path of length 15 when preemption is allowed as used in the solution of Exercise 7.18. In P_1, the second, third, and fifth requests should be granted, in order to grant as many requests as possible.

length 1 that intersect either with the first request or the second one are given; an example is shown in Figure 9.10.

For a given online algorithm BBDPAPREEMP, we again construct an online algorithm BGUESS as in the proof of Theorem 7.16. The difference is that, to guess a string of length n', instances on a path of length $\ell = 5n'$ are constructed, which weakens the lower bound. Consider two consecutive time steps T_i and T_{i+1} with i being odd and $1 \leq i \leq 2n' - 1$ (that is, within P_1). After T_{i+1}, BBDPAPREEMP can have accepted at most one of the two requests given in T_i and T_{i+1}. BGUESS guesses 0 in time step $T'_{(i+1)/2}$ if and only if BBDPAPREEMP grants the first subpath. Note that we can assume without loss of generality that BBDPAPREEMP always grants one of the two, since it is never better off by granting neither (due to the preemption). If a correct guess is made, BBDPAPREEMP can grant one of the requests in T_i and T_{i+1} and two additional requests in P_2. On an incorrect guess, it can grant at most two requests. Note that, in contrast to the proof of Theorem 7.16, the gain of an optimal solution is fixed for a fixed ℓ, namely $3n'$.

For the competitive ratio c of BBDPAPREEMP, we have

$$c \geq \frac{\text{gain}(\text{OPT}(I))}{\text{gain}(\text{BBDPAPREEMP}(I))} \geq \frac{3n'}{3n' - (1 - \gamma)n'} \,,$$

where BGUESS guesses $\gamma n'$ bits correctly; hence, $\gamma \geq 3/c - 2$. Since $\gamma \geq 1/2$, we require $c \leq 6/5$. This way, we obtain

$$\left(1 + \left(3 - \frac{3}{c} \right) \log_2 \left(3 - \frac{3}{c} \right) + \left(\frac{3}{c} - 2 \right) \log_2 \left(\frac{3}{c} - 2 \right) \right) \cdot \frac{\ell}{5}$$

as a lower bound on the number of advice bits required. Finally, we again note that the optimal gain grows with ℓ.

Exercise 8.1. As suggested in the hint of the exercise statement, we again define a function num: $\mathbb{N}^+ \to \mathbb{N}^+$ such that num(i) gives the minimum number of vertices required so that FIRSTFIT uses color i. This time, we show $\text{num}(i) \geq 2^{i-1}$ for $i \geq 2$ by induction on i.

Base Case. Since one vertex is clearly necessary to make FIRSTFIT use one color, and two vertices are needed to force FIRSTFIT to use two colors, we obtain $\text{num}(1) = 1 = 2^0$ and $\text{num}(2) = 2 = 2^1$, which covers the base case.

Induction Hypothesis. The claim holds for $\text{num}(1), \text{num}(2), \ldots, \text{num}(i-1)$.

Induction Step. Consider some time step in which a vertex v is given such that FIRSTFIT has to use color i. It follows that v is connected to at least $i-1$ vertices that were presented earlier such that these vertices are colored using colors 1 to $i-1$. Every such vertex needs to be in a different subtree of the whole graph G, because otherwise G contains a cycle and is therefore no tree.

Let $\mathcal{T}_1, \mathcal{T}_2, \ldots, \mathcal{T}_{i-1}$ be such trees, that is, $\mathcal{T}_j$ is colored with colors 1 to j with $1 \leq j \leq i-1$; it follows that $\mathcal{T}_j$ contains at least $\text{num}(j)$ vertices. By the induction hypothesis, we have that $\text{num}(j) \geq 2^{j-1}$. Since v is connected to all these trees, it follows that

$$\text{num}(i) \geq 1 + \sum_{j=1}^{i-1} 2^{j-1} = 2^{i-1} \ .$$

Observe that this is the same calculation as in the proof of Theorem 8.1. Indeed, we seem to be analyzing the same class of instances from another perspective.

As a result, if FIRSTFIT uses k colors, the number n of vertices has to satisfy $n \geq 2^{k-1}$, and thus we have $k \leq \log_2 n + 1$ as claimed.

Exercise 8.2. Consider the following online algorithm CLIN2 with advice. Again, the first vertex presented gets color 1, and thus no advice bit has to be read in the first time step. Next, one advice bit is read that is 1 if and only if the whole graph G is revealed such that there are at least $n-1$ isolated vertices. We distinguish two cases depending on the value of this bit.

Case 1. Suppose the bit is 1. Then the $n-1$ isolated vertices are all assigned the same color, say color 1. Since there is no edge between these vertices, this is optimal. At some point, a vertex may be presented that is not isolated. CLIN2 assigns this vertex color 2; clearly, this is also optimal. If no such vertex appears, the algorithm uses one color only. No further advice is needed to do this.

Case 2. Suppose the bit is 0. Then there at most $n-2$ isolated vertices. The idea is that CLIN2 only uses advice for isolated vertices; indeed, if these are colored correctly, non-isolated vertices can be colored optimally without advice. Since the first vertex is isolated and CLIN2 does not need any advice for it, it uses at most $n-3$ advice bits to color all isolated vertices optimally. In total, CLIN2 uses at most $n-2$ advice bits.

It follows that CLIN2 uses at most $n-2$ advice bits and produces an optimal solution on any instance.

Exercise 8.3. We again prove the claim using an idea we got from the simple knapsack problem. More specifically, we consider a probability distribution $\mathrm{Pr_{ADV}}$ over the (finite) set $\mathcal{I}$ that we used for the deterministic case (see Figures 8.6a and 8.6b), such that each instance is picked with probability $1/2$. This time, there are two *generic algorithms* for these instances; one takes the first edge $\{v_1, v_2\}$ and the other one does not. Without loss of generality, we assume that the algorithm that does not take the first edge always takes the two edges $\{v_1, v_3\}$ and $\{v_2, v_3\}$ if they are presented and thus computes a feasible solution in this case. Let ALG be one of these two algorithms; we distinguish two cases.

Case 1. Suppose that ALG takes the first edge. If the vertex v_3 is not presented, it has the optimal cost $1/\varepsilon$. If it is presented, however, ALG needs to use one of the edges that connect v_3 to v_1 and v_2, which leads to a cost of $1/\varepsilon + 1/2$, while the optimal cost is 1. Thus, its strict expected competitive ratio can be bounded from below by

$$\frac{1}{2} \cdot 1 + \frac{1}{2} \cdot \frac{1/\varepsilon + 1/2}{1} > \frac{1}{2\varepsilon} \, ,$$

which tends to infinity as ε tends to zero.

Case 2. Suppose that ALG does not take the first edge. If v_3 is not presented, it therefore does not compute a feasible solution and pays λ, while the optimal cost is $1/\varepsilon$. If v_3 is given, ALG pays the optimal cost 1. Hence, we obtain a bound of

$$\frac{1}{2} \cdot \frac{\lambda}{1/\varepsilon} + \frac{1}{2} \cdot 1 > \frac{\varepsilon \cdot \lambda}{2} \, ,$$

which tends to infinity for increasing λ (recall that λ is unbounded and can, for instance, be chosen as $2^{1/\varepsilon}$).

Following Yao's principle (more precisely, Theorem 2.3), we conclude that no randomized online algorithm is strictly competitive in expectation.

Exercise 8.4. We again use Yao's principle. Since we are dealing with an infinite number of instances, we apply Theorem 2.5; more specifically, as we will prove a lower bound on the expected competitive ratio that grows with n, we only need to show that (i) of Theorem 2.5 is satisfied (recall the discussion preceding the theorem). We construct sets of instances $\mathcal{I}_1, \mathcal{I}_2, \dots$ as follows. Every instance in $\mathcal{I}_i$ has a length of $n = 3i + 1$. We take i *widgets* $W_1, W_2, \dots, W_i$ such that every widget is either as in Figure 8.6c, which happens with probability $1/n$, or as in Figure 8.6d, which has probability $(n-1)/n$. These widgets are connected to an additional vertex via edges each of weight $1/i$ as in the proof of Theorem 8.6. Therefore, $\mathcal{I}_i$ is finite and contains 2^i instances.

Moreover, there are 2^i *generic algorithms* that, for each widget, either take the first edge or not. We assume that all these algorithms compute feasible solutions and hence take all i edges of weight $1/i$ each that connect the graph. Now consider any fixed deterministic algorithm ALG and a randomly chosen instance from $\mathcal{I}_i$. Suppose

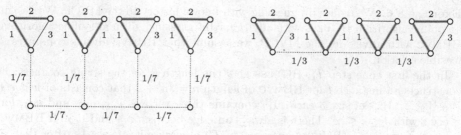

(a) The maximum degree is 3   (b) The maximum degree is 4

Figure 9.11. The widgets used in the solution of Exercise 8.5.

ALG takes the first edge $\{v_{j,1}, v_{j,2}\}$ with $1 \leq j \leq i$ for δ widgets. For every W_j, the edge $\{v_{j,1}, v_{j,3}\}$ has a weight of $1/2$ with probability $1/n$ and a weight of $n^2 - 1/2$ with probability $(n-1)/n$. Thus, ALG has cost n on δ widgets. On the other $i - \delta$ widgets, it has cost 1 with probability $(n-1)/n$ and cost n^2 with probability $1/n$.

Summing up, we can bound the expected cost of ALG from below by

$$\mathbb{E}_{\mathrm{ADV}}[\mathrm{cost}(\mathrm{ALG}(\mathcal{I}_i))] = \delta n + \sum_{j=\delta+1}^{i} \left(\frac{n-1}{n} \cdot 1 + \frac{1}{n} \cdot n^2 \right) + 1$$
$$\geq \delta n + (i - \delta)n$$
$$= i \cdot n .$$

The expected optimal cost on every widget is

$$\mathbb{E}_{\mathrm{ADV}}[\mathrm{cost}(\mathrm{OPT}(\mathcal{I}_i))] \leq \frac{n-1}{n} \cdot 1 + \frac{1}{n} \cdot n \leq 2 ,$$

and thus the total optimal cost is at most $2i + 1$ in expectation. As a consequence, the expected competitive ratio of ALG can be bounded from below by a function that grows with n.

Exercise 8.5. Instead of having one vertex w revealed in the last time step, we can connect the tree by a path that consists of k vertices and $2k - 1$ edges each of weight $1/(2k - 1)$, which all need to be part of any feasible solution; an example is shown in Figure 9.11a. Note that this makes the resulting lower bound weaker, because we increase the instances by a linear number of vertices that are not mapped to any guess. More precisely, we can do a reduction similar to the one in the proof of Theorem 8.9 with $n = 4n' + 1$. This is the only difference, however, since connecting all the widgets together to form a tree still only induces an additional cost of 1. As a result, the factor $(n-1)/3$ in the original theorem changes to $(n-1)/4$.

If we allow a degree of 4, we can even shrink the original instances by one vertex and directly connect the vertices $v_{i,3}$ with $1 \leq i \leq n$ by $k - 1$ edges each of weight $1/(k - 1)$; an example is depicted in Figure 9.11b. In this case, $n' = 3n$, and the bound even improves such that the aforementioned factor is replaced by $n/3$.

Exercise 8.6. We reduce bit guessing with known history to the MVCP. We design an online algorithm BGUESS with advice for bit guessing, given an online algorithm BBMVC with advice for the MVCP; we assume that BBMVC always computes a feasible solution.

In the first time step T_1', BGUESS gets the length n' of the string to guess; it constructs an instance I for BBMVC of length $n = 3n' + 2$ that consists of *widgets* $W_1, W_2, \ldots, W_{n'}$ of size 3 each. W_i contains three vertices $v_{i,1}$, $v_{i,2}$, and $v_{i,3}$, for every i with $1 \leq i \leq n'$. There is always an edge between $v_{i,1}$ and $v_{i,2}$. If BBMVC takes the vertex $v_{i,1}$, BGUESS guesses 0 in T_i'; otherwise it guesses 1. After that, a vertex $v_{i,3}$ is revealed together with either an edge $\{v_{i,1}, v_{i,3}\}$ if the correct guess of the ith bit is 0, or $\{v_{i,2}, v_{i,3}\}$ if the correct guess is 1. In the last two time steps T_{n-1} and T_n, two vertices w' and w are given; w is connected to all $v_{i,3}$ with $1 \leq i \leq n'$ and to w', which is only connected to w; see Figure 9.12. We distinguish two cases for every widget W_i.

Case 1. Suppose the correct guess is 0. In this case, an optimal solution takes the vertex $v_{i,1}$ and covers $\{v_{i,1}, v_{i,2}\}$ and $\{v_{i,1}, v_{i,3}\}$. This means it has cost 1 for W_i.

   Case 1.1. Suppose BBMVC also takes $v_{i,1}$. Then it also has cost 1 for W_i.

   Since BGUESS guesses 0 in this case, it has cost 0 in T_i'.

   Case 1.2. Suppose BBMVC does not take $v_{i,1}$. Then it has to take $v_{i,2}$ since otherwise the first edge presented in W_i is not covered. When $v_{i,3}$ is revealed, it also has to take this vertex to cover the edge $\{v_{i,1}, v_{i,3}\}$. Therefore, its cost is 2.

   Since BGUESS guesses 1 in this case, it has cost 1 in T_i'.

Case 2. Suppose the correct guess is 1. Then an optimal solution takes $v_{i,2}$ and has cost 1 in W_i. Similarly to the first case, it can easily be shown that if BBMVC has cost 1, BGUESS has cost 0, and if BBMVC has cost 2, BGUESS has cost 1.

When w' and w are finally revealed, both the optimal solution and BBMVC take w (unless BBMVC took all $v_{i,3}$ with $1 \leq i \leq n'$, in which case it can take w' instead). Suppose BGUESS guesses $\gamma n'$ bits correctly. Since the optimal cost is $n' + 1$, the competitive ratio c of BBMVC can be bounded from below by

$$
\begin{aligned}
c &\geq \frac{\text{cost}(\text{BBMVC}(I))}{\text{cost}(\text{OPT}(I))} \\
&= \frac{\text{cost}(\text{OPT}(I)) + (1 - \gamma)n'}{\text{cost}(\text{OPT}(I))} \\
&= \frac{(2 - \gamma)n' + 1}{n' + 1} \\
&\geq \frac{(2 - \gamma)n' + n'}{2n'} \\
&= \frac{3 - \gamma}{2},
\end{aligned}
$$

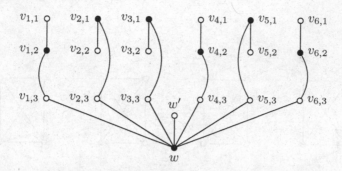

Figure 9.12. An instance used in the solution of Exercise 8.6. The optimal solution is marked by filled vertices.

and hence $\gamma \geq 3 - 2c$. Since $\gamma \geq 1/2$, we get $c \leq 5/4$, and from Theorem 7.8 it follows that at least

$$(1 + (1 - (3 - 2c)) \log_2(1 - (3 - 2c)) + (3 - 2c) \log_2(3 - 2c))n'$$
$$= (1 + 2(c - 1) \log_2(2(c - 1)) + (3 - 2c) \log_2(3 - 2c)) \cdot \frac{n - 2}{3}$$

bits of advice are necessary to be c-competitive. Finally, note that the optimal cost clearly grows with n.

Exercise 8.7. We reduce string guessing with known history and an alphabet size σ with $\sigma \geq 2$ to the MISP with preemption. We design an online algorithm SGUESS with advice that needs to guess a string of length n' over an alphabet of size σ; without loss of generality, let the alphabet be $\{1, 2, \ldots, \sigma\}$. The input I of length $n = \sigma(n' + 1)$ given to an online algorithm BBMIS with advice for the MISP consists of $n' + 1$ *widgets* $W_1, W_2, \ldots, W_{n'+1}$ that are each cliques of size σ. In every W_i with $1 \leq i \leq n'$, there is a *correct vertex*; the other vertices are called *incorrect vertices*. Every vertex from every subsequent widget is connected to all previously revealed incorrect vertices, but not to the correct ones. When W_{i+1} is revealed, BBMIS gets to know which vertex from W_i is the correct one; yet, since all vertices from W_{i+1} are connected to the same vertices that were previously revealed, there is no information about which is the correct vertex of W_{i+1}. This way, the correct vertices form an independent set of size n' in I, and every independent set that contains an incorrect vertex in some widget cannot take any other vertices of the following widgets. Note that also all incorrect vertices are connected to all vertices from $W_{n'+1}$; an example for $n' = 3$ is shown in Figure 9.13.

BBMIS is allowed to use preemption. However, it is not allowed to have any two vertices in its intermediate solution that are connected by an edge. Thus, after the last vertex of some W_i is presented, BBMIS took at most one vertex from W_i; without loss of generality, we assume that the algorithm takes one such vertex.

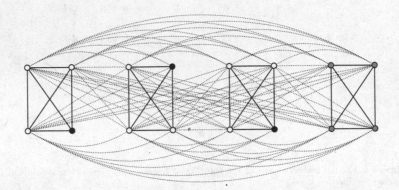

Figure 9.13. An instance used in the solution of Exercise 8.7. A maximum independent set contains a vertex from every widget; the vertices belonging to it are filled. Note that for the last widget, any vertex can be chosen.

In time step T_i', SGUESS presents W_i to BBMIS. The vertices of W_i are labeled $v_{i,1}, v_{i,2}, \ldots, v_{i,\sigma}$; afterwards, SGUESS guesses "j" in T_i' if and only if BBMIS chooses $v_{i,j}$ with $1 \leq j \leq \sigma$ for W_i with $1 \leq i \leq n'$.

Now consider any widget W_i with $1 \leq i \leq n'$. If the correct guess for T_i' was j with $1 \leq j \leq \sigma$, SGUESS connects all vertices $v_{i,j'}$ with $j' \neq j$ (that is, the incorrect vertices of W_i) to all incorrect vertices of subsequent widgets. If BBMIS chooses the correct vertex, its gain increases by 1, and SGUESS has cost 0 in T_i'. Conversely, if BBMIS chooses an incorrect vertex, it has two options. It can decide not to preempt the vertex chosen for W_i. In this case, it cannot take any other vertex in subsequent widgets (including $W_{n'+1}$). The algorithm can alternatively choose to preempt the incorrect vertex. In this case, it has no gain for W_i, but it can gain something for the following widget, and there is at least one widget remaining. Thus, this second option is always at least as promising as the first one.

The last $W_{n'}$ is an exception, where BBMIS can choose any vertex; by definition, no vertex from this widget is connected to any correct vertex. Since the optimal gain is $n' + 1$, we get for the competitive ratio c of BBMIS that

$$c \geq \frac{\text{gain}(\text{OPT}(I))}{\text{gain}(\text{BBMIS}(I))} = \frac{n' + 1}{\gamma n' + 1} \geq \frac{2n'}{\gamma n' + n'} \geq \frac{2}{1 + \gamma} \, ,$$

and thus $\gamma \geq 2/c - 1$. Since $\gamma \geq 1/\sigma$, we obtain $c \leq 2\sigma/(\sigma + 1)$. Using the result of Exercise 7.11, it follows that at least

$$\left(1 + \left(2 - \frac{2}{c} \right) \log_\sigma \left(\frac{2 - \frac{2}{c}}{\sigma - 1} \right) + \left(\frac{2}{c} - 1 \right) \log_\sigma \left(\frac{2}{c} - 1 \right) \right) \cdot \frac{(n - \sigma) \cdot \log_2 \sigma}{\sigma}$$

advice bits are necessary. The optimal gain again grows with n.

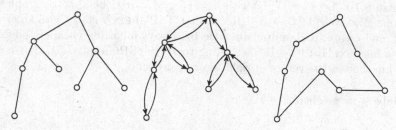

(a) The spanning tree S (b) The Eulerian cycle C (c) The Hamiltonian cycle H

Figure 9.14. Constructing a Hamiltonian cycle from a spanning tree as in the solution of Exercise 8.8; first, a spanning tree is computed, which is then converted to an Eulerian cycle, which is then again shortened to the Hamiltonian cycle.

Exercise 8.8. Consider the root v of the spanning tree S of the metric graph G. Suppose we perform a depth-first search on S, which leads to a directed Eulerian cycle C in the graph that is obtained from S by replacing the undirected edges of S by two directed ones that are in opposite directions. It follows that

$$\text{cost}(C) = 2 \cdot \text{cost}(S) .$$

Now we shorten C to a Hamiltonian cycle H in G. This is done by again starting at v and following C. Whenever we visit a vertex that we already visited before, we "jump" over it, that is, we remove it from the cycle and continue with the next vertex according to C. Shortening C this way does not increase the cost, due to the triangle inequality. The three steps to create H are shown in Figure 9.14. By applying this procedure, the resulting Hamiltonian cycle H is at most twice as expensive as the spanning tree S.

Exercise 8.9. Let DOUBLE be an offline algorithm which first computes a minimum spanning tree S_{opt}, which can be done in polynomial time as we know (see Exercise 1.3). After that, DOUBLE does a depth-first search on the metric input graph G and constructs a Hamiltonian cycle as in the solution of Exercise 8.8; this is the algorithm's output and we have

$$\text{cost}(\text{DOUBLE}(G)) \leq 2 \cdot \text{cost}(S_{\text{opt}}) . \tag{9.22}$$

Constructing DOUBLE(G) from S_{opt} can be done in polynomial time as well. Now let H_{opt} be a minimum Hamiltonian cycle in G. When removing an edge from H_{opt}, we obtain a path, and thus a tree S in G. As a result, we have

$$\text{cost}(H_{\text{opt}}) \geq \text{cost}(S) \geq \text{cost}(S_{\text{opt}}) ,$$

and together with (9.22), this proves that DOUBLE is a 2-approximation algorithm.

Exercise 8.10. Let $G = (V, E)$ with $V = \{v_1, v_2, \ldots, v_n\}$ be a metric graph with a weight function weight: $E \to \mathbb{R}^+$. Recall that TSPGREEDY starts with an arbitrary vertex, and creates a Hamiltonian cycle by always following cheapest edges. We define a function lab: $V \to \mathbb{R}^+$ according to $H := \text{TSPGREEDY}(G)$, that is, if the algorithm chooses the vertex v_j right after v_i, we set

$$\text{lab}(v_i) := \text{weight}(\{v_i, v_j\}) \ .$$

Hence, we have

$$\text{cost}(H) = \sum_{v \in V} \text{lab}(v) \ . \tag{9.23}$$

This time, we show that both conditions of Lemma 8.1 are met. Consider two vertices v_i and v_j such that, without loss of generality, TSPGREEDY chooses v_i before v_j. This means that, right after v_i was chosen, v_j was a candidate for the next vertex. Therefore, the edge $\{v_i, v_j\}$ has a weight that is at least as large as the one followed by TSPGREEDY, and thus

$$\text{weight}(\{v_i, v_j\}) \geq \text{lab}(v_i) \geq \min\{\text{lab}(v_i), \text{lab}(v_j)\} \ ,$$

which satisfies (i) of Lemma 8.1. Moreover, note that, for any such two vertices v_i and v_j, H_{opt} can be regarded as two disjoint paths that both connect them. Due to the triangle inequality, both these paths have a cost that is at least weight($\{v_i, v_j\}$), and thus

$$\text{cost}(H_{\text{opt}}) \geq 2 \cdot \text{weight}(\{v_i, v_j\}) \geq 2 \cdot \text{lab}(v_i) \ ,$$

using the same argument as above and that v_j was chosen after v_i. This implies that (ii) of the lemma is also satisfied.

Thus, we can use (9.23) and Lemma 8.1 to conclude that

$$\text{cost}(H) \leq (\lceil \log_2 n \rceil + 1) \cdot \text{cost}(H_{\text{opt}})$$

as claimed.

Exercise 8.11. The proof can be done analogously to that of Theorem 8.12. The only difference is that the algorithm EMBBIP with advice cannot immediately extrapolate the graph structure from knowing n. However, with another $\mathcal{O}(\log n)$ advice bits, the size of one of the shores can be communicated to the algorithm. Additionally, one bit encodes to which of the shores the first vertex belongs. If this is known, EMBBIP can embed the input graph and simulate ONKRUSKAL in exactly the same way as in the proof of Theorem 8.12.

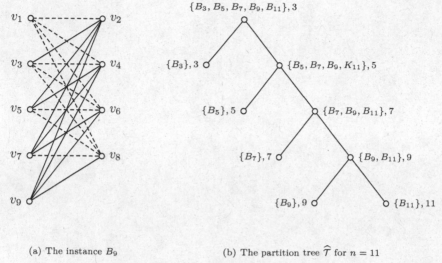

(a) The instance B_9 (b) The partition tree $\widehat{\mathcal{T}}$ for $n = 11$

Figure 9.15. The graph B_9 and a partition tree used in the solution of Exercise 8.12; again, edges of weight a are dashed and edges of weight b are solid.

Exercise 8.12. The claim can be shown using partition trees analogously to the proof of Theorem 8.13. For any odd n, consider the set of instances $\mathcal{I}^{(\leq n)}$ that consists of complete bipartite graphs $B_3, B_5, \ldots, B_n$. Every B_i with $3 \leq i \leq n$ consists of an odd number i of vertices $v_1, v_2, \ldots, v_i$ and $v_1 \prec v_2 \prec \ldots \prec v_i$. In the proof of Theorem 8.13, an algorithm essentially needed to know when the input ends to connect the last vertex with an expensive edge. Here, we follow a similar idea. The shore S_1 contains all vertices with an odd index, and the shore S_2 contains those with an even index. For every odd j with $1 \leq j \leq i$, the vertex v_j is connected to all vertices $v_{j'}$ with $2 \leq j' < j$ and j' even by edges each of weight b. Likewise, every vertex with an even index j is connected to all vetices $v_{j'}$ with $1 \leq j' < j$ and j' odd by edges each of weight a. B_9 is shown in Figure 9.15a.

The partition tree $\widehat{\mathcal{T}}$ for $\mathcal{I}^{(\leq n)}$ can be constructed analogously to the proof of Theorem 8.13; an example is shown in Figure 9.15b. This way, an online algorithm needs to know which one is the last vertex with odd index. The remainder of the proof can be done in an analogous way.

Glossary

General Symbols

α . . . . additive constant of the competitive ratio

$\textsc{Alg}$ . . . . deterministic online algorithm, online algorithm with advice

$\mathrm{amcost}(\cdot)$ . . . . amortized cost function of a minimization problem

B in the knapsack problem . . . . knapsack capacity

$b, b(\cdot)$ . . . . number of advice bits or random bits

c . . . . competitive ratio

$c_{i,j}$ in games . . . . the payoff of the adversary

$C_{\textsc{Alg}}$ . . . . configuration of $\textsc{Alg}$

$\mathcal{C}_{\textsc{Alg}}$ . . . . set of configurations of $\textsc{Alg}$

$\mathrm{cost}(\cdot)$ . . . . cost function of a minimization problem

$d_{\textsc{Alg}}$ in JSS . . . . number of diagonal moves of $\textsc{Alg}$

$\mathrm{dist}(\cdot)$ . . . . distance function of a metric space

e . . . . Euler's constant

$\mathbb{E}[\cdot]$ . . . . expected value

$\exp(\cdot)$ . . . . natural exponential function

$\mathrm{gain}(\cdot)$ . . . . gain function of a maximization problem

γ in bit guessing . . . . fraction of the input that is guessed correctly

γ in resource-augmented knapsack problem . . additive constant for overpacking

h in resource-augmented paging . . . . cache size of the optimal algorithm

H_{opt} . . . . minimum Hamiltonian cycle

$h_{\textsc{Alg}}$ in JSS . . . . number of horizontal moves of $\textsc{Alg}$

I . . . . input of current problem

$\mathcal{I}$ . . . . set of instances of current problem

$\mathcal{I}^{(n)}$ . . . . set of instances of current problem of length n

$\mathcal{I}_\phi$ . . . . instances that induce the same advice string ϕ

© Springer International Publishing Switzerland 2016
D. Komm, *An Introduction to Online Computation,*
Texts in Theoretical Computer Science. An EATCS Series,
DOI 10.1007/978-3-319-42749-2

k in k-server	number of servers
k in paging	size of the cache
k in set cover	size of the ground set X
k in ski rental	price to buy the skis
$\mu, \mu(\cdot)$	number of instances of given problem
l_i in paging	number of new pages in current phase
ℓ	size of strat(ALG) and strat(RAND) if finite
ℓ in paging	lookahead
λ in MSTP	penalty for infeasible solution
$\mathcal{M}$ in games	matrix representing the payoff of the players
$\mathcal{M}$	metric space
$\mathcal{M}_{[0,1]}$	metric space induced by real line between 0 and 1
m in JSS	number of machines
m in k-server	number of points of metric space
m in paging	size of the physical memory
m in set cover	size of the set family $\mathcal{S}$
n	input length
n in string guessing	length of string to be guessed
N in paging	number of phases
$\mathbb{N}$	natural numbers including 0
$\mathbb{N}^+$	natural numbers excluding 0
O	output for current problem
$\mathcal{O}(\cdot)$	class of functions that grow asymptotically at most as fast as ·
$\Omega(\cdot)$	class of functions that grow asymptotically at least as fast as ·
$\Theta(\cdot)$	class of functions that grow asymptotically as fast as ·
OPT	optimal (offline) algorithm for the given problem
ϕ	content of the random tape, content of the advice tape
Π	optimization problem
$\pi(\cdot)$	permutation
$\Phi(\cdot)$	potential
P in k-server	set of points
p_i in paging	ith page
p_i in k-server	ith point of metric space
P_i	ith phase of the input
$P_{\text{ALG},i}$	ith phase induced by ALG
$\mathcal{P}(\cdot)$	powerset of ·
$\Pr[\cdot]$	probability of the event ·
q	probability
R_i	ith round
RAND	randomized online algorithm
s in string guessing	string to be guessed
s_i in k-server	ith server
sol($\cdot$)	set of solutions for ·

solOpt($\cdot$) . . . . set of optimal solutions for ·
S_{opt} . . . . minimum spanning tree
strat(ALG) . . . . set of deterministic online algorithms ALG chooses from
strat(RAND) . . . . . set of deterministic online algorithms RAND chooses from
T_i . . . . ith time step
$\mathcal{T}, \mathcal{T}_v$ . . . . tree
$\widehat{\mathcal{T}}$ . . . . partition tree
v_{ALG} in JSS . . . . number of vertical moves of ALG
x_i . . . . ith request
X, X_i, Y . . . . random variables
y_i . . . . ith answer

Algorithms

ADIAG . . . . $(1 + 1/d)$-competitive for JSS; $b(n) \in \mathcal{O}(\log_2 d)$
AUG $(1 + 3\gamma/(1 - 4\gamma))$-competitive for the simple γ-knapsack problem; $b(n) \in \mathcal{O}(1)$
BGONE . . . . cost $n/2$ for bit guessing; $b(n) = 1$
BGRONE . . . . expected cost $n/2$ for bit guessing; $b(n) = 1$
BREAKEVEN . . . . $(2 - 1/k)$-competitive for ski rental
CBIP . . . . $2 \log_2 n$-competitive for coloring on bipartite graphs
CHASE . . . . $\lceil \lceil \log_2 k \rceil / (b' - 2) \rceil$-competitive for k-server; $b(n) = b'n$
CMP . . . . optimal for k-server on the real line between 0 and 1; $b(n) = n$
CLIN1 . . . . optimal for coloring on bipartite graphs; $b(n) = n - 1$
CLIN2 . . . . optimal for coloring on bipartite graphs; $b(n) = n - 2$
DCOV . . . . k-competitive for k-server on the real line between 0 and 1
DCOVP . . . . k-competitive for k-server on paths
DCOVT . . . . k-competitive for k-server on trees
DOUBLE . . . . 2-approximation for the TSP on metric graphs
DLIN1 . . . . optimal for DPA; $b(n) = n$
DLIN2 . . . . optimal for DPA; $b(\ell) = \ell$
EMB optimal for the MSTP on complete graphs with two weights; $b(n) \in \mathcal{O}(\log_2 n)$
FIFO . . . . k-competitive for paging
FIRSTFIT . . . . $(\log_2 n + 1)$-competitive for coloring on trees
FWF . . . k-competitive for paging; $k/(k - h + 1)$-competitive for (h, k)-paging
GLOG $(1 + \varepsilon)$-competitive for the (general) knapsack problem; $b(n) \in \mathcal{O}(\log_2 n)$
HALF . . . . $n/2$ correct guesses for bit guessing in expt.; $b(n) = n$
KNGREEDY . . . . not competitive for the knapsack problem
KNONE . . . . 2-competitive for the simple knapsack problem; $b(n) = 1$
KNLOG . . $(1 + \varepsilon)$-competitive for the simple knapsack problem; $b(n) \in \mathcal{O}(\log_2 n)$
KSGREEDY . . . . not competitive for k-server
KRUSKAL . . . . optimal for the offline MSTP
MSTGREEDY . . . . $\lceil \log_2 n \rceil$-competitive for the MSTP on metric graphs
MSTONE . . 1.4-competitive for the MSTP on metric graphs; $b(n) \in \mathcal{O}(\log_2 n)$

LFD . . . . optimal for paging

LFU . . . . not competitive for paging

LIFO . . . . not competitive for paging

LRU . . . . k-competitive for paging; $k/(k-h+1)$-competitive for (h,k)-paging

MARK . . k-competitive for paging; $k/(k-h+1)$-competitive for (h,k)-paging

MDIAG . . . . 4/3-competitive for JSS

PARENT . . . . optimal for spanning tree; $b(n) \in \mathcal{O}(n \log_2 n)$

PLIN1 . . . . optimal for paging; $b(n) = 2\lceil \log_2 n \rceil + n \lceil \log_2 m \rceil$

PLIN2 . . . . optimal for paging; $b(n) = n \lceil \log_2 k \rceil$

PLIN3 . . . . optimal for paging; $b(n) = n + k$

PLIN4 . . . . optimal for paging with $m = k + 1$; $b(n) = n \lceil \log_2 k \rceil / k$

RDIAG . . . . 1-competitive in expt. (and with prob. tending to 1) for JSS

RDIAG$_d$ . . . . $(1 + 1/d)$-competitive in expt. for JSS; $b(n) = \Theta(\log_2 d)$

RKNONE . . . . 2-competitive in expt. for the simple knapsack problem; $b(n) = 1$

RKNONE′ . . . 4-competitive in expt. for the simple knapsack problem; $b(n) = 1$

RMARK . . . $2H_k$-competitive in expt. (and with prob. tending to 1) for paging

RMARKBARELY . . . . $\mathcal{O}(\log_2 k)$-competitive in expt. for paging

RSKI . . . . $e/(e-1)$-competitive in expt. for ski rental

SCLIN1 . . . . optimal for set cover; $b(k) = k - 1$

SCLIN2 . . . . optimal for set cover; $b(m) = m$

SEG . . . . . $1/(1 - 2\sin(\pi/2^{b'}))$-competitive for k-server on the plane; $b(n) = b'n$

TSPGREEDY . . . . $(\lceil \log_2 n \rceil + 1)$-approximation on metric graphs

WALK . . . . k-competitive for paging

Bibliography

[1] Manindra Agrawal, Neeraj Kayal, and Nitin Saxena. PRIMES is in $\mathcal{P}$. *Annals of Mathematics*, 160(2):781–793, 2004. Cited on page 29.

[2] Sheldon B. Akers. A graphical approach to production scheduling problems. *Operations Research*, 4:244–245, 1956. Cited on page 181.

[3] Meike Akveld and Raphael Bernhard. Job shop scheduling with unit length tasks. *Theoretical Informatics and Applications (RAIRO)*, 46(3):329–342, 2012. Cited on page 182.

[4] Susanne Albers. BRICS – Mini-Course on Competitive Online Algorithms. http://www14.in.tum.de/personen/albers/papers/brics.pdf, 1996. Cited on pages 29 and 154.

[5] Susanne Albers. On the influence of lookahead in competitive paging algorithms. *Algorithmica*, 18(3):283–305, 1997. Cited on page 30.

[6] Susanne Albers. Online algorithms: A survey. *Mathematical Programming*, 97(1):3–26, 2003. Cited on page 29.

[7] Susanne Albers and Matthias Hellwig. Online makespan minimization with parallel schedules. In R. Ravi and Inge Li Gørtz, editors, *Proceedings of the 14th Scandinavian Symposium and Workshops on Algorithm Theory (SWAT 2014)*, volume 8503 of *Lecture Notes in Computer Science*, pages 13–25. Springer-Verlag, Berlin, 2014. Cited on page 182.

[8] Noga Alon, Baruch Awerbuch, Yossi Azar, Niv Buchbinder, and Joseph (Seffi) Naor. The online set cover problem. In Lawrence L. Larmore and Michel X. Goemans, editors, *Proceedings of the 35th Annual ACM Symposium on Theory of Computing (STOC 2003)*, pages 100–105. Association for Computing Machinery, New York, 2003. Cited on page 240.

© Springer International Publishing Switzerland 2016
D. Komm, *An Introduction to Online Computation*,
Texts in Theoretical Computer Science. An EATCS Series,
DOI 10.1007/978-3-319-42749-2

[9] Noga Alon, Baruch Awerbuch, Yossi Azar, Niv Buchbinder, and Joseph (Seffi) Naor. The online set cover problem. *SIAM Journal on Computing*, 39(2):361–370, 2009. Cited on page 240.

[10] Spyros Angelopoulos, Christoph Dürr, Shahin Kamali, Marc P. Renault, and Adi Rosén. Online bin packing with advice of small size. In Frank Dehne, Jörg-Rüdiger Sack, and Ulrike Stege, editors, *Proceedings of the 14th International Symposium on Algorithms and Data Structures (WADS 2015)*, volume 9214 of *Lecture Notes in Computer Science*, pages 40–53. Springer-Verlag, Berlin, 2015. Cited on page 210.

[11] Sanjeev Arora and Boaz Barak. *Computational Complexity*. Cambridge University Press, Cambridge, 2009. Cited on page 29.

[12] Kazuoki Azuma. Weighted sums of certain dependent random variables. *Tôhoku Mathematical Journal*, 19(3):357–367, 1967. Cited on page 83.

[13] Nikhil Bansal, Niv Buchbinder, Aleksander Mądry, and Joseph (Seffi) Naor. A polylogarithmic-competitive algorithm for the k-server problem (extended abstract). In Rafail Ostrovsky, editor, *Proceedings of the 52th Annual IEEE Symposium on Foundations of Computer Science (FOCS 2011)*, pages 267–276. IEEE Computer Society, Los Alamitos, 2011. Cited on page 154.

[14] Nikhil Bansal, Niv Buchbinder, and Joseph (Seffi) Naor. Metrical task systems and the k-server problem on HSTs. In Samson Abramsky, Cyril Gavoille, Claude Kirchner, Friedhelm Meyer auf der Heide, and Paul G. Spirakis, editors, *Proceedings of the 37th International Colloquium on Automata, Languages and Programming (ICALP 2010)*, volume 6198 of *Lecture Notes in Computer Science*, pages 287–298. Springer-Verlag, Berlin, 2010. Cited on page 153.

[15] Kfir Barhum. Tight bounds for the advice complexity of the online minimum Steiner tree problem. In Viliam Geffert, Bart Preneel, Branislav Rovan, Julius Stuller, and A Min Tjoa, editors, *Proceedings of the 40th Conference on Current Trends in Theory and Practice of Computer Science (SOFSEM 2014)*, volume 8327 of *Lecture Notes in Computer Science*, pages 77–88. Springer-Verlag, Berlin, 2014. Cited on page 267.

[16] Kfir Barhum, Hans-Joachim Böckenhauer, Michal Forišek, Heidi Gebauer, Juraj Hromkovič, Sacha Krug, Jasmin Smula, and Björn Steffen. On the power of advice and randomization for the disjoint path allocation problem. In Viliam Geffert, Bart Preneel, Branislav Rovan, Julius Stuller, and A Min Tjoa, editors, *Proceedings of the 40th Conference on Current Trends in Theory and Practice of Computer Science (SOFSEM 2014)*, volume 8327 of *Lecture Notes in Computer Science*, pages 89–101. Springer-Verlag, Berlin, 2014. Cited on pages 111 and 240.

[17] Dwight R. Bean. Effective coloration. *The Journal of Symbolic Logic*, 41(2):469–480, 1976. Cited on page 266.

[18] László A. Bélády. A study of replacement algorithms for a virtual-storage computer. *IBM Systems Journal*, 5(2):78–101, 1966. Cited on page 29.

[19] László A. Bélády, Robert A. Nelson, and Gerald S. Shedler. An anomaly in space-time characteristics of certain programs running in a paging machine. *Communications of the ACM*, 12(6):349–353, 1969. Cited on page 29.

[20] Shai Ben-David and Allan Borodin. A new measure for the study of on-line algorithms. *Algorithmica*, 11(1):73–91, 1994. Cited on page 29.

[21] Maria Paola Bianchi, Hans-Joachim Böckenhauer, Tatjana Brülisauer, Dennis Komm, and Beatrice Palano. Online minimum spanning tree with advice (extended abstract). In Rūsiņš M. Freivalds, Gregor Engels, and Barbara Catania, editors, *Proceedings of the 42nd International Conference on Current Trends in Theory and Practice of Computer Science (SOFSEM 2016)*, volume 9587 of *Lecture Notes in Computer Science*, pages 195–207. Springer-Verlag, Berlin, 2016. Cited on page 267.

[22] Maria Paola Bianchi, Hans-Joachim Böckenhauer, Juraj Hromkovič, and Lucia Keller. Online coloring of bipartite graphs with and without advice. *Algorithmica*, 1(70):92–111, 2014. Cited on page 266.

[23] Hans-Joachim Böckenhauer, Sascha Geulen, Dennis Komm, and Walter Unger. Constructing randomized online algorithms from algorithms with advice. Technical Report 48298, Department of Computer Science, ETH Zurich, 2015. Cited on page 112.

[24] Hans-Joachim Böckenhauer, Juraj Hromkovič, and Dennis Komm. A technique to obtain hardness results for randomized online algorithms – a survey. In Cristian S. Calude, Rūsiņš M. Freivalds, and Kazuo Iwama, editors, *Computing with New Resources: Essays Dedicated to Jozef Gruska on the Occasion of His 80th Birthday*, volume 8808 of *Lecture Notes in Computer Science*, pages 264–276. Springer-Verlag, Berlin, 2014. Cited on page 111.

[25] Hans-Joachim Böckenhauer, Juraj Hromkovič, Dennis Komm, Richard Královič, and Peter Rossmanith. On the power of randomness versus advice in online computation. In Henning Bordihn, Martin Kutrib, and Bianca Truthe, editors, *Languages Alive: Essays Dedicated to Jürgen Dassow on the Occasion of His 65th Birthday*, volume 7300 of *Lecture Notes in Computer Science*. Springer-Verlag, Berlin, 2012. Cited on page 111.

[26] Hans-Joachim Böckenhauer, Juraj Hromkovič, Dennis Komm, Sacha Krug, Jasmin Smula, and Andreas Sprock. The string guessing problem as a method to prove lower bounds on the advice complexity. In Ding-Zhu Du and Guochuan

Zhang, editors, *Proceedings of the 19th Annual International Computing and Combinatorics Conference (COCOON 2013)*, volume 7936 of *Lecture Notes in Computer Science*, pages 493–505. Springer-Verlag, Berlin, 2013. Cited on page 240.

[27] Hans-Joachim Böckenhauer, Juraj Hromkovič, Dennis Komm, Sacha Krug, Jasmin Smula, and Andreas Sprock. The string guessing problem as a method to prove lower bounds on the advice complexity. *Theoretical Computer Science*, 554:95–108, 2014. Cited on page 240.

[28] Hans-Joachim Böckenhauer, Dennis Komm, Rastislav Královič, and Richard Královič. On the advice complexity of the *k*-server problem. Technical Report 703, Department of Computer Science, ETH Zurich, 2010. Cited on page 154.

[29] Hans-Joachim Böckenhauer, Dennis Komm, Rastislav Královič, and Richard Královič. On the advice complexity of the *k*-server problem. In Luca Aceto, Monika Henzinger, and Jiří Sgall, editors, *Proceedings of the 38th International Colloquium on Automata, Languages and Programming (ICALP 2011)*, volume 6755 of *Lecture Notes in Computer Science*, pages 207–218. Springer-Verlag, Berlin, 2011. Cited on pages 111 and 154.

[30] Hans-Joachim Böckenhauer, Dennis Komm, Rastislav Královič, Richard Královič, and Tobias Mömke. On the advice complexity of online problems. In Yingfei Dong, Ding-Zhu Du, and Oscar H. Ibarra, editors, *Proceedings of the 20th International Symposium on Algorithms and Computation (ISAAC 2009)*, volume 5878 of *Lecture Notes in Computer Science*, pages 331–340. Springer-Verlag, Berlin, 2009. Cited on pages 83, 111, 181, 182, and 240.

[31] Hans-Joachim Böckenhauer, Dennis Komm, Rastislav Královič, Richard Královič, and Tobias Mömke. Online algorithms with advice. Technical Report 614, Department of Computer Science, ETH Zurich, 2009. Cited on pages 111, 182, and 240.

[32] Hans-Joachim Böckenhauer, Dennis Komm, Richard Královič, and Peter Rossmanith. On the advice complexity of the knapsack problem. In David Fernández-Baca, editor, *Proceedings of the 10th Latin American Symposium on Theoretical Informatics (LATIN 2012)*, volume 7256 of *Lecture Notes in Computer Science*, pages 61–72. Springer-Verlag, Berlin, 2012. Cited on page 210.

[33] Hans-Joachim Böckenhauer, Dennis Komm, Richard Královič, and Peter Rossmanith. The online knapsack problem: Advice and randomization. *Theoretical Computer Science*, 527:61–72, 2014. Cited on page 210.

[34] Allan Borodin and Ran El-Yaniv. *Online Computation and Competitive Analysis*. Cambridge University Press, Cambridge, 1998. Cited on pages 29, 82, and 210.

[35] Allan Borodin and Ran El-Yaniv. On randomization in on-line computation. *Information and Computation*, 150(2):244–267, 1999. Cited on page 82.

[36] Joan Boyar, Lene M. Favrholdt, Christian Kudahl, and Jesper W. Mikkelsen. Advice complexity for a class of online problems. In Ernst W. Mayr and Nicolas Ollinger, editors, *Proceedings of the 32nd Symposium on Theoretical Aspects of Computer Science (STACS 2015)*, volume 30 of *Leibniz International Proceedings in Informatics*, pages 116–129. Schloss Dagstuhl – Leibniz-Zentrum für Informatik, 2015. Cited on page 267.

[37] Joan Boyar, Shahin Kamali, Kim S. Larsen, and Alejandro López-Ortiz. Online bin packing with advice. In Ernst W. Mayr and Natacha Portier, editors, *Proceedings of the 31st Symposium on Theoretical Aspects of Computer Science (STACS 2014)*, volume 25 of *Leibniz International Proceedings in Informatics*, pages 174–186. Schloss Dagstuhl – Leibniz-Zentrum für Informatik, 2014. Cited on page 210.

[38] Joan Boyar, Kim S. Larsen, and Morten N. Nielsen. The accommodating function: A generalization of the competitive ratio. *SIAM Journal on Computing*, 31(1):233–258, 2001. Cited on page 29.

[39] Peter Brucker. An efficient algorithm for the job-shop problem with two jobs. *Computing*, 40(4):353–359, 1988. Cited on page 181.

[40] Peter Brucker. *Scheduling Algorithms*. Springer-Verlag, Berlin, 5th edition, 2007. Cited on page 181.

[41] Tatjana Brülisauer. Online minimum spanning tree with advice. Bachelor thesis, ETH Zurich, 2014. Cited on page 267.

[42] Niv Buchbinder and Joseph (Seffi) Naor. The design of competitive online algorithms via a primal-dual approach. *Foundations and Trends in Theoretical Computer Science*, 3(2–3), 2009. Cited on page 153.

[43] Elisabet Burjons, Juraj Hromkovič, Xavier Muñoz, and Walter Unger. Graph coloring with advice and randomized adversary (extended abstract). In Rūsiņš M. Freivalds, Gregor Engels, and Barbara Catania, editors, *Proceedings of the 42nd International Conference on Current Trends in Theory and Practice of Computer Science (SOFSEM 2016)*, volume 9587 of *Lecture Notes in Computer Science*. Springer-Verlag, Berlin, 2016. 229–240. Cited on page 266.

[44] Nicos Christofides. Worst-case analysis of a new heuristic for the travelling salesman problem. Technical Report 388, Graduate School of Industrial Administration, 1976. Cited on pages 29 and 267.

[45] Marek Chrobak, Howard J. Karloff, Thomas H. Payne, and Sundar Vishwanathan. New results on server problems. *SIAM Journal on Discrete Mathematics*, 4(2):172–181, 1991. Cited on page 154.

[46] Marek Chrobak and Lawrence L. Larmore. An optimal on-line algorithm for *k*-servers on trees. *SIAM Journal on Computing*, 20(1):144–148, 1991. Cited on page 154.

[47] Marek Chrobak and John Noga. LRU is better than FIFO. *Algorithmica*, 23(2):180–185, 1999. Cited on page 29.

[48] Richard W. Conway, William L. Maxwell, and Louis W. Miller. *Theory of Scheduling*. Dover Publications, Mineola, 2012. Cited on page 181.

[49] Thomas H. Cormen, Charles E. Leiserson, Ronald L. Rivest, and Clifford Stein. *Introduction to Algorithms*. The MIT Press, Cambridge, 3rd edition, 2009. Cited on page 181.

[50] János Csirik and Gerhard J. Woeginger. Resource augmentation for online bounded space bin packing. *Journal of Algorithms*, 44(2):308–320, 2002. Cited on page 30.

[51] Reinhard Diestel. *Graph Theory*. Springer-Verlag, Berlin, 4th edition, 2010. Cited on page 266.

[52] Stefan Dietiker. The advice complexity of the online disjoint path allocation problem. Bachelor thesis, ETH Zurich, 2013. Cited on page 240.

[53] Stefan Dobrev, Rastislav Královič, and Dana Pardubská. How much information about the future is needed? In Viliam Geffert, Juhani Karhumäki, Alberto Bertoni, Bart Preneel, Pavol Návrat, and Mária Bieliková, editors, *Proceedings of the 34th Conference on Current Trends in Theory and Practice of Computer Science (SOFSEM 2008)*, volume 4910 of *Lecture Notes in Computer Science*, pages 247–258. Springer-Verlag, Berlin, 2008. Cited on pages 110 and 111.

[54] Stefan Dobrev, Rastislav Královič, and Dana Pardubská. Measuring the problem-relevant information in input. *Theoretical Informatics and Applications (RAIRO)*, 43(3):585–613, 2009. Cited on pages 29 and 111.

[55] Jérôme Dohrau. Online makespan scheduling with sublinear advice. In Giuseppe F. Italiano, Tiziana Margaria-Steffen, Jaroslav Pokorný, Jean-Jacques Quisquater, Roger Wattenhofer, Roman Spanek, and Martin Rimnac, editors, *Proceedings of the 41st Conference on Current Trends in Theory and Practice of Computer Science (SOFSEM 2015)*, volume 8939 of *Lecture Notes in Computer Science*, pages 177–188. Springer-Verlag, Berlin, 2015. Cited on page 182.

[56] Reza Dorrigiv. *Alternative Measures for the Analysis of Online Algorithms*. Ph.D. thesis, University of Waterloo, 2011. Cited on page 29.

[57] Peter Elias. Universal codeword sets and representations of the integers. *IEEE Transactions on Information Theory*, 21(2):194–203, 1975. Cited on page 111.

[58] Yuval Emek, Pierre Fraigniaud, Amos Korman, and Adi Rosén. Online computation with advice. In Susanne Albers, Alberto Marchetti-Spaccamela, Yossi Matias, Sotiris E. Nikoletseas, and Wolfgang Thomas, editors, *Proceedings of the 36th International Colloquium on Automata, Languages and Programming (ICALP 2009)*, volume 5555 of *Lecture Notes in Computer Science*, pages 427–438. Springer-Verlag, Berlin, 2009. Cited on pages 111 and 240.

[59] Yuval Emek, Pierre Fraigniaud, Amos Korman, and Adi Rosén. On the additive constant of the k-server work function algorithm. *Information Processing Letters*, 110(24):1120–1123, 2010. Cited on page 153.

[60] Yuval Emek, Pierre Fraigniaud, Amos Korman, and Adi Rosén. Online computation with advice. *Theoretical Computer Science*, 412(24):2642–2656, 2011. Cited on pages 111, 154, and 240.

[61] Amos Fiat, Richard M. Karp, Michael Luby, Lyle A. McGeoch, Daniel D. Sleator, and Neal E. Young. Competitive paging algorithms. *Journal of Algorithms*, 12(4):685–699, 1991. Cited on page 82.

[62] Amos Fiat and Gerhard J. Woeginger. Competitive odds and ends. In Amos Fiat and Gerhard J. Woeginger, editors, *Online Algorithms, The State of the Art*, volume 1442 of *Lecture Notes in Computer Science*, pages 385–394. Springer-Verlag, Berlin, 1998. Cited on page 29.

[63] Amos Fiat and Gerhard J. Woeginger, editors. *Online Algorithms, The State of the Art*, volume 1442 of *Lecture Notes in Computer Science*. Springer-Verlag, Berlin, 1998. Cited on page 29.

[64] Michal Forišek, Lucia Keller, and Monika Steinová. Advice complexity of online coloring for paths. In Adrian-Horia Dediu and Carlos Martín-Vide, editors, *Proceedings of the 6th International Conference on Language and Automata Theory and Applications (LATA 2012)*, volume 7183 of *Lecture Notes in Computer Science*, pages 228–239. Springer-Verlag, Berlin, 2012. Cited on page 266.

[65] Christa Furrer. Online multiple knapsack. Bachelor thesis, ETH Zurich, 2015. Cited on page 210.

[66] Michael R. Garey, David S. Johnson, and Ravi Sethi. The complexity of flowshop and jobshop scheduling. *Mathematics of Operations Research*, 1(2):117–129, 1976. Cited on page 181.

[67] Heidi Gebauer, 2013. Personal communication. Cited on page 240.

[68] Heidi Gebauer, Dennis Komm, Rastislav Královič, Richard Královič, and Jasmin Smula. Disjoint path allocation with sublinear advice. In Dachuan Xu, Donglei Du, and Ding-Zhu Du, editors, *Proceedings of the 21st International*

Conference on Computing and Combinatorics (COCOON 2015), volume 9198 of *Lecture Notes in Computer Science*, pages 417–429. Springer-Verlag, Berlin, 2015. Cited on page 240.

[69] Sushmita Gupta, Shahin Kamali, and Alejandro López-Ortiz. On advice complexity of the k-server problem under sparse metrics. In Thomas Moscibroda and Adele A. Rescigno, editors, *Proceedings of the 20th International Colloquium on Structural Information and Communication Complexity (SIROCCO 2013)*, volume 8179 of *Lecture Notes in Computer Science*, pages 55–67. Springer-Verlag, Berlin, 2013. Cited on page 154.

[70] Venkatesan Guruswami, Atri Rudra, and Madhu Sudan. Essential coding theory. http://www.cse.buffalo.edu/faculty/atri/courses/coding-theory/book/, 2015. Cited on page 240.

[71] Grzegorz Gutowski, Jakub Kozik, Piotr Micek, and Xuding Zhu. Lower bounds for on-line graph colorings. In Hee-Kap Ahn and Chan-Su Shin, editors, *Proceedings of the 25th International Symposium on Algorithms and Computation (ISAAC 2014)*, volume 8889 of *Lecture Notes in Computer Science*, pages 507–515. Springer-Verlag, Berlin, 2014. Cited on page 266.

[72] András Gyárfás and Jenö Lehel. On-line and first fit colorings of graphs. *Journal of Graph Theory*, 12(2):217–227, 1988. Cited on page 266.

[73] Sven Hammann. The online vertex cover problem with advice. Master's thesis, ETH Zurich, 2015. Cited on page 240.

[74] Xin Han, Yasushi Kawase, and Kazuhisa Makino. Randomized algorithms for removable online knapsack problems. In Michael R. Fellows, Xuehou Tan, and Binhai Zhu, editors, *Proceedings of the 3rd Joint International Conference on Frontiers in Algorithmics and Algorithmic Aspects in Information and Management (FAW-AAIM 2013)*, volume 7924 of *Lecture Notes in Computer Science*, pages 60–71. Springer-Verlag, Berlin, 2013. Cited on page 210.

[75] Xin Han and Kazuhisa Makino. Online removable knapsack with limited cuts. *Theoretical Computer Science*, 411(44–46):3956–3964, 2010. Cited on pages 30 and 210.

[76] William W. Hardgrave and George L. Nemhauser. A geometric model and a graphical algorithm for a sequencing problem. *Operations Research*, 11(6):889–900, 1963. Cited on page 181.

[77] Wassily Hoeffding. Probability inequalities for sums of bounded random variables. *Journal of the American Statistical Association*, 58(301):13–30, 1963. Cited on page 83.

[78] John E. Hopcroft, Rajeev Motwani, and Jeffrey D. Ullman. *Introduction to Automata Theory, Languages, and Computation*. Prentice Hall, Upper Saddle River, 3rd edition, 2006. Cited on page 29.

[79] Juraj Hromkovič. *Algorithmics for Hard Problems*. Springer-Verlag, Berlin, 2nd edition, 2004. Cited on page 29.

[80] Juraj Hromkovič. *Theoretical Computer Science*. Springer-Verlag, Berlin, 2004. Cited on page 29.

[81] Juraj Hromkovič. *Design and Analysis of Randomized Algorithms*. Springer-Verlag, Berlin, 2005. Cited on pages 82 and 181.

[82] Juraj Hromkovič, Rastislav Královič, and Richard Královič. Information complexity of online problems. In Petr Hliněný and Antonín Kučera, editors, *Proceedings of the 35th International Symposium on Mathematical Foundations of Computer Science (MFCS 2010)*, volume 6281 of *Lecture Notes in Computer Science*, pages 24–36. Springer-Verlag, Berlin, 2010. Cited on page 111.

[83] Juraj Hromkovič, Tobias Mömke, Kathleen Steinhöfel, and Peter Widmayer. Job shop scheduling with unit length tasks: Bounds and algorithms. *Algorithmic Operations Research*, 2(1):1–14, 2007. Cited on pages 181 and 182.

[84] Oscar H. Ibarra and Chul E. Kim. Fast approximation algorithms for the knapsack and sum of subset problems. *Journal of the ACM*, 22(4):463–468, 1975. Cited on page 29.

[85] Makoto Imase and Bernard M. Waxman. Dynamic Steiner tree problem. *SIAM Journal on Discrete Mathematics*, 4(3):369–384, 1991. Cited on page 267.

[86] Sandy Irani and Anna R. Karlin. On online computation. In Dorit S. Hochbaum, editor, *Approximation Algorithms for NP-Hard Problems*, chapter 13, pages 521–564. PWS Publishing Company, Boston, 1997. Cited on page 29.

[87] Kazuo Iwama and Shiro Taketomi. Removable online knapsack problems. In Peter Widmayer, Stephan Eidenbenz, Francisco Triguero, Rafael Morales, Ricardo Conejo, and Matthew Hennessy, editors, *Proceedings of the 29th International Colloquium on Automata, Languages and Programming (ICALP 2002)*, volume 2380 of *Lecture Notes in Computer Science*, pages 293–305. Springer-Verlag, Berlin, 2002. Cited on page 210.

[88] Kazuo Iwama and Guochuan Zhang. Online knapsack with resource augmentation. *Information Processing Letters*, 110(22):1016–1020, 2010. Cited on pages 30 and 210.

[89] Bala Kalyanasundaram and Kirk Pruhs. Speed is as powerful as clairvoyance. In *Proceedings of the 36th Annual Symposium on Foundations of Computer*

Science (FOCS 1995), pages 214–221. IEEE Computer Society, Los Alamitos, 1995. Cited on page 30.

[90] Bala Kalyanasundaram and Kirk Pruhs. Speed is as powerful as clairvoyance. *Journal of the ACM*, 47(4):617–643, 2000. Cited on pages 30 and 210.

[91] Anna R. Karlin, Mark S. Manasse, Lyle A. McGeoch, and Susan Owicki. Competitive randomized algorithms for non-uniform problems. In *Proceedings of the 1st Annual ACM-SIAM Symposium on Discrete Algorithms (SODA 1990)*, pages 301–309. Society for Industrial and Applied Mathematics, Philadelphia, 1990. Cited on page 83.

[92] Anna R. Karlin, Mark S. Manasse, Larry Rudolph, and Daniel D. Sleator. Competitive snoopy caching. *Algorithmica*, 3(1):79–119, 1988. Cited on page 29.

[93] Richard M. Karp. Reducibility among combinatorial problems. In Raymond E. Miller and James W. Thatcher, editors, *Proceedings of a Symposium on the Complexity of Computer Computations*, pages 85–103. Plenum Press, New York, 1972. Cited on pages 29 and 266.

[94] Hans Kellerer, Ulrich Pferschy, and David Pisinger. *Knapsack Problems*. Springer-Verlag, Berlin, 2004. Cited on pages 29 and 210.

[95] Hal A. Kierstead and William T. Trotter. On-line graph coloring. *On-Line Algorithms, DIMACS Series in Discrete Mathematics and Theoretical Computer Science*, 7:85–92, American Mathematical Society, Providence, 1992. Cited on page 266.

[96] Donald E. Knuth and Andrew C.-C. Yao. The complexity of nonuniform random number generation. In Joseph F. Traub, editor, *Algorithms and Complexity: New Directions and Recent Results*. Academic Press, New York, 1976. Cited on page 82.

[97] Dennis Komm. *Advice and Randomization in Online Computation*. Ph.D. thesis, ETH Zurich, 2012. Cited on pages xi, 110, 112, and 182.

[98] Dennis Komm. Eine Einführung in Online-Algorithmen. Lecture notes of "Appromixations- und Online-Algorithmen" at ETH Zurich, 2013. Cited on page xi.

[99] Dennis Komm, Rastislav Královič, Richard Královič, and Christian Kudahl. Advice complexity of the online induced subgraph problem. Technical Report abs/1512.05996, CoRR, 2015. Cited on page 267.

[100] Dennis Komm, Rastislav Královič, Richard Královič, and Tobias Mömke. Randomized online algorithms with high probability guarantees. In Ernst W.

Mayr and Natacha Portier, editors, *Proceedings of the 31st Symposium on Theoretical Aspects of Computer Science (STACS 2014)*, volume 25 of *Leibniz International Proceedings in Informatics*, pages 470–481. Schloss Dagstuhl – Leibniz-Zentrum für Informatik, 2014. Cited on pages 83 and 182.

[101] Dennis Komm and Richard Královič. Advice complexity and barely random algorithms. In Ivana Černá, Tibor Gyimóthy, Juraj Hromkovič, Keith G. Jeffery, Rastislav Královič, Marko Vukolić, and Stefan Wolf, editors, *Proceedings of the 37th International Conference on Current Trends in Theory and Practice of Computer Science (SOFSEM 2011)*, volume 6543 of *Lecture Notes in Computer Science*, pages 332–343. Springer-Verlag, Berlin, 2011. Cited on pages 83 and 182.

[102] Dennis Komm and Richard Královič. Advice complexity and barely random algorithms. *Theoretical Informatics and Applications (RAIRO)*, 45(2):249–267, 2011. Cited on pages 83 and 182.

[103] Dennis Komm, Richard Královič, and Tobias Mömke. On the advice complexity of the set cover problem. In Edward A. Hirsch, Juhani Karhumäki, Arto Lepistö, and Michail Prilutskii, editors, *Proceedings of the 7th International Computer Science Symposium in Russia (CSR 2012)*, volume 7353 of *Lecture Notes in Computer Science*, pages 241–252. Springer-Verlag, Berlin, 2012. Cited on page 240.

[104] Elias Koutsoupias. The k-server problem. *Computer Science Review*, 3(2):105–118, 2009. Cited on page 153.

[105] Elias Koutsoupias and Christos H. Papadimitriou. On the k-server conjecture. *Journal of the ACM*, 42(5):971–983, 1995. Cited on pages 153 and 154.

[106] Elias Koutsoupias and Christos H. Papadimitriou. The 2-evader problem. *Information Processing Letters*, 57(5):473–482, 1996. Cited on page 154.

[107] Elias Koutsoupias and Christos H. Papadimitriou. Beyond competitive analysis. *SIAM Journal on Computing*, 30(1):300–317, 2000. Cited on page 29.

[108] Sacha Krug. Towards using the history in online computation with advice. *Theoretical Informatics and Applications (RAIRO)*, 49(2):139–152, 2015. Cited on page 240.

[109] Sven O. Krumke and Clemens Thielen. Introduction to online optimization. Lecture notes of "Online Optimization" at University of Kaiserslautern, 2012. Cited on page 83.

[110] Joseph B. Kruskal, Jr. On the shortest spanning subtree of a graph and the traveling salesman problem. *Proceedings of the American Mathematical Society*, 7(1):48–50, 1956. Cited on page 29.

[111] Lynn H. Loomis. On a theorem of von Neumann. *Proceedings of the National Academy of Sciences of the United States of America*, 32(8):213–215, 1946. Cited on page 82.

[112] Zvi Lotker and Boaz Patt-Shamir. Nearly optimal FIFO buffer management for DiffServ. In *Proceedings of the 21st Annual ACM Symposium on Principles of Distributed Computing (PODC 2002)*, pages 134–142. Association for Computing Machinery, New York, 2002. Cited on page 110.

[113] László Lovász, Michael Saks, and William T. Trotter. An on-line graph coloring algorithm with sublinear performance ratio. *Discrete Mathematics*, 75(1–3):319–325, 1989. Cited on page 266.

[114] Mark S. Manasse, Lyle A. McGeoch, and Daniel D. Sleator. Competitive algorithms for on-line problems. In *Proceedings of the 20th Annual ACM Symposium on Theory of Computing (STOC 1988)*, pages 322–333. Association for Computing Machinery, New York, 1988. Cited on pages 153 and 154.

[115] Alberto Marchetti-Spaccamela and Carlo Vercellis. Stochastic on-line knapsack problems. *Mathematical Programming*, 68:73–104, 1995. Cited on page 210.

[116] Lyle A. McGeoch and Daniel D. Sleator. A strongly competitive randomized paging algorithm. *Algorithmica*, 6(6):816–825, 1991. Cited on page 82.

[117] Jesper W. Mikkelsen. Randomization can be as helpful as a glimpse of the future in online computation. Technical Report abs/1511.05886, CoRR, 2015. Cited on page 112.

[118] Michael Mitzenmacher and Eli Upfal. *Probability and Computing: Randomized Algorithms and Probabilistic Analysis*. Cambridge University Press, Cambridge, 2005. Cited on page 82.

[119] Tobias Mömke. On the power of randomization for job shop scheduling with k-units length tasks. *Theoretical Informatics and Applications (RAIRO)*, 43:189–207, 2009. Cited on page 182.

[120] Rajeev Motwani and Prabhakar Raghavan. *Randomized Algorithms*. Cambridge University Press, Cambridge, 1995. Cited on page 82.

[121] John F. Nash. Equilibrium points in N-person games. *Proceedings of the National Academy of Sciences of the United States of America*, 36(1):48–49, 1950. Cited on page 82.

[122] Christos H. Papadimitriou. *Computational Complexity*. Addison-Wesley, Boston, 1993. Cited on page 29.

[123] Cynthia A. Phillips, Clifford Stein, Eric Torng, and Joel Wein. Optimal time-critical scheduling via resource augmentation. *Algorithmica*, 32(2):163–200, 2002. Cited on page 30.

[124] Michael L. Pinedo. *Scheduling: Theory, Algorithms, and Systems*. Springer-Verlag, Berlin, 4th edition, 2012. Cited on page 181.

[125] Marc P. Renault and Adi Rosén. On online algorithms with advice for the k-server problem. In Roberto Solis-Oba and Giuseppe Persiano, editors, *9th International Workshop on Approximation and Online Algorithms (WAOA 2011)*, volume 7164 of *Lecture Notes in Computer Science*, pages 198–210. Springer-Verlag, Berlin, 2011. Cited on page 154.

[126] Marc P. Renault, Adi Rosén, and Rob van Stee. Online algorithms with advice for bin packing and scheduling problems. *Theoretical Computer Science*, 600:155–170, 2015. Cited on pages 182 and 210.

[127] Daniel J. Rosenkrantz, Richard E. Stearns, and Philip M. II Lewis. An analysis of several heuristics for the traveling salesman problem. *SIAM Journal on Computing*, 6(3):563–581, 1977. Cited on pages 266 and 267.

[128] Sebastian Seibert, Andreas Sprock, and Walter Unger. Advice complexity of the online coloring problem. In Paul G. Spirakis and Maria J. Serna, editors, *Proceedings of the 8th International Conference on Algorithms and Complexity (CIAC 2013)*, volume 7878 of *Lecture Notes in Computer Science*, pages 345–357. Springer-Verlag, Berlin, 2013. Cited on page 266.

[129] Ivana Selečéniová. *Advice Complexity of Online Problems*. Ph.D. thesis, Comenius University, 2016. Cited on pages 111 and 240.

[130] Michael Sipser. *Introduction to the Theory of Computation*. PWS Publishing Company, Boston, 1996. Cited on page 29.

[131] Daniel D. Sleator and Robert E. Tarjan. Amortized efficiency of list update and paging rules. *Communications of the ACM*, 28(2):202–208, 1985. Cited on pages 29 and 30.

[132] Jasmin Smula. *Information content of online problems: Advice versus determinism and randomization*. Ph.D. thesis, ETH Zurich, 2015. Cited on page 240.

[133] Robert M. Solovay and Volker Strassen. A fast Monte-Carlo test for primality. *SIAM Journal on Computing*, 6(1):84–85, 1977. Cited on page 82.

[134] Andreas Sprock. *Analysis of Hard Problems in Reoptimization and Online Computation*. Ph.D. thesis, ETH Zurich, 2013. Cited on page 240.

[135] Björn Steffen. *Advice Complexity of Online Graph Problems*. Ph.D. thesis, ETH Zurich, 2014. Cited on pages 111 and 266.

[136] Philip D. Straffin. *Game Theory and Strategy*. Mathematical Association of America Textbooks, Washington, 1993. Cited on page 82.

[137] Włodzimierz Szwarc. Solution of the Akers-Friedman scheduling problem. *Operations Research*, 8(6):782–788, 1960. Cited on page 181.

[138] Alan M. Turing. On computable numbers, with an application to the Entscheidungsproblem. *Proceedings of the London Mathematical Society*, 42(2):230–265, 1936. Cited on page 28.

[139] Vijay V. Vazirani. *Approximation Algorithms*. Springer-Verlag, Berlin, 2003. Cited on page 29.

[140] John von Neumann. Zur Theorie der Gesellschaftsspiele. *Mathematische Annalen*, 100(1):295–320, 1928. Cited on page 82.

[141] David Wehner. Job Shop Scheduling im Dreidimensionalen. Bachelor thesis, ETH Zurich, 2012. Cited on page 182.

[142] David Wehner. A new concept in advice complexity of job shop scheduling. In Petr Hliněný, Zdeněk Dvořák, Jiří Jaros, Jan Kofroň, Jan Kořenek, Petr Matula, and Karel Pala, editors, *Proceedings of the 9th Doctoral Workshop on Mathematical and Engineering (MEMICS 2014)*, volume 8934 of *Lecture Notes in Computer Science*, pages 147–158. Springer-Verlag, Berlin, 2014. Cited on page 182.

[143] David Wehner. Advice complexity of fine-grained job shop scheduling. In Vangelis Th. Paschos and Peter Widmayer, editors, *Proceedings of the 9th International Conference on Algorithms and Complexity (CIAC 2015)*, volume 9079 of *Lecture Notes in Computer Science*, pages 416–428. Springer-Verlag, Berlin, 2015. Cited on page 182.

[144] Douglas B. West. *Introduction to Graph Theory*. Prentice Hall, Upper Saddle River, 2nd edition, 2001. Cited on page 266.

[145] Andrew C.-C. Yao. Probabilistic computations: Toward a unified measure of complexity (extended abstract). In *Proceedings of the 18th Annual Symposium on Foundations of Computer Science (FOCS 1977)*, pages 222–227. IEEE Computer Society, Washington, 1977. Cited on page 82.

[146] Xiaofan Zhao and Hong Shen. On the advice complexity of one-dimensional online bin packing. In Jianer Chen, John E. Hopcroft, and Jianxin Wang, editors, *Proceedings of the 8th International Workshop on Frontiers in Algorithmics (FAW 2014)*, volume 8497 of *Lecture Notes in Computer Science*, pages 320–329. Springer-Verlag, Berlin, 2014. Cited on page 210.

Index

Abramsky, Samson 328
Aceto, Luca 330
active page 97
active zone 173, 179
addition theorem 141
ADIAG 177, 325
ADIAG$_d$ 176, 177, 295, 297
adversary 22
    oblivious 34, 214
    randomized 47
advice bits 87
advice complexity viii, 72, 86, 88
advice tape 86
Agrawal, Manindra 327
Ahn, Hee-Kap 334
Akers, Sheldon B. 181, 327
Akveld, Meike xi, 182, 327
al-Khwārizmī, Muḥammad ibn Mūsā
    2
Albers, Susanne 29, 30, 154, 327,
    333
algorithm 2, 36
    ambitious 160
    approximation 5
    barely random 38, 64, 102, 171,
        193, 214

Christofides 5, 29, 267
consistent 4, 33, 45, 70
demand paging 22, 160
generic 50, 209, 300, 314
greedy 6, 116, 195
Kruskal's see KRUSKAL
lazy 116, 125, 160
marking 25, 64
    randomized 41
Monte Carlo 82
non-swapping 228
offline 2, 37
online 12
    with advice 87, 88
polynomial-time 4
Solovay-Strassen 39, 82
Alon, Noga 240, 327, 328
alphabet 212
altitude of a triangle 291
amortized cost 121
amplification 39, 40, 72
Angelopoulos, Spyros 210, 328
answer 11
AOC-complete 267
approximation algorithm see
    algorithm

© Springer International Publishing Switzerland 2016
D. Komm, *An Introduction to Online Computation*,
Texts in Theoretical Computer Science. An EATCS Series,
DOI 10.1007/978-3-319-42749-2

Printed in the United States
By Bookmasters

Printed in the United States
By Bookmasters